Sport in the Global Society

General Editor: J.A. Mangan

FLAT RACING AND BRITISH SOCIETY 1790–1914

SPORT IN THE GLOBAL SOCIETY

General Editor: J.A. Mangan

ISSN 1368-9789

The interest in sports studies around the world is growing and will continue to do so. This unique series combines aspects of the expanding study of *sport in the global society*, providing comprehensiveness and comparison under one editorial umbrella. It is particularly timely, with studies in the political, cultural, social, economic, geographical and aesthetic elements of sport proliferating in institutions of higher education.

Eric Hobsbawm once called sport one of the most significant practices of the late nineteenth century. Its significance is even more marked in the late twentieth century and will continue to grow in importance into the next millennium as the world develops into a 'global village' sharing the English language, technology and sport.

Other Titles in the Series

Footbinding, Feminism and Freedom
The Liberation of Women's Bodies in Modern China
Fan Hong

The Games Ethic and Imperialism
Aspects of the Diffusion of an Ideal
J.A. Mangan

The Nordic World
Sport in Society
Edited by Henrik Meinander and J.A. Mangan

The Race Game
Sport and Politics in South Africa
Douglas Booth

Rugby's Great Split
Class, Culture and the Origins of Rugby League Football
Tony Collins

Sporting Nationalisms
Identity, Ethnicity, Immigration and Assimilation
Edited by Mike Cronin and David Mayall

France and the 1998 World Cup
The National Impact of a World Sporting Event
Edited by Hugh Dauncey and Geoff Hare

Cricket and England
A Cultural and Social History of the Inter-war Years
Jack Williams

Scoring for Britain
International Football and International Politics, 1900–1939
Peter J. Beck

The First Black Footballer
Arthur Wharton 1865–1930: An Absence of Memory
Phil Vasili

FLAT RACING AND BRITISH SOCIETY 1790–1914

A Social and Economic History

MIKE HUGGINS

FRANK CASS
LONDON • PORTLAND, OR

First published in 2000 in Great Britain by
FRANK CASS PUBLISHERS
Newbury House, 900 Eastern Avenue
London, IG2 7HH

and in the United States of America by
FRANK CASS PUBLISHERS
c/o ISBS, 5804 N.E. Hassalo Street
Portland, Oregon 97213-3644

Website: www.frankcass.com

British Library Cataloguing in Publication Data

Huggins, Mike
Flat racing and British society, 1790–1914 : a social and economic history. – (Sport in the global society ; no. 12)
1. Horse racing – Great Britain – History – 19th century
2. Horse racing – Social aspects – Great Britain – History – 19th century 3. Social classes – Great Britain – History – 19th century 4. Popular culture – Great Britain – History – 19th century 5. Great Britain – Social life and customs – 19th century
I. Title
306.4`83

ISBN 0-7146-4982-1 (cloth)
ISBN 0-7146-8045-1 (paper)
ISSN 1368-9789

Library of Congress Cataloging-in-Publication Data

Huggins, Mike.
Flat racing and British society, 1790–1914 : a social and economic history / Mike Huggins.
p. cm. – (Sport in the global society, ISSN 1368–9789 : [vol. 12]).
Includes bibliographical references.
ISBN 0–7146–4982–1 (cloth). – ISBN 0–7146–8045–1 (pbk.)
1. Horse racing – Social aspects – Great Britain History. 2. Horse racing – Economic aspects – Great Britain History. I. Title.
II. Series: Cass series – sport in the global society : 12.
SF335.G7H84 1999
798.4`00941–dc21 99–37018
CIP

Printed in Great Britain by
Creative Print and Design (Wales) Ltd, Ebbw Vale

Contents

List of Illustrations

Between pages 144 and 145

List of Tables

Series Editor's Foreword

'O, for a horse with wings' pleaded Imogene in Shakespeare's *Cymbeline* – a plea that has echoed down the centuries. Horse racing is one of the oldest sports in the world with a known history in the West of almost 3,000 years. Records reveal that it was popular with the Greeks and Romans. In the East records of its popularity go back even further. In China it was popular during the Shang Yin Dynasty (*c.*1760–1122 BC) and apparently very popular in the Han Dynasty (206 BC–220 AD) of which it was recorded: 'In every city there is horse racing.' It has been the sport not merely of kings but of potentates, caliphs and emperors. Nevertheless, it is in England that horse racing in its modern form developed. The patronage of the English royalty and nobility for 400 years ensured England a leading place in horse racing by the nineteenth century.

The development of the sport was slow but sure. Organized English race meetings are recorded in the sixteenth century. Chester can lay claim to be the first on record in 1540. There were certainly race courses at Doncaster and Carlisle by the end of the sixteenth century. Under the patronage of kings and queens the growth of courses was steady. Charles II was responsible for Newmarket and his nickname of 'Old Rowley' is commemorated by the present mile course. By the end of the eighteenth century there were at least 72 race meetings in England. The Jockey Club was founded at Newmarket in 1750, the St. Leger was established at Doncaster in 1776 and the Oaks and the Derby at Epsom in 1779.

It is at this point that Mike Huggins, in his authoritative study of the social and economic history of flat racing between 1790 and 1914, takes up the story and sets the sport firmly in the life of *all* classes of society during the period when it developed from a people's recreation into a modern sport.

Not the least of Huggins' virtues is his desire to restore the history of horse racing to the people – working class *and* middle class – and to rescue it from historians with a preoccupation with middle-class reform movements based on evidence from the sober and earnest 'do-gooders' reported in parliamentary papers exhibiting the virtuous rhetoric of reform. He refuses to lock the pendulum of history on their side. He seeks to redress a partiality of perspective especially regarding the Victorian middle class. In doing so, to an extent, he puts both the cultural historian and the 'sports historian' right. Horse racing was popular with all classes as it evolved from folk festival to professional sport. Across the classes, and the sexes, racing was part of the pleasant reality of everyday life and 'part of the cultural fabric of all classes' (Introduction, p.4). Proscription by the moralist was simply not on. How could virtuous reformism triumph when the pleasures of horse racing were so deeply embedded in the cultures of the working class, the middle class and the upper class?

Huggins takes issue, rightly, with those autarkic historians who concentrate on the emergence of a working-class leisure culture that, among other things, puts over much emphasis on the gradual increase in real earnings, the reduction of working hours, the advance of technology and the resulting expansion of seaside excursions, music halls and professional soccer clubs, and those indignant historians who are too much concerned with suppression rather than appeasement. Theirs is a close, sometimes out of focus, view when a sharp, wide-angled view is required.

In horse racing at least, states Huggins, there was more continuity and less discontinuity than some historians appreciate. Efforts at hegemonic influence and social control in the interests of capitalism, morality and order more often than not failed. Negotiation rather than confrontation between employer and worker with the outcome frequently in favour of the proletarian racing enthusiast was the order of the day. Furthermore, claims Huggins, 'over concern with the experiences of the working classes has meant that middle-class leisure [in general] has been largely ignored' (Introduction, p.4). It is certainly a case of beyond one galaxy lay another and another. By way of example, what of intra middle-class attitudes and circumstances? What of the middle-class 'leisure culture' that was pleasure seeking, hedonistic and irreligious? High-minded moralists and 'time and motion' manufacturers did not get it all their own way – even in dealings with their own kind. And what of the significance of stages in the life cycle, geographical location and institutional opportunities? All good questions that exercise the pallial area of the brain. The middle class was hardly a fronde group in society!

And in passing, it should perhaps be noted that all these questions could be asked to good purpose, of the upper class – also largely overlooked by the historians of sport!

The neglect of middle-class leisure, however, is not the main concern of Huggins. He is acutely and properly concerned that horse racing has never been considered in its full complexity. What of the relationship of horse racing to 'leisure cultures' that cut across, never mind existed within, classes? What, he asks, of 'the national leisure culture with its conspicuous consumption; urban, middle-class culture; reformist leisure culture; artisan leisure culture; rural popular culture; and urban popular culture?' (Introduction, p.9). What of the relationships between owners, breeders, officials and investors? What of questions of crowd behaviour and control? What did horse racing mean to its various groups of supporters? How extensive was early commercialism? What, in fact, was horse racing's economic significance – local and national? What was its relationship to betting and gambling? Who were its opponents? What were their aims? How successful were they? What can be said about the 'moral conspiracy' that brought the racing fraternity together? Finally, what was the place of horse racing in society as a whole? On all these matters Huggins has something fresh and valuable to say. The purpose of this Series, of course, is to offer carefully chosen commentators, analysts and observers a stall on which to set out their academic wares offering depth, insight and originality. Huggins more than meets these criteria.

When the various complex issues are raised and considered, Huggins' forceful assertion remains in the mind; horse racing was a highly successful cross-class sport with a significant middle-class involvement. The rhetoric of the antagonists should not be confused with the reality of the participation of the protagonists. The strongest of Huggins' virtues is unquestionably his successful effort to bring subtlety to studies of Victorian and Edwardian sport through the medium of horse racing. Simplistic images of homogeneous class attitudes and actions are laid to rest. He offers us a chiaroscuro canvas of period images of horse racing that catches subtle variations and that reflects delicate shades. Particularly fascinating is his brushwork that reveals with telling clarity, images of working-class hostility to, and counter-images of middle class support for, racing and betting, and sharp portrayals of middle-class promotion of professional horse racing. Can this be the same middle class frequently associated by historians of sport with the perpetuation of 'closed-shop' amateurism?

How refreshing that Huggins is free of the recent affliction of some historians of sport who suffer, where the middle classes are concerned, from *pas trop de zèle* – indeed, an aversion to the bourgeoisie; how valuable for the history of sport that he seeks balance in inquiry; how providential for the history of sport that he reopens closed cupboard doors to shelves of cultural archives – working class *and* middle class. His contribution in this volume goes well beyond a consideration of horse racing. He brings a necessary and overdue balance to the social history of sport as well as a proper concern for complexity and caveat. Historians of sport owe him a debt of gratitude.

Huggins might well prove to be an antidote to the simplistic view that the history of sport owes its existence to a small cluster of historians with working-class interests; to adapt Robert Hughes, a view that serves as a prophylactic against understanding. The reality, of course, is a great deal more complex. Educational historians and cultural historians with a profound interest in the highly influential role of the English middle classes in the early evolution of modern sport played a far from insignificant part. To refresh the memories of the forgetful and to broaden the horizons of the unknowing, the *International Journal of the History of Sport* will shortly publish assessments of pioneers of the history of sport including the educational historian Peter McIntosh, the feminist historian Sheila Fletcher and the political historian W.F. Mandle, merely a handful of pioneers in the history of sport, who looked beyond a male working-class world.

Huggins could also be the catalyst who inspires a new interest not only in middle-class involvement but in the *complexity* of this involvement and in the *extensiveness* of this involvement. His forthcoming article in the *International Journal of the History of Sport* takes his arguments on horse racing and the middle class a good deal further than in this volume, setting them in the wider world of sport in general. It is a particularly challenging, provocative and subtle consideration of middle-class Victorian and Edwardian Britain and its sporting interests and activities.

Huggins ends with claims that there is a pressing need 'to explore in far greater detail the gap between rhetoric and reality in the leisure life of Victorian Britain' (p.240), and a need for a more detailed exploration of private practice rather than public pronouncement and regulatory action. In total, this stimulating, refreshing and sophisticated study of racing has profound implications for the historian's interpretations of leisure in culture.

Edward Gibbon once remarked, 'All that is human must retrograde if it does not advance.' Could it be that Huggins had Gibbon's remark, the history of horse racing and the history of sport in mind when he wrote this quite superb book?

J. A. MANGAN
International Centre for Sport, Socialisation and Society,
University of Strathclyde
September 1999

Acknowledgements

First and undoubtedly foremost I must thank my family, Jeff, Kath and Nicky, for their sacrifices and amused toleration during the long time this book was in maturation. I began by looking at one race meeting near our home, and somehow caught the racing bug. To my partner, Margaret, who sometimes missed the races as she helped me pursue more material, a special thanks. In writing this book so many libraries and archives throughout Britain have provided material and been helpful that space precludes thanking all of them, but the library staff of Lancaster University, St Martin's College and Charlotte Mason College gave particular support. I am especially grateful for the help and facilities offered by Dede Scott Brown of York Racing Museum, and by the staff of the Jockey Club, Newmarket. Mandy Whitham typed my material splendidly.

I should like to thank the following for granting permission to reproduce illustrations in this volume: the Doncaster Museum and Art Gallery (1); the Darlington Public Library (2); the British Library (5, 6, 7, 9, 10, 11, 15, 25); the History of Advertising Trust (16); the Radio Times Hulton Picture Library (17); the Durham Record Office, Strathmore Collection (19); the National Horseracing Museum (20); and the Cleveland Archives (24).

Horse racing is still treated with some levity by some staff in senior common rooms so I am particularly grateful to those fellow historians who have provided encouragement, morale boosts and critical challenge at the right time, especially Rob David, Tony Mangan, Jonathan Munby, Tony Pollard, John Tolson, Wray Vamplew and John Walton. Many of their ideas have been incorporated. Without them I would never have completed the book, although any errors that remain are definitely mine.

MIKE HUGGINS
August 1999

Introduction

The beginnings of this book came from my dissatisfaction with some aspects of the way in which the character of Victorian life has been interpreted by historians, and, in particular, the way in which the historical understanding of social formation and transformation has been shaped by an over-concentration on an agenda driven largely by the archive of Parliamentary Papers or the rhetoric of middle-class reformism.

The established picture that Victorian local and everyday life was controlled and defined by a moral and reforming hegemony seemed both problematical and unconvincing. The established resource base for historical interpretation fails to examine popular cultural practices in sufficient detail. We know more about the temperance movement and prosecutions arising from alcohol drinking than about everyday drinking. We know more about the social pathology of Victorian life than the everyday. We know more about how the working classes spent their time than we do about the supposedly respectable middle classes, thanks to the 'aversion of researchers to the bourgeoisie'.[1]

This case study of racing's enduring appeal to British society from 1790 to 1914 reveals just how partial many of the features that we have assumed as characterizing the totality of Victorian culture were.

Not long after Chartism had peaked and upper- and middle-class fears of revolution were still alive, W.P. Frith painted his picture of Derby Day. His canvas shows a lively panorama of the course, with a huge crowd, in the stands and right across the downs; carriages with fine ladies or prostitutes; Fortnum and Mason hampers, wine and beer; dozens of booths where food and alcohol were available; acrobats and gypsies; a group of thimbleriggers attempting to rook mug punters; the betting ring; a country lad and his lass; men, women and children of all classes with as much interest in all the other activities going on around them as in the race itself; the policemen keeping the course clear; their concentration on the race and toleration of a huge crowd, bent on gambling, drink and other sensual pleasures. Frith's picture has no sense of the moral dangers of the crowd;

it has no real sense of wrongdoing. Nor did much of his audience see it in those terms.

Such large crowds could be seen at many racecourses but were not perceived as dangerous, and most meetings were never in danger of being banned. Only a few months after the Peterloo massacre in Manchester (1819), when the magistracy had been in fear of riot and revolution, some hundred thousand people gathered on the moor for the races with no reports of violence or sedition. What was it about racing which enabled it able to survive?

In large part this was a shared sense right across the classes (and sexes) that racing was part of the common-sense reality of everyday life. Attempted prohibition and attacks by moral reformers or ideological defences of the sport were both largely irrelevant, since racing was part of the cultural fabric of all class groups.

Racing's success as a cultural practice also gained through its early introduction of modernizing elements. Like a number of other commercialized leisure activities, it provided a means of cultural and political entrance to the late modern age for groups in the middle and the working class otherwise excluded. The classes invested cultural capital in racing in different ways, and participation in racing often depended on the subtle negotiation of class differences. At a racecourse the top and the bottom of the social hierarchy shared a similar experience, and experienced a certain vicarious pleasure in travelling up and down the social ladder for the day. Race meetings provided a space for social play, where mobility was possible.

Yet cultural and leisure historians have chosen to ignore racing in favour of a more one-sided view, emphasizing the nature of pre-industrial leisure; the transformation of leisure under the twin processes of capitalism and industrialization; and the emergence of a modern working-class leisure culture. Academic interest has been mainly on the total pattern of working-class leisure during this period.[2] The historiography emphasized the suppression of many working-class leisure forms in the 1830s and the 1840s, the discontinuities between leisure in this period and more traditional leisure patterns, and the centrality of the middle years of the century as marking the slow emergence of more modern forms of leisure.[3] Certainly from the 1830s traditional, less respectable forms of leisure, such as pleasure fairs, came under increasing attack from vociferous and well-organized nonconformist, evangelical Anglican and other respectable working- and middle-class groups. There was a slackening of the grip of custom and community. At the same time, for some workers factory-imposed discipline limited the opportunities for free time. Leisure became constrained by these limits of space and time. Social control through state legislation and the activities of the new police forces in the interests of the maintenance of the moral order also played a part, while more improving and respectable recreations were offered as alternatives to the traditional pleasures of drink and gambling.

Historians have argued that the emergence of a more modern working-class leisure culture and a wider range of leisure forms came from the mid-century due to a slow increase in real earnings, a slow decrease in the hours of work, and the expansion of new technologies such as the railways and the telegraph. The last quarter of the nineteenth century saw the more rapid expansion of a number of key leisure activities, such as the growth in seaside trips and seaside holidays (especially in parts of north-west England),[4] the music hall,[5] or professional football.[6] These new forms were diverse yet extensive, more routinized and more homogeneous, many dominated by commercial leisure industries. Sport shared in this expansion, although much of it was aimed at the middle classes. The weekend became a time of leisure as working men gained a Saturday half-holiday, although this depended on geographical location, job or employers' attitudes.

This view is only partial; working-class attendance at race meetings fitted uneasily with the general pattern outlined above. Unofficial race-week holidays continued right through the nineteenth century. Local industries were forced to shut down whatever the attitudes of employers. The August races in the large north-eastern town of Stockton, for example, resulted in the partial shut down of all the local heavy industries during the meeting.[7] The enclosing of the course and the introduction of entrance fees by the 1860s reduced attendances but simply diverted absenteeism into other leisure channels such as seaside trips.

So racing does not match this conflict-based model. Any clash of interests between employers and workpeople was soon resolved in favour of acceptance by the employer of an enforced shutdown. Racing fits better into the more revisionist theme which some historians have developed from the early 1980s, examining the role of cultural continuities in terms of leisure formation and challenging the former stress on major discontinuities. J.M. Golby and A.W. Purdue, for example, argued that 'there was no sharp break with the past' in the nineteenth century and that 'many of the cultural phenomena of pre-industrial England were able ... to survive, adapt and thrive in new circumstances',[8] even if initially under some duress and modified appropriately in response to social and economic changes. They also pointed out that even before early industrialization a range of commercial leisure activities was emerging through popular demand, and this combination of popular demand and commercial supply produced new activities through the century. There was therefore evidence that the working classes were sometimes active in the making of their own leisure, as seemed to be much the case in Frith's picture.[9]

The ideological and theoretical debate about leisure has drawn heavily on E.P. Thompson's influential discussion of working-class experience under industrial capitalism, which took up a neo-Marxist position in relation to culture.[10] Most recent writers have seen culture as linked to the economic structural base, although some have seen it as only partially determined by it. A number of historians, most notably P. Joyce, have drawn on the apparent flexibility of Gramsci's concept of hegemony to examine the ways in which particular classes or powerful groups were able to establish their leadership, arguing that hegemony allowed dominant groups to impose authority by securing the consent of others.[11] Gramsci argued that the spontaneous consent of the great mass of the population to the general direction imposed on social life was caused by the prestige which the dominant group enjoyed because of its position and function in the world of production.[12] Hegemony was, in fact, never total, but achieved a 'moving equilibrium', as alignments and responses shifted among the classes. The response of subordinate groups could be resistant, disjointed or accommodating. Key emphases were therefore on consent and negotiation. This conceptualization has allowed historians to come to terms with the ability of working-class groups to be active in the making of their own leisure, while enabling neo-Marxist historians to argue for the position to be still one of class conflict.

The extent of such conflict at different points in the past is, however, still a matter of debate. In racing any attempt to impose a moral and reforming hegemony clearly failed. Racing cannot easily be fitted into this context of class struggle between the hegemonic bourgeoisie and a subordinate proletariat. Over-concern with the experience of the working classes under industrial capitalism has meant that middle-class leisure has been largely ignored. J. Lowerson's work on sport and the middle classes covers only the last 30 years of the nineteenth century and concentrated on more respectable sports, to the neglect of middle-class involvement in others.[13] Historians have overemphasized the ideological dominance of middle-class respectability, stressing the attempts to develop from the 1840s through the 1860s, 1870s and 1880s both what P. Bailey described as a 'rational recreation' approach to the 'improvement' of working-class recreation, and a respectable, dutiful and constrained leisure for their own class.[14] In devoting a whole book to leisure in Bristol between 1870 and 1914, H. Meller focused mainly on organized, institutional and respectable leisure forms and on those citizens who provided more 'cultural' facilities, excluding the day-to-day experiences of the majority of citizens.[15] There has been little recognition that, as Bailey observed, the middle-class ideologues of leisure did not always get the support that may have been expected, even from their own class. Some middle-class groups had a frank acceptance of more hedonistic leisure. Leisure may still have been a key battleground, but the simplicity of much discussion of class has obscured much of the complexity of intra-class attitudes. While there are undoubted difficulties of definition in terms of class structure and class relationships, it is becoming clear that, although middle-class leisure could be respectable, serious and nonconformist in character, there was another male leisure culture which was more pleasure-seeking, hedonistic and irreligious in certain contexts. Such contexts included certain times in the life cycle, a wide range of locational and associational forms, and the world of the imagination, characterized by the reading of various types of printed medium. In part this culture grew stronger as the century progressed, but there were also clear continuities with the Georgian period.

Writing on middle-class leisure has studiously ignored racing. Indeed, Lowerson, albeit on the basis of minimal evidence, was able to claim firmly that 'the growth of horseracing, attractive to both [the elite and the working-class] groups, was virtually without middle-class support'.[16] This was certainly not the case.[17] Racing had a solid basis of support across certain middle-class groups and reflected hitherto underestimated tensions in middle-class society. For many of the urban middle class there may have been some self-interest involved, through the commercial gains brought by the races, inter-generational gentrification or cultural accommodation. But many found the excitement of the course or of betting a worthwhile experience, and MPs, councillors, aldermen and magistrates all attended meetings.

Racing also formed part of aristocratic and gentry life. Aristocratic sports still await their historian, although beginnings have been made in the study of certain sports, especially hunting.[18] J.V. Beckett's study of the aristocracy in England makes only limited reference to the place of racing in its life but an examination of racing could shed light on the part sport played in aristocratic and gentry leisure.[19]

Equally, concern with the processes of industrialization and urbanization has led to concentration on the history of the larger cities and manufacturing towns. Here sport generally has often been regarded as marginal,[20] although more recent studies are beginning to give more serious academic attention to it.[21] Race meetings could be found in a range of settings, many relatively neglected, from cities to small market towns, while training and breeding were largely rural phenomena. A linked issue here stems from cultural geography: the whole question of physical and social space and their use in the study of leisure, social relations and cultural geography. Division of space and the meanings with which space is invested may both work as mechanisms of power and are therefore of central importance in both the experience and the consumption of leisure. That so many meetings took place on unenclosed moor, downland, winter-flooded river banks or beaches, where land ownership was less clear must be significant, and the types of space used for betting, racing and training need careful examination. Racing was an occasion for much dishonest activity. It was 'carnivalesque' and allowed temporary social mobility, the playing-out of roles, and the rehearsal for rather than simply the defusion of social transformation.

Finally, women's experience of leisure and sport is slowly being uncovered, although the process is often linked to female emancipation and it is still largely through an analysis of the experience of the more visible, middle-class women.[22] But women attended race meetings and were involved in betting, while racing was also associated with a range of female employments including prostitution, card-selling and stall-holding.

It is therefore the more surprising that earlier academic historians of leisure and sports historians have both ignored racing. The standard text on flat racing is still Wray Vamplew's *The Turf: A Social and Economic History of Horseracing* (1976), a scholarly, well-written book, but one published before many of the more recent developments in leisure historiography outlined above and now therefore somewhat dated.

Tony Mason, in his survey of the literature on football, had the challenge of struggling with a relatively weak, secondary literature and the thinness of organizational and manuscript material.[23] By contrast, the historian of racing has the opposite problem, with almost an excess of material. Racing, horse-breeding and betting were the focus of a range of Parliamentary Papers, including the reports of Select Committees and Royal Commissions, as well as debates, bills and acts. There is a wide range of late nineteenth-century secondary literature, especially memoirs and historical surveys. It is therefore all the more regrettable that the many histories of racing written by racing journalists in the present century have usually confined their research to a relatively limited range of these secondary works in which the same stories about the past are told again and again alongside a heavy reliance for further information on the standard texts of racing: the *Racing Calendar*, which gave annual details of winners, placed horses, and runners, together with owners and jockeys for all races at major courses, and the *Stud Book*, which gave information about breeding. The vast majority of these sources, albeit written in the late nineteenth century, looked to the past through rose-coloured spectacles. To a more limited extent these sources also used *Ruff's Guide to the Turf*, a specialist, annual, racing publication which from the 1840s gave information about top jockeys and trainers, auction prices of thoroughbreds and top stallion stud fees. Other monthly London-based newspapers and magazines were used by these sources to a much lesser extent. The weekly newspaper *Bell's Life in London* was founded in 1822 and covered horse racing, pugilism and other interests of the fancy. The monthly *Sporting Magazine* provided a broad coverage of the gentry's sporting interests from the late eighteenth century, and *Baily's Magazine of Sports and Pastimes*, appearing from 1860, gave coverage to racing matters alongside other horse, hunting, sporting and leisure matters of interest to aristocratic, gentry and middle-class and predominantly conservative readers.

In general, such sources are useful but biased, presenting a predominantly London-, southern- or Newmarket-based and upper- or upper-middle-class view of racing, written for a particular reading public which shared common understandings, as much of what was unsaid as what was said. They concentrated much more on the major events at Newmarket, Ascot, Epsom and Doncaster, and on successful owners, trainers and jockeys, to the relative neglect of the lesser provincial meetings and less successful participants which provided the mainstay of racing in the country and for the population as a whole.

Here sources have been sought outside the conventional racing archives, most especially contemporary newspapers. These fell into two classes. First there were newspapers with a specialist focus on racing which emerged early. Weekly sporting papers, such as the *Sunday Times* and *Bell's Life in London*, were among a number of London-based, sporting papers first emerging from the 1820s with a great deal of racing information aimed at a literate, middle-class betting audience.

Secondly and more importantly, use of the regional and local press has shed new light on provincial racing matters hitherto neglected. This complements the more national approaches of earlier racing historians. Vamplew, for example, believed that up to and beyond the 1840s 'racing columns were not a regular feature' of provincial newspapers.[24] He fails to recognize that in areas such as Yorkshire, where there was a long tradition of interest in racing, regional weekly newspapers such as the *York Herald*, the *Yorkshireman* or the *Doncaster Gazette* reflected the widespread interest in racing with a turf column giving details not only of racing in the particular area but also much further afield from well before this date. Local papers everywhere had turf articles at the time of their local meetings, while local papers serving training areas, such as the *Malton Messenger*, also contained much information of interest.

From the 1870s the specialist racing press, first exemplified by the *Sporting Life* and *Sportsman*, was rapidly expanding, not just in London and Manchester, the two major English betting centres, but throughout the major industrial towns. Such contemporary newspapers were used less systematically but extensively. They present a challenge to the non-racing historian since they are texts with a number of levels of meaning and often signal a range of dishonesty and malpractice to the experienced turfite quite unperceived by readers from outside the sport. What is often unclear to non-turfites is that horses were regularly deliberately run to lose and that jockeys were expected to conceal their horses' form, even when winning, for future betting advantage. Racing sources do not speak of this overtly, but words or phrases such as 'pulled', 'dead meat', 'all Johnny Armstrong', 'came where nature and intention coincided', 'stiff 'un', 'a clever second' and many others signal such movement. A key word in racing literature was 'clever' (applied to bookmakers, owners, jockeys and trainers) but its meaning was complex, varying from writer to writer, often needing to be teased out from knowledge of the context, the writer and the period, but often suggesting some kind of activity which might be seen by some as dishonest. Racing morality in terms of betting and racehorse management was a special kind of morality which was rarely spoken of directly. Many racing works have a comment somewhere which indicate that the writer's memories are restricted to 'things I can tell'.[25] The representation and interpretation of meaning through such texts is therefore important for the historian.

Racing records survived for a number of courses, more especially when the local corporation played a major role in their survival, and were extremely useful for economic issues. Some joint-stock company details were held in the Public Record Office (the BT31 files), and were a useful source for the later nineteenth-century thoroughbred breeding companies as well as grandstand and racecourse companies. Court records have also been used, providing an insight not only into betting and racecourse offences but also other aspects of racing life. Litigation between trainers, betters, jockeys or owners gave at times a real window into attitudes and values. Another hitherto relatively unexploited source was gentry and other family archives. The retention of documents relating to betting, training bills and attendance at meetings, or correspondence relating to racing was characteristic of many gentry families. Diaries from a number of points in the social structure sometimes made reference to attendance at meetings and shed further light on the social class of attenders, while the wills of some racing participants such as bookmakers, trainers and jockeys gave their estates at death. Census enumerator records provide details of the social structures of breeding and training. Small, local case studies have been used to flesh out our existing understanding of the social organization of the fascinating microcommunities and shed new light on the people involved.

The use of this much wider range of sources has made possible an approach to racing which investigates the view from the crowd as much as from the grandstand; from the racing insider's perspective as much as from that of the convinced nonconformist anti-gambler; and from the provinces as much as from London.

Notions of social class have been used to help to organize the text, but a study of racing suggests that while nineteenth-century society was not empty of classes, neither the working nor the lower middle classes had any readily perceptible cohesion of consciousness or culture in terms of their attitudes to racing. Within both classes there were quite clear fractures and splits, from which sprang both strong support and strong opposition. The approach adopted has been to explore the relationship of racing to notions of leisure cultures which H. Cunningham and others have attempted to identify: the national leisure class with its conspicuous consumption; urban, middle-class culture; reformist leisure culture; artisan leisure culture; rural popular culture; and urban popular culture.[26] Here again, however, racing presents a challenge to such theoretical constructs in their present state of development. Cunningham has attempted to avoid the issue by arguing, for example, that social mixing at race meetings was either 'infrequent, and on that ground acceptable' or that it was 'of relatively minor importance in the context of the full range of leisure activities in which people engaged'.[27] This argument marginalizes any social actions not fitting the model. This is entirely inappropriate. Instead, the model needs to be modified to fit the findings of empirical research.

Such issues are given full attention in the conclusion; but before doing so more basic questions needed to be addressed. In terms of social issues there was a need to demonstrate the cross-class nature of race-meeting attendance and the several groups involved in other participatory ways as owners, breeders, race officials or investors, or in becoming involved in betting on racing results. Related social questions were also examined: the attractions of going to meetings and changes in their character; the part played by betting on and off the course; problems of crowd behaviour and how they were dealt with; the role of racing in the towns with racecourses, in other urban areas, and in those country areas where training and breeding took place. It is important to confront the issue of the different meanings of racing for the several social groups who rendered it their allegiance.

A second set of questions concerned economic issues, with the commercialization of racing. Racing was more commercialized in the early part of the century than has been realized. Its organization was such as to ensure that profits were made; but it is important to identify those who set out to make a profit from the sport and the extent to which they were successful. Did racehorse owners have an opportunity to profit or to recoup expenses, or were they expected to pay for their pleasure? What was the economic contribution of betting to the sport?

Other questions were political in nature, concerned with the distribution of power and authority within and over racing. Conventional wisdom sees the Jockey Club as having a key role, even at times able to control legislation. The Club's role is reassessed here, challenging the accepted chronology and arguing that it was relatively powerless across the majority of the country meetings until well after mid-century. To understand this we need to understand who controlled the sport and the range of ways in which different forms of control were exercised. How was control exercised at the level of individual meetings, in terms of the power of stewards, clerks and other officials? Externally, who were the social groups who opposed it and its associated betting, and what forms did this opposition take? How successful were they?

In attempting to answer such questions two aspects of racing have been excluded from the discussion. First, Irish racing has yet to be covered, in part because of the sheer bulk of the sources available, but more importantly because of its limited impact on Irish society for much of the period. One usually authoritative writer has asserted that 'up to 1888 the public who went racing in Ireland might be described as horsey people only. Breeders, owners and trainers attended. The stakes were small and the gate infinitesimal.'[28] Telegraph traffic figures show that there was little off-course Irish interest in results. Secondly, there is no consideration of National Hunt racing because it has received recent attention in an important work by R. Munting.[29]

Although this study contributes significantly to a number of debatable aspects of continuity, change and social relations within racing, its reconceptualization and the novelty of the conclusions also contribute to a number of important, broader, historical debates and raise questions in relation to our understanding of the part racing played in society as a whole. It employs a far wider range of sources than previous studies have. It pushes back the accepted chronology of racing, arguing that working-class betting was playing a major role in some towns even in mid-century; that racing had major commercial features in the early nineteenth century; and that the apparent ruling group in racing, the Jockey Club, had only limited power before the 1860s. The history of racing is in part the history of attempts to control racing and betting by three groups: the anti-betting minority, Parliament and the Jockey Club; yet these attempts were constantly subverted or the outcomes different from what might be expected. A knowledge of racing also challenges our assumptions about leisure during the last century. Racing was a cross-class sport with significant middle-class involvement. Many members of the latter espoused leisure and sporting values very different from those held by the more vociferous, 'respectable', evangelical opponents of much sport or supporters of the 'amateur' ethos and they have been hitherto neglected. Racing morality challenged respectable morality head-on. The cross-class support for racing, the clear attraction of racing to large numbers of people, and the complex range of reasons why it was easily able to survive as a major sport and industry all suggest that the 'respectable' group may have triumphed in ideological terms but was far less successful in reality in British society. Within the sport itself vertical ties of common interest often bound competing groups, and there were only limited examples of class conflict or hegemonic practice. Not all leisure forms were a focus for class conflict, while a study of racing also suggests that notions of leisure cultures need much further refinement and that the hitherto accepted relationships between social class and some forms of leisure are more problematical than has been realized. Not all popular leisure activities were respectable, wholesome acts that cultivated the mind, body or spirit. Favourite pursuits might also include drunkenness, whoring or gambling, and these may well have been attractive to wider groups than just urban working men, just as racing certainly was.

The following chapters examine these questions in some detail. The first provides the non-racing reader with an overview of flat racing between 1800 and 1914, concentrating on a basic social, geographic and economic description of the industry at three key stages; pre-railway, the period from about 1840 to about 1880, and the period from around 1880 to 1914. Major aspects of racing and its associated activities (breeding, ownership and training) are documented and the key changes in the nature of the industry over time are explored.

The following three chapters present new and important evidence to demonstrate that support for racing came from right across the social structure and could be found within a range of leisure cultures, including sections of the national leisured classes, some middle-class groups, artisan leisure culture, and rural and urban popular culture.[30]

Thoroughbred racing had its origins in aristocratic sport and this group continued to play a major role in breeding and racing through the period, as is shown in Chapter 2. Indeed, they were more successful in the classic races towards the end of the period than earlier. The wide range of motives for upper-class involvement and its complex nature are addressed through a structure which first explores the forms of involvement with the races themselves, such as investment in meeting organization, the purchase of shares in grandstand companies, subscriptions towards the prize money or attendance at meetings. Sociability, membership of race clubs and the role of the house party are also discussed. A following section assesses involvement in thoroughbred breeding, racehorse ownership and betting, exploring the range of motivation – from those primarily intent on making money from the sport, to those who were more intent on achieving success or other non-monetary forms of satisfaction.[31]

The urban middle classes have hitherto been seen as the most strongly and fiercely opposed to racing, but Chapter 3 makes clear how many within that group made a variety of positive contributions and had an attachment to the sport throughout the century. By its end they dominated racehorse ownership; throughout the century grandstands sheltered them at the meetings; they acted as bookmakers or backers of horses in the betting market; middle-class share ownership was becoming common from the 1860s; they played a part in the industry; and they dominated the ranks of racing officials. Much of such activity came from the ranks of the urban middle classes, although some occupational groups played a larger part than others, and the picture overall is a complicated one. Many of the rural middle classes also supported racing, while the wealth, income and status of some trainers, breeders and jockeys also put them into this group.

Racing and betting were also in part unashamedly populist, a key part of urban popular culture, and this aspect is looked at in Chapter 4, which examines the role of spectatorship and on-course and off-course betting. The chapter argues for the crucial importance of the period from around 1840 to the 1870s in providing the underpinning for the growth of later mass betting. It took a variety of forms, but initially ante-post betting and sweepstakes on major races such as the Derby or St. Leger were the most common. The 1853 Betting House Act had only a brief impact and the expansion of betting news in the press, given powerful impetus by the electric telegraph, saw a further growth in working-class betting from the late 1850s, often but not solely among skilled workmen. Shops and public houses continued to be used, but this could be a risky strategy and in most larger towns street betting was more common, socially zoned and tolerated. Local authorities employed by-laws to control it but only spasmodically, while some magistrates were reluctant to convict. A more rapid expansion of betting from the 1880s caused sufficient concern for the government to pass the Street Betting Act of 1906, but the impact on betting was only marginal. There was a range of clear reasons for betting in working-class urban communities, and by the First World War betting was a dominant leisure feature of working-class urban life, although not of more rural communities, whose inhabitants had attended meetings in some numbers up to the 1860s.

The racecourse and racecourse life lie at the heart of racing. Chapter 5 argues that, while there were changes in the size and nature of the crowd and in the range of facilities offered, there were also major continuities, especially in terms of food and drink, betting, prostitution and entertainments. The races had large elements of carnival, up to and beyond the mid-nineteenth century, although processions and ceremonial features also helped to confirm the established order. Informal social zoning created order from disorder, while the grandstands provided shelter, food and a privileged view and were linked to the mid-century development of the parade and the betting ring. On-course betting inside and outside the ring became more organized through the century, supported by information provided by tipsters, card sellers and the sporting press. Despite the large crowds and carnival atmosphere, major disturbances on courses were extremely rare. Most courses survived the attacks on popular recreations which characterized the period from 1820 to 1850 unscathed. There were occasional flare-ups stemming from resistance to attempts at crime control by the authorities, while later disturbances included elements of social conflict, especially clashes between minority groups such as the navvies or the Irish and locals, as well as a range of brief disturbances including organized robberies or anger at suspected dishonesty. There was a range of crowd-control measures carried out by the police but right through the century there were few arrests at any one meeting.

To see racing as merely a sport underestimates its importance. It was also a major British industry. As G. Cross has shown, most societies of leisure were transformed by modern technology and economic organization.[32] Racing has been seen as becoming significantly more commercialized over the century, albeit on the basis of limited evidence from the earlier period, but in Chapter 6 a substantial range of evidence is presented to indicate that local race meetings in the earlier period were already adopting a commercial approach. The chapter examines the ways in which meetings were organized and the ways in which money was raised to run them and meet the various costs associated with them. Key questions such as who profited and how that profit was made are explored. Finally, the economics of ownership, breeding and training are discussed.

According to D. Cannadine, the aristocracy continued to exercise substantial political power until the end of the century.[33] Racing also has a political dimension, especially in terms of power and control, and it has often been portrayed as an activity where the aristocracy were able to play a dominant role, not least through the Jockey Club and its Newmarket base. But Chapter 7 provides a critical reassessment of the Club's role, drawing on a wider range of contemporary sources to demonstrate that its path to power was slower and much more problematic than has been generally thought. At first, any power it held was solely over Newmarket racing, although it was extended to Ascot and Epsom by the 1830s and at times to courses elsewhere where individual members had strong links. The Club began making changes to more general rules in the late 1850s and only really began attempting to extend its power to courses more broadly from 1870. Racing remained in large part dependent on local political conditions and local market forces for much of the century. After 1870 the Club's authority and power grew rapidly, thanks in large part to the power vacuum at the heart of the sport. The Weatherby publishing family, through their control of entries in the *Racing Calendar* and the *Stud Book*, their official position *vis-à-vis* the Jockey Club at Newmarket and their management of much racing correspondence were far more important definers of reality to most racing men. The Jockey Club itself was not united but divided largely by its members' betting interests and was only rarely purposeful. Its members' betting interests were often best served in the longer term by doing nothing. Social control often involved maintenance of a moral order, but the Jockey Club often reflected the same sets of values as racing at large. Through its upper-house representation, however, it was able to control legislation to a limited extent and no major nineteenth-century legislation on racing ever challenged its interests.

Beyond the course in society as a whole there was a range of views on racing. As we have seen, its adherents could be found right across the class system, but so could its opponents, and the forms and strength of their opposition is assessed in Chapter 8. Some social groups were strongly opposed to the races and particularly strongly opposed to gambling and to betting, on or off the course, on the results. This group comprised those espousing reformist leisure culture, alongside a range of others, ranging from some among the urban elite to more respectable artisans and workers. Opposition stemmed partly from fear of the crowds, their language and behaviour, together with broader concerns about absenteeism from work, working-class spending on pleasure and the travelling criminals who followed the races. The whole apparatus of rational, recreationalist argument was marshalled against the races to try and eliminate them. It took a variety of forms, including preaching, petitions, anti-race demonstrations, counter-attractions and trips, and the formation of the National Anti-

Gambling League. The anti-race group did have some limited success. A few courses were closed down thanks in part to their efforts; local authority by-laws were strengthened; and some legislation was passed against working-class betting. It is argued however, that this was a minority group which failed to sway public opinion as a whole.

Chapter 9 shows how the findings shed light on the larger question of why racing survived despite the opposition. The reasons are complex and varied from meeting to meeting. Race meetings often contributed significantly to local economies; police control and other forms of supervision may have become more effective; aristocracy, gentry and local politicians exercised social and political patronage; there was almost always cross-class support; a semi-professionalized course management group from early in the century often showed sound economic and commercial acumen; and racing provided a key context for gambling. By the later nineteenth century there was a growing recognition that races were a 'workfolk's holiday'.

It also ties the study back to the Introduction, beginning with a re-emphasizing of some key themes: those of continuity as much as change and the importance of early commercial features. Racing was transformed to only a minor extent by the processes of capitalism, urbanization and industrialization. It had many of its key features from the early nineteenth century, and, unlike most other sports, had a stress on speculation equally as much as competition and pleasure. It was among the earliest of populist, commercial, leisure activities, yet it provided a refuge for an annual carnival of drink, betting and other more dubious pleasures. Absenteeism for the races was common throughout the century and employers were faced by worker resistance to any attempts to stop it. Racing fits only with difficulty to a model premised on class conflict, because relationships were different within racing.

Two other understandings are necessary for the reader. First, being individualistic, the turf was also characterized by shifting allegiances which were not necessarily those of class. Class distinctions were much looser on the turf, even though participants were well aware of them and would often observe them scrupulously in other contexts. Betters or owners might temporarily work together to ensure that a horse won (or lost), and might well need the assistance of trainers, commission agents or jockeys and might even socialize with them, while trying to outdo other such constellations of racing power. Like Harold Perkin's 'old society', it was based on vertical ties but with a major difference, being founded not on permanent ones of deference but of shifting ones of common interest.

Secondly, racing had an important publicly unacknowledged but privately integrating feature. Nearly all racing insiders tried constantly to indicate that the sport espoused amateur, manly, honest, respectable and sportsmanlike values, while really accepting that the reality was otherwise, thus also avoiding potential libel actions. When Wildrake produced a description of events on the turf in the 1830s and the early 1840s he was careful to state that he had 'assiduously endeavoured to avoid giving offence to any; and sought to bury all unpleasant reminiscences with the bones of the by-gones'.[34] Sir Loftus Bates, a major figure on the northern circuit in the early twentieth century admitted, 'If I put all I knew into print, half of those on the Turf stage would be warned off.'[35] Warning off was used only when even the lax morality of the turf was shocked and this suggests a very high level of dishonest practice at one time or another. To make a valid complaint about someone else's winner was often to risk a later, equally valid complaint in return. Memoirs of the turf and racing newspapers hint at dishonest practices but were always concerned about libel or causing upset to families. Suspicion was one thing, proof was another. Almost everyone living the world of the turf relied upon a conspiracy of silence; Lord Rossmore's chosen title in his memoirs of the turf, *Things I Can Tell* (1912), indicates the limited access which the public were permitted to this secret world.

NOTES

1. R. Holt, 'Sport and history; the state of the subject in Britain', *Working Papers in Sport and Society*, Vol.3 (University of Warwick, 1995), p.5.
2. For a review of leisure historiography up to 1989 see P. Bailey, 'Leisure, culture and the historian: reviewing the first generation of leisure historiography in Britain', *Leisure Studies*, Vol.8 (1989), pp.107–27.
3. R.D. Storch, 'The roots of working class leisure; some roots of middle class moral reform in the industrial north', in A.P. Donajgrodzki (ed.), *Social Control in 19th Century Britain* (1977); E. Yeo and S. Yeo (eds), *Popular Culture and Class Conflict: Explorations in the Study of Work and Leisure 1590–1914* (Brighton, 1981).
4. J.K. Walton, *The English Seaside Resort: a Social History 1750–1914* (Leicester, 1983).
5. P.C. Bailey (ed.), *Music Hall, the Business of Pleasure* (Milton Keynes, 1986).
6. T. Mason, *Association Football and English Society 1863–1915* (Brighton, 1980).
7. M.J. Huggins, 'Stockton race week', *Journal of Regional and Local Studies* (June 1985).
8. J.M. Golby and A.W. Purdue, *The Civilisation of the Crowd: Popular Culture in England 1750–1900* (1984), p.12.
9. See, for example, H. Cunningham, *Leisure in the Industrial Revolution c. 1780–c. 1880* (1980); J.K. Walton and J. Walvin (eds), *Leisure in Britain 1780–1939* (Manchester, 1983).
10. E.P. Thompson, *The Making of the English Working Class* (1963).
11. P. Joyce, *Work, Society and Politics; the Culture of the Factory in Later Victorian England* (Brighton, 1980).
12. R. Williams, 'Base and superstructure in Marxist cultural theory', *New Left Review*, No. 82 (1973), p.8.
13. J. Lowerson, *Sport and the English Middle Classes* (Manchester, 1994), p.5.
14. P. Bailey, *Leisure and Class in Victorian England: Rational Recreation and the Contest for Control, 1830–1885* (1978).

15. H. Meller, *Leisure and the Changing City 1870–1914* (1976).
16. See Lowerson, *Sport*, p.5.
17. M.J. Huggins, 'Culture, class and respectability; racing and the English middle classes in the nineteenth century', *International Journal of the History of Sport*, Vol.11, No.1 (April 1994), pp.19–41.
18. D.C. Itzkowitz, *Peculiar Privilege: a Social History of English Foxhunting 1753–1885* (Brighton, 1977); J.M. Mackenzie, *The Empire of Nature: Hunting, Conservation and British Imperialism* (Manchester, 1988).
19. J.V. Beckett, *The Aristocracy in England 1660–1914* (1986).
20. Early urban historians such as Briggs made minimal reference to sport; A. Briggs, *Victorian Cities* (1963). Even Meller (*Leisure and the Changing City*) makes only passing references to sport in Bristol.
21. E.g., M.J. Huggins, 'Leisure and sport in Middlesbrough 1840–1914', in A.J. Pollard (ed.), *Middlesbrough: Town and Community 1830–1950* (Stroud, 1996).
22. E.g., K. McCrone, *Sport and the Physical Emancipation of English Women 1870–1914* (1988).
23. T. Mason, *Association Football and English Society 1863–1915* (1980), pp.6, 175–95.
24. W. Vamplew, *The Turf: a Social and Economic History of Horse Racing* (1976).
25. Even more modern writers still do this, e.g., J. Fairfax-Blakeborough, *History of Horseracing in Scotland* (1973), p.ix. Early writers were often quite explicit. 'Wildrake', *The Cracks of the Day* (1843), p.ii, in a survey of classic winners claimed that he had 'assiduously endeavoured to avoid giving offence to any and buried all unpleasant reminiscences'.
26. H. Cunningham, 'Leisure and Culture', in F.L.M. Thompson, *The Cambridge Social History of Britain 1750–1950*; Vol. 2, *People and Their Environment* (Cambridge, 1990).
27. Ibid., p.319.
28. London and County Press Association, *Racing at Home and Abroad*, Vol. II (1927), p.236.
29. R. Munting, *Hedges and Hurdles: a Social and Economic History of National Hunt Racing* (1987).
30. See Cunningham, 'Leisure and Culture'; this provides descriptions of a number of what he terms 'leisure cultures'.
31. W. Vamplew, *Pay Up and Play the Game: Professional Sport in Britain 1875–1914* (Cambridge, 1988), Ch.8.
32. G. Cross, *A Social History of Leisure since 1600* (State College, PA, 1990), p.225.
33. D. Cannadine, *Lords and Landlords; the Aristocracy and the Towns 1774–1967* (Leicester, 1980).
34. See Wildrake, *Cracks of the Day*, p.ii.
35. N. Fairfax-Blakeborough (ed.), '*J. F.-B.*', p.106.

1

Racing: An Overview, 1800–1914

The cross-class nature of racing, most especially the upper- and middle-class involvement, its early commercialization and the importance of betting are important themes which helped to ensure its popularity; these are developed in subsequent chapters, when the place of racing in British society is examined in more detail.

Before doing so, however, some background information may be helpful for the non-specialist reader. First, to understand racing it is necessary to understand the major changes in betting over the period and a brief account is therefore provided. Secondly, although many changes in racing were clearly linked to broader economic and social changes in British society, they cannot be fully understood without some reference to key technologically driven instruments of change: transport, the electric telegraph and the sporting press, and these are next reviewed. Finally, the chapter provides a quantitative, descriptive overview of some key dimensions of the sport and its development as a preparation for the later discussion of social and commercial changes in racing.

Around 1800 annual races between thoroughbred horses, predominantly owned by the upper classes and ridden by diminutive, professional jockeys, were the highlight of the entertainment calendar in many towns throughout Britain. Drinking, eating and a wide range of other ancillary entertainments accompanied the races, which were already commercial enterprises, organized and run by those who might benefit from the increased spending races stimulated. Owners ran their horses for prize money to which they contributed, but which was often also raised locally to attract runners and hence profit to the town. At Newmarket races were organized by the Jockey Club, but elsewhere, although a gentry-dominated committee decided some details, much of the organization was carried out by a clerk of the course and a committee of local business people whose interests were commercial, as Chapter 6 will show. Races required capital outlay. Revenue could not come direct from the crowd; the poverty of many of those attending made them unwilling to pay an entrance fee. But rich owners staying in town for a week spent a great deal of money, and annual race meetings, like annual fairs, were occasions for which socially-mixed crowds were prepared to save and then spend their money. They were occasions for local holidays; mills, mines and manufactories and some shops closed; country people also attended. The money spent in the towns and on the course during the race week made them a magnet for a travelling population of turfites, thimbleriggers, card sellers, prostitutes and others with commercial interests. Most towns held only one meeting a year; local populations could not afford to spend their money on two such events. Most betting then took place only at the local races, since most people had no access to any wider information about horses and their form.

By 1914 racing had changed greatly; changes in commercial practice created meetings which were either fully enclosed or partially enclosed, charging admission to spectators, many of whom had travelled from a distance. With the introduction of an entry charge the crowd had become increasingly male and there was more focus on the racing itself. Yet interest in race meetings reached new heights and coverage in the daily newspapers reflected this. Thus Emily Davidson's choice of the King's horse in the Derby to make her suffragist demonstration in 1913 got high publicity, although public sympathy for her was not widespread.[1] Wider information about racing, disseminated in the popular press and gained from telegraphed reports, had led to betting on racing becoming common in British society, most especially among the working classes.

Such changes were related to broader social and economic changes.[2] In 1800 there was insufficient aggregate discretionary spending power to make more than one meeting a year economically possible and regular sports spectatorship was unknown. After the mid-1840s even the most pessimistic of historians of the standard of living accepts that real wages rose, by which time Britain was becoming an increasingly industrialized and urbanized nation and factory employees were no longer such a minority of workers. Even in 1851, however, agriculture remained the largest single category of employment, and the majority of workers were not subject to factory discipline. Increases in spending power, sufficient leisure time and improved transport led to some limited increases in the number of meetings in large urban areas and in attendance at them, and, as we shall see in Chapter 4, to the beginnings of growth in working-class betting. Despite cyclical and technological unemployment, real wages for most workers generally rose in the last decades of the nineteenth century, before levelling off or declining, while commercial spectator sport for the mass market became one of the economic success stories of later Victorian Britain. More regularly held, highly-capitalized meetings, increasingly held on Saturday afternoons, and the rapidly steepening growth in working-class betting from the 1870s were both consequences of this rise in disposable wealth.

Despite these changes, racing had a large measure of continuity across the period. Betting lay at the heart of its popularity. Competition between horses was the major sporting feature. Many of the ancillary entertainments present on the courses show little change through the period and the atmosphere of the course remained one of rush and excitement, turmoil and din, coming from a crowd whose main aim was pleasure. Racing was closely connected with the selling of alcohol and the making and taking of bets. Shared enthusiasm, interests, values, attitudes and a resulting solidarity of interest bound the followers of racing together – even though competition divided them – and were important in ensuring a continuing support for racing.

I

Betting was the *raison d'être* of racing and its operation was complex. Around 1800 there was already an inner turfite betting group and some horse owners were already taking or laying odds on a number of horses in a race to minimize potential losses or maximize their profits, recording bets in their betting books, since betting was credit betting paid on a post-race 'settling day'. Although most owners were upper- or middle-class, by 1800 a relatively few working-class 'bookmakers', described as 'legs', were also involved in this 'betting ring'.[3] Although modern bookmakers lay (offer odds against) all horses in the field, this was much more difficult in the smaller betting market then existing. Some of both the upper-class group and the more plebeian 'legs' with whom they associated would both lay against and back a number of horses as the odds changed, betting with each other in a cross-class way, often in temporary alliance with others. Ideally, they balanced the betting book and took sufficient bets to make a profit. This could be done by backing a single horse at long odds, and then 'hedging' the bet by laying the horse at shorter odds, so that money was not lost if the horse lost but was won if the horse won. Or it could be done by taking sufficient bets against all horses, 'betting round', so no matter what horse won the income would exceed the money paid out. Unfortunately, there was usually insufficient money in the betting market to do this. When Birmingham won the St. Leger in 1830, the 'Warwickshire gentlemen' were 'almost the only winners', so few had backed him.[4] Even in the 1820s the number of 'betters rounds' was estimated as few more than a baker's dozen.[5]

The size of this central turfite group could be measured in a few thousands. Many knew each other. Tattersall's, the Hyde Park Corner subscription betting rooms, had a predominantly upper-class London and Newmarket-based membership of around 200 in the 1830s. The number of racehorse owners was under 500 for much of the first two decades. There was a fluctuating annual figure of fewer than 1,500 subscribers to the annual *Racing Calendar* between 1814 and 1834, but this was also used by those more interested in breeding than racing. Most betters were upper-class, but there were also more proletarian betters including trainers and jockeys. 'Betting commissioners', from all classes, placed bets for others. Sometimes this was to conceal the origins of support for a horse, but bets were also posted to commissioners by country betters. This gave them more opportunities of betting round, if they had the right connections. The Derby betting books of the working-class 'leg' John Gully reveal that he laid or backed horses with some hundred others in 1810 and with nearly 150 people in 1825.[6] Ante-post betting, from up to and beyond a year before, often at long odds, took place on a small number of major races and this allowed some very big money wins. Single winning bets quoted for the Derby or the St. Leger were often between £20,000 and £40,000.

Turf morality was much the same among members of all classes. The 'knowing ones' were those who were most aware of the true form and fitness of horses entered in the major races.[7] Both aristocratic betters and 'legs' were anxious to manipulate the betting to their own advantage.[8] Information was crucial, since it was by betting against horses which the bookmaker had good reason to consider safe because they were not good enough, injured, unfit or not meant to win by the owner (or the trainer or jockey) that money was best made. So public trainers were expected to keep their horses' owners in touch with relative racing form, and the most successful public trainers with many horses were crucial in helping the careful manipulation of betting odds. For a major race, such as the St. Leger, there might be a number of horses entered; but most would not finally run because all the stables' owners would be made aware of their relative merits. Of the 19 horses entered from John Scott's Malton stables in 1835, where some ten or more owners had horses, only the best-fancied two actually ran. So bets could be made against the rest quite safely. But could the trainer always be trusted? The Day family, for example, were involved in many racing scandals in the mid-nineteenth century, and John Barham Day's nickname 'Honest' was well recognized as 'a facetious soubriquet', not least since he was sometimes prepared to put his own betting interests above those of his owners.[9] A poor horse's form could be 'puffed up', a good one's merits concealed. If a stable favourite lost form or was injured attempts would be made to lay against it before this became public knowledge. Where the stable had two good horses in a race and felt that they could win with either, the better, shorter-odds horse might be held back by the jockey to allow the other, longer-odds, well-stable-backed one to win. Horses could be bet against, and subsequently withdrawn (since under 'play or pay' betting the bet was lost if the horse did not win whether it started or not) or pulled during the race. A good horse owned by an opponent could be purchased and then withdrawn. Information about other horses could be purchased from horse watchers or 'touts'. Such strategies were common among all parties on the turf and those owners who ran their horses without resorting to such activities were often singled out as exceptional.

It was the increasing information about form and betting odds that allowed betting to expand beyond this turfite group. The first races of wider betting appeal were the Derby and the St. Leger, where reports on form could be gathered for over a year before. Regional papers were including the Derby and St. Leger results as well as those of the local races even in a relatively non-racing area such as south Westmorland as early as the 1820s.[10] The St. Leger result was conveyed by the next coaches on all the major coaching routes, while dogs following a trail, riders or carrier-pigeons were used to get the results to major towns.[11] But while betting information was limited and the newspapers and magazines which provided it costly, more widespread, off-course betting on racing was still limited to a relatively narrow and often relatively wealthy group of turfites.

By the 1850s the number of major races where ante-post credit betting began anything up to a year before the race, or when weights were published in handicap events, had widened. As betting information became more readily available betting became more popular.[12] The inner group of turfites was still comparatively small, but the greater access to information gave increased rationality and a businesslike, profit-driven focus, attracting more middle- and working-class bookmakers. Betting information printed in London newspapers about the changing odds now came not just from Tattersall's but also from the City, the West End and London clubs. Tattersall's provided what the Druid described as a 'great betting mart, whose quotations are to racing men what those of Mart Lane are to the farmer, Lloyd's to the insurer'.[13] Tattersall's opened new and enlarged subscription rooms in London in 1865 to cater for the demand. Outside London the Manchester betting rooms provided a focus for northern turfites and northern papers listed its odds from the 1830s.

Information was obtained largely from newspapers. These had brought betting information to a reading public from early in the century. In

Yorkshire, for example, weekly papers such as the *York Herald,* the *Yorkshire Gazette,* or the *Doncaster Gazette* provided full betting, breeding, and other racing information. In London two weekly sporting papers, the *Sunday Times* and *Bell's Life in London* provided betting information superior to that of the *Racing Calendar* sheet from the late 1820s, and had a wider circulation, although at five pence a copy it was not cheap. Monthly magazines, such as the *Sporting Review,* contained interesting but out-of-date racing material, at a cost well outside the pockets of most working men.

Following the abolition of advertising and stamp duty in the 1850s, the growing market for racing news built by the extension of telegraphic results was fed by the London-based *Sporting Life* (founded in 1859) which published first weekly and then twice weekly at a cost of a penny. By 1860 it claimed a readership of 260,000.[14] Its first major competitor, the *Sportsman*, was first published in 1865 twice a week, becoming a daily in 1874. The first provincial racing paper was Hulton's Manchester-based *Sporting Chronicle,* first published in 1871.

Greater information about form soon began to drive down individual amounts won and lost. By 1853 it was argued that in the major classic races 'the general information which prevails ... operates materially against bookmaking ... those which are worth backing are constantly brought forth as prominent favourites'.[15] Owners now had more chance of manipulating odds in handicaps by concealing horses' form until weights allocated were low enough to give a real chance of winning.

Among the wider population betting was also growing in popularity. As we shall see in Chapter 4, the working classes were increasingly interested in wider betting, especially in northern England and London. Sweepstake betting on big races was one example of this, and even in 1848 the *Sporting Magazine* claimed with pardonable exaggeration that 'nine tenths of the males in every parish in the north of England' were personally interested in the St. Leger result.[16] In contrast, a reduction in the numbers of prestigious Scottish owners had contributed to a decline in the interest in betting in Scotland. In England betting lists were increasingly to be found in public houses, barbers or other places of association where bets could be placed with bookmakers, although odds were poor, and bets had to be in cash.

In London list houses included the Coach and Horses in Piccadilly, where the 'leviathan' bookmaker of the 1850s Davis was to be found.[17] Bookmaking was, however, still a risky business. It was not always possible to 'get round', given the size of the betting market, and if odds were laid to unlimited totals against anything backed a bookmaker could lose heavily. Government anxieties about the increased popularity of list houses led to the Betting House Act in 1853, which made them illegal. This had some temporary impact in London where there were a number of prosecutions,[18] but there were few elsewhere.

As betting information was becoming quicker to gain access to and more easy to obtain there was a clear shift away from big-money credit ante-post betting. The yearling books made on the classic races by the turfite group were disappearing, while the regular publicity given to horses puffed up in the market for handicaps and then either withdrawn or pulled during the race to ensure profits by owners working with bookmakers made 'pay or play' bets more obviously risky.[19] With the increasing interest in betting only near the start of the race the *Sporting Chronicle* began giving starting prices in 1871. Those betting by post with 'commission agents' found this a fairer system than relying on the commissioner's claim that he had obtained the best possible odds, a move open to fraud. By 1876 Tattersall's and clubs' ante-post returns were increasingly meagre and unsatisfactory, with the majority of bets, formerly in hundreds of pounds, now between £5 and £20. Most betters now bet on the basis of starting-price odds then appearing in the papers, where bets were void for non-runners. Training reports were giving the public more chance of picking the winner and making it more difficult for owners and betters to exploit public ignorance of true form and manoeuvre horses in the market.[20]

It was the shift to starting prices, and not Jockey Club action, that eliminated some of the more obvious manoeuvres with 'dead meat', 'dead 'uns' and other pre-start tricks, and made racing a little more honest.[21] The shift also forced a change in the nature of bookmaking, with books on races being opened only two or three weeks before, and bookmakers beginning to lay off money and balance their books.

Ever greater newspaper coverage of racing from the 1860s both responded to increased working-class interest in betting and contributed to it. Working-class betting expanded in the 1860s and 1870s, and expanded even more rapidly thereafter. Increasing publicity contributed to increased concerns from the anti-gambling minority by the 1880s (see Chapter 8). These led to the formation of a powerful pressure group, the National Anti-Gambling League in 1890, which was increasingly vociferous in arguing for radical legislation to deal with it.

The opposition to racing had little effect in the face of now widespread support for racing and betting in British society as a whole, and by the first decades of the twentieth century racing enjoyed high status. For the upper classes its main events were part of the social calendar, attracting an elegant and fashionable attendance; while the ownership of top horses was dominated by aristocratic owner-breeders, together with a number of rich newcomers. By contrast, upper-class betting was becoming less significant; gentlemen now placed their bets not with each other but with credit bookmakers. By 1902, according to Sir James Lowther, bets between gentlemen were very rare and had, like matches, faded out, as this 'avoided social argument'.[22]

II

While betting was one important agent of change in racing, three others significantly affected racing's development. Transport changes from the 1830s and the 1840s, the electric telegraph from the 1850s, and the growth of the popular press from the 1860s were all important.

In 1800 deficiencies in transport significantly restricted spectator catchment areas. Most people attended only their local meeting, unless they could afford the high costs of post-horses or coaches; and while horses had to walk between courses most raced only within a regional racing circuit. Newmarket was the key racing centre for the southern upper classes and by the 1830s had seven meetings a year. Many owners ran their horses only there, perhaps occasionally extending their interest to Epsom and Ascot. It was therefore highest in status, not least in the sheer numbers of races and because so many horses were trained there. It was there that both the general rules of racing and the Jockey Club rules were developed, although, as we shall see in Chapter 7, the Club had little power outside Newmarket until well after mid-century. By the 1860s it was becoming increasingly powerful, and by the 1870s it introduced a series of rule changes which were widely adopted by higher-status courses and drove out a number of the smaller ones, although these sometimes continued as unrecognized meetings.

Not all owners/trainers restricted their horses to a single circuit, since running a horse where local opposition was weaker or where its form was unknown increased the chances of prize money or of winning bets, especially since betters took longer to gather information on form or results when they were reliant on the mailcoach. Horses were walked significant distances as a result. In 1826, for example, one Middleham trainer ran his horse Truth at Catterick, Middleham, Epsom and Ipswich.

In the late 1830s there was a change by some owners from having horses walked to meetings to having them taken by specially constructed racehorse vans. This stemmed from Lord George Bentinck's conveyance of his horse Elis from Goodwood some 250 miles in three days, having got odds of 12–1 against its winning the 1836 St. Leger. Most layers had assumed that the horse would not arrive in time. Vanning, however, was costly. Elis's trip, using relays of post-horses, probably cost about £90.

But by this time the spread of the railways was changing the sport by increasing spectator numbers, aiding the rapid transport of horses between meetings and thereby increasing the numbers of entries and conveying betting information. As early as 1831 the Liverpool and Manchester Railway had 26 cotton wagons fitted up temporarily as second-class carriages to run to and from Liverpool and Manchester to Newton races in June. Numbers were at first not large (about 2,500 tickets were printed each day), but by 1835 the line's race traffic had expanded significantly.[23]

From small beginnings in the 1830s, there were nearly 2,400 miles of lines by 1846, and about 6,000 by 1850. By this point a sufficiently extensive railway network was in place to ensure that many meetings received special trains from a significantly expanded regional catchment area. Rising real wages meant that urban dwellers could attend rural meetings elsewhere. In 1853, for example, the small meeting at Ripon in north Yorkshire attracted special trains from the towns of Hartlepool and Stockton in Durham and from York and Leeds in Yorkshire.[24] The expansion of the railways therefore increased spectator levels and indirectly helped to raise both commercial revenue for those interested in profiting from racing and prize money at meetings.

More indirectly, the railway boom of the early 1840s contributed to a broader moral climate which revolved around the urge to speculate and make money fast. Railway mania, with a series of distorted, exploitive railway projects often designed to defraud the public, reached a head in 1844, the same year as the notorious 'Running Rein' Derby, with its substitute horses and deliberate dishonesties.[25] Racing dishonesty, with aristocratic owners, bookmakers, trainers and jockeys all involved, received temporary publicity, although this had little long-term effect.

Increased entries were a second major effect. Southern horses were more able to run at northern meetings and vice versa, while there was also a related growth in the proportion of two-year-old races, since previously these young horses had been unable to stand the strain of long-distance walking. Horses could now leave their stables quite close to the race, decreasing the chances of illness, injury or of being 'got at' *en route*. More entries helped to boost the earnings of top jockeys who could now, with swifter travel, get more rides. Thirdly, transport innovation encouraged the spread of thoroughbred breeding by enabling owners to send their mares to the most fashionable and successful stallions. Finally, railways encouraged a wider interest in racing through their making more readily available daily papers with racing news for a wider clientele.

But what really generated public interest in wider betting was not the railway but the electric telegraph. It provided a rapid results service and reduced betting dishonesty. As newspapers became increasingly able to gain reports from the training areas by telegraph, the manipulating of horses in the betting market became less easy.

Derby and St. Leger results were being transmitted to and from London as early as 1847, thus 'frustrating the manoeuvres of private speculators'.[26] The result of the St. Leger was sent to London from Doncaster in the same year. *Ruff's Guide* was offering to supply betting news and results by telegraph 'on moderate terms' in 1850.[27] The Electric Telegraph Company (ETC) laid a line direct from a racecourse – Doncaster – in 1852, and by 1858 the British and Irish Magnetic Company also had permanent offices there.[28] Epsom had a temporary office in 1853 and a permanent circuit in 1857.[29] Ambitious provincial race committees were quick to want the same service, while there was greatly increased pressure to run races on time because betters elsewhere expected telegraphic results messages.[30]

But the companies were slow to expand. There were still only 2,040 stations open to the public in 1865 and so the number of public messages concerned with racing expanded relatively slowly over the period 1855–65.[31] Geography and ease of access still limited the potential of the telegraph for betting information and the use which could be made by newspapers of racing results. The real boom for betting came in 1868 when the Post Office took over the several telegraph companies and began a rapid expansion.

The impact of more immediate news on the world of racing and betting, and hence upon wider society, was soon noticeable. In 1870 114,479 messages were sent from 135 meetings in the United Kingdom.[32] By 1875 a total of 436,603 were sent from 264 meetings. Certainly in the early 1870s much of the traffic at meetings was still generated by bookmakers, owners and other regular racegoers, but the volume of press messages was growing relative to it. The impact varied with the perceived general importance of the race result. This may be seen clearly by a comparison of public and press messages for 1870 and 1875 in Table 1.

The telegraph made reports by touts on the horses' progress almost immediately available to the daily papers, making information on form more widely available, if the tout were honest and the horse's form clear. It also encouraged the move to starting prices among urban working-class betters.

Two principal associations, the Press Association and the Central Press, soon had a major impact on the transmission of racing news by telegraph. In 1868 the telegraph companies had sent news to only 144 towns and to

TABLE 1
TELEGRAPH MESSAGES FROM UNITED KINGDOM COURSES, 1870–75

Racecourse	Public messages 1870	Public messages 1875	Press messages 1870	Press messages 1875
*Newmarket	30,168	71,716	3,499	15,280
*Aintree	3,635	22,275	213	5,477
*Doncaster	7,677	17,932	616	2,979
*Epsom	5,660	17,081	c230	2,492
*Goodwood	2,632	14,432	365	1,797
*Warwick	5,930	12,182	707	3,718
*Ascot	3,700	12,812	100	1,715
York	4,585	11,011	503	2,015
Chester	4,626	10,812	389	1,172
Lincoln	1,259	9,188	204	2,243
Shrewsbury	3,435	8,773	302	1,681
Newcastle	1,414	8,300	160	1,717
Brighton	2,327	7,816	256	1,869
*Croydon	n.a.	4,554	n.a.	3,443
*Lewes	n.a.	5,569	n.a.	1,813
*Windsor	1,897	4,687	214	1,680
*Sandown Park	n.a.	4,439	n.a.	1,900
Bristol	n.a.	4,537	n.a.	1,030
Northampton	n.a.	4,063	n.a.	543
*Stockbridge	1,178	3,249	150	1,263
Nottingham	1,915	3,397	266	1,096
Other meetings in England served by special staff	13,974	42,163	3,115	32,356
Scotland	1,401	5,557	603	3,404
Wales	1,614	7,922	651	6,961
Ireland	169		40	
Meetings in UK worked only by local staff		13,729		8,060
Small meetings in several areas	1,800		200	

Source: Report of Select Committee of the House of Commons on the Post Office Telegraph 1876 (357),Vol.XIII.

* Either no or only limited local staff; minimum charge for telegrams was 1s. for 20 words plus the address.

173 newspapers; by 1870 the Post Office was sending it to 365 towns and to 467 newspapers at a lower rate. The special rates for news brought in the halfpenny evening paper with its racing results. In 1870 there were two and by 1893 about 70 such papers, often with several editions to update results.[33] The evening paper brought more immediacy to betting. Bets could be placed during the day and the result known that evening; the attraction

of this to working-class communities may be seen in the rise of betting alongside the growth of the evening press.

The railways had important effects on attendance at meetings, but it was the combined impact of the telegraph and cheap newspapers which forced racing information more firmly into social consciousness. They contributed to a growing opposition to racing from anti-gambling groups. More importantly, they facilitated the growth in betting and helped to popularize the sport more widely. But these changes also affected the nature of racing itself directly. To understand this, the reader needs some quantitative data about meetings, races and racehorses.

III

This section covers important aspects of the changes taking place in racing over the period from about 1800 to 1914 and provides some background information concerning key questions. Where were race meetings held? How many meetings in Britain? How often in a year? How many days did meetings last? What types of race? Over what sort of distances did horses race? How old were the horses?

Racing in Britain already had a long history, with some courses established by corporations as early as the sixteenth century for commercial reasons and others by royalty, the aristocracy and the gentry.[34] Ownership of thoroughbred bloodstock was predominantly for the rich and race meetings were often linked to towns which had close connections with upper-class landowners. Many nomination boroughs held race meetings. In Yorkshire, for example, regular meetings were held at Malton, Northallerton, Pontefract, Richmond and Ripon, occasional ones at Thirsk and Boroughbridge, and only Aldeborough and Knaresborough were non-racing boroughs. Most race meetings were held near county centres, not all of which were shire towns, and were focal points for county social life.[35] Many other races were held near market towns, since these could provide a range of support services such as stabling, accommodation and entertainment. A few meetings were held at more remote training areas. Land used for the races came from a variety of sources, including a range of unenclosed, poor, agricultural land on moorland, heath or downland or on river flood plains; corporation land; or on land owned by local farmers or gentry families favourably disposed to racing. At seaside venues races were sometimes on the beach, when the start depended on low tide.[36]

Although the heartlands of racing were then in Newmarket and in the north, there were significant intercounty variations in the numbers of meetings held, due to differences in size, regional interest or disinterest, or the relative suitability for breeding and training. Surrey had around four and Yorkshire about 20 towns where racing took place. Towns would only organize meetings, with all the costs they entailed, if sufficient money would be spent by those attending to make it worthwhile.

Weatherby's *Racing Calendar* gives a useful overview of the changing numbers of British courses where most races were for thoroughbreds, although there were always many other meetings of lesser importance.[37] At the beginning of the nineteenth century fewer than 80 courses were reported annually. Thereafter, despite some annual fluctuations, the trend was slowly upward, reaching 90 in 1808, passing 100 in 1820 and reaching 120 in 1826. From a peak in 1830 of 125 towns with races, there was a slight decline to 114 in 1833 as some upper-class owners quit racing following the 1832 Reform Act and the sport took a short while to recover.[38] Townsfolk felt that it was not worthwhile to invest money to support the races if insufficient wealthy visitors could be attracted. The introduction, first in 1836 of horse-vanning and secondly of an expanding railway system in the early 1840s, pushed the number of courses up to 151 in 1841, although most new ones did not attract sufficient entries and hence visitors to be commercially successful. Growing urbanization and industrialization, the growing reputation of racing for dishonesty, and the large proletarian crowds brought by train to small, distant, rural, race meetings drove away some upper-class attendance, and the trend thereafter was down for some time. By 1844 there were just 120 courses; by 1850 there were 100; and by 1863 just 96. Of this total, 45 were core meetings, mostly longstanding, with perhaps another ten or so which nearly attained this level of continuity. The rest were a mixture of traditional meetings which suffered breaks in continuity and more temporary ones entering the *Racing Calendar* in a much more irregular way. Sixty-two new meetings emerged in the 1850s and 99 in the 1860s. By now, however, the population rise, increases in living standards and the expansion of interest in betting were affecting racing, and the number of courses rose once again, reaching a peak of 144 in 1869. The increasing exercise of Jockey Club power and the introduction in 1870 of new rules which forced those courses included in the *Calendar* to recognize the Club's authority then affected the total, and the number of courses listed had dropped to 104 by 1876. The Club then demanded that all courses should provide sufficient added money to ensure that each race was worth £100 to the winner. This forced out of the *Calendar* many long-established courses, often near rural market towns, and numbers dropped once more. There were 73 courses listed in 1878, 64 by 1880 and only 49 by 1900. These were the elite of the courses, although there were other 'unrecognized' ones, under less onerous rules, often racing on Saturdays or holidays.

In 1809 Newmarket, home of the Jockey Club, had 39 days racing, spread over a number of meetings. York (10), Doncaster (6), Chester (5), Ascot and Ayr (4 each) or Epsom (3) which came next in status had far fewer. By 1839 Newmarket had 30 days, while Liverpool and York (7 each), Epsom, Chester and Doncaster (5 each), Ascot, Goodwood and the Royal Caledonian Hunt meeting (4 each) were next in status. Most courses had only one or two days' racing a year at their single meeting. But the growing interest in racing and the influence of railway building then began to make it commercially possible and socially acceptable to have two or more meetings at a small number of courses beyond Newmarket. By 1869 several London venues were holding three or more meetings a year, as were York, Manchester and Liverpool. Holiday resorts, such as Margate or Scarborough, which had increasingly begun to run meetings once they were accessible by rail, were another more commercially-orientated group now increasingly found in the lists (see Table 2).

TABLE 2
ANNUAL FREQUENCY OF MEETINGS

Date	One meeting (% of course)	Two meetings (% of course)	Three meetings	Four meetings	Five meetings	Six meetings
1839	92	7	York	–	–	Newmarket
1869	78	16	Chelmsford Kingsbury Margate Liverpool Manchester	West Drayton Bromley		Newmarket Croydon

Source: Racing Calendar.

Even in 1880 only 12 courses had three or more meetings a year. But by the 1890s, although there was an even smaller number of courses, mostly enclosed, 22 of them had three or more meetings a year. Nearby courses which fed the needs of London racegoers – Lingfield, Sandown, Windsor, Kempton Park and Hurst Park – had five or more flat meetings each year, as well as further meetings under National Hunt rules. Only Newmarket had more meetings. These new courses were highly capitalized and most were limited companies. They were major investments, required substantial levels of capitalization and were highly commercial ventures. Where possible, they had fixtures at the beginning and the end of the week. Hurst

Park had obtained fixtures on the Bank Holidays, on Whit Monday and the first Monday in August. Provincial meetings also expanded, although at a slower rate. Manchester had four meetings a year by 1880. Although most meetings proved highly successful, there was no guarantee of this and insufficient demand in some urban areas such as Birmingham quickly forced several newly-formed courses out of business. Competition from these new, enclosed courses forced even old-established, high-status meetings such as Epsom or Doncaster to create more enclosures, improve and rebuild stands and increase the proportion of services for which a charge was levied.

The number of days over which races were run was initially associated with their status in terms of aristocratic attendance, numbers of entries and the prize money offered. The poorest-quality meetings, with the smallest crowds, were single-day events, often organized either by minor gentry in search of prestige or for more purely commercial reasons by innkeepers and others. Very occasionally, a poorer meeting would stretch its few races over more than one day, especially early in the century, when seven or eight races were sometimes spread over six days at Scottish meetings. Even as late as 1839 at Eccles the four races were spread over four days in an attempt to gain extra income. Much more usually, however, three days or more usually signalled a more prestigious meeting and more races. Newmarket, Epsom, Ascot and Doncaster were of highest status, but York, Chester, Newcastle, Goodwood, Liverpool, Manchester, Coventry and Warwick were sometimes of more than regional importance. Up to 1869, as Table 3 makes clear, the bulk of additional meetings were shorter and hence less prestigious.

From the 1870s there was increased standardization and most recognized meetings lasted only two days. Events of three days or more were mostly associated with high-status, partially unenclosed, meetings at courses such as Newmarket or Ascot, which could attract the leisured rich.

Over the period the age of the horses running slowly declined. This was linked to more commercial attitudes among owners and to the generating of

TABLE 3
NUMBERS OF DAYS OVER WHICH MEETINGS WERE HELD 1809–69

Date	1 day (%)	2 days (%)	3 days (%)	4 or more days (%)	
1809	5	33	42	19	n = 99
1839	20	60	12	8	n = 168
1869	30	55	8	7	n = 184

Source: *Racing Calendar*.

betting gain since the form of younger horses was less clear. In the eighteenth century most races were for older horses, and in 1807 two-year-old racing was rarely found outside Newmarket and, more rarely, Yorkshire. But the proportion of two-year-old races was increasing even before the railways began to spread, especially with the introduction of high-status races such as the Criterion Stakes at Newmarket in 1827. Racing younger horses meant that the investment in bloodstock stood the chance of a quicker return and was attractive to gamblers. Young horses coped badly with walking between meetings but with the extension of the railway network they could race more easily (see Table 4).

TABLE 4
PERCENTAGES OF PARTICIPATING RACEHORSES BY AGES 1817–97

Date	2-yr olds	3-yr olds	4-yr olds	5+yr olds	Numbers
1817	10	39	22	30	n = 800
1837	18	27	17	38	n = 1,213
1859	35	30	15	20	n = 1,636
1877	39	29	15	16	n = 2,057
1897	39	27	17	17	n = 3,506

Source: *Ruff's Guide.*

As more younger horses competed, the length of the races slowly shortened. In 1800 most were run over two miles or more, except for Newmarket where the early introduction of two-year-old racing to make betting more uncertain skews the figures. By 1820 about 60 per cent of races elsewhere were run over a distance of between one and two miles, although only about 6 per cent were under this distance.

Longer distance races, for older horses, were more common at smaller events where more of the races were in heats. Although classed as a single race, heat races were repeated until a horse had won the event twice. This generated more betting when there were fewer horses. In 1809 all meetings in the *Racing Calendar* had some heat races except the high-status events at Newmarket, Ascot, York, Chester and Brighton. In 1820, 52 per cent of meetings still had a majority of their races in heats. Increased numbers of entries of younger horses following the railway expansion decreased the number of longer-distance heat races for older horses, and by the later 1840s turf reformers were arguing that they were outdated.[39] Although in 1850 almost a fifth of all flat races recorded in the *Racing Calendar* still had heats, by the late 1860s heats had almost entirely disappeared.

Once younger horses could travel by rail, sprint races (under a mile) with younger horses began to replace longer-distance events, and sprint races attracted the betting public. The first burst of change came in the period after mid-century and by its end the proportion of sprint races had almost doubled from what it was in 1850 (Table 5).

TABLE 5
PROPORTION OF RACES RUN BY DISTANCE, 1850–93

Date	Less than 1 mile (%)	Between 1 and 3 miles (%)	More than 3 miles (%)
1850	30	67	3
1865	49	49	2
1893	58	41	1

Source: *Ruff's Guide*.

The shift to sprint racing had two consequences. First, the government's support for long-distance racing, supposedly to improve the breed and hence the supply of cavalry horses through the provision of prizes in the form of 'royal plates', became less important and held less interest for British owners. By 1872 there were still 17 Queen's plates for Ireland and two in Scotland, but of the 33 plates in England four were no-contests and a further ten attracted only two runners each.

It also led to changes in starting, since with sprint races a bad start was disastrous. Around 1800 the starter had simply said 'Go!' and removed and waved his hat. The starting gate was an attempt to make the procedure fairer. It had been used in Australia for some time before it was provided at Epsom in 1898 'to be used at the discretion of the starter for any five-furlong races in which unnecessary delay is caused at the post'. In 1899 it was approved by the Jockey Club for all two-year-old races to be run and was in general use by 1901.

One of the questions to be addressed later is the extent to which owners were motivated by profit, and the keenness of owners to gain prize money as well as the status of winning lay at the heart of several changes in the types of race. In 1800 many individual races were matches (two owners each racing a single horse for a stated sum over a stated distance). Even then most were either at Newmarket, with its seven meetings a year, or similar high-status gatherings, and were linked to the aristocratic group. The entrance of more middle-class owners and more betting by upper-class owners put such matches into steep decline – not least because they offered few opportunities for others to profit from betting. By the 1830s too, gold cups and plates, previously important status prizes at courses, were beginning to be replaced by cash.

Instead there was an increased emphasis on sweepstakes and handicaps.

Sweepstakes were races where all those subscribing put up a given amount of limited stake money some time before the race, thus risking only a little but in return having a chance of winning a much larger sum. Handicaps, initially seen as an inferior, end-of-the-day race, were races where horses carried different weights, depending upon their previous public form and therefore (in theory) gave all the horses an equal chance to win. Their numbers increased slowly up to the 1830s and more rapidly thereafter. They were attractive to some because of the element of betting uncertainty; to owners because a horse carrying a light weight after its form had been concealed in earlier races offered the possibility of a coup; and to bookmakers because they could sometimes profit through their access to betting information about such horses (see Table 6).

TABLE 6
PROPORTION OF RACES AS SWEEPSTAKES, PLATES, HANDICAPS AND MATCHES, 1809–69

Date	Sweepstakes (%)	Plates, purses, cups, etc. (%)	Handicaps (%)	Matches (%)
1809	28	32	4	36
1839	61	18	13	7
1869	39	10	47	3

Source: *Racing Calendar.*

Matches had disappeared from almost everywhere except Newmarket by the 1850s. Another form of race took their place. This was the selling race the conditions of which required that the winner be sold at auction for a specified sum, and any money difference between the actual and the nominated price split between the race fund and the owner of the second horse. For owners there was the possibility of making money in a range of ways: selling the horse, prize money won by a poor horse in an even poorer entry, or by careful manipulation of the odds to ensure a betting profit.

Attempted betting profit was important for most owners. As one commentator in the 1860s admitted, 'if betting were done away with ... there would be very few noblemen or gentlemen found willing and many unable to keep and run racehorses.'[40] Twenty-three per cent of races were sellers by 1869. From the 1880s the mainstays of enclosed course racing were handicaps and sweepstakes, to which prize money was normally added.

In 1800 most horses at a meeting came from nearby. Horses were often not privately trained on aristocratic estates but based at one of some 200 training centres scattered throughout the country. These provided the bases from which horses were walked to the six overlapping regional racing circuits to compete for prizes.[41] Improved transport facilities brought horses from further afield, including some from abroad. Irish-bred horses were the first to be successful, with classic wins as early as the 1840s, and by 1877 Volume XIII of the *General Stud Book* remarked on the growing number of stallions and mares in Britain that had been bred abroad, especially in France. In 1865 the French horse Gladiateur had won three classic races.[42] The 1890s also saw what has been termed 'the American invasion', although American owners had already been racing in Britain for many years.[43] The 1897 Volume XVIII of the *General Stud Book* took explicit notice of the increasing number of horses and mares bred in the USA and Australia which had been imported into Britain. More owners too were arriving, sometimes bringing their trainers and jockeys. American trainers brought in better techniques in horse care and greater skill in horse doping. American jockeys popularized a new riding style, riding short in a crouched position, and achieved quick success. By 1900 five of the top ten jockeys were Americans, including the champion jockey Lester Reiff.[44] Better sea and rail connections enabled the first American-owned, French-trained horse to win the Derby, to a most subdued reception, in 1914.[45]

By this time the combined impact of changes in transport, the electric telegraph and the press had transformed the nature of racing and betting in British society, as well as encouraging such foreign competition. These and other themes will be developed in subsequent chapters.

NOTES

1. *Daily Sketch*, 5 June 1913.
2. For a wide-ranging discussion of the ways in which sporting activities more generally were linked to economic and social changes, see W. Vamplew, *Pay Up and Play the Game* (Cambridge, 1988), Part II. The following paragraph is based largely on this.
3. Admiral Rous later claimed that bookmaking came into vogue in 1804 due to the growing importance of the Derby, a claim often interpreted as a reference to working-class 'betters round' taking bets against all horses in a race; Admiral Rous, 'On the past and present state of the turf', quoted in *Yorkshire Herald*, 29 December 1855. The claim is not to be relied upon.
4. *The Times*, 24 September 1830.
5. Goldfinch, 'Racing in 1825 and racing in 1850', *Sporting Magazine*, February 1851, p.146.
6. For Gully's life see B. Darwin, *John Gully and His Times* (1935). Some of Gully's Derby betting books survive in the Jockey Club Rooms, Newmarket.
7. *The Times*, 24 September 1825.
8. E.g., *The Times*, 22 September 1825; *Liverpool Mercury*, 8 July 1829.
9. Sylvanus, *The Byeways and Downs of England* (1850), p.176; R. Mortimer *et al.*, *Biographical Encyclopaedia of British Flat Racing* (1978), pp.162–4.
10. *Westmorland Advertiser*, 22 September 1821.
11. *The Times*, 24 September 1825 gives details of dog use.
12. *Manchester Free Lance*, 25 May 1868 provides a late description of the rooms.
13. The Druid, quoted by P. Willett, *The Story of Tattersall's* (1987), p.36.

14. T. Mason, *Sport in Britain* (1988), p.47.
15. Cecil, 'The Turf Exchange', *Sporting Magazine*, October 1853, p.257.
16. Ibid., August 1848, p.232.
17. *Bell's Life*, 13 April 1845; *The Times*, 20 May 1858.
18. Ibid., 17 October 1854.
19. For the 1866 Northumberland Plate, one of the great betting races in the north-east, it was reported that 'although nearly a score of horses had been in the betting the event proved that not more than three or four were ever really meant. How the owners can possibly reconcile such nefarious doings ... with common decency we are at a loss to conceive'; 'Our Van', *Baily's Magazine*, September 1866. See 'Our Van', ibid., December 1875, p.62 for similar comments more generally about the 1875 season.
20. 'The Ring and the Book', ibid., March 1876, pp.189ff.
21. 'Dead meat' or 'dead 'uns' were horses not intended to win which could be safely bet against.
22. 1902 Select Committee on Betting; evidence of Sir J. Lowther, Q2438.
23. R.H.G. Thomas, *The Liverpool and Manchester Railway* (1980), pp.199ff.
24. *Ripon Chronicle*, 7 August 1858.
25. M.J. Huggins, 'Lord Bentinck, the Jockey Club and racing morality in mid-nineteenth century England: the "Running Rein" Derby revisited', *International Journal of the History of Sport*, Vol.13, No.3, December 1996, pp.432–44.
26. *Manchester Courier*, 22 May 1847; *The Times*, 15 September 1847.
27. *Ruff's Guide*, Spring Edition 1851, p.199.
28. Doncaster Record Office, AB 2/2/5/1, Minutes of General Purpose Committee, 30 August 1852; 3 May 1858.
29. *The Times*, 25 May 1853; E.C. Baker, *Sir William Preece, FRS: Victorian Engineer Extraordinary* (1976), p.61. Preece was a key figure in the development of the telegraph and the telephone.
30. At Manchester in 1869 they set aside a room and tried every effort to 'secure either the Electric or United Telegraph Company's wires'; *Manchester Courier*, 20 May 1869.
31. Parliamentary Papers, Reports from Mr Scudamore to the Postmaster General with appendices, 1867–68 (202), Vol.XLI, Appendix D, pp.73–4.
32. Parliamentary Papers, Report by Mr Scudamore on the Reorganisation of the Telegraph System of the United Kingdom, 1871 (c304), Vol.XXXVI, p.36; Report of the Select Committee on the Post Office (Telegraph Department), 1876 (357), Vol.XIII, Evidence of Mr Johnston, Q1765.
33. J.L. Kieve, *The Electric Telegraph: A Social and Economic History* (1973), gives details.
34. R.W. Thomlinson, 'A geography of flat racing in Great Britain', *Geography*, Vol.71, No.3, 1986, pp.228–30.
35. P. Borsay, *The English Urban Renaissance* (Oxford, 1989), pp.180ff.
36. At Scarborough in 1839 the races 'had no option in fixing the hour of starting' at the early hour of half-past eleven, 'it being the low water', *Yorkshireman*, 31 August 1839.
37. See M. Huggins, 'Horse racing on Teesside in the nineteenth century: change and continuity', *Northern History*, Vol.23, 1987, pp.98–118.
38. This temporary decline in national interest in racing is seen in a range of sources, including the circulation of the *Racing Calendar*, the stamps issued for which dropped from 30,650 in 1830 to 26,358 in 1836. These figures are derived from Parliamentary Papers giving returns relating to the stamps issued for newspapers in Great Britain and Ireland, 1830–38.
39. *Sporting Magazine*, July 1848, p.9.
40. Anon., *Horse Racing: Its History and Early Records* (London, 1863), p.326.
41. There was a Scottish circuit, based predominantly round Gullane; a northern English circuit centred on Beverley, Middleham, Richmond and Malton; a west-Midlands circuit centred on Cannock Chase; south-east and south-west circuits; and a sixth circuit centred on Newmarket.
42. The 'heavy blow to our national pride and vanity' even led to an unfounded objection to the horse by a gin distiller at Doncaster; 'Our Van', *Baily's Magazine*, February 1876, p.180; J. Fairfax-Blakeborough, *York and Doncaster* (1950), p.380.
43. See W. Vamplew, *The Turf : A Social and Economic History of Horse Racing* (1976), Ch.4.
44. In October 1901 he was warned-off for pulling a horse at Manchester, amid rumours that this was a common occurrence for the stable; *Daily Express*, 2 October 1901.
45. *The Times*, 28 May 1914.

2

Racing and the Upper-class Fast Set

Although much has been written about elite culture, there have been fewer attempts to set leisure development explicitly in the context of class relationships. Research on upper-class leisure is still among the 'obvious limitations in leisure historiography'.[1] Nevertheless, despite the problems of definition associated with the identification of this group, there has been some recognition by historians of the eighteenth century of the part played by the upper classes in the development of increasingly commercialized race meetings and the complex part racing played in social relationships, including patronage and deference.[2] It has been recognized too that by the nineteenth century racing had become a key means of consolidating upper-class primacy.[3] Social mixing at meetings helped to sustain social deference.[4] It was also a major element of upper-class sociability and leisure and, like hunting and shooting, exhibited conspicuous consumption patterns.[5]

The themes of patronage and cross-class mixing, investment and consumption, sociability and pleasure run through this chapter, and help to provide a better understanding of the complex social and cultural motives at stake. Such motives include the part racing played in reinforcing social norms and status in society and its use as an emblem of self-identification, its role as an upper-class citadel and safe haven of exclusivity at one level and as an opportunity for more ambivalent relationships with the middle and working classes, monetary motives for involvement, seeking profit through prize money or gambling for some, prestige, honour, love of sport or conspicuous consumption for others. These highly complex motives for upper-class involvement are addressed through a structure which first explores the various forms it took with the races themselves, such as investment in meeting organization, the purchasing of shares in grandstand companies, subscribing towards the prize money or attendance at meetings, and the motivations associated with these. A following section assesses involvement in the three key aspects of the sport: thoroughbred breeding; racehorse ownership; and betting, again attempting to explore the range of motivations, which ranged from those aimed at making money from the sport to those which were more intent on achieving success or other non-monetary forms of satisfaction.[6]

First, however, a definition of the upper classes themselves must be attempted. Several writers have indicated their complex nature and the way in which they contained a subtle hierarchy of status groups, not all of whose memberships had titles.[7] The definition of 'upper-class' used here follows Beckett in arguing that that the chief requirement was significant land ownership, followed by acceptance within county society, or membership of a governing elite.[8] Land carried both economic and political power and social prestige. Around 1800 there were over a thousand great landowners and wealthy gentry in England alone with an annual income each of over £3,000 and a further three or four thousand members of the squirearchy with incomes each over £1,500.[9] In the later nineteenth century the onset of agricultural depression hit those without industrial or urban property, but this was probably offset by the entry, from the mid-1880s, of new men with new titles, many of them industrialists.

The complex motives lying behind upper-class involvement were often concealed behind a series of public rhetorics of justification, many linked to the key dimensions of involvement, ownership, breeding and spectatorship, rather than to betting or profit. The former were often seen as associated with other 'diversions of a manly character' such as hunting or shooting and as giving a wide range of pleasures and enjoyments.[10] Racing's classical associations gave it the respectability of antiquity. It was described as a purposeful hobby for gentlemen, an antidote to boredom, especially for those who did not take part in more robust field sports. Involvement was supposedly an example of conspicuous consumption, when 'the gentry no more thought of deriving profit from racing than from their opera boxes'.[11] The sporting writer 'Nimrod' argued that racehorse ownership furnished the lord, the squire and the yeoman with a common recreation, while racing as an activity promoted mutual goodwill among local inhabitants.[12] In order to look beyond such justifications and tease out the key aspects of involvement and motive in more detail we turn first to involvement in the meetings themselves.

I

Over time this took a variety of forms. In the early part of the nineteenth century a minority of meetings were actually organized by the upper classes, some with races solely for 'gentlemen' riders. In Wales, the

Morgans at Tredegar Park arranged meetings partly to sell horses, with entry generally open only to house guests and army officers from Newport, and partly to allow them to ride their own horses without competing with jockeys.[13] Lambton Park, built by Lord Lambton in 1821 for the Lambton Racing Club, was open to neighbouring gentry and their friends.[14] In Scotland, the Earl of Eglinton organized private races on his estate in the late 1830s and the 1840s. But while there were exceptions, such as Goodwood, most such meetings away from population centres survived only as long as the estate owner's money and interest.[15] By 1850 'gentlemen riders' were mostly restricted to Newmarket, estate races such as Croxton Park or the several hunt meetings set up by gentlemen for gentlemen. Fewer than 10 per cent of the total number of races in the *Racing Calendar* were of this type, with professional jockeys carrying extra weight when they were allowed to enter or with similar forms of special restriction. In 1869, for example, the Perth meeting had some races restricted to 'horses belonging to and ridden by officers in garrisons in the Edinburgh and Glasgow districts'.

While most upper-class turfites found the arranging of a meeting too major an expense, some were prepared to contribute financially by subscription to grandstands, the purchase of shares or donations towards prize money. Motives here were mixed: the enjoyment of spectatorship, profit or the encouragement of local deference. Most grandstands erected in the period 1750–1820 were built by upper-class subscription, which gave free entrance for the subscriber and his family and ensured a socially-segregated area. When at Beverley in 1767 silver tickets were sold to defray the cost of the grandstand, 'almost every gentleman in the East Riding became the owner of one'.[16] At this stage subscription may be seen both as a gesture of support and as a way of securing a regular, future place in the stand. In the years around 1850 many new urban grandstand and racecourse companies, although predominantly composed of more middle-class shareholders, also had some landed shareholders and directors. Recent research reveals that such share purchasing was partly profit-driven, but also a gesture of support.[17] Dividends were limited (often to 5 per cent) and a proportion of the shares were annually repurchased by the company, after which profits were used for added money. The new enclosed English courses of the later nineteenth century showed a revival of aristocratic share ownership, while in Scotland both Lanark and Ayr racecourses were dominated by aristocratic and gentry shareholders in the period 1900–14.[18] The enclosed courses had a clearer business orientation, with more frequent meetings, more use of Saturday racing, better use of marketing and an emphasis on the attracting of larger numbers of upper- and middle-class women. Material motivations should not be overstated, however. The Jockey Club imposed a higher dividend limitation of 10 per cent and free admission was often an added bonus. Upper-class control of a number of enclosed courses allowed them to run poorer quality but well-attended races at Whitsuntide or on Saturdays to build up sufficient profit to subsidize more select meetings at other times when the upper-class members attended and entered more of their own horses.[19] Even so, local loyalties can still be seen. In the period 1870–1900 a number of wealthy landowners subsidized struggling open meetings on or near their estates. In the 1880s the rural course at Catterick Bridge was heavily subsidized by Sir John Lawson even after its enclosure. On 26 May 1886, for example, he gave £640 towards the meeting.[20] Towards the end of the century, however, most were reconsidering, sometimes for financial and sometimes for social reasons. At Richmond in Yorkshire, once the course was enclosed, local subscriptions began to dry up and with only some 4,000 spectators the course was increasingly unviable financially, unless Lord Zetland increased his existing contribution, which he was unwilling to do.[21]

In the period 1800–70 subscription was the main form of support for open meetings. Up to the 1850s the sport would have collapsed without such patronage. Local magnates often donated towards the races near their estates. Stewards often provided a cup.[22] Stewardship of meetings and race-meeting subscription was an important way of showing the local community who was at its head. Both cost money, especially early in the nineteenth century, when in addition to cups, plates or subscriptions to the fund, money towards a race ball or supper might also have to be found.[23] Although the stewards were in theory the ultimate decision-makers at meetings, the posts were honorary and some did not even attend.[24] Others were ineffective.[25] Local race committees normally approached the local aristocracy and gentry and, although some were clearly reluctant, as correspondence reveals, most grudgingly accepted the honour.[26] Cups were falling out of use by the 1850s, since most owners preferred cash.[27] Legacies were occasionally left. William Watt in 1874 left £3,000 to Beverley to be invested for an annual prize plate.[28]

Many upper-class owners saw it as important also to send their own horses to ensure that the clerk had sufficient entries. At Richmond in 1814 a local writer praised the 'gentlemen of the neighbourhood who made a point of sending horses to contribute to the amusements of the day' and supported the meeting by their exertions.[29] The motives lying behind such actions were often paternalistic. John Bowes, in a letter to the *Sportsman* in 1875, claimed that he sent horses to the racecourses in the northern districts with which he was connected and was willing to run them without regard for his betting book, because he believed that 'the public who attend these races feel an interest in my horses ... and consequently make small speculations'. He was anxious to avoid any disappointment to them.[30] Later in the century owners sometimes sent horses substantial distances by rail just to keep up entries, although they sent up more when attending personally.[31]

Giving financial support could be seen merely as an example of paternalistic patronage; attending the races was important to upper-class sociability. In the early nineteenth century, when horses were vital to the local economy and horseracing had long been an aristocratic amusement, it was expected that the great local families would come together to attend local races, although Lord Milton, enjoying his holiday on the Cleveland coast, wrote to his father Earl Fitzwilliam that 'I hope not to receive any recommendation to go to York races as I am so occupied and pleased here that I have no intention to stir unless very much pressed.'[32]

Before the railway came, London, or 'town', was the focus for many upper-class families from April to July, and attendance at Epsom and more particularly Ascot was socially important. At Ascot in the first half of the century carriages would be lined along the inside of the track for anything up to a mile and five to ten deep if facing the royal box, although only 20 or so carriages would be found on a rain-soaked Friday not attended by any royals.[33] In the north of England, York and Doncaster fulfilled similar functions. At such major races lists of the 'company' attending were often printed in the local papers and upper-class women attended these events in some numbers.[34] Ascot, with its royal enclosure and lawn, attracted large numbers of the aristocracy of both sexes. Smaller meetings attracted only local gentry. At Carlisle there were 'but seven carriages on the ground' in 1833.[35] The extent to which meetings attracted the gentry depended on whether they had the active support and attendance of the major county territorial magnates, since they drew others to their house parties. Aintree increased rapidly in status in the late 1830s because, through its substantial prize money, the meeting attracted two key supporters – the Earl of Sefton and Lord Stanley, who filled their country houses with members of the aristocracy and 'persons of distinction'.[36] Absence of a society leader could have a marked effect. When the Duke of Rutland did not attend Leicester in 1850 upper-class attendance fell and it was complained that 'the county gentlemen and ladies seem entirely to have forsaken our racecourse'.[37]

There is an important distinction between those who went only to local meetings or to great national events such as Ascot, often for a mixture of social reasons and as part of their obligations as magnates or as opportunities to display wealth and status, and the almost entirely male group who were more closely involved in the turf. The latter generally had a greater interest in betting as well as breeding and racing and could be found at a wider range of meetings. Racing, with its secret world, was also largely a social activity. Friendships were often close. A small group might travel together, lodge together and use the same betting commissioner or the same trainer. Most, but not all, were unmarried. Before the spread of the railways, some of this group attended and entered their horses mainly at regional races. In the period 1817–30 the Shropshire landowner John Mytton watched his horses running in a circuit bounded by Manchester, west Wales, Warwick and Lichfield, although he also attended Doncaster, travelling there and back in his own coach.[38] By contrast, his wealthier contemporary Lord Derby helped to establish the Aintree course and attended north-western meetings but also major, upper-class meetings at Newmarket, Epsom, Ascot, Doncaster, York and Goodwood.[39]

For the increasing numbers of owners based in the south, Newmarket, with its many days of annual racing, its successful training stables and its Jockey Club rooms, was already a key base for sociability in the early nineteenth century. Although its popularity declined somewhat around mid-century, it revived again with renewed classic successes and the opening up of railway connections to London. Doncaster upper-class attendance likewise dropped somewhat around 1850, despite increases in prize money and the greater ease of travel the railways provided.[40] The railways, which also brought increased numbers of unruly, urban, working-class excursionists, were a two-edged sword. There were, however, sufficient upper-class turfites now attending a greater number of meetings because of the railways to ensure that any drops in local support were partly balanced out. Lord Chetwynd, Jockey Club steward in 1878, went from Harry Chaplin's house at Blankney to Lincoln, and then his upper-class group hired a special train to the Liverpool races.[41]

Although the grandstands had often been relatively exclusive at the beginning of the nineteenth century, they had become much more socially mixed thereafter, despite rising entrance costs, because of the greater interest in racing among the population and through rising real incomes. This had deterred some upper-class women from entering many course grandstands, although carriages and private or stewards' stands were used. As racing again became more attractive to upper-class families in the 1870s, attempts were made to cater for that need. A number of the new enclosed courses used a combination of pricing and blackballing to create more select areas in the form of what they often termed 'county' or 'members' stands at meetings. Sandown formed yet another male racing club with its own stand but vetted membership carefully; members were entitled to two ladies' badges free if they paid the higher rate of membership. York founded a new club around 1884 with a committee of management distinct from the race committee and a separate club stand, the county stand, for its members and friends.[42]

For the turfite group, racing played a key role in terms of elite sociability.[43] One area hitherto ignored by historians has been the important factor of the male membership of racing clubs, especially in the first half of the nineteenth century. These clubs varied in their level of exclusivity; not all were upper class. For males who were not staying at nearby country houses they sometimes provided lodging as well as food and drink. The Jockey Club was the most exclusive, with its club rooms at Newmarket; this is dealt with in more detail in Chapter 7. The annual Jockey Club dinner was a major event, attended successively by George III, George IV, William IV and Edward VII.

Scotland had its parallel to the Jockey Club in the exclusive Royal Caledonian Hunt, founded in 1777 and based on Scottish birth and land ownership. Its only club house was in Edinburgh. One of its stated objectives was to encourage horseracing and breeding in Scotland, although it had little interest in controlling racing. It had an itinerary of eight or nine centres and each year hunted and raced for a fortnight at a chosen one, endowing races in the process. It also inaugurated an annual cup in 1818, restricted to horses bred in Scotland. It had its own rituals, uniform and social activities. In the early nineteenth century it gave significant support to important Scottish meetings such as Ayr or Edinburgh. By the 1840s, however, there was less interest in racing among Scottish landowners and its exclusive membership was in decline, although it still had an annual subscription in 1863 of 10 guineas (£10.10s). Its dominance was challenged by the less socially exclusive Border Racing Club, founded in 1854 'for the purpose of giving increasing encouragement and support to racing in the east part of Scotland and northern parts of England'. It had a subscription of three guineas.[44]

Club rooms or houses of a more local nature could be found at many meetings, although membership was often only limited by the ability to pay the subscription, often of two or three guineas, and betting debts. Some clubs were simply ways of creating a betting market. An elegant subscription club house was built near the assembly rooms in York in 1828, with a betting room as an additional inducement to noblemen and gentlemen. Doncaster's betting rooms were so crowded in 1827 that 'noble lords were constrained to stand on tables and chairs' in their eagerness to bet.[45] Entrance was a guinea, and by 1831 'upwards of 600 noblemen had entered their names in the subscription book'.[46] The rooms were open until after midnight just before, during and after race week, including the Sunday during service times.[47]

Some turfites paid subscriptions to several clubs. John Bowes in 1845 was a member of the Jockey Club at Newmarket and the other relatively exclusive racing club – the Bibury Racing Club – but he was also a member of Tattersall's and of the Doncaster and Stockton Racing Clubs where membership was more mixed.[48]

The membership of most clubs was small, and excluded women. This may well have been an attraction to some in the inner turfite group, but was common to many clubs of the time; racing clubs were therefore not unusual. Indeed, the Jockey Club rules even banned women from owning horses. Later in the nineteenth century several notoriously did, including the Duchess of Montrose, but the Club, as usual, turned a blind eye so long as appearances were preserved. Gendered identity rules may even have fostered the ready investment in racing among the well-to-do.

In England a small but significant number of clubs linked horseracing and hunting, especially in the period 1830–60, organizing races for hunters or gentlemen riders. The clubs, with their distinctive clothing, provided both exclusivity and a context for evening conviviality.[49] In Cheshire, the Tarporley Hunt Club organized races of more local importance and placed great stress on hunting, drinking and the singing of hunting songs.[50]

London racing clubs emerged more slowly since existing clubs such as Brooks fulfilled many of the same purposes. But increasingly manipulative upper-class betting needed to be cross-class because of the need for information from bookmakers, commission agents and 'legs'. London meeting points such as Tattersall's were vital. The Victoria Club, founded in 1860 with an even more mixed clientele, was predominantly a betting club, charging a membership fee of ten guineas plus an annual subscription of six.[51] Its success contrasts with the social exclusiveness of the 1876 Turf Club in Piccadilly, with its predominantly 'gentlemen' membership, which aimed (unsuccessfully) to promote weight-for-age races, encouragement for gentlemen riders and the raising of handicap weights.[52]

Some stayed at club rooms during meetings, but most stayed elsewhere. In the late eighteenth and the early nineteenth century some upper-class turfites still owned town houses as well as country mansions; some stayed at house parties on nearby estates; others at larger hotels in the vicinity or in private lodgings in the town. At the beginning of the nineteenth century even Earl Fitzwilliam took lodgings in Doncaster's High Street. Hotels were preferable since they allowed greater freedom, less ceremony and convivial drinking. At York's Black Swan Lord Glasgow reportedly threw a waiter out of the window, breaking his arm, and was billed for an extra £5 as a result. Hotels also encouraged cross-class mixing. The 1851 visitors' book included the 'legs' John Gully and Padwick, as well as Prince Henry of the Netherlands, the Earls and Countesses of Zetland and Eglinton, and other notables. Block hotel bookings were possible; in the later 1860s Lord Falmouth, George Payne, Lord Westmorland and others formed a party at the Station Hotel.[53]

The races were associated with other urban social activities arranged to allow upper-class society to enjoy itself and give status-conscious townfolk opportunities for social mixing, perhaps eating together at 'ordinaries' organized by local inns, or attending balls. At the end of the eighteenth century many assembly rooms were built, often by subscription, for just such a purpose.[54] With the increase in popularity of race meetings, even small market towns such as Malton, whose assembly hall was built in 1815, followed suit. Balls were a social highlight, with added opportunities for upper-class matchmaking. At Doncaster 'nearly all the nobility were at the ball' on Monday in race week 1829.[55]

But as the races lost their central place in the social calendar around the mid-century as towns expanded and the influx of excursionists increased, balls and ordinaries became less common. The reduction in such ancillary social activities reduced some of the interest in racing, more especially among women. Even staying in town for social meetings as in Doncaster became less fashionable around mid-century, and for a number of decades the majority of upper-class attenders travelled in each day from their estates or house-parties elsewhere.

Such social attendance became increasingly popular once again in the last three decades of the nineteenth century, partly through social emulation of the Prince of Wales and his high-spending circle. At Doncaster in 1888 more upper-class attenders stayed locally than had been known for some time, while special trains from nearby country houses contained much of the northern aristocracy.[56] By 1891 the *Doncaster Gazette* had both a visitor list for those staying in the town and a second one of house party attenders.[57] House parties in the country were becoming increasingly popular. Train travel provided the means, horseracing the favourite excuse, a leisure context providing excitement and the opportunities for betting, dressing up, sexual intrigue and gossip. Some parties, such as those of the Duke of Richmond at Goodwood House, ended with a ball, showing continuity with the earlier period. Maintenance of social position still depended on conspicuous consumption and ostentatious display. In the early nineteenth century the Lowthers had given significant personal and financial support to meetings at Kendal and Carlisle. At the end of the century Hugh Lowther, 5th Earl of Lonsdale, spent his wealth on a more national scale.

Although racing was by no means his chief extravagance, his striking racing colours of canary yellow even adorned his carriage at Ascot and he entertained lavishly at Epsom and other courses, although he did not bet and never had a large string.[58]

A wide range of memoirs show the key role of the house party in upper-class life at this period, reflecting the power, wealth and self-confidence of this class.[59] Country houses became centres of consumption and local employment. To stay at Windsor for Royal Ascot was the height of social acceptability, followed by admittance to the royal enclosure, for which written application had to be made. Racing house parties were popular with ladies, especially in comparison with shooting parties. Racing was a summer activity which allowed the wearing of decorative and fashionable dresses, and racing itself was watched in comfort, while lavish picnics were transported to the course. Dresses for Ascot or Goodwood were fully described in the press.[60] Not all meetings attracted such activity, and Henry Chaplin's house party at Blankney in the spring was for the select few, but by Ascot in June the season was in full swing. The Newmarket July meeting and Goodwood, at the end of the month, were both popular, partly because they were less formal than Ascot, while Doncaster in September was the last major social event of the season.[61] Beyond such British-wide social events, local magnates would have house parties for their own nearby meetings. The previously small August meeting at Redcar on the north-east coast became a meeting more for the upper classes than the masses, with 'much of the blue blood of the north' staying at Wilton Castle, with others such as the Earl of Durham staying at nearby seaside resorts.[62]

On Edward VII's accession in 1901 the spending on such parties if anything grew yet more intense and the potential benefits of hosting such parties became increasingly apparent to plutocrats intent on gaining entrance to upper-class society. Solly Joel, the diamond producer, began giving huge parties at Maiden Erleigh before Ascot; William James, the American industrialist, bought West Dean Park in Sussex because of its proximity to Goodwood and hosted a house party there. Their conspicuous display of wealth, central heating, telephones and hot baths made house-party life yet more comfortable. Such parties were given significant coverage in the national press up to 1914.[63] Edward's racing friends included the Tottenham Court Road furniture magnate Sir John Maple, who had three classic successes in the 1890s; Lucien and Maurice de Hirsch, the Austro-Jewish railway contractors, who had racing success in the 1880s and 1890s; and the Joels, sons of an East End publican, who made a fortune out of the South African diamond fields before taking up racing in 1900.

The upper-class house party provided a socially exclusive context for racing, one in which women played a more major role. Attendance at meetings and betting on horses could, however, have a range of other social functions. Race meetings provided an opportunity for people with shared interests and aspirations to meet, to debate local issues, promote capitalist ventures or political alliances, cement family bonds or existing friendships, or cultivate acquaintance with powerful local families.

Some, although not all, upper-class turfites mixed socially with working- and middle-class turfites, some of whom had accumulated wealth on the turf and had developed the appropriate social skills. As early as the late eighteenth century John Hutchinson, a former stableboy, jockey and trainer from the most proletarian of backgrounds, had accumulated sufficient wealth through his turf exploits to become an owner, mixing and betting with the upper classes. One memorialist, writing in 1826, ignored his background and claimed that his fortune was gained by 'skill and good breeding', arguing that 'the notice he obtained from lords and men of high degree shewed how high he stood'.[64] Later examples included John Gully, the former butcher, pugilist and 'leg', who became MP for Pontefract in 1832 and a major landowner.

Not all of the socialization with more plebeian turfites was in the privacy of the racing clubs and betting rooms. Sam Chifney junior, the jockey, used to stay for weeks with the Duke of Cleveland at Raby Castle and they often dined alone together after hunting.[65] In 1856 the Earl of Derby made a point of inviting race officials, jockeys and others to a dinner at Knowsley.[66] It is clear from the correspondence of these trainers, jockeys and officials with wealthy owners that they were conscious of status differentials, yet also that attitudes varied. Derby's relationship with John Scott, the famous northern trainer, was a case in point. According to *Baily's Magazine* there 'existed between the owner and his trainer the most perfect understanding and mutual respect which the one felt for the other. There was *none of that undue familiarity* [author's italics] which too frequently exists between an owner and his trainer'. His visits to Whitewall were among the most gratifying of his recreations, exhibiting 'the enjoyment of a schoolboy' in his inspection of the stables.[67] Derby may have been statesmanlike in the House of Lords but in the privacy of the Newmarket betting rooms he was described as 'in the midst of a crowd of blacklegs, betting men, and low characters of every description, in uproarious spirits, chaffing, roaring and shouting with laughter'.[68]

Such social mixing declined as betting became increasingly carried out at a distance by post, telegraph and telephone with credit bookmakers.[69] The social exclusiveness promoted by house parties also had an influence. By contrast, however, some of the upper classes were beginning to become more involved in racing professionally by the 1880s. Lord Marcus Beresford became an official Jockey Club starter in 1885 and by 1893 it was claimed that the nobility and gentry were competing for such posts.[70] There was also an influx into training. Although upper-class men had sometimes earlier acted as racing managers, their role had been more in placing horses and instructing trainers rather than actual hands-on activity. In 1872, when the gentleman rider Arthur Yates began training professionally, he felt that because of his family's objections it was necessary to train under a false name.[71] By 1893, however, when George Lambton, a younger son of the Earl of Durham, began training for the Earl of Derby there was increasing participation by upper-class young men.[72]

II

The last section explored the range of motivations and involvements with the races themselves. But in order to understand the place of racing in upper-class life more broadly the class's involvement in thoroughbred breeding, racehorse ownership and betting, and the motivations involved in these activities are also important. Vamplew's application of economic theory to British sports in the late nineteenth century has suggested that some of those involved in racing sought to make money, while others sought success measured in terms of wins, applying all their resources to that end.[73] Clearly there were examples of upper-class attempts to profit from racing, an issue discussed in Chapter 6. There is a more limited aim here: to examine the non-monetary motives for participation.

The range of motivations lying behind breeding were concealed behind a rhetorical facade. According to one writer, breeding was 'not only national but patriotic' since it had improved the breed of horses so that they were unrivalled, 'the admiration indeed, of the whole of Europe'. It was 'fraught with usefulness, as well as with pleasures and enjoyments of more than an ordinary character'.[74] Improving the breed of horses generally was a key part of the rationale for racing, a point brought out in the meetings of the Select Committee on Laws Respecting Gaming in 1844 and subsequent Commissions on Horse Breeding.[75] But in fact such arguments were hypocritical since increasingly immature, half-grown animals were the main ones raced. One of Admiral Rous's letters makes the point: 'I always suspect that the improvement of the breed of horses means to get the best horse and to win the most money. I never met a man whose sole object was the improvement of horses except Lord Glasgow and the late Duke of Portland.'[76] It may also be, as R.F. Moore-Colyer has argued, that behind the breeding of the thoroughbred lay a profound, almost anthropomorphic motivation for the aristocracy and gentry, and that the breeding of thoroughbred horses was a possible way of celebrating one's belief in the hereditary principle, thus helping to justify disparities in wealth.[77] The undoubted fact that some gentlemen preferred to breed their own racing stock may be offered in support of this view, as may the large amount of material many families accumulated about their studs and horse pedigrees.[78] But Moore-Colyer also showed that many Welsh gentlemen who entered breeding were motivated by profit, although few actually made any. It is possible that the rhetoric of profitability was necessary in order to justify what was really a pleasure.

Both the size and the success of such breeding studs varied.[79] Few owners had more than 20 mares, only a small number had fewer than four.[80] Success varied still more. Despite maintaining large studs, the Earl of Glasgow had little turf success over his 50 years of private breeding, while George Bentinck, despite other successes, never realized his dream of a Derby win.[81] But many sent their mares, at first by road and later by rail, long distances to be covered by the most fashionable and successful stallions.[82]

Wealthy breeder-owners often bred patiently from their own stock for the speculative success of classic middle-distance events. Such breeding was costly, but as other breeders increasingly concentrated on sprints and handicaps, their chances improved. Lord Falmouth, breeding at Mereworth, had 16 classic successes between 1863 and 1883. Between 1880 and 1900 the Duke of Westminster, the Duke of Portland and the Earl of Rosebery bred and owned the winners of 29 classic races. The Earl of Rosebery's 1896 York Gimcrack speech summarized his philosophy. He claimed not to stay in the turf for gain. It was 'a most discouraging amusement'. His love lay 'in the breeding of a horse .... the brood mare and foal; in watching the development of the foal, the growth of the horse, and the exercise of the horse'.[83] Most titled owners sold only their poorer yearlings and kept their more promising ones.

In terms of racehorse ownership, although wealthy owners regularly featured in magazines such as the *Sporting Magazine* or *Country Life,* quantitative data are difficult to ascertain.[84] In the period 1800–50 lists of owners in the *Racing Calendar* are a relatively useful source of evidence, identifying the titled, officers (who often came from similar backgrounds, especially when commissions had to be bought) and 'esquires', a term then used fairly consistently to denote a wealthy, land-owning background.[85] Some 30 members of the Jockey Club were described as such in the period around 1840. Even before mid-century, however, the term was dropping out of use and the more general title 'Mr' then conceals wealthy landowners such as Henry Chaplin, making identification more problematic.

The *Calendar* evidence shows that the raw totals of titled and officer owners in Britain fluctuated around the low hundreds up to the 1860s and then began to rise, but only very slowly. The rise in the numbers of esquires, from a base of around 120 at the start of the century, had begun by the 1840s but at much the same limited rate. Since racehorse ownership was growing, this meant that the *proportion* of upper-class owners was constantly falling. It fell from 20 per cent in 1809 to 11 per cent in 1839, with a rapid increase in the owners of lower social background, and then slipped to 10 per cent by 1869. The proportion of officer owners, by contrast, rose, but only slightly; 5 per cent in 1809, 6 per cent in 1839 and 7 per cent in 1869. By 1899 changes in compilation make the data less clear, but the proportion of titled owners had probably fallen still further, perhaps due to the long agricultural depression which reduced some upper-class rent rolls.

But the picture is complicated by regional variation. In the North Riding, for example, a survey of trainers' masters listed in *Ruff's Guide* suggests a steeper absolute and proportional decline in upper-class ownership over the century. In 1848 over 21 per cent of owners were titled or officers. By 1858 this had dropped to 17 per cent, and the decline thereafter was rapid. By 1888 it was down to 7 per cent and by 1898 to 3 per cent.

As with breeding, the reasons underlying racehorse ownership were complex. One sporting writer, 'Amphion', writing in 1876, suggested four main ones. The first, he implied, was the main upper-class reason, which was the innate love of the horse 'which animates the vast majority of the wealthy landed proprietors and capitalists of England' and the associated desire to 'share in the pleasures and glories popularly supposed to attend the possession of a large racing stud'. The others were vanity and love of notoriety; 'pleasant opportunities for gambling'; and the 'long firm whose prey is their fellow men', who manipulated horses in the market for betting profit and who would nobble horses if necessary.[86]

Although in reality all such attitudes could be found among them, the first was the one most commonly espoused in public by and about such owners. Such owners had 'integrity' and were 'sportsmen who run for honour and the pure love of sport'.[87] There were clear links between landowning and position in society and for this group their ownership of horses and attendance at meetings reinforced the social hierarchy. For some wealthy owners racehorse ownership and breeding could be a hobby. The diaries, day books and other manuscript material held by upper-class owners clearly show the pleasure it gave and many of them kept meticulous records.[88] It was clearly a hobby that took much time, played an important role in conversation, and in many cases combined family tradition and sentiment. One Duke of Portland was wealthy enough reputedly to give all his earnings to charity.[89]

As a hobby, it was often an expensive one. Even though only their better horses would be trained, training costs were quite substantial. Owners paid for training fees by the week and some other costs incurred at the stables, further costs incurred in travelling to courses, and course expenses, which included entries and forfeits and on-course stabling. Jockeys were also a significant extra cost with fees for races and trials and presents. The training fees charged by public trainers rose through the century, although with some variation between trainers, depending upon their professional standing. Although in 1779 fees were only a guinea (21 shillings) a week per 'horse and boy' during the racing season at Epsom, by 1822 they had risen to 36 shillings, when the Newmarket fee was already 46 shillings.[90] In the 1830s and the 1840s top trainers charged from 35 to 42 shillings, but by the 1890s 50 shillings had become an average fee, while top trainers obtained three guineas, plus in some cases a salary and a proportion of the stakes won by horses.[91]

As well as such fees, owners also had to meet a number of further costs, paid out by the trainer on their behalf, such as charges for the use of training-area gallops, or travelling and living expenses related to taking the horse and van to the races. Some owners even hired special trains to and from meetings to get a horse there at the appropriate time. Men had to be hired to lead the animals if they were being walked, and they needed accommodation *en route*. Whether by rail, van or on foot costs were considerable. There were extra costs for the course blacksmith, saddler, training liquor and watchmen to prevent the horse from being nobbled. Other money was also laid out at the meetings, including stabling costs and payments to clerks and other officials.[92] Expenses incurred by winning the Derby and the St. Leger were particularly high, and required gifts to officials and celebratory drinks. For a landowner's tenantry the celebrations of classic wins often rivalled those of the eldest son's coming of age and were important events in estate life.[93]

Total annual costs of keeping horses in training were high and rising. In 1844, in his evidence to the Select Committee on Gaming, Richard Tattersall expressed the view that no man could keep a racehorse in training for less than £230, not including jockeys' fees.[94] By 1905, however, it cost more than £366 to have a horse in training.[95] In the same year the mean prize money per horse was only £149, which indicates how difficult it was to make a profit.

Only about a third of horses running each season ever won a race, and although the proportion of prize money varied from course to course, Vamplew has estimated that generally about two-thirds of prize money routinely came out of owners' pockets in the form of race entry fees or forfeits.[96] Early in the nineteenth century sweepstakes and matches probably demanded an even higher contribution.

Since prize money could normally do no more than offset some of the costs of ownership, this suggests that owners' economic motivations were not concerned with profit maximization. Moore-Colyer argues that for the Welsh gentry families which he studied profit was a useful rather than an essential adjunct to their activities, and that for many horse breeding and racing lay outside economic considerations.[97] Maintaining a small stud at relatively low cost might realize a modest profit, but the large racing studs maintained by richer owners was another matter. One of the most successful, Lord Derby, who raced between 1842 and 1863, won £94,003 in prize money; but since Scott trained 243 horses of his at an estimated average cost of £407 per horse, that is £98,901 in total, even he did not profit overall.[98]

Money here was being spent to maximize the chances of a horse winning something, and for many landed owners the glory and prestige of winning major races were always clearly important. One of the best northern horses of the early nineteenth century, Dr Syntax, owned by Ralph Riddell of Felton Park, rarely ran more than four times a year between 1816 and 1823 but made a speciality of competing for gold cups. John Bowes in the 1840s and the 1850s consistently aimed at the classic races.

There was certainly an emphasis on winning, although also on prize money, in the press from the mid-nineteenth century. Lists of winning owners were published, with the totals of stakes won. This may have influenced some owners, anxious to enjoy the publicity and status. But success cost money. The most successful owners almost always had large training establishments. When Monsieur Lefevre topped the table in 1873 with £25,813 in stakes, the *Pall Mall Gazette* questioned whether it would cover a quarter of his costs.[99] In 1881 Stirling Crawford topped the table with £17,919 but had nearly a hundred horses in training. In general, about a quarter of all stakes were won by the top dozen owners, most of whom were wealthy men well-prepared to pay for their pleasure. The income other owners received could therefore not even have covered the training and travelling fees alone of a horse, never mind entrance money or forfeits. Even for the richest owners it proved difficult to win consistently. The Duke of Westminster won £23,016 in 1896, but only £4,218 the following year. The Prince of Wales won £26,819 in 1896, but only £2,189 in 1899.

Because purchase was often a quicker way to success, wealthy breeder-owners often used their wealth and influence to help them to purchase top yearlings. C.W. Orde, whose filly Beeswing was outstanding on the turf, got letters from Lord Clifden, Lord Eglinton and others enquiring after the cost of her stock.[100] Eglinton also entered into an agreement with the owner of another top mare to give £1,000 each for all her foals.[101] With the introduction of auctions, fashionable yearlings and foals became even more expensive. In 1890 Baron de Hirsch paid 5,000 guineas for La Fleche as a yearling.

Great aristocratic owners were keen both to breed and own the best horses of the time. Lord Rosebery, in a turf apologia, conceded that the rewards, as compared with the disappointments of racing, were only about 1 per cent and that the turf should not be pursued for gain; but described his ultimate ambition as to breed and own the horse of the century.[102] When Lord Bentinck's one-time horse Surplice, sold when he decided to enter politics, went on to win the Derby he was inconsolable: 'All my life I have been trying for this, and for what have I sacrificed it?'[103]

So they hired top trainers and often left them to manage their horses. For many years Scott had the sole control over Lord Derby's stud.[104] Lord Palmerston's instructions to William Day were to 'run them where you like and when you think best only let me know when they are worth backing or that you have backed them for me'.[105] Some allowed others of their class to manage their studs. Greville managed the Duke of York's stud from 1821, and Rous managed the Duke of Bedford's Newmarket horses, engaging them and matching them from 1840.[106]

Although a proportion of aristocratic and gentry owners may have run simply to achieve prestige, for many others the appeal of the turf lay in betting. Admittedly there were some who either did not bet or only rarely betted. Major Yarborough, at Heslington Hall near York, was 'a much respected old gentleman, who supports the turf for the sole sake of sport, unbiased by the least gambling or speculative consideration'.[107] But such men were rare. Admiral Rous, an opponent of heavy betting, argued convincingly in 1856 that betting was 'a necessary adjunct to racing' and without it 'four-fifths of the racecourses would be ploughed up'. Approaches varied: some bet in a small way, as part of the fun of ownership; some were high-stakes plungers, who usually lasted only a short time on the turf; some sought to profit from their fellows by acting as a bookmaker and betting round; some manipulated their horses in the betting market to ensure a profit. Betting behaviour of varying honesty was all acceptable inside the world of the turf, which affected the way horses were run.

Unless an owner betted on a grand scale he could scarcely hope to train and run horses without being seriously out of pocket. Betting on horseracing had been prevalent among the upper classes right through the eighteenth century, part of a wider passion for gaming and 'deep play'.[108] Aristocratic bets were high, often for £500 or more a match or at long odds well before a race.[109] The introduction of sweepstakes races, especially the St. Leger (1776), the Oaks (1779) and the Derby (1780), began to change the nature of upper-class betting, since for such races horses were entered as yearlings, with a much larger potential field. Ante-post betting began many months before, when information about the horses involved was sparse and odds were long. For layers this offered the possibility of a large win for a limited expenditure. Most owners backed their horses cheaply at long odds at this stage. If a horse began to show form and the ante-post odds dropped, an owner could 'lay' against the horse and thus hedge his bet, covering his initial stake if the horse subsequently lost and still make a profit if it won. This more rational approach to betting depended upon a combination of larger fields of horses, information about them, and places where betting owners could associate, such as assizes or clubs.

By the beginning of the nineteenth century betting on racing was already substantial.[110] But such *reported* betting was composed of relatively small numbers of bets, often for extremely high stakes made at long odds well before the race, so the actual outlay of the backer was not high, although losing layers might pay substantial sums after the race.

Some bet on their own horse and ran it straight. 'Sylvanus', only too aware of the dishonesty of many on the turf, saw Lord Eglinton as a 'most straightforward, unimpeachable, bona fide gentleman'.[111] At racecourses before the widespread availability of training reports the public would back their horses because they knew they would be run to win.[112] Others would bet more heavily on their own horse when they thought the odds were good, and for most a bet was part of the attendance at a meeting.[113]

Such bets could be for significant amounts, but not heavy when compared to the betters' income. Heavy betting flew in the face of dominant middle-class and reformist ideology and was seen as a poor example to workers. *The Times* admonished, 'were gentlemen to remember that racing is a recreation and were they to speculate less deeply, they would set a better example'.[114] Nevertheless, there was often confusion since many big wins were a result of small sums wagered at long odds well before a race.

Upper-class wealth sometimes resulted in high stakes betting. Some won large amounts, some lost them. Some could afford to, but others could not. For such plungers there was little rationality. Some were in it for the excitement, others needed a large sum of money and risking money on a long-odds bet was one way of getting it. When George Moore won some £17,000 on a Chester race in 1845 at 44–1 he was delighted. It gave him the money to pay his debts, feed his Irish tenantry and give to the poor.[115] But Georgian attitudes, enjoyment of drink, betting, gaming and other such activities were reflected in numerous examples of turfites rapidly dissipating their fortunes. Colonel Thornton sold his Yorkshire estate and died in France.[116] Colonel Mellish, who won two St. Legers, and was one of the heaviest wagerers of his day, rarely betting less than £500 a race, had lost his entire fortune and was living on a small farm when he died at the age of 37 in 1817.[117] George Henry Fitzroy, a compulsive gambler, son of the 3rd Duke of Grafton, incurred debts of over £38,000 when he lost heavily over the Derby of 1827 and attempts to recoup his losses at Doncaster failed.[118]

Jockey Club members were not immune. The suicide of the Hon. Berkley Craven in 1836, after having become inextricably involved in betting, was on account of Derby losses.[119] George Payne, on the turf from 1840 to 1870, lost two fortunes there and at the card table. Heavy plungers in the 1860s included the Marquess of Hastings, the Dukes of Beaufort and Carlisle, and the Chaplin-Machell confederacy.[120]

Betting could become addictive and Greville was probably referring to betting when he wrote in 1838 that racing was 'just like dram drinking; momentary excitement and wretched intervals; full consciousness of the mischievous effects of the habit and equal difficulty in abstaining from it'.[121] Greville often bet on horses he owned, when he knew their form and chances, but some upper-class betters were acting almost as modern bookmakers, betting round, taking bets against all horses, even in the early part of the century. Indeed, this led William Garforth, High Sheriff of Yorkshire in 1815, to quit the turf in 1820 claiming that 'no honourable man ... could train either with confidence or satisfaction when even Gentlemen betted round and made up their books as a matter of business'.[122] Although working-class 'legs' were joining them by this time, upper-class bookmakers taking bets against and backing a number of horses dominated the limited betting market, sometimes to the surprise of sporting writers who through the century kept believing that upper-class bookmakers were a new phenomenon. The *New Sporting Magazine* in 1842 was surprised that 'now ... noblemen make books'.[123] Richard Tattersall in 1865 claimed that bookmaking had 'sprung into prominence only of late years', and had only recently 'passed from noblemen and gentlemen of high standing and means to persons of lower rank'.[124]

Profit from betting was more likely if the odds could be manipulated. The writer 'Nimrod' in the 1830s admitted that gentlemen on the turf 'swerved from the straightforward course', excusing them by suggesting that they had been exploited unjustly by others.[125] Lord George Bentinck and others were quite prepared to disguise the horses running, hold horses back, or otherwise manipulate odds, while it was claimed that working-class legs such as Hill were employed by 'men who profess to keep their escutcheon unstained' to do 'the work of darkness' in the 1840s.[126] 'Sylvanus' made the point that gentlemen cheated too in 1850.[127] Examples of upper-class dishonesty may also be found in the second half of the century. In 1887 it was claimed that the dishonesty of some of the most prominent upper-class patrons of the turf was 'a matter of public notoriety'.[128] In the same year the disreputable Marquess of Ailesbury, a 'sharp among sharpers', was warned-off after his jockey confessed to a catalogue of such activities, while Sir George Chetwynd's stable was accused by his fellow Jockey Club member Lord Durham of similar offences.[129] In the early 1900s the Druid's Lodge confederacy, a group of upper-class owners, became well-known as a result of their carefully-planned betting coups, usually on handicaps, where their horses' form had been deliberately concealed.[130]

Betting required places of association where betters could meet, and there were a range of such in the early nineteenth century. The assizes, political meetings or social events such as the theatre are all examples. Another was horse sales, and a more formal betting system was introduced in London in 1815 when Tattersall's opened special subscription betting rooms at Hyde Park Corner for the settlement of betting debts. The membership was mixed. It included peers, baronets, MPs and gentlemen but also others from lower social classes who had made money on the turf and were reliable payers. Odds laid at Tattersall's were reported in the press regularly by the 1820s. When in 1865 Tattersall opened new and larger rooms at a cost of £30,000, the membership was still socially mixed, although wealthy, and the healths of Padwick and Hill, two well-known 'legs', were among those drunk at the opening.

The London clubs provided another betting market from early in the century. White's maintained a betting book on the Derby for its members and by 1811 was also running a 10-guinea Derby sweepstake.[131] In 1824 nine London clubs subscribed to the *Racing Calendar* and interest grew thereafter. By 1853 *The Times* was quoting ante-post prices in the City and the West End.[132] Eighteen clubs subscribed to the *Calendar* by 1854, and 29 by 1874.

Those more deeply involved in the turf also associated in betting rooms, where entry was by subscription in order to restrict entry. Such rooms were specially constructed as commercial enterprises at a number of towns, following Tattersall's example, but often open only just before and during race weeks. Doncaster betting rooms were filled with the 'noble and wealthy of the land' in 1825.[133] They had nearly 600 socially-mixed subscribers by 1827.[134]

Tattersall's was frequented by four main groups – owners of racehorses and amateur betters, young men of fashion and sporting ambition, commission agents acting for others who were unable to attend personally or who wished to keep their knowledge private, and the 'legs'.[135] There had been initial attempts to keep out the 'legs' by a minority of members through blackballing, but the legs' willingness to bet round and their prompt payment facilitated betting so that they were given a separate room in Tattersall's in 1818, and were soon a regular general presence in the subscription rooms.

The cross-class nature of the betting market was necessary because otherwise upper-class owners could not put sufficient money on the horses they wished to back or lay bets with others. The limited numbers of betting books which survive clearly show this. John Bowes bet not only with fellow Jockey Club members but also used working-class betters such as John Gully as commissioners; Bentinck used Gully and Hill as commissioners; Sir Joseph Hawley used Swindell.[136] Betting information was actively sought by many, and before the newspaper training reports were published some even employed their own private touts to watch horses and acquire it.[137] Upper-class owners often allied with working-class commissioners in their betting operations. George Payne, a well-known Jockey Club member, had been given good reason to believe by Gully that Jerry, the 1824 St. Leger winner, would not win the race again and lost £26,000 on the race when the jockey was changed. Naturally, he claimed to be unaware that the jockey had been nobbled.[138] They also allied with trainers and jockeys to ensure betting success. The *Sporting Magazine* of 1844 claimed 'we could name Dukes and Lords ... not only agents but confederates' with the latter.[139]

Up to the 1870s the subscription betting rooms at Newmarket, London and Manchester were regularly frequented by upper-class wagerers, some betting large amounts. But by 1876 *Baily's Magazine* could claim that Tattersall's and other clubs' returns were 'meagre and unsatisfactory', money was coming in in 'fivers and the occasional monkey [£20]' and the 'swells were no longer forthcoming'.[140] There were a number of reasons for this. Much publicity had been given to some of the high-stake plunging characteristic up to the late 1860s. The death of the Marquess of Hastings in 1868, after he had vainly tried to recoup immense losses with a final series of desperate plunges, was perhaps the most significant in this respect.[141] A comment on 1873 betting suggested that it was 'little marred by ephemeral plungers or by foolish youths squandering an ancestral inheritance'.[142] Upper-class young men often came to betting early, most probably through the socializing influences of family, public school and university. Certainly in 1900 the Rev. J. Wood, the Harrow headmaster, admitted that pupils whose parents bet and took them to meetings also bet, but 'less than formerly'.[143]

Then too, better information about horses became available. Horses could no longer be nursed in the market and their chances exaggerated when they were unfit. The new press coverage of racing gave more publicity to horses which were withdrawn at the last minute after the owners had bet against them and to the dishonesty and pulling of horses, and contributed to a recognition of the risks of the 'play or pay' system whereby once a bet was taken then the result was all that mattered.[144] There was a steady move to starting-price betting, where a horse had to start for a bet to stand, and to betting with bookmakers rather than the betters' own social group.

Control over credit betting at Tattersall's and the Newmarket subscription rooms was also strengthening. Both had originally been run by upper-class committees which tried to control the course betting in the rings and provide rulings regarding betting disputes, as well as the betting itself. The Newmarket subscription room committee had had a powerful voice in warning-off courses everywhere those defaulters who failed to pay up on settling day, since its membership was closely linked with that of the Jockey Club. Tattersall's committee in London also arbitrated on a range of betting disputes. In 1899 the two merged, but membership of the new committee suggests that the previous upper-class dominance was weakening, since it contained three Jockey Club members and four gentlemen owner-breeders but also a sports journalist, two commission agents, a town councillor and a representative of the ring.[145]

Plunging did not completely disappear. In 1878 Sir Charles Nugent suffered heavy losses.[146] In 1887 Lord Rodney, the 7th Baron, won the St. Leger and the Cesarewich, but thereafter plunged heavily and soon had to sell up.[147] By 1893 there were complaints that gentlemen 'welshers' from Tattersall's were becoming more and more common, and that bookmakers often let them go on in default unblushingly year on year for fear that if the bookmakers pressed too hard for payment their high connections who did pay might then refuse.[148]

Between 1870 and 1914 upper-class betting involvement continued to have a significant social context often involving the membership of clubs, which also included credit bookmakers from more plebeian backgrounds.

By 1901 clubs such as Tattersall's, the Albert, the Victoria (founded 1860) and the Beaufort with their upper-class and bookmaking membership were highly respectable, credit-betting venues which few in the provinces could rival.[149]

In terms of motivation, therefore, while profit-maximization can be found it is likely that for most racing men ownership, breeding and betting consumed fortunes, and there was clearly a substantial element of conspicuous consumption involved in such behaviour, as there was in attendance at and the financial support of meetings. For some of its adherents the demands of the racing lifestyle pushed expenditure far too high for their incomes to bear, leading to increasing indebtedness. But for many of the upper-classes the hope of breeding or owning a successful horse was a great attraction, and the jubilations, disappointments and pleasures of turf life were clearly worth paying for.

III

This chapter has shown that racing helped to reinforce social norms and status, although alongside the battle for continuing social exclusivity there were elements of an ambivalent relationship with the middle and the working class in a racing context. Racing remained a focus of sociability, allowing the upper classes to cohere informally despite subtle status distinctions. Earlier in the nineteenth century the several racing clubs allowed social and betting intercourse in a partially controlled setting. The race meeting, partly supported by upper-class contributions, allowed conspicuous consumption and display, the reaffirmation and reinforcement of 'traditional' authority, yet also some social mixing. By the Edwardian age the country house, with its gatherings for local race meetings and its breeding stud or training stable, had assumed a more important place. Breeding, racing and betting could be a pleasurable hobby for upper-class males, with success measured in a variety of ways, and the sporting, social and cultural motives for being involved were, despite the gambling culture, more important than the monetary motives.

But below such generalizations remained the realities of regional, personal and chronological variation, change and continuity. The North and the East Riding of Yorkshire had a series of large estates, far more race meetings and far more families involved in racing than the more fragmented and industrial West Riding. Beyond that, each family's involvement varied both from individual to individual and through an individual's lifetime. The 12th Earl of Derby raced horses from 1776 and supported Preston races in particular, although his racing days had ceased before his death in 1834.[150] The 14th Earl had horses with John Scott for some 21 years, but the 13th Earl had limited interest and the 15th Earl had a lifetime suspicion and dislike of the turf. The surviving correspondence of the 3rd and the 4th Earl of Grafton in the early nineteenth century revealed an intense interest in the turf and betting, but the 1836–49 journals of the 5th Earl contain mainly religious reflections.[151] There were, however, other aristocratic families who maintained a close connection with racing throughout the period. Richard, 1st Earl Grosvenor, a major better, established a stud at Eaton, near Chester in about 1780 and on his death in 1802 had spent an estimated £250,000 on racing. His son, created Marquess of Westminster in 1831, bred Touchstone, the 1834 St. Leger winner the same year, and won further classic races in 1841 and 1842. His interest declined in later years, but the next Marquess revived the stud and, as Duke of Westminster, bred and raced successfully for classic races.[152] The Dukes of Rutland showed a keen interest in Leicester races through the nineteenth century.[153]

A comparison between the *Racing Calendar* lists of owners and published lists of great landowners and the very wealthy during the nineteenth century shows a substantial measure of overlap.[154] But lists of subscribers to the *Calendar,* where the titled were until 1888 listed first before a breakdown of the other subscribers by county of residence, also suggest something of changing patterns of upper-class involvement. In 1814 about one-third of all dukes, marquesses and earls subscribed.[155] Between 1834 and 1854 there was a sharp decline in subscriptions, almost certainly due in part to the effect of the railway in increasing the working-class presence at meetings, growing middle- and working-class ownership of horses, an increasing public awareness of turf dishonesty and dislike of high-stakes plunging (see Table 7).

TABLE 7
TITLED SUBSCRIBERS TO THE *RACING CALENDAR* 1814–74

	1814	1834	1854	1874
Duke or marquess	16	19	15	11
Earl	27	28	24	21
Viscount or baron	48	48	21	26
Honourable	30	29	20	21
Knight	59	49	28	31

From the 1870s, however, there was a renewed interest in the turf among the upper classes. This raises an interesting question. Cannadine has demonstrated a late nineteenth-century decline in aristocratic power which seems to be associated here with a renewed interest in racing, breeding, and house-party sociability. Sociability was a potentially important factor in class cohesion, as Thompson has demonstrated.[156] This heightened interest may mark a return to upper-class estates and core leisure concerns.

Finally, the theme of the openness of the elite to outsiders has a respectable historical pedigree and is worth considering from a racing perspective. Most writers have laid some stress on social emulation as an important adjunct to patronage and the achieving of a social entrée into the ranks of the nobility, although the degree of openness is open to dispute and, as Beckett has pointed out, racing, horse-breeding and betting could become aids to social success.[157] Following the initial involvement of the Rothschild family in racing and the Mentmore stud in the 1860s, Leopold de Rothschild's election as a member of the Jockey Club in 1891 marked a key point in their acceptance into upper-class society.[158] Racing involvement of the right sort may be seen as another channel of admission, like political and state service, local office or marriage. This theme of intergenerational gentrification links with the next chapter, where middle-class racing involvement is examined.

NOTES

1. P. Bailey, 'Leisure, culture and the historian: reviewing the first generation of leisure historiography in Britain', *Leisure Studies*, Vol.8, No.2, 1989, p.118. Cunningham's work revived an earlier term – 'the leisure classes' – to describe this group, but gave their leisure only limited consideration; H. Cunningham, 'Leisure and culture', in F.M.L. Thompson (ed.), *The Cambridge Social History of Britain 1750–1950*. Vol.II. *People and their Environment* (1990), p.290. See also Cunningham, *Leisure in the Industrial Revolution* (1980). There are however some earlier exceptions, such as D.C. Itzkovitz, *Peculiar Privilege: A Social History of English Fox Hunting* (1977); L. Davidoff, *The Best Circles* (1973).
2. For a summary of his views see J. Rule, *Albion's People: English Society 1714–1815* (1992), pp.159–60. Borsay, in a wide-ranging survey of cultural life in provincial towns in the eighteenth century, has argued that racing was showing signs of commercialism by the 1760s; P. Borsay, *The English Urban Renaissance: Culture and Society in the Provincial Town 1660–1770* (Oxford, 1989). See also M. Girouard, *The English Town* (Milan, 1990), pp.50–6.
3. Thompson has argued that such activity consolidated the primacy of the aristocracy just as much as its involvement with other patronage and public utilities; F.M.L. Thompson, 'Some nineteenth century horse sense', *Economic History Review*, Vol.29, 1976.
4. J.V. Beckett, *The Aristocracy in England 1660–1914* (Oxford, 1986), pp.358–9. It had the added advantage of linking the rural and the urban.
5. F.M.L. Thompson, *English Landed Society in the Nineteenth Century* (1983), pp.183–8.
6. W. Vamplew, *Pay Up and Play the Game: Professional Sport in Britain 1875–1914* (Cambridge, 1988), Ch.8.
7. Beckett, *The Aristocracy in England*, pp.16–42, provides a good review of the literature. M.P. Filby, 'A Sociology of Horse Racing in Britain', PhD thesis, University of Warwick (1983), Ch.2, discusses some of the subtleties of the interrelationship of racing and elite culture and the problems of definition.
8. See Beckett, *The Aristocracy in England*, pp.21–2. Such a group lay at the heart of a wider group of clerics, lawyers, diplomats and military men (linked through kinship) and a small group of wealthy newcomers.

9. D. Sutherland, *The Landowners* (1988), pp.21–2. Thompson, *English Landed Society,* gives an overview.
10. *Doncaster Gazette*, 3 September 1841.
11. Craven, *Sporting Magazine*, November 1848, p.306.
12. Nimrod, *The Chace, the Turf and the Road* (1852 edn), p.143.
13. R.F. Moore-Colyer, 'Gentlemen, horses and the turf in nineteenth century Wales', *Welsh Historical Review*, Vol.16, 1992, p.50.
14. T. Rose, *Westmorland, Cumberland, Durham and Northumberland Illustrated*, Vol.1, 1832, p.20. See also C.N. New (ed.), *Lord Durham: An Autobiography of John George Lambton* (1968), pp.72, 82–4, for Lambton's racing involvement. Heaton Park was built as an enclosed, gated course in 1827; Love and Marnton, *Manchester as It Is* (Manchester, 1839), p.144.
15. Sir William Chaytor founded a racecourse near the Croft Spa Hotel in 1845 in an unsuccessful attempt to bolster its fading popularity. *Yorkshire Gazette*, 4 January 1845.
16. Anon., *Sketches of Beverley and the Neighbourhood* (Beverley, 1882), p.61.
17. M.J. Huggins, 'Culture, class and respectability', *International Journal of the History of Sport*, Vol.11, No.1, 1994.
18. See Vamplew, *Pay up*, pp.292, 300. At Chester eight of the ten directors of the Chester Race Company in 1892 were of an aristocratic or gentry background; Chester City Record Office, CR 543, Chester Race Company Articles of Association, 1892.
19. M.J. Huggins, 'Mingled pleasure and speculation; the survival of the enclosed courses on Teesside 1855–1902', *British Journal of Sports History*, Vol.3, No.2, September 1986, pp.157–72.
20. North Yorkshire Record Office, ZRL 4/7/1, Lawson family papers.
21. He was willing to do this only if he was allowed to build a private stand so that his party did not have to share the socially-mixed grandstand. When the Corporation refused he withdrew his support. *Darlington and Stockton Times*, 19 July 1890. Lord Legh subsidized the Newton-le-Willows meeting but lost money, before the purchase of nearby Haydock Park as an enclosed course in 1898; C. Ramsden, *Farewell Manchester* (1966), p.21.
22. There is correspondence relating to the anxiety of Lords Milton and Monson, the two stewards, not to order two cups from Garrards the jewellers by mistake in 1808; North Riding Record Office, DC/RMB, Richmond racing papers .
23. At Winchester the committee decided to cease such support in 1822 because of its 'great expense'. *Sporting Magazine*, July 1822, p.207.
24. None attended at Catterick in 1834; *Yorkshireman*, 13 April 1834.
25. See Vamplew, *The Turf*, p.127.
26. For Welsh cases see Moore-Colyer 'Gentlemen, horses and the turf', p.52.
27. Not all stopped giving cups. Lord Londesborough, who had estates at Scarborough, gave a cup there in 1851; *York Herald*, 6 June 1851. The Duke of Westminster, who continued to play a key role at Chester after its enclosure in 1893, was then still subscribing £200 towards the Chester Cup; R.M. Bevan, *The Roodee: 450 Years of Racing at Chester* (Northwich, 1989), p.84.
28. Hull University Archives, DDGE (2) 7/3, Will of William Watt, 1874.
29. C. Clarkson, *History of Richmond* (Richmond, 1814), p.328.
30. *The Sportsman*, 19 May 1875.
31. Lord Zetland and James Lowther sent up 19 horses to the August races at Redcar, when they had house parties nearby, but only five at the more popular Whitsuntide meeting; Huggins, 'Mingled pleasure and speculation', p.168.
32. Sheffield Archives, WWM F128–62, Fitzwilliam papers.
33. D. Laird, *Royal Ascot* (1976), p.44.
34. At Doncaster in 1841 there were 30 titled members of the male nobility, plus the Duchess of Cleveland, Lady Charlotte Fitzwilliam and ten other ladies. There were 17 honourables, 23 knights and 61 officers, some with their wives, as well as substantial numbers of the minor gentry from Yorkshire and beyond; *Doncaster Gazette*, 17 September 1841.
35. *Carlisle Patriot*, 28 September 1833.
36. *Sporting Magazine*, July 1838, p.255; *Yorkshireman*, 20 July 1839; *York Herald*, 10 July 1841.
37. J. Crump, 'The great carnival of the year: the Leicester races in the nineteenth century', *Transactions, Leicestershire History & Archaeological Society*, Vol.58, 1982–83, p.61. In 1895 the absence of the Princess of Wales and closing of Goodwood House due to a death led to

marked gaps in the ranks of the aristocracy and 'the long lines of matrons of high degree' at Goodwood; 'Our Van', *Baily's Magazine*, September 1895, p.224.

38. Nimrod, *The Life of John Mytton Esq.* (1835), p.62.
39. M. Cox, *Derby: the Life and Times of the12th Earl of Derby* (1974), p.105.
40. Cp. *Doncaster Gazette*, 17 September 1841 and 19 September 1851 lists of attendees.
41. Chetwynd seems to have attended about ten meetings a year in England, with occasional visits to continental meetings; Sir George Chetwynd, *Racing Reminiscences*, Vol.1 (1891), pp.72–110.
42. J. Fairfax-Blakeborough, *York and Doncaster* (1950), p.180.
43. This continues through the twentieth century and is one of the central points made by Filby (see n. 7).
44. For Scottish racing clubs see J. Fairfax-Blakeborough, *History of Horseracing in Scotland* (1973), pp.171ff.
45. *The Times*, 18 September 1827.
46. *Yorkshire Gazette*, 24 September 1831.
47. Select Committee of the House of Lords. Reports and Minutes of the Laws Respecting Gaming First Report 1844 (468) VI; Second Report 1844 (544) VI; Third Report (604) VI.
48. Durham County Record Office, D/St/C1/16/556, Strathmore papers.
49. The Yorkshire Union Hunt Club established an October meeting in 1835. Like a number of others, it included a Champagne Stakes in which the winner gave a specified amount of champagne for the Club's evening dinner. Thereafter it organized two days' racing at York each year, attracting a fashionable attendance, with a dinner, a meet and a hunt ball at the Assembly rooms on the first night, which drew 'the belles and beaus' of Yorkshire; See Fairfax-Blakeborough *York and Doncaster*, p.39. Very much an exclusive club for the gentry, it had a membership of over 300, with a subscription of three guineas and a uniform and button. The races ceased in 1856 and the Club then merged with the Yorkshire Club (founded 1839) whose rooms became a rendezvous for prominent upper-class turfites and hunting men while in York; see Fairfax-Blakeborough *York and Doncaster*, pp.121–4.
50. G. Fergusson, *The Green Collars: the Tarporley Hunt Club and Cheshire Hunting History* (1995), *passim.*
51. Report of Select Committee of the House of Lords on Betting 1902, evidence of J. Bain, Q2820.
52. Our Van, *Baily's Magazine*, April 1876, p.309.
53. See Fairfax-Blakeborough, *York and Doncaster*, pp.46, 163 give details of York Clubs.
54. York Assembly Rooms were built in 1732 in part 'for the entertainment of the nobility, gentry etc., who usually honour our horse races with their presence'; See Fairfax-Blakeborough, *York and Doncaster*, pp.51ff.
55. *The Times*, 21 September 1829. At Doncaster the Mansion House was used, illustrating yet again the close links between the Corporation and the races. See E. Miller, *History and Antiquities of Doncaster* (Doncaster, 1802), p.140.
56. See Fairfax-Blakeborough *York and Doncaster*, p.409.
57. *Doncaster Gazette*, 11 September 1891.
58. D. Sutherland, *The Yellow Earl* (1965); R. Hale, 'Horse Racing in Cumbria, the Development and Survival of Racing in Carlisle 1580–1900', undergraduate dissertation, University of Lancaster, 1989.
59. For instance, Sir J. Astley, *Fifty Years of My Life* (1894); W. S. Churchill *Lord Randolph Churchill* (1906); Lady A. Fane, *Chit Chat*, 1926; H. Leach, *The Duke of Devonshire* (1904); Marchioness of Londonderry, *Henry Chaplin* (1926); Princess Daisy of Pless, *What I Left Unsaid* (1936); Duke of Portland, *Memoirs of Racing and Hunting* (1935) and *Men, Women and Things* (1937); Countess of Warwick, *Afterthoughts* (1931).
60. For Ascot and Goodwood dresses in 1911 see *The Times*, 14 June 1911; 28/29 July 1911.
61. G. Plumtre, *The Fast Set: the World of Edwardian Racing* (1985), Ch.2 provides a good overview of the house-party world.
62. M.J. Huggins, 'Horse racing on Teesside in the nineteenth century', *Northern History*, Vol.23, 1987, p.109. 'Our Van', *Baily's Magazine*, September 1895.
63. *The Times*, 15 June 1912; 29 July 1912; 5–7 September 1912.
64. 'York in Town', *Sporting Magazine*, May 1826, p.253.
65. D. Laird, *Royal Ascot* (1976), p.64.
66. *The Times,* 14 July 1856.

67. 'The late Earl of Derby', *Baily's Magazine*, November 1869, pp.234–5.
68. Greville Diaries, quoted in T.H. Bird, *Admiral Rous and the English Turf 1795–1877* (1939), p.143.
69. In the years after 1898 R.C. Vyner had accounts with Edwards at the Wilton Club in Manchester and with both Pickersgill and Spruce in Leeds. West Riding Record Office Leeds, D NH 141, Newby Hall records box has his very full correspondence.
70. R. Black, *Horse Racing in England* (1893), p.225.
71. B. Blunt, *Arthur Yates: Trainer and Gentleman Rider* (1922), p.105.
72. The Hon. G. Lambton, *Men and Horses I Have Known* (1924) provides a good account of the world of Edwardian racing.
73. See Vamplew, *Pay Up*, pp.100–11.
74. *Doncaster Gazette,* 3 September 1841.
75. Royal Commission on Horse-Breeding, 1st Report 1888 (C.5419) XLVIII.I; 2nd Report 1888 (C.5595) XLVIII.II; 3rd Report, Minutes of Evidence and Index (C.6034-I) XXVII.319, 327; 4th Report, Appendices 1893–4 (C.6897) XXXI.871; 5th Report 1895 (C.7811) XXXV.365; 6th Report 1897 (C.8593) XXXIV.233; 7th Report 1899 (C.9487) XXXIII.1029.
76. Quoted by Bird, *Admiral Rous and the English Turf*, p.123.
77. Moore-Colyer, 'Gentlemen, horses and the turf', pp.61–2. See also H. Ritvo, *The English and Other Creatures in the Victorian Age* (Harvard, 1987).
78. The Londonderry papers, for example, show significant personal interest in this side of racing; Durham County Record Office, D/Lo/F, pp.653–4.
79. When Lord Egremont in the first decades of the nineteenth century kept five stallions and 35 mares in 'princely magnificence' this was seen as a large stud; *Sporting Magazine,* April 1824, p.3. In 1844 Sir Gilbert Heathcote kept 20 brood mares and two stallions; M. Seth Smith, *Lord Paramount of the Turf* (1971), p.93.
80. E. Conran, *John Bowes, Mystery Man of the British Turf* (Middlesbrough, 1985), pp.4–5, suggests that Bowes usually had only four brood mares. Cookson, at Neasham, never exceeded eight; *The Times*, 15 June 1865. Monck rarely had more than five, 'Sir Charles Monck', *Baily's Magazine*, December 1862, pp.271–4.
81. J. Kent, *The Racing Life of Lord George Cavendish Bentinck MP* (1892), p.235.
82. Northumberland Record Office Gosforth, NRO. 1356/D/11, expenses incurred for Beeswing, a mare walked from Northumberland to Eaton Hall in Cheshire. Lord Fitzwilliam in 1852 sent his 13 mares to four separate stallions, matching them up carefully. Sheffield Archives, WWM, Ledger for keeping horses at stud 1852–57.
83. Quoted by J. Osborne, *The Horse Breeder's Handbook* (1898), p.xciv.
84. E.g., *Baily's Magazine*, December 1875, pp.2, 64, had features on the Marquis of Hartington and Sir George Chetwynd.
85. Vamplew's figures for upper-class titled ownership are heavily inflated since he uses the *Racing Calendar* lists of owners with registered colours, some of whom could well not have raced for some time, rather than those actually running horses in a particular year. See Vamplew, *The Turf*, p.178.
86. Amphion, 'A character', *Baily's Magazine*, February 1876, p.126.
87. L.H. Curzon, 'The horse as an instrument of gambling', *Contemporary Review,* Vol.30, August 1877, p.383.
88. J. Fairfax-Blakeborough, *Sykes and Sledmere* (1929), provides a detailed account of one wealthy gentry family's ownership and breeding activities through the period under discussion.
89. F. Bonnett, 'Racing', in *Victoria County History of Nottinghamshire,* Vol.2, 1910, p.397.
90. *Sporting Magazine*, May 1822, p.91. Many horses went back to their owner's estate during the winter.
91. A range of accounts give details of training costs, e.g., Sheffield Record Office, WWM Fitzwilliam accounts in connection with stud, 1762–69; *Sporting Magazine*, May 1822, p.91; North Yorkshire Record Office, ZPB III 6/4/4; Northumberland Record Office, 1356/D/15. John Smith's accounts show that stable lads were earning from 7 shillings a week to 8 shillings and 6 pence plus board and lodging in 1808; see Durham County Record Office, Strathmore Papers, D/St/C1/10/61. See also Leeds Record Office, NH 141, for Vyner's training bills from Mat Dawson; The Druid, *The Post and the Paddock* (1862), p.29; A.E.T. Watson, *The Turf* (1898), p.151. For more general details of training costs in Yorkshire see M.J. Huggins, *Kings of the*

Moor: North Yorkshire Racehorse Trainers 1760–1900 (Middlesbrough, 1991).

92. The stall costs paid out by Sir W.W. Wynn in the 1840s alone varied from £7.10s to £10 per meeting; Moore-Colyer 'Gentlemen, horses and the turf', p.58.
93. Processions on the course and celebrations of classic wins were all part of the pageantry of upper-class life and a celebration of family pride. For a discussion of the role of formality and festivals see J.M. Robinson, *The English Country Estate* (1988), Ch.7.
94. Bowes's training accounts during the same period show annual average training costs of only £110 per horse, although this includes horses who spent only a short time in the stables and never raced, and excludes general expenses; Durham County Record Office, Strathmore Papers.
95. See Vamplew, *Pay Up,* p.104.
96. Ibid., p.105.
97. Moore-Colyer 'Gentlemen, horses and the turf', p.59.
98. 'The late Earl of Derby', *Baily's Magazine*, p.229.
99. Quoted in *The Times*, 20 December 1873.
100. Northumberland Record Office, NRO. 1356/D/7 correspondence re. foals of Beeswing 1848–53; and NRO. 1356/D/9 correspondence from Lord Eglinton and others re. horses 1851–53.
101. See Bird, *Admiral Rous*, pp.100–1.
102. 'Memorative biography of Lord Rosebery', *Bloodstock Breeders' Review*, 1929, in L. Rasmussen and M. Napier, *Treasures of the Bloodstock Breeders' Review* (1990), pp.225–6.
103. See Kent, *Lord George Cavendish Bentinck MP*, p.253.
104. Vandriver, *Baily's Magazine*, November 1869, p.270.
105. W. Day, *Reminiscences of the Turf* (1886), Ch.X1.
106. Seth Smith, *Lord Paramount*, pp.26, 55.
107. *Yorkshireman*, 21 September 1839.
108. C. Chinn, *Better Betting with a Decent Feller*, pp.9–10.
109. North Yorkshire Record Office, ZNK X1/14 2–3, 11–20 Notebook for bets 1769, 1783, settlement with Mr Wentworth to 1773.
110. The *York Herald* of 23 August 1806 claimed that 'never have we known more betting than for the ensuing St. Leger stakes. We have little doubt but that upwards of one million guineas is already laid.'
111. Sylvanus, *The Byeways and Downs of England* (1850), p.80.
112. See, for example, the comments on Sir Charles Monck, *Baily's Magazine*, December 1862, p.273.
113. The Irish peer Lord Rossmore in his memoir refers to his own bets and those of the Earl of Enniskillen and the Duchess of Montrose, quoting bets of £50 through the hundreds up to £800; Lord Rossmore, *Things I Can Tell* (1912).
114. *The Times*, 4 June 1874.
115. M.G. Moore, *An Irish Gentleman: George Henry Moore* (n.d.), pp.104–6.
116. See Fairfax-Blakeborough, *York and Doncaster*, p.109.
117. J. Fairfax-Blakeborough, *Northern Turf History*. Vol.1. *Hambleton and Richmond* (1948), p.207.
118. Suffolk Record Office, HA 513/5/172, Grafton papers.
119. See Seth Smith, *Lord Paramount*, p.40.
120. See Fairfax Blakeborough, *York and Doncaster*, p.401.
121. Certainly he was slowly betting more from the 1820s to the 1850s. In the 1820s and the early 1830s wins were mostly hundreds. In 1834 he was in credit to £7,000 at the end of the year. But by the 1840s and the 1850s wins were more significant – £9,000 on the 1846 St. Leger and £14,000 on one race in 1851.
122. J. Fairfax-Blakeborough, *York and Doncaster,* p.45.
123. 'The Statistics', *New Sporting Magazine*, February 1840, p.140. In 1850 Craven commented that legging was practised 'by the patrician who has won the silken garter'; Craven, 'The New Year', *Sporting Magazine*, January 1850.
124. J. Rice, *The History of the British Turf*, Vol.2 (1879), p.305.
125. Nimrod, *The Chace, the Turf and the Road*, pp.77, 129.
126. See M.J. Huggins, 'Lord Bentinck, the Jockey Club and racing morality in nineteenth century

England', *International Journal of the History of Sport*, Vol.13, No.3, December 1996, pp.432–44. For Hill, see *The Satirist*, quoted in Bird, *Admiral Rous*, p.149.
127. Sylvanus, *The Byeways and Downs of England*, p.234.
128. 'Turf reforms and legislation', *Baily's Magazine,* Vol.48, November 1887, p.227.
129. See Fairfax-Blakeborough, *York and Doncaster*, p.150. For Chetwynd, see Vamplew, *The Turf*, pp.105–6.
130. P. Mattieu, *The Druid Lodge Confederacy: the Gamblers who Made Racing Pay* (1990).
131. Cox, *Derby*, p.111.
132. *The Times*, 23 May 1853.
133. Ibid., 23 September 1825.
134. *York Chronicle*, 27 September 1827.
135. *Illustrated London News*, 25 March 1843.
136. John Gully's betting books for several years are preserved in the Jockey Club rooms at Newmarket and provide a fascinating account of the betting market with whom he dealt.
137. The Druid, *The Post and the Paddock*, p.177.
138. See Fairfax-Blakeborough *York and Doncaster*, p.283.
139. *Sporting Magazine* December 1844, p.354.
140. 'The Ring and the Book', *Baily's Magazine*, March 1876, pp.189ff.
141. Plumtre, *The Fast Set*, pp.43–4.
142. *The Times*, 1 December 1873.
143. Report of the Select Committee of the House of Lords on Betting 1902.
144. For a description of an 1875 Liverpool Cup 'full of dishonesty' see Our Van, *Baily's Magazine*, December 1875, pp.55–62.
145. Report of the Select Committee of the House of Lords, 1902, evidence of C. Fludyer, Q1–5.
146. *The Times*, 23 May 1878.
147. See Fairfax-Blakeborough, *York and Doncaster*, p.407.
148. See Black, *Horse Racing in England*, p.271.
149. Lord Durham's view, 1901 Select Committee, p.17, Q183.
150. *Sporting Magazine*, December 1834, p.148.
151. Suffolk Record Office, e.g., HA 513/5/ 78, 164, 172, Grafton papers.
152. E. Moorhouse, 'The Eaton Stud and its memories', *Bloodstock Breeders Review* (April 1914).
153. Crump, 'The great carnival', p.59.
154. E.g., W.D. Rubinstein, *Men of Property: the Very Wealthy in Britain since the Industrial Revolution* (1981) provides one definition; J. Bateman, *The Great Landowners of Great Britain and Ireland* (1883) provides a contemporary view.
155. J. Cannon, *Aristocratic Century: The Peerage of Eighteenth Century England* (1984), p.15; Beckett, *The Aristocracy*, pp.486–7.
156. F.M.L. Thompson, 'Social agencies and institutions', in Thompson (ed.), *The Cambridge Social History of Britain*, Vol.3.
157. See Beckett, *The Aristocracy*, pp.7, 356–8.
158. 'The death of Mr Leopold de Rothschild', *Bloodstock Breeders' Review*, 1917.

3

The Middle-class Supporters of Racing

By comparison with both the upper and the lower levels of nineteenth-century society, the middle classes have received relatively little attention. In part this is because, as some writers have argued, there are serious problems in identifying a coherent and united middle-class group.[1] The bourgeoisie was complex and fragmented, with tensions and clear differences in wealth, income, influence, importance and status between large and small employers, the professions, large retailers, shopkeepers and clerks. The professional, commercial and industrial groups were different and potentially challenged by intergenerational gentrification or a slide into the working classes.

The work by R.J. Morris and others exploring bourgeois culture has concentrated on more formal, institutional and respectable recreations, such as the voluntary societies.[2] This has led to a view that bourgeois culture in the nineteenth century was dominated by improvement, religion and respectability, a culture 'concerned with higher things', one of 'art exhibitions, museums and civic buildings'.[3]

Here again, use of a partial source archive has distorted interpretation. In reality, honesty, sobriety, sexual prudity and an opposition to gambling were not always characteristics of this group. A wider conception of leisure provides a necessary and salutory corrective to the over-simplified view of the bourgeoisie, a view which can even be seen to an extent in the explorations of middle-class involvement in sport, where the historiographical stress hitherto has been on more amateur activities or the usually socially exclusive, suburban recreations which were emerging to meet middle-class needs.[4]

This one-sided view of middle-class culture is especially problematic in terms of male leisure, where at certain times in the life cycle, in certain cultural contexts, and in certain occupations, life could be more hedonistic and much more complex than has been portrayed. Racing provides a case study of middle-class culture existing outside the narrow picture of respectable leisure forms which has hitherto predominated.

Through an over-concentration on middle-class investment in improvement, religion and respectability, most historians have overlooked the middle-class involvement in racing. Although R.W. Malcolmson, in his study of leisure between 1700 and 1850, recognized that racing had followers drawn from all social levels,[5] work on middle-class leisure and sport during the Victorian period has suggested that racing was 'virtually without middle-class support'.[6] Bailey believed that by the 1850s city meetings were almost exclusively proletarian occasions, and R. Holt accepted that 'the bulk of middle class opinion ... tended to frown upon the sport'.[7] Cunningham went further and explicitly contrasted it with the 'respectable credentials' of sports in middle-class, urban culture.[8]

Such views are incorrect. Both the invisibility of the middle classes and the lack of respectability of racing were more apparent than real, a product of limited research. There were a variety of ways in which some groups among the middle classes could be involved in racing, as attenders, shareholders, organizers and managers, owners or betters. Racing can therefore be firmly linked to the broader debate about culture, class and respectability.[9]

As we shall see in Chapter 8, hostility to racing and betting among some middle-class groups was vociferous but had only a limited effect. More illuminating than the anti-racing views expressed in the columns of the liberal, non-conformist sections of the press, is the successful pro-racing support found in the majority of traditional racing towns. Although the numbers of racecourses open varied through time, there were major elements of continuity about the existence of most courses, and few closed simply because of opposition from protesters.

The predominantly middle-class local authorities, who controlled a significant range of executive functions, varied in their attitude to the races. Their financial support was erratic, but corporation support for the local race committees in those towns with a tradition of racing was often strong and on a fairly continuous basis. Up to the 1835 Municipal Corporations Act many towns offered corporation cups or funds and corporation members were often attenders at the races. At Mold in 1800 the local corporation even laid on a public breakfast at the Black Bull Tavern.[10] At Richmond the mayor opened a new judge's box in 1814, and by the early 1820s the town clerk was also clerk of the course.[11] At Doncaster the aldermen got free grandstand tickets for themselves, their wife and children.[12] The provisions of the Municipal Corporations Act no longer allowed for direct financial support from the rates, but there were ways its constraints could be avoided.

Many corporations and councils continued their links well after this date, and some into the twentieth century. Doncaster, York and Chester provide good examples. At Doncaster the town council clearly saw the meeting as benefiting the town. From early in the nineteenth century up until 1860 the Corporation had a sub-committee of the General Purpose Committee to deal with the races, using grandstand revenue for support. Surviving minutes document their decisions.[13] After 1860 the Corporation formed a powerful, special race committee, composed of the mayor and ten councillors, to make decisions. Doncaster Corporation contributed financially to the races through a range of means and profited from them overall.[14] The anti-racing group on the town council who wanted funding and support to be withdrawn were always well outvoted.

At York the corporation held the Knavesmire course on behalf of the Micklegate ward freemen, leasing the grandstand and leaving the actual organization to a race committee. Early in the century they made annual subscriptions to the races.[15] Later on the watch committee reports show that the policing was organized by the city, and the race committee always contained councillors or aldermen. At Chester the municipality financially supported the races directly until 1836 and continued to subscribe thereafter in a less formal fashion. Later on the town council and its officers were represented on the board of the racecourse company which operated the racing. During the 1850s and the 1860s the chief constable, a former acid works owner, was personally responsible for collecting subscriptions.[16] Thereafter the Corporation, which controlled the Roodee course, were active in the management of the annual meeting and in 1888 the council set up a special race committee.

At Leicester the council, and especially its estate committee, was sympathetic to the race meeting and loaned money for the rebuilding of the stand.[17] At Newcastle the herbage committee controlled the Town Moor and gained revenue from tents and stands. The Newcastle Corporation made a regular contribution even after 1835. According to the *Racing Calendar*, they gave a contribution of 60 guineas in 1839 and were still giving a similar contribution in 1869. At Morpeth the Corporation leased the land to the race organizers. Here, as elsewhere, individual mayors often gave active, public support, which indicates how race meetings were seen as a respectable cultural activity. In Ripon the mayor laid the foundation stone of a new stand in 1865. At Morpeth in 1875 the mayor laid the stone on behalf of the community, arguing that 'it had been decided by a majority of the inhabitants that a race meeting should be held', that it would be 'conducted respectably' and would 'encourage the old English sport in all its manliness and purity', clearly here using rhetoric designed to locate racing within the frame of respectable middle-class sport.[18] By the later nineteenth century there were many such examples of mayoral support. In

1884, for example, the mayor of Durham, even though 'not a racing man', nevertheless gave support to the meeting,[19] while at Newcastle the mayor attended the meeting with a party of ladies.[20]

In the great majority of towns with a single, long-standing, annual meeting, the races were the 'nearest approach' to a 'real holiday' of the year.[21] They benefited the towns economically and were generally supported, both by the residents as a whole and the Corporation. In 1850 a Doncaster public meeting to oppose the races was organized by clergymen, a Unitarian minister, industrialists, Chartists and other 'respectable parties', but the meeting was rowdily broken up and the organizers pelted.[22] At Ripon an attempt to have the races discontinued in 1845 'met with the most determined opposition from the bulk of the inhabitants, who have risen *en masse*'.[23] At Lancaster, when in 1840 the Liberal council passed a motion to abolish the races, they were voted out of office as a result.[24]

Although the local and the regional press varied in its attitude to racing, the early nineteenth-century regional press gave racing its support and provided good coverage, especially where the sport had deep roots, as in the North Riding, the East Riding and Lancashire. The London *Times* slowly extended its coverage from Brighton, Newmarket and York races in 1810 to Ascot, Doncaster, Epsom and Newmarket in 1820, but was covering even such small events as Coothill and Thirsk by 1841, reflecting a growing interest among sections of its middle- and upper-class readership. The cheaper local press which grew up following the Stamp Act repeal was split. At Doncaster the *Gazette* was strongly pro-racing, while the *Reporter*, albeit with a much smaller circulation, was strongly opposed. The same pattern can be found elsewhere. This again strongly implies a division among the educated readership. Editorial attempts to attack betting by refusing to print racing results were ineffective. As the popularity of betting spread, the majority of newspaper editors found themselves engaged in a circulation war in which anyone failing to give the results saw a loss of circulation, and the practice was soon discontinued. When the Middlebrough watch committee asked the editor of the *York Herald* to stop placing racing result telegrams in his Middlesbrough office window in order to reduce the crowds, the response stated the paper's concern to 'maintain our position in Middlesbrough by not giving our local contemporary such a palpable advantage as it would have if we discontinued'.[25] The committee accepted the view.

Although the reformist, anti-racing group tried to categorize racing as lacking respectability, those of the middle classes involved in the sport suffered no diminution in general respectability. Perhaps one example makes the point: James Bake, as a young man in the early nineteenth century, went through an apprenticeship as a saddler, setting up in business himself subsequently. Alongside his business he had an interest in betting and was responsible for bringing the news of the St. Leger winner to Manchester on relays of horses each September. He disposed of the business to become a publican, eventually to become the landlord of the Post Office Hotel, where the Manchester betting rooms were housed, and organized racing sweeps from there by 1841.[26] He was the key figure in Manchester's growing prominence as the centre of the northern betting market. He was clerk of the course at the Manchester Castle Irwell course from 1847. He retired with a 'competency' from the Post Office Hotel in 1849, still associated with list house betting, and represented first the Oxford and then the Cheetham ward as a Manchester councillor in the 1850s. He was a key member of the Manchester race committee when elected alderman in 1865. He also held the post of clerk at the Newton meeting and died wealthy.[27] Racing and respectability could go hand in hand.

This point cannot be too heavily stressed. There were middle-class groups who strongly opposed the races. But there were many others who gave active support, through attendance, contribution to funds, share ownership, organization, office holding, racehorse ownership or by betting. Such activity reflected tensions in middle-class society, encompassing intergenerational gentrification at its higher levels and cultural accommodation. Ripon's race ball list of attenders in 1855 was full of the local gentry, military and middle classes.[28] Association with racing was no bar to success in local government. As we have seen, many magistrates and councillors supported it.

To what extent did the middle classes actually attend meetings? While it is impossible to quantify – since the social composition of crowds in terms of age, sex and status is an important but notoriously difficult area of research – there is a great deal of evidence to demonstrate that they did attend.

General descriptions of open meetings in the first half of the century regularly refer to all 'classes' attending, even at the height of the supposed attack on working-class recreations in the 1830s and the 1840s. In 1831 the expected attendance of 'merchants and manufacturers from the large towns' was numerous at Doncaster.[29] Even when attendances were down nationally in 1832, at Epsom, although fewer 'of rank' attended and the 'neighbouring peasantry disappeared', the 'middle classes, who always put the best face on things … increased in numbers' and were 'most agreeably sober'.[30] When in 1844 two skeleton stands collapsed at Newcastle, those injured included 'men in respectable stations', and poor quality races such as those at Horwich still attracted the 'respectable families' of the district.[31] Even the strong opponent of racing the Revd Dr T. Houston was prepared to concede that some of those 'in business or professional pursuits ... and farmers, merchants and tradesmen' went racing in the early 1850s.[32] Races in county and market towns attracted farmers, their families and the middling ranks of county society, and the last mixed with more aristocratic supporters at the balls and ordinaries always associated with the meetings in the early part of the century. The letters, pocket-books and diaries of the Crompton banking family, who dealt with and mixed with both the major and the minor Yorkshire gentry in the first half of the nineteenth century, show them regularly attending York races and the associated social activities and going to other meetings elsewhere.[33] The diary of a Suffolk farmer's wife, with a cultivated world view, is similarly typical. Her sons were taken out of school to go with their parents to Ipswich races, which were one of the high spots of her social calendar in the 1850s.[34] Meetings with famous races such as the Chester Cup attracted the middle classes from further afield. The diary of William Andrews, a Birmingham factory manager in the 1850s with a range of cultural interests, shows him taking a day's holiday to go to Chester races, and making a special trip to Epsom to see the Derby.[35]

By this time the data provided by the long newspaper lists of attenders in the grandstands, when matched with local directories, more explicitly show middle-class attenders, as well as the gentry and aristocracy who dominated the lists. These lists, like resort visitors' lists, reflect views about status. Middle-class attenders perhaps gained status from their association with the gentry and the aristocracy, as well as excitement from the races themselves. Councillors, magistrates, aldermen and mayors may fall into this group, as do the many military men who appear on all lists, although, given the social background of this group, it is also possible that some were related to the aristocratic and gentry group. Such attenders would take advantage of the segregation provided by the main grandstand at the smaller meetings, while at the larger ones such as Epsom or Doncaster they would use the smaller stands. MPs were well aware of the need to appear in the grandstand. During the 1865 general election campaign at Newcastle 'even preparations for the approaching general election had to be postponed and hon. candidates ... might today have been seen out around the grandstand forgetting their political and party feelings.'[36]

Further evidence is provided by the reports of prosecutions or accidents occurring on or around racecourses. These show clearly that open meetings were an occasion for local holidays and were cross-class in their attendance, acting as a magnet for middle-class visitors from further away. At the 1875 Beverley races, for example, a Hull chimney-sweep's wife died when a cart carrying her family and their manservant overturned on the way home from the races, while a Hull manufacturer was charged with assaulting a woman in one of the drinking booths.[37]

Powerful evidence of middle-class attendance is also supplied by the anti-race writers themselves. The crusading Liverpool journalist Hugh Shimmin, totally against the 'vicious practices' and 'questionable pursuits' of racing, still accepted that 'crowds of people from every class' attended Aintree in the 1850s.[38] The picture which emerges from such descriptions is of a section of the Victorian middle class who worked hard and played hard, playing one role at work and a quite different one in their leisure. Shimmin described 'more respectable people ... merchants who on the Exchange and at home pass for gentlemen' engaged in 'indecorous and unbecoming' dalliance in a notorious brothel-keeper's booth, and 'members of parliament, magistrates, aldermen, town councillors, merchants, brokers, publicans, businessmen of every grade, and many men of questionable character' betting in the ring. He contrasted that with their work on county sessions, their speeches at public meetings on the need to purify and regenerate society, their support for missions, religious and benevolent associations, and their political ambitions.[39] Similar examples came from Manchester. A series of articles in *The Free Lance* painted an unregenerate middle class, bent on pleasure and described the Manchester grandstand as 'graced, or otherwise, by a great many who regard themselves as the aristocracy from a monetary and cottonian point of view'.[40] Equally, the large number of racing pictures and prints which show crowds at meetings, even though focusing more on classic races with a more upper-class crowd background, still show many apparently middle-class attenders.

Top trainers, jockeys and race officials were middle-class in terms of income. Racing provided the means of social mobility. Race officials had to be literate, numerate, men of probity, with good organizational skills. To begin with such posts were part-time, although good officials were officiating at more than one course even at the beginning of the nineteenth century, and they increasingly carried out their duties at a range of courses as full-time occupations from the 1870s. Of those race officials whose original occupations can be identified, almost all had solid, respectable, middle-class backgrounds, often being from the professions. Some had legal training.[41] Several were originally teachers, including one of the most successful northern clerks, Thomas Craggs, who was reputed to have left £40,000 on his death in 1885.[42] Joseph Lockwood, the clerk and judge at Doncaster (1803–31), was elected an alderman in 1821. His son, who succeeded him, was a sculptor.[43] J.F. Clark, the Newmarket judge after 1852, saw no incongruity as an architect in specializing in the design of 'churches, chapels and race stands'.[44] Others were shopkeepers, printers or innkeepers who gained financially from the races through the presence of visitors. William Loftus, the Newcastle clerk from 1790 to 1825, ran and owned posting-houses. Some top trainers and jockeys likewise had high incomes and employed servants.

The composition of race committees, whose chief responsibility was raising sufficient 'added money' to ensure good entries, was also predominantly middle class and often consisted of prominent townsfolk. While the clerk of the course did much of the day-to-day administration, the spirit and energy of race committees were important in encouraging local support. Sometimes a committee had a membership which included both the gentry and the wealthier townspeople; sometimes there were two separate committees – one representing the country gentry who sent their horses, arranged the stakes and the dates, and a town committee who liaised with them, raised money and promoted improvements.[45] At York the urban members of the race committee organized the appointment of a committee of county noblemen and gentlemen in the 1840s 'to communicate from time to time with the present Racing Committee and to set on foot an annual county subscription' and to help 'the ancient capital of this great county ... to boast an August meeting equal to its former importance and celebrity.'[46]

The evidence does not allow us to determine the extent to which interest and profit or love of racing were motives lying behind committee membership. Racing writers often claimed that committee members had little thought of financial return.[47] But certain occupations, such as brewers, inn- and hotel-keepers, wine and spirit merchants, lawyers and solicitors, Tory newspaper publishers and surgeons occur frequently on membership lists and some of these may well have profited indirectly. Membership of local race committees was always dominated by prosperous townsmen. As early as 1791 the original 20 proprietors of the Preston Grandstand included a majority who may be identified from contemporary directories as local merchants, manufacturers or in commercial occupations, and the first race committee was formed predominantly from these groups.[48] When aristocratic support was withdrawn from Preston in 1831, the strengthening of this management committee resulted in the races being continued 'with renewed vigour'.[49] In the later nineteenth century, as surviving meetings grew in status, the standing and wealth of race committee membership rose alongside. Membership of most committees included councillors and magistrates of both Liberal and Tory views. At Leicester, Joseph Underwood, hosiery manufacturer, leading Liberal councillor and mayor, and Thomas Milligan, a leading Tory councillor, were dominant figures, and here there were clear links with the Liberal bourgeoisie.[50] At Manchester a leading figure on the late nineteenth-century committee was J.E. Davies, a magistrate, secretary of the Salford Liberal Association and councillor.[51]

Nineteenth-century subscription lists provide further evidence of middle-class support for racing, with money added by MPs, local magnates, tradesmen and innkeepers, partly through the self-interested need to 'encourage the races' and to achieve potential profit.[52] At Preston innkeepers, the butchers and some of the shopkeepers were all expected to contribute.[53] At Knutsford the meeting was revived in 1849 following a requisition signed by 59 of the inhabitants, and a subsequent meeting in the court room of freeholders, shopkeepers, publicans, tradesmen and other residents.[54] Many contributors seem to have given partly out of a willingness to support a sport which they enjoyed, as at Chester, where the 250 tradesmen subscribers included a significant number for whom any pay-off was unlikely.[55] At Blackburn in the 1840s a leading figure in race organization was the leading employer in the town, W.H. Hornby.[56]

The occupational background of grandstand and race company shareholders was predominantly middle-class – unsurprisingly, since although share costs varied, the median cost was £5 (see Table 8).

TABLE 8
OCCUPATIONAL STRUCTURE BY PERCENTAGE OF RACE COMPANY SHAREHOLDERS OF SELECTED COMPANIES BETWEEN 1859 AND 1894

Date	1859	1865	1869	1873	1874	1881	1881	1883	1884	1885	1894
Aristocracy, gentry	9	6	35	41	29	25	11	47	17	14	17
Upper professional	15	19	10	4	18	18	6	13	11	2	20
Lower professional	0	0	5	0	0	0	3	0	0	0	0
Drink trade	15	21	10	4	12	0	25	0	26	28	9
Manufacturers' traders, shopkeepers	48	51	30	26	0	57	28	10	20	35	11
Managers, higher administration	0	0	5	0	0	0	0	0	2	0	3
Clerical	6	1	5	9	0	0	1	0	2	0	3
Skilled manual	0	0	0	0	0	0	6	0	2	2	0
Semi-skilled manual	0	1	0	0	0	0	4	0	2	2	0
Unskilled	0	0	0	0	0	0	1	0	2	0	0
Farmers, yeomen	6	0	0	11	29	0	14	0	2	12	20
Unknown	0	1	0	5	12	0	0	30	13	5	33
Total: n=	33	136	20	76	17	28	71	40	46	43	64

Source: Sample of northern grandstand or racecourse companies from the Public Record Office, BT31 file: Stockton, Newcastle, Carlisle Grandstand Company, Scarborough, Ripon, Whitehaven, Chester, Hull, Morpeth and Carlisle Racecourse Company.

Although the aristocracy dominated the shareholding at a minority of courses, overall it was the group of merchants, tradesmen and shopkeepers who were the most numerous, and the drink trade, professional men and farmers were not far behind. The drink trade everywhere, except in Manchester, played a major role, as was to be expected, especially in initially buying shares in the newly enclosed grounds. At Leeds, for example, the ill-fated Leeds Racecourse Company was dominated by three innkeepers and a maltster.

Financial returns were not necessarily high, although shareholders got free entry and at some courses shares were to be redeemed as soon as possible, after which profits were to be applied to the benefit of the races. The secretary of the Stockton company wrote in 1878 telling the registrar that 'the shareholders who took shares for the good of the races have had their shares redeemed and paid off with the exception of very few'. At many courses the interest on shares had not to exceed 5 per cent, with anything in excess going to further the objects of the meeting. Share purchase may thus be seen as a commitment to and a gesture of support for the races, as well as an investment.

What did directors of limited companies gain? As with the capitalization of football and cricket, the love of the sport, the hope of influence or social prestige were at least as important as financial return for many, although there was often a higher proportion of gentry in the directorate than in shareholders generally. At Newcastle, the 1864 directorate included two 'gentlemen', along with two colliery owners, three manufacturers, an ironmaster, a solicitor, a baker and wine merchant. Being on the directorate was an unpaid task, involving substantial work. The chairman at the final winding-up of the Durham meeting, Alderman A.O. Smith, a local solicitor, claimed that directors 'had filled, without favour or reward, and with a positive loss to themselves, functions that in other companies were invariably discharged by salaried officials'.[57]

Being on directorates or race committees was an opportunity for exercising patronage, and another middle-class opportunity to sponsor, through their support and organizational skill, approved activities. In many ways it paralleled the unpaid voluntary work associated with mechanics institutes, temperance societies, Sunday-school associations and the like. Not all the urban middle class espoused the rhetorical claims of the bourgeois culture of 'art exhibitions, museums and civic buildings' and concern with 'higher things'.[58] The sporting world was also run by the middle classes. Football, with its professionalism, working-class fanatical spectatorship and play-to-win philosophy, was organized and run by a similar group to that which ran racing.[59]

The extent to which the middle classes owned racehorses is a question fraught with difficulty. Neither the *Stud Book* nor the *Racing Calendar* give more than names, some of which are assumed. Nevertheless, the index of owner names in the *Calendar* is indicative. As early as 1809, 54 per cent were titled, military or 'esquires', a title used to denote those with substantial wealth, position or land, implying that some of the rest were from middle-class backgrounds.

The earliest discernible large group were the 'legs', more interested in betting than in horse ownership, although they often kept horses in several major stables to gain from inside stable knowledge. Many of this group, while working-class in origin, had a wealthy lifestyle and employed servants. Early nineteenth-century examples included John Gully, later Pontefract MP and colliery owner; Crockford and the Blands who ran gambling 'hells'; and the Huddersfield clothier Pedley.[60] Mid-century betting owners included a London businessman, lawyer and money lender, who became a magistrate and deputy lieutenant of Sussex; the London businessman Parker; an Epsom surgeon; and a Northleach solicitor.[61] Most stayed at the same hotels as the aristocracy, mixed with them in certain social settings, and often aped the gentry's patterns of lifestyle and consumption. The betting link with ownership was a clear example of continuity. Later in the nineteenth century it was a common practice for wealthier bookmakers, property-owning and servant-employing, to own and run horses. John Jackson, owner of Fairfield Hall and stud near York, the 'Leviathan of the North' and worth over £40,000 on his death in 1869, was an early example from the 1860s.[62] John Devereux, the Stockton bookmaker, was running horses all over the north in the early 1880s. Joe Pickersgill of Leeds, ex-butcher's boy, registered his colours in 1881 and was worth £746,459 on his death. Another Leeds bookmaker, George Drake, built his own stables at Middleham.[63]

Beyond this group were others. A number of early owners were innkeepers, who used their stables, often located on the coaching routes or near racemeetings, for breeding. What might be termed the rural middle classes often owned horses. Trainers, whom I have described elsewhere as 'marginal men' since they were both the servants of owners and yet wealthy servant employers themselves, were often extremely successful.[64] Chifney, Day, Dawson, Scott, I'Anson and other trainers achieved classic successes and wealth. Some of the wealthier jockeys were also owners. The ex-stableboy John Hutchinson won the St. Leger as early as 1791; another, the high-betting Jack Hammond, won the 1884 Derby. The other group which tended to be successful were the wealthier tenant farmers. The horse Alice Hawthorn, bred and owned by the North Riding farmer John Plummer, won 52 of her 71 races in the 1840s.

Lists of urban, middle-class urban owners can be identified most commonly when press references show them running at their local meetings, although also, less commonly, in the writings of those with racing interests. A significant number of urban owners were brewers, distillers or licensed victuallers. Among the local owners at Thirsk, recalled by William Allison in his memories of his 1870s childhood near Thirsk, alongside his father's solicitor partner who ran horses under an assumed name, was Sammy Cass, a Liberal brewer, and William Rhodes, brewer and 'backbone of the local Conservative party'.[65] The distiller Mr Graham operated under an assumed name, treating racing partly as a pleasure and partly as business, but backed only his own horses.[66] A number of racecard printers owned horses. Industrialists, merchants and manufacturers who were on the way up in status often bought property and turned to racing, as a way of gaining respect and status. Examples from early in the century abound. Thomas Houldsworth, a Manchester cotton manufacturer, ran horses from 1804, bought Sherwood Hall, Nottingham, and became an MP in 1818.[67] The 'railway king', James Hudson, ex-linen draper, owned horses and officiated as a steward at northern meetings after buying Newby and Londesbrough Parks. Mr G. Foster, well known in the Newcastle iron trade, won the Northumberland Plate in 1857, 1858 and 1859. R.C. Naylor, a Liverpool banker, High Sheriff of Chester in 1856 and the purchaser of Hooton Hall, won the Derby in 1863. In the second half of the century a number of wealthy Scottish owners entered racing successfully, including the Glasgow brewer Frederick Gretton. The Scottish ironmaster James Merry, son of an itinerant pedlar, had seven classic successes. The iron-founder and millionaire George Baird reputedly wasted his fortune on 'horse racing, prize fighting, and harlotry'.[68]

Some wished for social status, some for pleasure, while others were out to profit from racing, either through betting or prize money. The Middleham businessman Tom Masterman attempted both. In 1869, for example, his horse Honesty ran in 36 races in England and Scotland, winning 15. By the end of the century, in the north at least, many owners were described as either 'men making a business of the sport' or 'commercial men with local associations who find the turf a pleasant recreation after the cares of business'.[69] The excitements and uncertainties of ownership and association with the famous and the infamous had their own rewards. And there was always the possibility of winning. The cups and plates, pictures and photographs, still in the possession of some racing families today, handed down as heirlooms, indicate that ownership was more than a mere 'business'. There was a clear pride in racing success. The will of the Newcastle chemist, druggist and alderman Antony Nichol, for example, left an estate of £60,000 and made explicit provision for his wife to inherit his racing cups from Stockton and York and for his daughter to have them on his wife's death.[70] By the 1860s those described as merely 'Mr' dominated the lists of owners. In 1869 83 per cent of owners were described as such, and the proportion grew thereafter.

To what extent were middle-class punters involved with on- and off-course betting? Research has tended to focus on the working classes. But there was certainly middle-class betting both on- and off-course from the early nineteenth century.

On-course betting was such an accepted part of course life that there is little direct evidence about it, although the scattered entries in some diaries indicates that it was attractive. Early in the century the yeoman George Browne (1741–1804) of Townend in Westmorland, an area with little tradition of thoroughbred breeding, attended races at Kendal and Lancaster, where he 'cleared £5 or £6' besides his expenses.[71] There are isolated references to a wide variety of middle-class occupational groups in court cases, usually where there was involvement with welshers, throughout the period. The three-times mayor of Richmond Michael Brunton was laying the odds at country meetings all over the north in the 1820s, and by the 1840s a range of evidence shows that middle-class men were entering the emerging profession of 'legging'. Indeed, by mid-century it was being complained that clerks and small shopkeepers were 'making a social sort of business' of it.[72] The evidence of the sweeps also almost certainly indicates middle-class interest. In the 1840s these were widely advertised in the press, at prices between £1 and £10 a ticket, well beyond the means of working men.[73] By early April 1845 Paul Ashley, a prominent Sheffield sweep organizer, had already filled one £5 Derby sweep and was on to his fifth £1 sweep.[74] Sweeps were illegal but ignored by local magistrates; this fact and the pricing indicating their widespread support. The London prosecutions in 1848 had little effect beyond. In Hartlepool surviving printers' material contains a significant number of tickets for several sweeps over the period 1850–56 covering the classics, the Cesarewitch and the Cambridgeshire stakes, mostly between 150 and 500 members, at between 1 shilling and half-a-crown each, with 5 per cent held back for the organizer.[75] Such lower stakes reveal target marketing lower down the wealth structure.

But there were also increasing numbers of places in larger towns where racing lists were being exhibited and bets taken on future races. 'Sylvanus' claimed in 1850 that in York there were 'many retail shops that would give odds on horses' and druggists, publicans, and yeomen-traders who would back them.[76] Such list houses were illegal after 1853, although they continued clandestinely. It may be that they continued to be used by the middle classes. But there were other options which were less risky.

One was to bet in betting rooms or clubs. Tattersall's was the most important club for those centrally involved in betting and some of its members were certainly middle class. Mr Perry, for example, who was one of the few to back Imperieuse in 1857, was on the Stock Exchange.[77] In the north, at Manchester's Post Office Hotel, the bookmakers and backers found there were 'self-made men', including employers as well as clerks and other employees.[78] By the 1860s many major bookmakers were abandoning the notion of using betting rooms and were using office premises as well as on-course betting in Tattersall's ring, almost certainly catering for wealthier upper- and middle-class patrons. The memoirs of James Peddie, a London-born turf commission agent, make clear that, beside his own firm, there were major (illegal) offices taking postal cash bets in Covent Garden, Great Russell Street, Jermyn Street, Fulwoods Rents and Farringdon Street, while the firm of Holt and Crook were established at Leeds.[79] Unfortunately, as betting historians concede, there is little firm evidence of their clientele,[80] although a punter could bet only once credit was established, or by sending cash through the post, so punters were more likely to be middle-class. These offices were hit hard by renewed police prosecutions in London in 1869. According to Peddie, these began following pressure brought to bear on Downing Street by Sir Joseph Hawley, a Jockey Club member, who was being forestalled in backing his horses by one of these agents. Peddie then moved to Scotland and began advertising his services in the *Sporting Life*, soon turning over about £100,000 annually.[81] Over the next few years other commission agents followed, advertising extensively in the national sporting press. To deal with this a new Betting Act was introduced in 1874 (37 Vic. cap.16). It prohibited the publication or distribution of material advertising methods of betting, by placard, handbill, card or advertisement which had been prohibited by the 1853 Betting Act. Circulars sent by post were to be deemed advertisements. It also extended the 1853 Betting Act to Scotland. Bookmakers were to be liable to a fine not exceeding £30.[82] Most of these major commission agents then moved to Boulogne or the Netherlands in order to be out of the reach of the Act, advertising particularly in the new sporting papers such as *Sporting Life* (1859 to the present) or *Sporting Times* (1865–1930). Many of these commission agents were highly reliable. Valentine, Hardaway and Topping, a firm first founded in 1850 as 'commission agents', were members of Tattersall's, and operated as credit bookmakers out of London, but were running services from Boulogne and Flushing, widely advertised in the press, *Ruff's Guide* and elsewhere in the

1880s, taking cash in the form of postal orders. They sent out a free daily *French and English Sportsman* on receipt of an address. They were often used by people in the country who had no access to street bookmakers or by young middle-class males who could not get credit and who would not have penetrated into the world of the list and street bookmaker. Topping and Spinder, based in Flushing, and James Webster of Middleberg, maintained a large postal business and were advertising in papers such as the *Financial Times* as well as *The Sportsman* in the late 1890s.

Legal credit bookmakers were operating in the larger towns by the 1870s. Shepherd and Son in Blackpool date from 1876, while Manchester bookmakers such as A. Magnus, T. Gibbons and W. Vincent were well known throughout the north by the 1880s.[83] They received instructions by letter or telegraph and offered starting-price bets based on course information. Their punters were drawn from people met in the Ring, the known wealthy and local small tradesmen, the shopocracy and wealthier clerks. Joe Pickersgill ran a credit office in Leeds which drew on many wealthy Yorkshire landowners and later numbered the Prince of Wales among his Tattersall's clients, although he gained his initial capital by being a street bookmaker.[84] Some middle-class clubs were also opening during the same period with a betting focus and bookmaker members. At Manchester the Wilton Club was a popular betting place in the 1880s, with many of its clients self-made men.[85]

Betting started early. Children of those of the middle classes who were part of the turf world often went with them to the stables and to the races. William Allison, whose solicitor father worked in the racing town of Thirsk and owned horses, was, like some of his friends, betting with Crook at Boulogne in 1870, while by 1901 the Master of Harrow saw the increase in betting among his pupils as due to parents who encouraged it, sweepstakes and circulars from foreign betting houses.[86] Some young men reacted against the dominant ideology of their non-conformist parents.[87] By the end of the century a 'reformed' bookmaker was describing many of his customers as having 'made money in trade or business', citing a draper, a grocer, a solicitor, a chemist and a market gardener as examples.[88] Several of those giving evidence to the 1902 Lords Select Committee claimed that clerks were especially prone to betting, while one tipster stated that even clergymen used his services.[89]

Views among the magistracy were mixed. Anti-gambling magistrates were common enough to put some list bookmakers on the street where they had more chance of avoiding the police, who generally left them alone. But many magistrates were unwilling to deal firmly with illegal betting unless there was strong public pressure to do so. Some recognized that legislation had a class base. As one pro-racing Middlesbrough councillor said in 1880, 'if they were going to stop betting they should stop it not only among the working men but in the clubs and the higher grades of society'.[90] Significantly, even here in a town whose early history was dominated by Quakers, the watch committee voted 11 to nine not to deal more stringently with persons betting. Councillor Weighell, a racehorse owner himself, paid tribute to the street bookmakers as 'honourable men who paid 20 shillings to the pound' while another councillor, one of the largest employers in the area, said that many of the betters were among his 'very best and most respected workmen'. The middle-class bench here, as elsewhere, displayed mixed attitudes to betting. The extent to which fines varied, depending upon which magistrate was sitting, shows this clearly. In Lambeth some magistrates would refuse to convict unless all the writing in a betting book was clearly in a bookie's writing.[91]

Equally, although some newspapers attacked betting, most consistently printed racing information. Here material interest was at stake. Editors knew that there was more demand for racing information than there was for negative comments about racing. This view may be found even in the most antagonistic of papers. The *Doncaster Reporter*, the only local paper opposing the races and betting, was selling views of the grandstand and course, playing cards and betting books at the paper's office at the height of its campaign.[92]

There was, as we shall see, an anti-racing group, with a bourgeois vision of civilization and moral improvement, composed of a group of churchmen and dissenters, and their manufacturer, industrialist and shopkeeper supporters. Suspicious of the moral temptations of the emerging leisure world, often liberal in their politics, some were trying to construct a new religious identity. Others saw themselves as economically disadvantaged by the races. The key question is whether this group was actually as typical as it has appeared to be. Another middle-class lifestyle, perhaps more unregenerate, or more bent on pleasure, may be seen in certain locations, at certain points in the lifestyle, in certain associational and in certain occupational settings.

Although many people may not have held strong views on racing, there was certainly a strong base of public support for its continuance. Even firm anti-racing writers regretfully admitted, 'it is no use discussing the question as to whether the races exert a bad or a beneficial influence on society in the face of the fact that by far the greater portion of society appears not only to countenance but to support them',[93] and that 'all classes of society' were attracted to them.[94] A study of support for horseracing suggests that our picture of middle-class leisure may have in the past been too one-sided.

There is a need for more recognition of cultural complexity and diversity and more subtle definitions in any discussion of nineteenth-century social class which attempts to relate it to culture. The 1845 revival of the races at Derby shows this clearly, at a time when the conventional chronology of leisure sees popular recreations as under severe pressure from middle-class evangelicanism and industrial capitalism. At Derby a clear majority of the town council voted for reintroduction. The pro-racing group, led by the Mayor William Mousley, a wealthy solicitor and pewholder in the parish church, was composed of professional men, manufacturers, tradesmen and shopkeepers. It was opposed by a similarly mixed, propertied and prosperous evangelical group, indistinguishable in terms of occupation, property and social standing. As A. Delves has pointed out, here any consensus was both relative and finite, and there were real differences of social identity.[95]

A study of racing, therefore, has implications for wider debates about culture and class. R.J. Morris felt able to identify an independent, middle-class, respectable culture in Victorian Leeds.[96] More recent work has offered a more measured and subtly qualified view.[97] While an earlier emphasis tended to be on such determining factors of middle-classness as utilitarianism or evangelicalism, or work in local government and politics, racing and other leisure activities show the need for an increased awareness of cultural complexity and the tensions of cultural aspiration. Manchester shows this. Even in the 1830s such highly respectable industrialists and manufacturers as the factory owner Thomas Houldsworth, the calico printer Robert Turner, or the printer James Patrick were heavily involved in racing life.[98] Manchester was the key northern centre of racing and betting, with clear evidence of middle-class involvement with no loss of respectability, except in the eyes of a minority, anti-racing group. It is therefore not surprising that the Manchester middle classes had a 'complex and contradictory matrix of values, practices and institutions'.[99] Everywhere respectability was both complex and contested. Anti-racing pressure could usually be exercised only on those in certain positions, as with the Revd Mr King, who was pressed into resigning his living after his horse won the 1874 St. Leger. Both the support for racing and the vociferous opposition to it shows that at times middle-class consensus and hegemony were more limited than many historians have recognized.

Contrary to established belief, racing had a solid basis of support among certain middle-class groups, especially those more avowedly materialistic or secular in attitude, who could see financial, social and cultural capital in it. This included many MPs, councillors, aldermen, magistrates, doctors, factory managers and even occasionally clergymen. Some gained through the commercial benefits brought by the races; some used them as a vehicle for social mobility, social recognition or for intergenerational gentrification. It is clear that racing and betting involvement was no bar to success in life and business. Many enjoyed racing or betting. Racing provided a context where notions of class identity were under negotiation and contested. Social status, pleasure and profit were interrelated and contributed to the increasing legitimacy of and cross-class access to racing. Such access included that of the working classes, and it is to them that we now turn.

NOTES

1. N. McCord, *British History 1815–1906* (1991).
2. R.J. Morris, *Class, Sect and Party, the Making of the British Middle Class: Leeds 1820–1850* (Manchester, 1990).
3. S.J.D. Green, 'In search of bourgeois civilization; institutions and ideals in nineteenth century Britain', *Northern History*, Vol.28, 1992, pp.228ff.
4. J. Lowerson, *Sport and the English Middle Classes 1870–1914* (Manchester, 1993).
5. R.W. Malcolmson, *Popular Recreations in English Society 1700–1850* (Cambridge, 1973).
6. Lowerson, *Sport and the English Middle Classes*, p.5. See W. Vamplew, *The Turf* (1976), pp.133–4.
7. P. Bailey, *Leisure and Class in Victorian England* (1978), p.22; R. Holt, *Sport and the British: A Modern History* (Oxford, 1989), p.181.
8. H. Cunningham, 'Leisure and culture', in F.L.M. Thompson, *The Cambridge Social History of Britain 1750–1950;* Vol.II. *People and their Environment* (1990), Ch.6, pp.305–9.
9. For an earlier version of the discussion below see M.J. Huggins, 'Culture, class and respectability: racing and the middle classes in the nineteenth century', *International Journal of the History of Sport*, Vol.11, No.1, 1994.
10. R.J. Moore-Colyer, 'Gentlemen, horses and the turf in nineteenth century Wales', *Welsh Historical Review*, Vol.16, 1992, p.49. At York the Corporation always gave an annual payment to the August meeting in the first three decades of the nineteenth century. See York Archive Office, YCC York Chamberlain's Books and Accounts, e.g., 11 August 1826.
11. North Yorkshire Record Office, DC/RMB, Richmond racing papers.
12. First Report of the Royal Commission on the Municipal Corporations of England and Wales, Vol.30, 1835, Q1502. It also provides numerous other examples of corporation involvement.
13. It is clear that in the details of the arrangements they were relatively deferential to the opinion of the stewards. For an example concerned with the appointment of officials see Doncaster Record Office, AB 2/2/5/1, Minutes of the General Purposes Committee, 10 December 1852.
14. By 1887 the Corporation was making a profit of approximately £10,000 after stakes and expenses were paid, and 'at least six times as much' was left 'sticking to the pockets' of the inhabitants. *Baily's Magazine*, Vol.57, October 1887, p.130.
15. E.g., York Archive Office, YCC Chamberlain's Books and Accounts, 11 August 1826.
16. F. Simpson, *Chester Races: Their Early History* (Chester, 1925), p.8.
17. J. Crump, 'The great carnival of the year', *Transactions of the Leicestershire History and Archaeological Society* (1982–83), p.66.
18. *Newcastle Daily Journal*, 15 February 1865; *Morpeth Herald*, 21 August 1875.
19. *Durham Chronicle*, 25 July 1884.
20. *The Northumbrian*, 28 June 1884, p.56.
21. 'Holiday Times', *Household Words* (1853), p.329.
22. *Doncaster Gazette*, 7 September 1850.
23. *Yorkshire Gazette*, 5 April 1845.
24. R. Hale, 'The Demise of Horse Racing in Lancaster and Preston', Lancaster University BA dissertation 1991, p.28.
25. Minutes of Middlesbrough Watch Committee, 7 October 1890.

26. *York Herald*, 7 July 1841.
27. J.T. Slugg, *Reminiscences of Manchester Fifty Years Ago* (Manchester, 1881), p.112; E.A. Axon, *The Annals of Manchester* (Manchester, 1886), p.372; *Manchester Courier*, 3 June 1869.
28. *Ripon Chronicle*, 20 October 1855.
29. *Doncaster Gazette*, 16 September 1831.
30. *Sporting Magazine*, Vol.V, 2nd Ser., 1832, pp.153, 490.
31. *Yorkshireman*, 29 June 1844; T. Hampton *History of Horwich* (Wigan, 1883), pp.229ff.
32. T. Houston, *The Races: The Evils Connected with Horse Racing and the Steeplechase and Their Demoralising Effects* (Paisley, 1853), pp.34–6.
33. M. Ashcroft (ed.), *Letters and Papers of Henrietta Matilda Crompton and her Family* (Northallerton, 1994).
34. S. Hardy (ed.), *The Diary of a Suffolk Farmer's Wife 1854–1869* (Basingstoke, 1992).
35. V. Chancellor (ed.), *Master and Artisan in Victorian England* (1969).
36. *Newcastle Daily Journal*, 28 June 1865.
37. *Beverley Guardian*, 19 June 1875; 26 June 1875.
38. J.K. Walton and A. Wilcox (eds), *Low Life and Moral Improvement in Mid-Victorian England: Liverpool through the Journalism of Hugh Shimmin* (1991), pp.72–3.
39. Ibid., pp.75–6, 79.
40. *The Free Lance*, 15 June 1867; see also 9 February 1867.
41. J. Fairfax-Blakeborough, *History of Horseracing in Scotland* (1973), p.130.
42. *Middlesborough Daily Exchange*, 28 December 1885; 29 January 1886.
43. J. Fairfax-Blakeborough, *York and Doncaster* (1950), p.246.
44. *Baily's Magazine*, June 1876, p.385.
45. *Sporting Magazine*, August 1838, p.368 provides a Liverpool example.
46. York Racing Museum, Minutes of York Racing Committee, 5 October 1843.
47. J. Fairfax-Blakeborough *Thirsk Races* (n.d.), p.20.
48. Lancashire Record Office, Preston; DDX 103/4, Fulwood Race Minutes 1790–1829.
49. *Yorkshire Gazette*, 30 July 1831.
50. J. Crump, 'The Great Carnival of the Year', p.60; C. Ramsden, *Farewell Manchester* (1966), pp.19–21, cites good Manchester examples. This applied even to small unrecognized meetings such as Blaydon; see J. Gale, *The Blaydon Races* (Newcastle, 1970), p.36, for membership of the 1891 committee.
51. Ramsden, *Farewell Manchester*, p.17.
52. North Yorkshire Record Office, DC/RMB, Richmond Racing Papers.
53. Lancashire Record Office, DDX 103/4, Minutes of the Race Committee, 9 July 1829.
54. Cheshire County Record Office, D4222/24, Knutsford Race Committee Minutes, 1849–52.
55. R.M. Bevan, *The Roodee: 450 Years of Racing in Chester* (Northwich, 1979), p.47.
56. G. Miller, *Blackburn: the Evolution of a Cotton Town* (Blackburn, 1951), p.373.
57. *Durham County Advertiser*, 8 June 1888.
58. S.J.D. Green, review article: 'In search of bourgeois civilisation: institutions and ideals in nineteenth century Britain', *Northern History*, Vol.28, 1992, p.232.
59. See T. Mason, *Association Football and English Society 1863–1915* (Brighton, 1980), pp.37ff.
60. B. Darwin, *John Gully and his Times* (1935) gives details.
61. W. Day, *Reminiscences of the Turf* (1886), pp.3–34, 158–80. J. Fairfax-Blakeborough, *Northern Turf History,* Vol.III., *York and Doncaster* (1950), p.360; Select Committee of the House of Lords. Reports and Mimutes of the Laws Respecting Gaming Third Report 1844 (604) VI. Evidence of J. Day, Q.923ff.
62. For obituary see *Newcastle Daily Chronicle*, 28 January 1869.
63. J. Fairfax-Blakeborough, *The Analysis of the Turf* (1927), pp.262–3.
64. See M.J. Huggins, *Kings of the Moor: North Yorkshire Racehorse Trainers 1760–1900* (Teesside, 1991), p.46.
65. W. Allison, *My Kingdom for a Horse* (1919), pp.37–9.
66. 'A Character', *Baily's Magazine*, February 1876, p.130 .
67. R.W. Proctor, *Memorials of Manchester Streets* (Manchester, 1874), p.83.
68. For details of these and others see R. Mortimer, R. Onslow and P. Willett, *Biographical Encyclopaedia of British Flat Racing* (1979).
69. R. Ord, 'Horseracing in the North of England', *Badminton Magazine*, Vol.19, 1902, p.172.

70. Northumberland Record Office, Will of A. Nichol, 1881.
71. S. Scott, *A Westmorland Village* (London: Archibald Constable, 1904), p.112.
72. *Sporting Magazine*, Vol.125 (1854), p.140; *Sporting Magazine*, December 1848, p.459.
73. E.g., *York Herald*, 7 July 1841.
74. *Yorkshireman*, 6 March 1845; 12 April 1845.
75. Robert Wood Collection, Gray Art Gallery, Hartlepool. See also *Newcastle Weekly Chronicle*, 6 August 1864: 'The Next Great Monster Draw on the St. Leger has 5,000 shares now at 5/- each, with a first prize of £500'.
76. Sylvanus, *The Byeways and Downs of England* (1850), pp.1–20.
77. *The Times*, 18 September 1857.
78. *Free Lance*, 25 May 1868.
79. J. Peddie, *Racing for Gold: Incidents in the Life of a Turf Commissioner* (1891).
80. M. Clapson, *A Bit of A Flutter: Popular Gambling and English Society c1823–1961* (Manchester, 1991), p.28, summarizes the position. Clapson's treatment of the earlier nineteenth century is highly cursory.
81. Peddie, *Racing for Gold*, pp.1–8.
82. *The Times*, 1 April 1874; 1 August 1874.
83. Clapson, *A Bit of A Flutter*, p.38.
84. Fairfax-Blakeborough, *The Analysis of the Turf*, p.280.
85. *Burnley Express and Advertiser*, 27 August 1887.
86. Allison, *My Kingdom*, p.22. B.S. Rowntree (ed.), *Betting and Gambling: a National Evil* (1905), Appendix.
87. E.g., N. Gould, *The Magic of Sport* (1909), for a description of his early betting life at boarding school.
88. A Bookmaker, 'The Deluded Sportsman', in Rowntree (ed.), *Betting and Gambling*, p.92.
89. Select Committee on Betting, 1902, Evidence of C. Gould Surrey, Q.1472; J. Orr, Chief Constable of Glasgow, Q.2164–5; A.G. Markham, Q.3074.
90. *Cleveland News*, 1 May 1880.
91. Select Committee on Betting, 1902, Evidence of Superintendent Shannon of Lambeth, Q.1726.
92. *Doncaster Reporter*, 11 September 1867.
93. *Middlesbrough Weekly News*, 17 August 1866.
94. Houston, *The Races*, p.8.
95. A. Delves, 'Popular recreation and social conflict in Derby 1800–1850', in E. and S. Yeo (eds.), *Popular Culture and Class Conflict 1590–1914* (Brighton, 1981), p.110.
96. R.J. Morris, 'Middle-class culture 1700–1914', in D. Fraser (ed.), *A History of Modern Leeds* (Manchester, 1980); idem, *Class, Sect and Party*.
97. E.g., P. Joyce, 'In pursuit of class: recent studies in the history of work and class', *History Workshop Journal*, No.25, 1988; idem, *Visions of the People: Conceptions of the Social Order in England before 1914* (Cambridge, 1990).
98. Slugg, *Reminiscences of Manchester*, pp.8, 34, 89.
99. A.J. Kidd, 'Introduction: the middle class in nineteenth century Manchester', in A.J. Kidd and K.W. Roberts (eds.), *City, Class and Culture: Studies of Cultural Production and Social Policy in Victorian Manchester* (Manchester, 1985), p.17.

4

Racing and Betting: A Key Part of Urban Popular Culture

Working-class participation in the aspects of racing culture most open to them (betting and spectatorship) testify to an heterogeneous picture of working-class life, varying from region to region and with local economic life.[1] Yet several critical points emerge. First, both working-class forms of participation reflected both a desire for and at least a partial achievement of self-organization and autonomy in this leisure area. Secondly, racing and betting reinforced regional social cohesion within and between classes, offsetting the potential for class conflict and division and playing a key part in gossip and talk. Thirdly, bookmaking allowed for local control of an important industry within working-class communities.

When discussing leisure a number of writers have argued that there were two popular cultures, one perhaps resting on drink, gambling and sport, and one on the chapel, respectability, temperance and the mechanics institute, contending for much of the nineteenth century.[2] This chapter therefore uses culturalist analysis to examine the links between racing, the world of work and broader cultural life and leisure, drawing heavily on Cunningham's recent notions of 'leisure cultures' which examined nineteenth-century social experience and described different ways of life.[3] Two of these cultures are particularly relevant. The first, 'reformist' culture, with both religious and secular forms, refers to groups within the middle and the working class which provided a more purposeful, self-improving, political and pious approach to life, opposed to both race meetings and to betting; this is dealt with in Chapter 8.

The activity of the reformist group may be interpreted not simply as an attempt to control the leisure interests and behaviour of the lower classes, but also as a fear of pleasure, irrationality and carnival. From this perspective, racing may be seen as a source of resistance to reformism and rationalization and was used to this end by some working-class spectators.

Cunningham also identifies what he calls 'urban popular culture' and his three approaches to it are relevant here. The first emphasizes commercial activity, requiring consumption and absence from work with participants in the role of spectators, or purchasers of goods or services. Race meetings clearly fall into this category. His second approach, examining activities generated in the local community or neighbourhood, is related to betting, and working-class bookmakers were soon involved in the commercial provision of betting services. His third explores the role of women, who played a role in both the making and the taking of bets in the home and on the street.

Much of the commentary on racing and betting is 'former golden age' antiquarianism, or alarmist tracts about betting's pervasiveness. Only the most recent writing has related betting to broader economic, social and cultural changes.[4] This research has unsurprisingly largely focused on the relationship of mass betting to working-class living standards and is significantly stronger on the last decades of the nineteenth century than earlier in the period. Working-class involvement in racing had two theoretically separate but overlapping dimensions, with different chronologies: attendance at local and regional meetings, which almost always involved betting, and off-course betting by men and women who might rarely if ever attend a single meeting and the chronology of these dimensions has previously been insufficiently explored, while overuse of a fairly limited range of largely metropolitan sources has also distorted the picture.

In fact, the sporting press and other cultural institutions which supported working-class betting and attendance at meetings were already developed by the 1840s and the 1850s in some regions of Britain. This chapter fleshes out and develops existing understandings, giving more emphasis to the early period, since the later nineteenth and the early twentieth century world of working-class betting is now well-trodden ground.

I

The working-classes played no substantial part in the organization of meetings. They were largely spectators, and right through the nineteenth century racing attendance and support had a clear regional dimension.[5] The thoroughbred had originated in Yorkshire and support was greatest there for much of the century, with large crowds at major meetings and press interest in off-course betting information. Knowledge of racing was particularly rooted in the North and the East Riding, which had the majority of courses and training establishments. Even in the early part of the century there was also interest in some West Riding urban centres such as Sheffield or Leeds. Working men walked through the night from Sheffield to Doncaster to see the St. Leger.[6]

Lancashire crowds were also large for major meetings, with Manchester a major racing and betting centre. Lancashire, like Yorkshire, hosted large numbers of meetings. This may well link to broader political attitudes. Conservatives were stronger supporters of racing than Liberals. Lancashire was still an important centre of Conservative strength in the later nineteenth century and notable racehorse owners, such as the Earl of Derby or W.H. Hornby, MP, the Blackburn textile manufacturer, also enjoyed significant political influence. The third key area was London, the centre for the inner, often upper-class turfite group, and generated an associated, wider, working-class interest.

Racing also provided a focus for regional identity.[7] In the early part of the nineteenth century rivalry between northern- and southern-trained horses was significant within the world of the turf, affecting jockeys, trainers, owners and spectators. This made it difficult for a good southern horse to win in the north, and vice versa. At Doncaster, where the St. Leger was a focus of widespread regional interest, northern jockeys colluded at the start to hold back southern riders.[8] The attitudes of the crowds reflected this same regional bias; the more so in the north, a significant factor, as Malcolmson points out, in reinforcing regional, social cohesion, identity and togetherness.[9]

The races also attracted country people. Horses were bred and trained in rural surroundings so the rural working classes were often interested. In recent years the reassessment of rural discontent has been an important focus of revisionist approaches to rural society, demonstrating how protest against aristocratic landed interests ran through English and Welsh society from the Napoleonic period onwards, although it appears to have been more common further south than in Scotland and northern England.[10] Racing provides a context where class relations were less conflictual. Many men had a keen eye for a thoroughbred. Farmers often kept a thoroughbred mare from which to breed, while wagering was also part of social interaction. At Coxwold in the North Riding in the 1860s, for example, almost ‘any of the old inhabitants could talk with intimate knowledge of north country horses’ and it was the ‘favourite topic’ in the public house.[11]

In training towns or in towns associated with racehorse owners, they were keenly interested in local successes. Burnley bells rang in both 1861 and 1863 when Townley horses won the Derby, the Oaks and the Doncaster Plate.[12] Where horses were bred and trained on great estates this made a contribution to the local economy, while the public training stables were often of central social and economic importance, providing significant local employment in towns such as Newmarket, Malton or Middleham.

The next chapter will deal with course life, but it is worth emphasizing that numerically the working classes were the greatest patrons of the races throughout the period. Going to the races was a special, ever-new, annual day (or days) out, a shift away from the everyday. Races were a calendared event, central to the notion of the British holiday, and show the adaptability of popular culture.

Even at the beginning of the nineteenth century there was significant popular interest in the local races. Like the local fairs, working people looked forward to such events, and they were relatively peaceable. The races at Manchester after the deaths at Peterloo could have become a focus for demonstration, but did not since popular interest in racing overrode political attitudes. In Newcastle the over-exuberant celebration of the coronation of George IV led to a riot which forced even the local yeomanry into retreat, but the riot died down of its own accord in the afternoon with a general exodus to the town moor for the races.[13] Working-class support for racing may also be seen in the reaction to anti-racing groups when they attempted to curtail long-standing local races. In 1850 at Doncaster an anti-racing group meeting at the Guildhall found themselves assailed with a burst of uproar whenever they attempted to address the meeting, which broke up with the organizers pelted with stones.[14] In the south as early as the 1840s the Derby had become a major popular occasion, and continued so throughout the rest of the period. Middle-class observers focused upon the hedonistic behaviour of race days or on its carnival features. Taine, visiting in the 1840s, described it as a Saturnalia, with crowds of nearly 200,000, including 'numerous poor', with fighting, people relieving themselves publicly, enormous losses and violent feelings, and betting associated with 'the sensation of an enormous risk'.[15] According to *The Times*, the 'whole metropolis ... goes mad in concert, and becomes boisterous, extravagant and noisy without restraint ... all London seems under the influence of a great mania.'[16]

But references to 'mania' or the 'annual Saturnalia' were only part of the story.[17] Sociability was a key part of race-going and many people went to the races in groups. Some walked and others everywhere seem to have ridden in large carts, crammed together.[18] Large crowds who could not afford the trip often began assembling to watch their passage quite early in the morning and were equally keen to watch their return.[19] Some non-race-going observers saw the equipages and the liquor and heard the raucous music as groups of working-class spectators made their way through the city to the course, and associated behaviour with irrationality. In fact, some London groups were organized months before. Every expense, down to the turnpike charges, was carefully calculated. The proportion that each person would bear was identified so that a steady payment to the common fund would allow a committee to make all the preparations needed.[20] In Liverpool in the 1850s it was not uncommon in workshops for money clubs to be formed or saving boxes established.[21] It paralleled Lancashire holiday clubs established for wakes weeks and provides another example of self-help in working-class life, but not in a way which middle-class reformers could understand: thrift in pursuit of 'irrationality'.

To spend money during race weeks, conscious budgeting efforts were made. Diminished turnover in local shops reflected the need to save up for the races and the domestic economy it entailed. Where overtime was available, as at Leicester, factory operatives used this as a means of being able to take time off later.[22] This meant that race meeting crowd size was linked to trade cycles. When Hull suffered depression in the shipping trade in 1884, with hundreds of men rendered unemployed, it was reflected in a drop of over 3,000 in the railway traffic to the nearby Beverley races.[23]

This illustrates the importance of race meetings as times of a recognized break, not just in the town itself but in the surrounding area, and the part played by travel. People went from London to Epsom; from Sheffield to Doncaster; from Hull to Beverley. R. Poole has shown how the Bury cotton operatives used Radcliffe wakes races as their summer holiday.[24] The 'mechanics of the great iron districts' were major attenders at Walsall races in the 1850s.[25]

Annual race meetings were important customary holidays, especially for many of those not actively making money out of the races, although the nature of such holidays varied both in status and duration. Absenteeism was partly sanctified by tradition, but where race meetings were newly set up there was often an initial, widespread opposition to absenteeism from many local employers. But even in the face of legal restraint and labour discipline, large-scale absenteeism was widespread. For many urban dwellers the race week was the major popular holiday. The time taken off seems to have varied. On Teesside trade reports show that in the 1850s, when the races were revived, employers fought hard to keep men at work, but unavailingly, and by the 1880s the mills, forges and foundries were all closed for the greater part of the week. The shipyards and one steelworks remained open, although with high absenteeism.[26] Where meetings were long-standing the holiday was taken for granted, although this was more problematic when fixture dates were changed. At Durham in 1881 a late change of date meant that the suspension of the collieries and works could not be relied on, but the commercial importance to the city was such that all the influential tradesmen did what they could to support the meeting by closing their businesses.[27]

Urban residents were not the only ones affected by the races, although the rural working classes came in less often, often attending the races in the afternoon of the town's market day. Nevertheless, their attendance was regular. Around Epsom by the 1840s farmhouse servants built attendance into their hiring-day agreement.[28] Nearby industrial villages also fed in spectators, although this was more commonly a day or half a day's absence from work to see a major race such as the St. Leger. Pitmen and handicraftsmen in the north-east sacrificed 'half a day's pay' to see the Northumberland Cup.[29] The special nature of life in mining communities often meant that miners were great gamblers, keen on deep play, and most descriptions of racing at meetings in mining areas make reference to their presence. A German coalminer living and working in the Northumberland coalfield saw betting on races as a central part of mining culture. It was part of the propensity for deep play, high stakes and excitement, giving status and reward in the community.[30] At Stockton 'the toiling miners of Cleveland, the pitmen of Durham' all 'poured into the town in droves' for the big race.[31] Large numbers of working-class excursionists from other urban areas introduced other accents, other working-class sub-cultures and helped the process of social mixing and increased mobility that characterized Victorian Britain.

Opposition to the races often led to attempts to take children and their parents away from the race meetings. Sunday-school trips to the seaside and the country played a significant role in socializing the working classes first into the seaside trip and later the seaside holiday. The numbers going away grew through the century, reflecting the population growth, the rise in working-class real incomes and the increasing tendency for whole communities to take the week for leisure, whether they wished to go to the races or not. Manchester by 1878 had large numbers of Sunday-school excursions during race week and over 22,000 took advantage of them.[32]

The introduction of enclosed courses, which moved racing from a free event with a vast range of ancillary commercial attractions, to a sport relying on admission fees, diminished the impact of such popular holidays only in part. Where a nearby enclosed meeting took over from a traditional open one, businesses still sometimes shut, although at Leicester, where the course was two miles away, business carried on as usual. At many towns the pattern of holidays was sufficiently strong to maintain the holiday. At Newcastle, although the shift to enclosed Gosforth Park changed the nature of attendance, the old town moor still had sports and entertainment, now organized by the Sunday schools, in an attempt to keep spectators away. Generally, therefore, the impact of the meetings continued. The enclosed courses put on the types of racing which were most popular, with increased prize money and more handicap and sprint races, where the outcome was uncertain, to attract betting interest. The newspapers were sensationalizing racing, making top horses and jockeys household names. Fred Archer's death led to demonstrations of feeling quite unprecedented in Victorian Britain.[33] Crowds flocked to courses to see these sporting heroes.

Race weeks had become traditionalized, a key part of the working-class leisure calendar. The railway companies soon responded to demand and from the 1860s working people were using the race-week holiday as a cheap opportunity to visit other places. This was not necessarily reformist and oppositional. One member of the Leicester race committee even suggested that 'there are ten drunken persons who go by special train to one seen on the racecourse'.[34] By the 1890s at Newcastle nearly 12,000 people were taking advantage of cheap railway company trips during race week.[35] Nearby resorts often had added attractions, and, although trips were more expensive than a day at the races, tripper numbers peaked during nearby race holidays.[36] This indicated that among the working classes significantly large groups were prepared to save and then spend on race-week leisure.

II

Horseracing's location in working-class culture was also mediated through betting.[37] R. McKibbin has even argued that mass betting was the most successful example of working-class self-help in the modern era. Discussions on its chronology and extent have been heavily distorted by the use of the material produced by the Anti-Gambling League in the 1890s and the evidence given to the Select Committee of the House of Lords in 1902. Both were concerned to stress the apparent consensus between the police and the magistracy that betting was 'until recently ... almost exclusively the sport of the wealthy, but now it has through the instrumentality of horseracing, become a popular passion'.[38] The House of Lords Select Committee report argued that 'betting is generally prevalent in the United Kingdom and that the practice has increased considerably of late years, especially among the working classes'.[39] But the evidence presented to it was limited and much was of the nature of special pleading. Certainly the last quarter of the nineteenth century was when debates about gambling came into prominence but, although McKibbin and R. Miller stressed the 1880s as the point when betting became a major factor in working-class life, more recent commentators have been more cautious, suggesting that working-class betting went on throughout the century, although providing little supporting evidence.[40] This section demonstrates that a gambling industry was already beginning to grow up around racing by the 1840s, and a clear culture of working-class betting emerged in the period from about 1840 until 1880. Working-class betting was not new in the 1880s; it was already there.

This commercialized, capitalistic betting industry depended for its existence on technological advances such as the growth of the railways and the electric telegraph. As the century progressed and betting information became more readily available, it espoused the rational values of middle-class ideology, as betters made choices on the basis of information and notions of probability. Its emergence reflected the tensions inherent in middle-class culture. Most working-class betting was, from 1853, illegal, yet the police rarely prosecuted and many magistrates' attitudes were ambivalent, with some highly unwilling to convict and others issuing minimal fines.

Unfortunately, key questions such as the numbers of people who bet, who they were, the frequency with which they bet or who was most likely to bet, prove to be almost impossible to answer with high levels of confidence, even later in the period where evidence is fuller. Police statistics on prosecutions and investigations into domestic budgeting are almost entirely useless.[41] Middlesbrough, a town where street betting was endemic from the 1870s, illustrates how unreliable the use of such evidence would be. In 1880 an attempt to introduce a by-law dealing more stringently with street betting was defeated by a small majority in full council, reflecting the feeling that 'unless there were an absolute nuisance it would be better to leave the betting men alone'.[42] The Middlesbrough police rarely acted against betting unless pressed to do so; indeed, they had to be warned against betting on duty on at least one occasion,[43] while in a privately-brought court case in 1898 police evidence revealed that they patrolled the 'betting ground' regularly only to see that good order was kept.[44] Lady Bell's 1907 study of Middlesbrough's workers devoted a whole chapter to the place of betting and drinking in working-class life yet her examples of working-class budgets omitted it entirely.[45]

Early in the nineteenth century almost all betting was confined to the local meeting, although working-class jockeys, stable lads and others within the racing world were already taking an interest in betting. The diary of Thomas Greathead, a servant to the Earl of Strathmore, for instance, records a number of bets. On 26 March 1799, for example, he bet that Diamond would not have beaten Hambletonian the previous day at Newmarket, and on the next day recorded that he had 'got an account of that Hambletonian won, by the guard'.[46] The coaches' guards in the pre-railway era provided access to betting information in provincial towns and *en route* between them. In Yorkshire, until their demise, 'what's won?' was invariably the first question asked of them from April to November.[47] The early 'legs', found at London, Newmarket and in the north, were of mixed social origins, although of as dubious integrity as many of those for whom and with whom they bet, but almost all were working-class.

The first significant, more general, working-class, off-course betting came in the form of the sweeps, which had a similar appeal to the state lottery abolished in 1826, largely because of working-class gambling associated with it, which had nurtured a nascent interest in betting.[48] For the sweeps the names of horses in a particular race, most commonly the Derby or the St. Leger, were drawn by participants. While winning was based on chance, tickets for well-fancied horses could be sold on before the race. The fashion for sweeps caught on first in London and those larger towns, such as Doncaster, Leeds, Newcastle and York, which had a racing tradition. By 1844 sweeps and lotteries were being got up in almost all cities and were spreading into the rural horseracing and training centres. In 1846 the training town of Middleham had sweeps organized at both the White Swan and the Old Commercial Hotel, both with dinners associated with them, which the winner of the sweep was expected to give.[49] Early sweeps were aimed more at wealthier customers, but by about 1846 sweeps were available at prices affordable by working-class punters and could be found organized by a wide range of public houses, some advertising in the sporting press.[50]

Unless stirred into action, the magistracy and the state placed a low priority on enforcing existing laws against gambling, under which organized sweeps could have been prosecuted, so sweeps were initially tolerated. Their move down the social scale led to increased concern with both the social-class and the moral dimension, even from some within racing. The journalist 'Craven', writing in *The Sporting Magazine*, began a campaign in 1848, believing that it was bad for the turf that publicans should run large sweeps for profit, and that such 'speculation' was against the ethos of the sport.[51] The editor of *Bell's Life* had no objection when 'respectable licensed victuallers got up sweeps of moderate amount'. His concern was that, more recently, 'instead of being confined to this respectable class of men, the getting up of sweeps was made a trade of itself and fictitious names were put forward to call attention to schemes equally fictitious'.[52]

Questions were then asked in Parliament and the Home Office advised the Solicitor of Stamps that journals containing advertisements for racing sweeps should be prosecuted. By December 1848 prosecutions were being reported.[53] Advertisements for sweeps temporarily disappeared as a result, although ingenious sweepstake promoters soon found ways of wording them to avoid the risk of prosecution.[54]

This fashion for sweeps was already being accompanied by an increase in more organized, urban betting, and between around 1840 and 1860 betting was becoming well-rooted in urban society. In the earlier nineteenth century bookmakers had dealt mainly with that relatively small circle of racing insiders, where individuals were known and betting was on credit. By the 1840s there was an increasing interest in racing across all classes and in the major urban areas a new type of cash bookmaker emerged to meet their needs.[55] Even in 1840 it was being reported that almost as much heavy betting was taking place in Liverpool, Manchester and Birmingham on the leading turf events as in London, and that there were one or more 'sporting public houses' in all great towns.[56]

Racing information was also increasingly available. National newspapers and some regional ones had full coverage of national racing, including regular reports from their 'own correspondent' at major meetings. At a cost of 4½ pence a week, these would still have been a significant element of spending by a single individual, although purchases may have been pooled. Even so, by 1848 the *Sporting Magazine* was already bemoaning not just the growth of lotteries and sweeps on the major races, but also that of popular betting and other racing ventures 'for the poor'.[57] The St. Leger, for example, had become of such widespread interest that carrier pigeons were released to bring the news to 'the great manufacturing towns of Yorkshire, Lancashire and Northumberland'.[58]

In London the effect of banning the sweeps was an increase in the exhibition of betting lists, especially in public houses, where the position and wealth of the landlord was a guarantee of payout.[59] In turn, the efforts of licensing magistrates who put pressure on landlords to stop exhibiting lists led to the opening of 'list houses', some of dubious honesty and reliability and some fraudulent. List bookmakers posted lists of odds on named horses in specified races in key places of urban association – the public house, the tobacconist, billiard rooms or barbers' shops, and took ready-money bets. Betting lists were being reported in the London and the Manchester press from the mid-1840s.[60] List houses became so popular that some members of Tattersall's opened offices in self-defence.[61] One early York list bookmaker was Thomas Holtby, the ex-coachman of the London and Edinburgh mail, who had carried information about racing matters and gained information from passengers *en route* to and from meetings. Holtby advertised his new business as the 'Ebor Betting Office', informing his friends that 'his lists are now open on all the forthcoming events for the ensuing year ... Tattersall's odds laid ... commissions promptly executed on receipt of cash'.[62]

List bookmaking was at its most effective when most of those placing bets knew little about the horses. For many major races entries were made many months before, the horses' future development was uncertain and few would actually run. Bets were 'play or pay' so a better lost the bet if the horse did not run. So the list proprietors stood a reasonable chance of a profit, especially since the odds were usually ungenerous. There was less of a potential profit on minor events, where few horses were backed. The winning of a favourite might not be covered by money on other horses, so lists tended to focus on major races. In Yorkshire, where there was more knowledge of racing, the system took off slowly, 'as the tykes generally knew too well what horses were in work'.[63]

As betting moved into working-class areas, London-based, upper-class racing writers viewed the growth of 'racing clubs and betting offices that pollute our streets, our lanes and alleys' or the 'betting dens' in Cheapside and elsewhere with increasing alarm.[64] It was perceived as problematic and therefore potentially criminal. It was conspicuous, commercial and complained of. Just as before with sweeps, growing governmental anxieties over 'list houses' in London led to action, this time legislation. The 1853 Act for the Suppression of Betting Houses was an attempt to deal with this new betting form. According to the Attorney General, it was 'servants, apprentices and workmen', including 'vast numbers of youths' who were tempted to risk a small sum for the opportunity of a large one.[65] Betting failed to foster the virtues of self-denial, hard work and saving and thus threatened the social order. The working classes would lose money. Betting would corrupt the young. Losses might lead to the robbing of employers.

In large part the Act may be seen as class discriminatory, a paternalistic concern for the poor. The Act was interpreted as meaning that it was legitimate to bet off-course on credit, a possibility open only to the better-off in regular work, but not in cash. Since racecourse betting was not mentioned in the Act, it was accepted that on-course betting in the enclosures remained legal.

Following an initial surge of prosecutions, mainly of those houses more flagrantly catching the attention of the anti-betting public and police, the Act had little effect even in London, and even less elsewhere. Most police and magistrates had more urgent priorities.[66] Indeed, the racing editor John Corlett felt that for the following 20 years the act 'was practically speaking a dead letter'.[67] Zealous magistrates and officious policemen were rare. Spasmodic bursts of prosecutions were only occasionally seen.[68]

Between the 1850s and the 1870s, several working-class contexts for betting and gambling on racing developed: on-course betting apparently legal, but sweeps, list bookmakers and the still relatively rare street bookmaker illegal. Both sweeps and early bookmakers found a handy, ready-made and mutually beneficial outlet for betting activities in public houses, a key location of working-class sociability during this period, especially when there were attempts to modify popular culture.[69]

Sweepstakes, more often aimed at the artisan class, attracted those punters relying on sheer chance, a flutter at long odds. They were sometimes advertised by poster or in the regional press.[70] More commonly they were organized by publicans issuing printed tickets. A collection of Hartlepool printers' materials contains a significant number of tickets for sweeps over the period 1850–56 covering the classics, the Cesarewitch and the Cambridgeshire stakes, mostly of between 150 and 500 members, at between 1 shilling and half a crown each, with 5 per cent held back for the organizer.[71] In Liverpool a monster sweep for the Chester Cup in 1856 had 500 members at 1 shilling each, winning £5 for the first and £3 for the second horse.[72] Despite occasional moves against sweeps in the late 1860s, they continued in such widespread popularity right through the century with such rare prosecutions that in 1883 one prosecuted publican could claim that 'in all hotels and public houses ... and all provincial towns, including Stockton, sweepstakes are got up', and that he did not know they were illegal.[73] Publicans made a profit out of running them so long as the tickets were all sold. They also attracted company to the public house and thereby increased the money spent and the drink consumed. Sweeps, however, were usually arranged only for the major races which attracted national interest.

The most significant expansion of working-class betting took place below this level. The Betting Houses Act of 1853 was largely ignored. Many large towns had their own, albeit illegal, small-scale, local, cash bookmakers, continuing to operate the 'list' bookmaking approach, despite its illegality, but seldom bothered by the police, although not all towns had sufficient clients interested in racing. It was later claimed that in Edinburgh in 1857 there were no places in which to place a bet.[74] Local interest was variable, but increased betting information in the press helped betters to make more rational decisions. Some working-class urban betters were drawn to following the fortunes of the horses of a well-known magnate in the region, either through the traditional Toryism of many of this group, the survival of deference or local loyalty to a sporting lord who had the reputation for running his horses honestly. Rumours from the great house could have reached the towns that a horse had been backed heavily and had good current form. Certainly there were many examples where the winning of a major race by such magnates was greeted with popular enthusiasm in nearby areas. When the result of Colonel Townley's 1861 Derby win was telegraphed to Burnley, the nearest town to his estate, the news was reportedly received with great rejoicing, the church bells rang and a dense crowd assembled. Local 'gentlemen' at the Bull Inn celebrated with champagne and barrels of ale were drunk. The horse's success 'had won many persons in Burnley substantial sums of money'.[75] In Dunsop, where Townley's stud farm was located, practically 'the whole assets of the village had been staked'.[76]

In the period 1850 to 1860 betting on horseraces became a popular urban diversion. The strength of potential demand for betting services was increasingly from among the urban, lower middle and upper working classes. Just as Blackpool grew up to meet the needs of a new group of holiday makers, each spending a small amount, but a large one in total, the list bookmakers provided an alternative new form of excitement. Although individual bets might be small, much more in total was in circulation. Daily newspapers became important in carrying up-to-date news about the results of races, training reports and the horses withdrawn from engagements. Rising real incomes among the urban masses, the attraction of risk and uncertainty and a possible windfall all made their presence felt in stimulating demand.

A mere three years after the 1853 Act, a journalist campaigner against betting houses argued in the *Liverpool Mercury* that they were still 'more numerous in Liverpool than is generally supposed' and were a 'large and growing nuisance'. Liverpool list houses were used by males from a wide variety of occupations, from shopkeepers' assistants to merchants, from clerks to car-drivers and from brewers to billiard players. The betting houses were socially ranked. Some were associated with prostitution and other forms of 'low life'. Some appeared 'old-fashioned, clean looking and respectable', others catered specifically for the nearby drapers and other shop assistants or were described as 'working man's betting houses'.[77] The writer claimed that magistrates must have known that betting was regularly practised, contrary to the Act.

In London too, the Betting House Act was largely ignored, despite occasional police raids which revealed that public houses were still commonly used for betting purposes. Indeed, it was variously alleged that there were 'hundreds' or 'thousands' of public houses in the West End where bets were nightly made.[78]

In Manchester many 'list' houses were public or beer houses, while others were described as cigar shops, butchers and private houses. The first Manchester prosecutions occurred in 1858–59 and after that they were left alone. According to the Manchester *Free Lance* in 1868, 'the swarm of clerks, operatives, stable men and even women ... pass in and out in an unceasing stream' into the list houses, and spent a minimum of 2 shillings.[79]

A series of London prosecutions stirred the Manchester police into action once more in May 1869.[80] Perhaps tipped off by sympathetic officers, some bookmakers had taken flight before the arrival of the police.[81] Fifteen men were charged and the police described how they saw men sit at a desk or table surrounded by betting lists and racing cards. People enquired what odds were offered, staked money, got a card with a number on it and the bet was entered in a book.

One bookmaker, Aaron Worsley, in pleading guilty, admitted that he had been convicted for a similar offence in 1859, but having seen betting carried on by other people and 'thinking that the Act had become either a dead letter or that the practice was winked on by the authorities he again opened his office'. The word 'office' emphasizes the business connection in such bookmakers' minds. But the magistrates, being 'determined to put down the nuisance of betting which has grown to a great height in this city and which has been the cause of ruin to so many clerks and servants', imposed fines of £100 or £75 plus costs.[82] Both the large fines and the bookmakers' ability to pay them give some indication of the money being turned over.

The business approach, the utilization of public houses and the spasmodic action by the police and the magistracy were typical of other northern urban areas. In 1861 in Leeds bookmakers at the King Charles I public house were fined and had their betting books confiscated and the magistrates, as elsewhere, claimed to be 'determined to put down betting on horseracing, especially in public places'. This was their first prosecution, yet evidence was put forward that the place was notorious for betting.[83] In Newcastle in 1861 a letter to the press complained that there were in the town 'about forty or fifty betting houses ... who will be applying for a renewal of their licences'.[84] When there were prosecutions by the Newcastle police in 1865 this simply forced bookmakers to take bets in the street before the subsequent races.[85] The list bookmakers prospered because they were known to their customers, living in a local community and hence less likely to welsh on bets. They dealt in cash, not credit, and it was they who sustained the growth in betting. The *Free Lance* admitted that 'we have no hesitation in saying that there are hundreds of thousands of people in the habit of backing horses at list houses who would not know a trustworthy layer of odds if they saw him and would not bet at all if it were not for the facilities afforded them by list houses.'[86]

In his study of sport, Holt has reminded us how strongly rooted in working-class life were the public house and the street, so it is unsurprising that street betting grew in popularity. There are references to betting in the streets in London in the 1840s and the 1850s, although it is unclear whether this refers to organized pitches, and by the late 1850s the police were using obstruction of the street prosecutions to attack bookmakers who betted 'on the London pavement' in defiance of the law.[87] Here certain areas, such as Bride Lane, Fleet Street and Bridge Street, were becoming bookmakers' haunts, to the dismay and complaint of some local inhabitants.[88] Lists were also exhibited in Hyde Park and other open ground.[89] There is further evidence of street bookmaking in large towns such as Newcastle or Manchester which were associated with major race meetings and where, as a result, racing knowledge was more widespread and betting had long been popular, indeed *Bell's Life* was publishing betting information from Manchester by the 1840s. Some bookmakers had been forced on to the street by the closing of premises, but it can be argued that the move also signified an expansion of betting within the local community since some were bookmakers starting up in a small way without premises, taking smaller amounts of cash. In Manchester tradesmen were already complaining of the 'betting nuisance' which blocked the streets in 1859.[90] By the 1860s the open yard beside St Paul's church was a recognized centre. At its edge were 'timber erections' where men would 'book the shillings of pickpockets, mechanics and mechanics' wives with the greatest complacence'.[91] The owner of the Castle Irwell course in Manchester, Mr P. FitzGerald, MP, claimed in the same year that 'betting on the large and numerous scale is spreading ... and large numbers of our workmen catch the frenzy'.[92] Thereafter street bookmaking spread, first through major urban areas and then beyond. By 1876 it was claimed that even the larger villages had local bookies.[93]

This evidence suggests a gradual build up of working-class betting from the 1840s, rather than a sudden expansion in the 1880s. It lends further support to the work already carried out by such writers as C. Chinn and M. Clapson, although both underplay the continuing role of the sweeps in working-class public houses. Sweeps accented one half of punters' culture, the belief in luck, at the expense of the more 'rational' study of form. There were occasional prosecutions. In 1869 the government initiated a series of renewed prosecutions of racing lotteries and sweeps on the Derby and put a temporary stop to the many shilling, half-crown and five-shilling private sweeps usually got up.[94] Defending landlords at later nineteenth-century prosecutions claimed that public house sweeps were quite general.[95]

By the beginning of the 1870s there was already a clear culture of urban betting. It was cross-class in that it involved both those with 'big money' and those who could afford only their humble shillings, yet it had its own internal forms of stratification. The references to women are also important in indicating a broader spread to betting than has previously been thought. Betting had already moved from a pre-industrial, informal, 'sporting' model to an urban, industrialized, commercialized, mass-market model. The very occasional opposition and the law were largely ignored. Betting reflected a different value position from that of the moral campaigners. It was a key concern for those who took part, an integral part of their lives. Although a cross-class activity, it showed significant numbers of the working class active in the making of their own leisure, despite its illegality.

The nature of betting was also changing. By the 1870s the sporting press was increasingly arguing that 'milking operations' and 'dirty work' by owners, trainers or bookmakers could be avoided by using starting-price odds.[96] The move from list prices, a reflection of the bookmaker's assessment of the odds, to starting prices in the ring at the relevant meeting, took place gradually over the 1870s, in the view of the correspondent of a daily newspaper. The London firm of Valentine and Wright was probably the earliest exponents of this approach, initially offering the facility for postal bets.[97] Working-class betters soon realized that by this means they could literally be sure of getting a run for their money.[98] Starting prices further boosted working-class betting, particularly in the towns, but also in the country. The trainer John Porter believed that there had been an increase in his own village of Kingsclere as a direct result of the introduction of starting prices.[99] Thanks to the telegraph, papers could now print training reports so that the public had more information and a much better chance of picking a winner. The use of starting prices telegraphed from the course to the newspapers from the early 1870s quickly led to the disappearance of illegal list houses run by bookmakers exhibiting their own odds. A new hierarchy of bookmakers emerged in the changed betting conditions of the period, using starting prices instead of calculating their own odds.

The disappearance of list houses was exacerbated by renewed prosecution of them by the police in the 1870s. Since lists were commonly displayed in public houses, some of this renewed persecution was a consequence of the Licensing Act of 1872. In response came an increasing relocation by bookmakers on to the streets in some although not all towns. The social geography of betting which was to characterize much of the twentieth century was first laid down in the 1870s and the 1880s, thereafter only increasing in extent. Working people needed to know where to go to place a bet. An examination of summonses shows that everywhere such places included patches of waste ground, public houses and shops, and particular streets.

Open spaces were most commonly used because the bookmakers could disperse quickly in case of a police raid. By the early 1880s spaces such as The Midden in Leeds, the Quayside at Stockton or Newcastle or the Middlesbrough Marshes had become well-known bookmaker sites where they were rarely disturbed, since police raids simply resulted in an increase in betting on the main streets and more complaints from shopkeepers or their more respectable customers.

The public house played a key role in all kinds of social activity in the nineteenth century and its role in terms of a centre for the taking of bets should not be underestimated. Some of them acted almost as sporting clubs on the model of those in London. There had been mid-nineteenth-century sporting public houses, such as the Adelphi in Liverpool or the Post Office Inn in Manchester, and the numbers of these expanded. Betting at such clubs was difficult to prevent. Ready money was rarely overtly staked and members knew each other. Where people were prosecuted, it was sometimes argued that it was unfair to allow betting at places such as Tattersall's yet attack it elsewhere. In Sheffield the Exchange Club and Newsroom was established expressly by betting men 'as a consequence of the recent magisterial decisions against betting' in 1869.[100] On Teesside by 1880 the Albert Club in Middlesbrough and the White Hart Inn in Stockton were both sporting clubs, normally left alone. In Liverpool Williamson Street and Tarleton Street contained 'authorized' betting clubs in 1884.[101]

Throughout Britain many landlords acquiesced in betting. In some cases, the landlord himself acted as the bookmaker, taking bets over the counter, in others the bookmaker would take bets in the landlord's presence.[102]

Shops used as betting centres were usually ones where large numbers of men might legitimately enter, such as tobacconists or barbers. In Manchester the 1860s list houses in Thomas Street and Turner Street claimed to be cigar shops, and this pattern could still be found in the 1900s.[103]

Police action against public houses and shops did not solve the problem, it simply relocated it. Raids on working-class betting houses in London in 1865 and a spate of arrests in Manchester in the early 1870s merely put bookmakers on the streets instead, leading to an 1875 by-law against street betting.[104] In both cases the effect was temporary. In Burnley the new Chief Constable began prosecuting bookmakers for obstructing the pavements in 1890 because earlier prosecutions had forced them 'out of the public houses on to the street.'[105] In Manchester further action against list houses led to more betting in betting clubs, and in 1885 a great raid on betting clubs by 170 police led to 200 arrests.[106] Here the final shift to street bookmaking took place only in the 1890s.[107]

Most commonly it was in the 1870s when certain streets in larger towns were becoming key bookmakers' haunts, although the chronology varied. In Middlesbrough, Richmond Street, South Street, Sussex Street and

Snowden Road, all increasingly working-class residential areas, were centres for bookmaking from the mid-1870s.[108] As bookmaking expanded in the 1880s and the 1890s individual bookmakers, like policemen, increasingly had their own beats, particularly the public houses and streets which were their territory.

In Stockton the first betting prosecutions were in the 1870s, and were of public houses such as the Blue Post, the Ship Inn yard and the Red Lion.[109] Police interference eventually led to the bookmakers moving on to more open spaces, first to the Market Cross and then to two sites, one above Dovecot Street, near to the White Hart Inn, an acknowledged 'sporting' centre, and to the Stockton quayside, near to where boats from Middlesbrough arrived, where the magistrates felt they were best left alone.[110] The Victoria Club was set up in the early 1880s as a betting club. By the 1890s each bookmaker had his own street territory. In 1897, the 'well-known' bookmaker A.B. Todd frequented Christopher Street and the neighbourhood of Blairs Works.[111] To follow the court careers of the Stockton bookmakers through the 1870s and the 1880s provides an instructive insight into bookmaker life, which proved to reflect working-class traditions of hardness and street-fighting. Bookmakers had to be tough to earn a living and quarrels over bets were not uncommon.

In Britain as a whole the numbers of those involved in betting seems to have been rising from the 1870s to 1914, and it has been estimated that by the latter year up to four million were betting regularly and others were having an occasional flutter on the Derby, the Grand National or the St. Leger.[112] There were significant regional variations. The pressure of anti-gamblers in the Metropolitan Police District forced up convictions there.[113] In terms of convictions London, Manchester and then Liverpool had the highest rates. In 1911 the Manchester police arrested 387 bookmakers and the Liverpool police 190. Lancashire had the highest rates outside London, followed at a distance by Yorkshire.[114] Different groups within the working classes had different degrees of involvement. The skilled working classes and young men were most involved in betting, since they were the groups most likely to have surplus, disposable income.

Many references to those betting on Teesside in the 1870s and the early 1880s are to skilled artisans and youths.[115] The numbers interested were substantial. At Stockton, in 1880 on Manchester Cup day there was a crowd of about a thousand in Dovecot Street, while 'bookmakers and backers were ... anxiously awaiting the receipt of telegrams and discussing the merits of various horses'.[116] Betting was also following the Manchester example with significant numbers of women involved. In 1882 a prosecution witness told Stockton magistrates that 'large numbers of men, women and youths assembled in Dovecot Street and Central High Street for the purpose of betting'.[117] In the 1890s betting was very much a cross-class activity, but kept up by the 'sixpences and shillings here and half crowns and crowns there, paid by the working classes'.[118]

By 1914 betting represented a small but regular charge on most working-class wages. The evidence of betting slips seized by the police may not be reliable, but it is consistent and suggests that the normal stake was between sixpence and a shilling. It could be only a couple of pence. Occasionally it could be as much as half a crown.[119] There is little evidence to suggest excessive spending. Most wagered only what they could afford. Despite the arguments of anti-gambling writers, no serious research has been able to demonstrate any clear connection between betting and working-class poverty or crime.

The question of how betting fitted into working-class culture and the domestic economy is important in this connection. Betting was perhaps the most widespread and important of working-class hobbies. It was small in stakes, regular and rational, and, despite the attacks on gambling by the press and rational recreationalist writers, it is clear that few gambled compulsively. McKibbin argues that betting was a rational hobby, drawing on the increased literacy of the working class in an era of mass education.[120] It could be studied and calculated, based on a wide range of variables such as previous form, breeding, age, weight, handicap, money won, position in the draw, the state of the going, knowledge of trainer, the jockey and the likely odds. These variables had to be weighted according to the circumstances in an attempt to eliminate chance from the bet as much as was possible, which could only be done through hard work, concentration and reading. It became possible on a mass scale when working people had sufficient time and sufficient free cash, as well as access to the racing information provided in the sporting press and local and national papers. By 1895 all three main racing papers had circulations of over 300,000.[121] Successful betting therefore required skill, sharpness and keenness, and the ability to read and understand a mass of statistical information. Many who became skilled at it probably only rarely attended a meeting and may have showed little profit on their betting, but they acquired status among their peer group.

For those who found this too difficult, a range of how-to guides were published on ways to make fortunes on the turf, nearly all based on some system and requiring the use of a particular method and set of information.[122] For those who wanted someone else to do the work, racing tips could be purchased. Some tipsters worked hard to provide information, others were self-proclaimed experts out to exploit the gullible. Tipsters were a common feature of the sporting press as early as the 1850s, although they were often seen by sporting writers as exploitive. J. Rice, writing in the 1870s, felt that 'the ignorance of servants and others of the least intelligent class fell an easy prey'.[123] By the early 1890s tipsters were also advertising in many regional and local papers on a regular basis.[124] Those using tipsters perhaps doubted their own ability to master the range of information required, or evinced a faith in the 'expert'. Others preferred luck and chance rather than rationality, and enjoyed the sweeps or the choice of a horse with a lucky name.

Many anti-gambling commentators failed to recognize that betting was attractive because it fitted the economics of working-class life and linked with the endemic uncertainty characterizing much working-class employment. Income was often irregular in boom and slump conditions. Working-class families already invested in burial insurance, but saving was generally incompatible with much of their culture, except for those attracted to temperance who were in any case less likely to bet.[125] Clapson makes the significant point that once real wages increased, money spent on bets was likely to increase alongside an increase in savings.[126] When working men did bring off a win at reasonable odds they acquired a lump sum available in no other way, supplementing income, tiding a family over or breaking the debt–credit cycle.

Betting also provided excitement, because of its risk and uncertainty. It produced thrills, excitement and stimulation. Lady Bell, no supporter of gambling, described the Tees ferry crossing to Middlesbrough full of anticipatory Port Clarence ironworkers. A man of about 60 stood facing them, a paper in his hand:

> In one word he gave them the answer, the word they were waiting for – the name of a horse. It ran through the crowd like the flash of a torch, lighting up all the faces with a nervous excitement; and it seemed to the onlooker that there was not a man there whom that name did not vitally concern. The moment of tense expectation before the result was known was to many of the hearers part of the pleasure they were buying and paying for.[127]

Culturally, betting and work overlapped. Betting could be an antidote to the tedium of work. Even anti-betting campaigners sometimes accepted that betting was attractive for 'people who wanted a little more variety in the dead monotony of life'.[128] For others the workplace was a central part of their lives. Recent research has indicated that pride in craft skills, in physical strength and endurance, and in machines and their handling could all be found in the settings of work.[129] In a work context, where routines were increasingly controlled by others, with resultant loss of autonomy, betting provided a combination of intellectual initiative and spontaneity within a structured framework. Racing and betting were regular features of work conversation, newspapers were read to gather information. Employees collected bets at lunchtime to take to bookmakers or bookmakers waited at the gate, meeting men coming to or from work.

For the street bookmaker, betting *was* work, and the language of work, such as 'office', 'speculation' or 'profit', was commonly used within the trade. Street bookmaking was impossible to stop. There were inconsistent attempts to control it, using the existing laws on the obstruction of pavements and street gaming, although municipal by-laws directed against betting varied in scope and in their penalties.

Prosecutions were therefore related to the attitudes of magistrates and the police at a local level. The Metropolitan Police, tacitly recognizing that the law was unenforceable, made only sporadic efforts to suppress betting, when public outrage and agitation could plausibly justify it.[130] The year 1883 saw a burst of prosecutions of London street bookmakers because of 'complaints about betting men'.[131] In most places laws against betting and bookmaking were enforced extremely spasmodically, usually only in response to specific complaints. In 1875, for example, 'numerous complaints' were received by the Middlesbrough police against men standing in the streets betting and the resulting fines were seen as 'a caution to others'.[132] By the late nineteenth century it was also clear that some policemen were unwilling to act, while police–bookmaker collusion had become an open secret.[133]

Some magistrates and chief constables showed strong, often class-based opposition. A Middlesbrough magistrate told a bookmaker in 1877 that he 'strongly deprecated the idea of a man making his living by betting with the working classes', and the chief constable was 'determined to stop the betting taking place ... and intended to keep constables on the watch to prevent it'.[134] However, on most watch committees and among JPs there was not always a clear majority sufficient to enforce firmly the local by-laws which allowed prosecutions for obstructing the pavement and thus there were few. Stockton Petty Session records show few prosecutions specifically associated with betting and substantial variations in penalties over the period. Although the first prosecutions occur in 1872, the next burst came in 1878–79, and then another offensive in 1882, by which time the police 'had already summonsed fifty or sixty offenders'. The police then put in further efforts to halt what the press described as 'the Betting Mania' as a result of a petition from about 20 of the leading tradesmen, complaining of 'loss, inconvenience and annoyance' as a result of the presence of loiterers.[135] There were only occasional prosecutions until 1892 and then one or two of groups of men each year thereafter. One major bookmaker explained the few prosecutions by arguing that 'for some years we were undisturbed on a pitch on the quayside... The magistrates agreed we were better left alone down there.'[136] Even when people were prosecuted the fines varied substantially. Innkeepers using premises for betting were fined the substantial total of £10 plus costs in October 1879, while bookmakers obstructing the pavement in Dovecot Street were fined 6 shillings. In the 1890s obstruction fines ranged from 5 shillings down to one in mid-decade, but bookmakers were being fined from £5 to £3 by its end. Clearly this reflected changes in the magistrates' attitudes. In the urbanized area around Stockton, which included the industrial ironworks town of Port Clarence, well described by Lady Bell in *At the Works* where betting was known to be rife, as well as the villages of Norton and Billingham, the surviving session records of 1883–90 show no prosecutions whatever.[137] In the early twentieth century the introduction of sliding scale penalties had little effect, since bookmakers were increasingly able to afford repeated fines. London evidence shows this clearly. One London bookmaker had been convicted 54 times over the period 1903–05; see Table 9.

TABLE 9
CONVICTIONS FOR STREET BETTING IN LONDON 1903–05

Date	1903	1904	1905
Number of convictions	4,085	5,574	6,263
Number of persons convicted	1,629	1,827	1,882

Source: Return of Summary Convictions for Street Betting in the Metropolitan Police District, House of Commons Paper 179 (1906).

The 1906 Street Betting Act made all street betting illegal, but, while the police generally welcomed the new powers, it was still impossible to stop such betting. Local communities did not support the police; indeed, as local small businessmen bookmakers were often protected by their customers. Larger bookmakers used runners, often part-time employees, the unemployed or the old, or used agents in factories and workshops; others, as we know from local newspapers, oral testimony, autobiographies and police evidence, operated from terraced backrooms.[138] Despite the emphasis on street betting, many of the prosecutions still involved bookmakers operating in licensed premises, and in 1907 hatters' and grocery shops and private houses were also used in London, according to *The Times*.[139]

The Act also had more far-reaching consequences in further

criminalizing the working classes and reinforcing antagonism against the police, since post-1906 betting involved a more or less permanent conspiracy against the law by a majority of the working population.[140] The Act made little practical difference in London or elsewhere, and in 1911 Sir Edward Henry, the Metropolitan Chief Commissioner, admitted that it was widely disregarded. London was 'one enormous betting ring'.[141] Even in Manchester, despite the anti-gambling activity of both the police leadership and leading city churchmen in the Edwardian years, a modest flutter had become an acceptable part of the fabric of everyday life. Both bookmakers and punters simply ignored the law.[142]

III

Writing about leisure has tended to focus more on male working-class culture, neglecting divisions by sex and women's contribution to working-class life. There are scattered references to women betting from the 1860s onwards, although whether this reflected the limited numbers of them doing so or not is difficult to establish, since police prosecutions tended to be of bookmakers, not their customers. Women were betting in Manchester in the 1860s.[143] It is, however, difficult to be sure whether they were putting on bets on behalf of someone else or on their own behalf. In the 1890s, following its foundation, the National Anti-Gambling League (NAGL) made constant references both to betting by children on behalf of parents or as bookies' runners, and to women's role in betting. One of its supporters, J.M. Hodge, claimed that gambling among women had increased in recent years. He cited evidence from South Shields, Jarrow, York and Leeds, pointing to police reports that women were pawning possessions in order to meet gambling debts.[144] Such evidence may be special pleading, calculated to generate more widespread opposition to betting.

There was a tendency to believe that women must have been led astray by evil men. *The Times* in 1902 alleged that bookmakers were 'entrapping men, boys and even girls'.[145] In 1913 a Manchester canon claimed, not only that women's betting had increased fiftyfold since 1895, but that mill girls and women were forced to bet by foremen.[146] Such cases are difficult to substantiate and were probably few and far between.

Increased reports on women betting may be simply a product of a growth in public awareness. But certainly a study of the local press supports the view that women were betting, although some of the evidence was hearsay. 'We hear that there are some districts in Burnley where married women actually call bookmakers into their house to make bets', the *Burnley*

Express claimed in 1890.[147] Nevertheless, observers from a number of areas of Britain reported that crowds where bookmaking was taking place often included women. In Stockton, the Quayside betting had 'a number of women ... taking as much interest in the proceedings as were many of the men'.[148] In London, an observer reported to C. Booth that 'all must bet; women as well as men',[149] while Lady Bell was noting the 'systematic betting' of women near Middlesbrough sometime later, with and without their husband's knowledge.[150]

By the beginning of the twentieth century the NAGL claimed that female bookmakers were also emerging, although the first example reported in *The Times* came only in 1907.[151] Early examples were often of women who ran small shops in working-class communities, but betting businesses could also be run from the front rooms of terraced houses.[152] For women, the boundary between home, the street and work was perhaps more fluid. Social pressures would have made it more difficult to visit predominantly male haunts, such as public houses, tobacconists or barbers, and it may also be, as Clapson has suggested, that many women preferred to bet with a female bookie.[153]

IV

Boundaries of class are not entirely helpful once we move outside the world of work, since such boundaries were only partially reproduced in leisure, and leisure itself had an impact on them. Some writers such as Thompson or McKibbin have tended to portray a uniform, working-class culture.[154] However, in the work of more recent writers, there are signs of a weakening emphasis on class alone as a means of investigating society. Hill and Williams, for example, have suggested that identities of neighbourhood, workplace, town, region, religion and nation are all possible analytical tools.[155]

This chapter has examined three important ways in which racing impacted on the working classes: their role as spectators in race meetings; the ways in which betting became rooted in the local community or neighbourhood, and the growth of working-class bookmaker services; and (more briefly) the role of women.

All three indicate the desire of working people for autonomy and self-organization in leisure. In large measure they achieved it. In attendance at meetings, workers were far from powerless and dependent wage-hands; they were able to maintain a regular holiday in the face of opposition, and organize themselves effectively to enjoy their leisure. Racing was a major popular recreation, with its origins predating the industrialization of many of the towns in which it was set. It adapted to industrialization and expanded thereafter with very minor concessions to reformist leisure culture.

In examining betting, this chapter has argued for the crucial importance of the period from *c.*1840 to the 1870s in providing the underpinning for the growth of later mass betting. The view put forward is that working-class gambling shifted into horseracing alongside the growth of better press coverage and information, and the emergence of more opportunities to bet within local communities. In the 1840s and 1850s these opportunities, outside those of meetings themselves, mainly took the form of sweeps and list bookmakers. The amount of working-class betting increased between the 1840s and 1900 as real wages improved and working hours were modestly reduced. It is still, however, difficult to establish the extent of that increase, and further work still needs to be done here. In 1902 John Corlett, a former betting reporter, argued that betting had not increased in magnitude but had merely become more visible, a perception of increased betting following more prosecutions as a result of the 1853 Act, and subsequent county and local authority byelaws.[156] He was only partly correct. While betting was certainly common in some large urban areas like Manchester, London or York quite early in the nineteenth century, these were areas with a long-standing interest in racing. Thereafter expansion was more gradual, although by the 1880s betting had spread to urban areas throughout Britain.

By then, however, the earlier emphasis on attendance at local meetings, with their contribution to locality, regional identity, and racecourse drinking, eating and other forms of sociability, had shifted. Mass betting developed strong new forms of sociability, playing its part in pub and workplace gossip, and in conviviality, and although male-dominated, it was an activity in which women could play a role both in the making and the taking of bets in the home and in the street. Working-class betting, generated by local interest, was sustained by local working-class bookmaker businessmen, a local underground economy, unlicensed and under the control of the community rather than the local elite or local authority.

NOTES

1. A study of racing lends support for the view that working-class culture was neither uniform nor homogeneous. See P. Joyce, *Visions of the People: Conceptions of the Social Order in England before 1914* (Cambridge, 1990) *passim.*
2. See N. McCord, *British History 1815–1906* (1991), p.334; F.L.M. Thompson, *The Rise of Respectable Society: a Social History of Victorian Britain 1830–1900* (1988), Ch.6.
3. H. Cunningham, 'Leisure and culture', in F.L.M. Thompson (ed.), *The Cambridge Social History of Britain 1750–1950.* Vol.II. *People and their Environment* (1990), pp.279ff.
4. M. Clapson, *A Bit of a Flutter: Popular Gambling and English Society c.1823–1961* (Manchester, 1992), p.2, reviews the literature. Other relevant material used in the following section includes D. Dixon, *The State and Gambling: Developments in the Legal Control of Gambling in England 1867–1923* (Hull, 1981); idem., *Illegal Gambling and Histories of Policing in England* (Hull, 1984); D.C. Itzkowitz, 'Victorian bookmakers and their customers', *Victorian Studies*, Vol.32, No.1, 1988; C. Chinn, *Better Betting with a Decent Feller: Betting and the British Working Class 1750–1990* (Hemel Hempstead, 1991).
5. See Anon., *Horse Racing: Its History and Early Records of the Principal and Other Race Meetings* (1863), pp.121–2, 248 for examples.
6. The Druid, *The Post and the Paddock* (1862), pp.1–4, provides a useful overview of views on regional variation in racing interest at that time.
7. J. Hill and J. Williams (eds), *Sport and Identity in the North of England* (Keele, 1996), provides an overview of this theme but ignores racing.
8. J. Kent, *The Racing Life of Lord George Cavendish Bentinck MP* (1892), pp.87, 305.
9. R.W. Malcolmson, *Popular Recreations in English Society 1700–1850* (Cambridge, 1973).
10. D.J.V. Jones, *Rebecca's Children: a Study of Rural Society, Crime and Protest* (Oxford, 1989); J.E. Archer, *'By a Flash and a Scare': Incendiarism, Animal Maiming and Poaching in East Anglia 1815–1870* (Oxford, 1990); M. Reed and R. Wells (eds), *Class, Conflict and Protest in the English Countryside 1700–1880* (1990).
11. W. Allison, *My Kingdom for a Horse* (1919), p.58.
12. W. Bennett, *The History of Burnley from 1850* (Burnley, n.d.), pp.239–40.
13. R. Colls, *The Collier's Rant* (1977), pp.67–72.
14. *Morning Post*, 7 September 1850.
15. R. Taine, *Notes on England* (New Jersey, 1958 edn), pp.32ff.
16. *The Times*, 20 May 1858.
17. Ibid., 6 June 1874.
18. For a Manchester example, see 'How Manchester is amused: a correct card of the races', *The Free Lance*, 15 June 1867.
19. 'Epsom', *Household Words*, Vol.3, No.63, 7 June 1851.
20. *The Times,* 1 June 1865.
21. 'The Aintree carnival', in J.K. Walton and A. Wilcox (ed.), *Low Life and Moral Improvement in Mid-Victorian England: Liverpool through the Journalism of Hugh Shimmin* (1991).
22. J. Crump, 'The great carnival of the year: Leicester races in the nineteenth century', *Transactions, Leicestershire History & Archaeological Society*, Vol.58, 1982–83, p.62.
23. *Beverley Guardian*, 14 June 1884.
24. R. Poole, *The Lancashire Wakes Holidays* (Preston, 1994), p.22.
25. *Sporting Life*, 1 October 1859.
26. M.J. Huggins, 'Stockton Race Week 1855–1900: the growth of an unofficial holiday', *Journal of Regional and Local Studies*, Vol.6, No.1, Spring 1986.
27. *Durham Chronicle*, 8 April 1881.
28. Evidence of R. Tattersall, before the Select Committee on Gaming 1844, quoted in full in V. Orchard, *Tattersalls: 200 Years of Sporting History* (1953), p.296.
29. 'North country sport', *Baily's Magazine*, Vol.48, December 1887, p.318.
30. E. Duckershoff, *How the English Work and Live* [trans. C.H. d'E Leppington (1899)], p.36.
31. *Stockton Herald*, 23 August 1890.
32. *Manchester Courier*, 10 June 1878.
33. *The Times*, 9 November 1886; 13 November 1886.
34. J. Crump, 'The great carnival of the year', p.63.

35. *Newcastle Weekly Chronicle*, 24 June 1893.
36. M.J. Huggins, 'Victorian seaside resorts around the mouth of the Tees', *Northern History*, Vol.20, 1984. p.194.
37. R. McKibbin, *The Ideologies of Class: Social Relations in Britain 1880–1950* (Oxford, 1990), p.131.
38. E. Bowden Rowlands, 'A glance at the history of gambling', *Westminster Review*, Vol.135, 1891, p.659.
39. House of Lords, Select Committee on Betting, 1902, Report p.5.
40. R. Miller, 'Gambling and the British Working Class 1870–1914', University of Edinburgh, MA thesis, 1974; R. McKibbin, 'Working class gambling in Britain 1880–1939', *Past and Present*, No.82, 1979; Clapson, *A Bit of a Flutter*; Chinn, *Better Betting*, pp.12–17; R. Munting, *An Economic and Social History of Gambling in Britain and the USA* (Manchester, 1996).
41. See McKibbin, *Ideologies of Class*, p.106.
42. *Cleveland News*, 1 May 1880.
43. *North-Eastern Daily Gazette*, 13 March 1893.
44. Ibid., 5 August 1898
45. Lady F. Bell, *At the Works*, 1907.
46. Durham Record Office, Strathmore material, D/X872/1.
47. T. Bradley, *The Old Coaching Days in Yorkshire* (Leeds, 1889), p.64.
48. See J. Raven, 'The Abolition of the English State Lotteries', *Historical Journal*, Vol.34, No.2, 1991, pp.371–90.
49. *Wensleydale Advertiser*, 3 February 1846; 29 September 1846.
50. Itzkowitz, 'Victorian bookmakers'.
51. *Sporting Magazine*, October 1848, p.227; November 1848, p.206.
52. *Bell's Life in London*, 10 September 1848.
53. 'The racing season of 1848', *Sporting Magazine*, December 1848, p.383.
54. E.g., *Bell's Life in London*, 22 April 1849.
55. One sporting barber in York became 'the field of considerable speculation' by the late 1830s, while another bookmaker was based at or near the railway refreshment rooms. See *Yorkshireman*, 22 June 1844; 18 May 1844.
56. J.C. Whyte, *History of the British Turf*, Vol.II (1840), pp.261, 625.
57. *Sporting Magazine*, November 1848, pp.306ff.
58. J. Fairfax-Blakeborough, *Northern Turf History*, Vol.III. *York and Doncaster* (1950), p.346.
59. C. Sydney, *The Art of Legging* (1976), p.46, dates the first appearance of lists to the period 1815–20.
60. Itzkowitz, 'Victorian bookmakers', cites a number of examples.
61. *Sporting Magazine*, September 1853, p.256.
62. *York Herald*, 13 February 1851.
63. The Druid, *The Post and the Paddock* (1856), p.68.
64. Craven, 'The state of the turf in 1851', *Sporting Magazine*, March 1851, p.164; idem., 'The turf in 1852', *Sporting Magazine*, January 1853, p.7; Craven, 'Clubs as Accessories of the National Sports', *Sporting Magazine*, March 1853, p.169.
65. Quoted in R. Munting, 'Social opposition to gambling in Britain: a historical overview', *International Journal of the History of Sport*, Vol.10, No.3 (1993), p.303.
66. For unsuccessful appeals against betting house prosecutions see *The Times*, 17 October 1954; 17 November 1854.
67. Select Committee on Betting, 1902; John Corlett, Q.3343.
68. See for a burst of London examples of list house prosecutions *The Times*, 22 July 1865; 1 August 1865.
69. P. Bailey, *Leisure and Class in Victorian England: Rational Recreation and the Contest for Control* (1978).
70. E.g., *Newcastle Weekly Chronicle*, 6 August 1864.
71. Robert Wood Collection, Gray Art Gallery, Hartlepool.
72. H. Shimmin, *Liverpool Life: Its Pleasures, Practices and Pastimes* (Liverpool, 1856), p.122.
73. *Cleveland News*, 28 April 1883.
74. 'About the profitable prophets', *Baily's Magazine* Vol.48, November 1887, p.219.
75. *Burnley Advertiser*, 1 June 1861.

76. Oral recollections of one villager, *Clitheroe Times*, 6 June 1924.
77. See Shimmin, *Liverpool Life*, Ch.XV–XIX.
78. *The Times*, 19 July 1856; *Penny Bell's Life*, 9 April 1859; 13 April 1859.
79. *The Free Lance*, 25 May 1868.
80. For the London prosecutions see Itzkowitz, 'Victorian bookmakers'.
81. *Manchester Courier*, 18 May 1869.
82. Ibid., 19 May 1869. The defence lawyer during the contemporary London prosecutions made a similar point. There was sufficient interest in prosecutions for subsequent Manchester ones to be reported elsewhere. See *Newcastle Daily Journal*, 10 June 1869.
83. *Yorkshire Gazette*, 1 June 1861.
84. *Newcastle Daily Chronicle*, 23 August 1861.
85. *Newcastle Journal*, 28 June 1865.
86. *The Free Lance*, 22 February 1868 .
87. *Penny Bell's Life and Sporting News*, 24 March 1859; *Sporting Life*, 14 September 1859.
88. *Sporting Life*, 30 March 1859.
89. See Sydney, *The Art of Legging*, p.52.
90. *Sporting Life*, 21 September 1859.
91. *The Free Lance*, 25 May 1868.
92. P. FitzGerald, MA JP, Letter addressed to a member of the Manchester Racing Association, c.1876 (Salford Library).
93. 'The Ring and the Book', *Baily's Magazine*, March 1876, p.193.
94. *Manchester Courier*, 27 May 1869.
95. E.g., *Morpeth Herald*, 25 June 1870; *Redcar Gazette*, 28 April 1883.
96. 'The common sense of touting', *Baily's Magazine*, June 1876, pp.400ff.
97. See Sydney, *Art of Legging*, p.58.
98. 'The Ring and the Book', *Baily's Magazine*, March 1876, pp.189ff.
99. Select Committee on Betting, 1902, John Porter, Q.3491.
100. *Newcastle Daily Journal*, 31 May 1869.
101. See Clapson, *A Bit of a Flutter*, p.25.
102. For Hartlepool examples see *Cleveland News*, 19 October 1877; *North-Eastern Daily Gazette*, 5 August 1898.
103. C. Waters, 'All sorts and any quality of outlandish recreations: history, sociology and the study of leisure in England 1820–1870', *Historical Papers*, 1981, p.13.
104. *Sporting Life*, 12 July 1865; *The Porcupine*, 10 March 1877.
105. *Burnley Express*, 31 May 1890.
106. J. Caminada, *Twenty-five Years of Detective Life. A Fascinating Account of Crime in Victorian Manchester* (Manchester, 1985), pp.7–17.
107. Evidence of E. Hulton, Select Committee on Betting, 1902, Q.2550.
108. *Middlesbrough Weekly News & Cleveland Advertiser*, 7 May 1875; *South Bank Advertiser*, 18 May 1877; *Guisborough Weekly News*, 6 April 1876; 20 July 1877; *Cleveland News*, 17 April 1880.
109. Records of Stockton Petty Sessions are held in Middlesbrough Record Office. They show one prosecution in 1872, and others in 1878–89. See *Cleveland News*, 25 October 1879.
110. J. Fairfax-Blakeborough, *The Analysis of the Turf*, p.268.
111. *North-Eastern Daily Gazette*, 4 June 1897.
112. See McKibbin, *Ideologies of Class*, pp.109–10.
113. S. Petrow, *Policing Morals: the Metropolitan Police and the Home Office 1870–1914* (Oxford, 1994), p.250.
114. M. Clapson, 'Playing the system: the world of organised street betting in Manchester, Salford and Bolton c.1880–1939', in A. Davies and S. Fielding (eds), *Workers' Worlds: Cultures and Communities in Manchester and Salford 1880–1939* (Manchester, 1992), p.157.
115. For Teesside examples see *Middlesbrough Weekly News & Cleveland Advertiser*, 7 May 1875; *Cleveland News*, 11 October 1879.
116. *Cleveland News*, 25 May 1880.
117. Ibid., 8 April 1882.
118. *North-Eastern Daily Gazette*, 20 October 1893.
119. See McKibbin, *Ideologies of Class*, pp.110–12.

120. Ibid., pp.116–21.
121. W.J.K., 'Betting and gambling', *Westminster Review*, Vol.140, 1895, p.146.
122. See McKibbin, *Ideologies of Class*, pp.119–20.
123. J. Rice, *History of the British Turf.* Vol. 1 (1879), p.225.
124. See, for example, the three tipster advertisements in the *Newcastle Daily Journal*, 16 June 1893.
125. See McKibbin, *Ideologies of Class*, pp.114–16.
126. See Clapson, *A Bit of a Flutter*, Ch.3.
127. See Lady Bell, *At the Works*, p.264.
128. The Lord Bishop of Newcastle in a sermon on betting, *Newcastle Weekly Chronicle*, 24 June 1893.
129. See McKibbin, *Ideologies of Class*, pp.152–7.
130. Petrow, *Policing Morals*, pp.239–93.
131. *Newmarket Journal*, 12 May 1883.
132. *Middlesbrough Weekly News*, 7 May 1875.
133. See A. Davies, 'The police and the people: gambling in Salford 1900–1939', *Historical Journal,* Vol.34, No.1, 1991; Clapson, 'Playing the system', p.166.
134. *Guisborough Weekly Exchange*, 6 April 1876.
135. *Cleveland News*, 8 April 1882.
136. See Fairfax-Blakeborough *Analysis of the Turf*, p.268.
137. Stockton and District Petty Session records, 1870–1914, Cleveland County Archives, Middlesbrough.
138. M. Clapson, 'A bit of a flutter', *History Today* (October, 1991), p.41.
139. *The Times*, 15 August 1907; 19 September 1907; 19 October 1907.
140. Quoted by D. Dixon, 'The Street Betting Act of 1906', *International Journal of the Sociology of Law*, Vol.8, 1980, p.103.
141. Public Record Office, HO45/10682/221977.
142. Clapson, 'Playing the system', pp.157–8.
143. *The Free Lance*, 25 May 1868.
144. J.M. Hodge, 'Gambling among women', in B.S. Rowntree (ed.), *Betting and Gambling* (1905), p.72.
145. *The Times*, 5 July 1902.
146. Clapson 'Playing the system,' p.159.
147. *Burnley Express*, 10 September 1890.
148. *North-Eastern Daily Gazette*, 20 October 1893.
149. C. Booth, *Life and Labour of the People in London*, Vol.17, 1902, p.57.
150. See Lady Bell, *At the Works*.
151. *Bulletin of the National Anti-Gambling League*, Vol.2, No.21, November 1900; *The Times*, 5 August 1907.
152. *Manchester Evening News*, 27 August 1912.
153. Clapson 'A bit of a flutter', p.41.
154. Thompson, *Rise of Respectable Society*; McKibbin, *The Ideologies of Class*; M. Savage 'Urban history and social class: two paradigms', *Urban History*, Vol.20, April 1993, pp.61ff, provides a discussion of the recent ways class structure and action has been examined.
155. J. Hill and J. Williams (eds), *Sport and Identity in the North of England* (Keele, 1996), p.2.
156. 1902 Select Committee on Betting, evidence of John Corlett, Q3304–3367.

5

'The Greatest Carnival of the Year': The Racecourse and Racecourse Life

In an age of increasing embourgeoisiement, the races offered an opportunity for release. Even when working-class leisure was most under threat, from the 1830s to the 1850s, in many towns throughout Britain races were a calendared event. The holidays observed in nearly all trades in the Black Country, for example, were then midsummer, Christmas and three days racing in August.[1] Meetings provided the major setting for local social gathering and cross-class mixing. More importantly still, they were a privileged site for ludic behaviour, an arena where the bonds of convention and respectability could, if wished, be temporarily laid aside and where risk and the *risqué* coincided.

Meetings presented a range of attractions to a socially mixed, all-age crowd until the majority of courses became enclosed in the period after 1875. Despite the crowd sizes and the alcohol sold, there were rarely problems of behaviour which could not be dealt with adequately by tactful policing. Much of the attraction of the races was their carnival spirit, their loosening of the bonds of convention and respectability, and betting, gaming, food, liquor and prostitution all played their part in creating that spirit. The races countenanced behaviour normally seen as offensive to some social groups. This chapter examines the ways in which the races offered an encouragement to excess and for all social groups to escape the restrictions of sobriety, sexual prudery, moderation and respectability. It explores the way in which racing undermined so many of the apparent reformist beliefs. While racing could also be a venue for display and status distinction by the upper classes, they too were also revelling in indulgence, conspicuous consumption, betting and other forms of excess, a rejection of conventional bourgeois behaviour.

Racecourse life was not immune from change. As we have seen, at first meetings drew many of their crowds from the surrounding area, but the railways, bringing new crowds from a wider region, were clearly important by the 1840s, while the increasing pattern of enclosure of courses radically changed the size and the composition of the crowd from the 1880s, finally making it one predominantly composed of 'racing' men. Nevertheless, most courses provided a shelter for a rich variety of less 'respectable' activities right through the century.

Between 1800 and the early 1840s England had a rich calendar of race meetings with a number of distinctive features. Although some appealed beyond the locality, all were predominantly local, social gatherings. For many of those attending, with no direct involvement with racing and with little information upon which to place a bet besides their own knowledge of horseflesh and the appearance of the animal, betting on the horses was not necessarily the major attraction. News travelled slowly. Newspaper information was out of date and, until the abolition of stamp duty, also expensive. So unless they were racing insiders, most of the crowd could bet only on the basis of their own eyes and with very limited rationality.

Ancillary, competitive, betting events accompanied the racing. Cockfighting was a common betting spectacle at meetings up to the 1830s, although gamecocks were often owned by rival land-owning magnates, and mains ran over several days. At Preston the 12th Earl of Derby, the owner of at least 3,000 fighting cocks, was a great supporter up to 1830. Mains organized between groups of county gentlemen needed large numbers of birds and an expensive infrastructure of purchasing, breeding and feeding. At Lancaster mains were between 'the Gentlemen of Lancashire' and those of Cumberland or Yorkshire. Newcastle and Durham races featured mains between the 'gentlemen of Durham and Northumberland', although the support of the north-east gentry declined after 1812.[2] Cockfighting was still important enough in York for a new pit to be built adjoining the Assembly Rooms and the betting rooms in 1828 with mains during the spring meeting.[3] So there was a strong territorial emphasis at each meeting. Like racing, cockfighting was rooted in gambling, attractive across the social scale and a natural adjunct to racing. The prize money, which could be about £200 the main, was a further attraction. By the 1820s there were signs of its declining popularity. It was claimed to be 'nearly obsolete' in many parts of the country by 1822, although the *Sporting Magazine* was still reporting major mains at races at Newcastle, Manchester, Buxton and Lancaster, and minor ones at Chelmsford, Brighton and Lewes.[4] But the sport certainly featured less in the 1830s, surviving longest at north of England meetings. Prizefighting too was associated with the races, often in an *ad hoc* manner through the raising of a subscription purse among grandstand spectators.

At the smaller local meetings there were also sporting events for the poorer sections of the population. These ranged from footraces, sackraces and catching a soap-tailed pig to smoking matches, wheelbarrow races, donkey races and women's races for print silk dresses.[5] At Carlisle, while the races engendered interest among the gentry, 'immense numbers' of 'people from the country ... flooded in from all quarters to see the wrestling which seemed to hold much greater charm for them than the Tradesman's Cup'.[6] Indeed, in Cumbria the greater popularity of wrestling competitions contributed to the supersession of racing at smaller Cumbrian races such as Kendal, Ambleside and Penrith.[7]

Races provided a day out, entertainment and a carnival atmosphere. They were 'a rendezvous where long-parted friends could see each other and exchange greetings; members of families and once fellow villagers separated during the rest of the year and dwelling far apart were sure of meeting one another'.[8] There were other ludic attractions too. Manchester's pre-1847 Kersall Moor races were fondly remembered as having melodramatic exhibitions, 'monstrosities of nature', sparring exhibitions and 'gypsy kettles cooking'.[9] At Stokesley in 1846 when entries were of poor quality the normal crowds deserted the meeting for the greater attraction of a nearby 'company of equestrians, elephants and camels'.[10]

Despite such alternative attractions, there were many regions where horseracing itself was of particular spectator interest, and provided a shared, socially-linking enthusiasm quite apart from the betting. The North and the East Riding of Yorkshire, Lancashire and the London area had larger crowds at major meetings and had early local and regional press coverage of races elsewhere. Even at the start of the century Epsom, Doncaster, York and Manchester all had crowds estimated at over 100,000 for major races, the poorer people walking many miles to see them. At Manchester, according to Engels, the moor was the 'mons sacer' for the city.[11] Even before the arrival of Doncaster's railway, the St. Leger attracted 'visitors from the south' travelling by a mixture of 'mail or coach, [steam] packet or railway', and visitors from the manufacturing districts, including Liverpool and Manchester, as well.[12] Even medium-sized races such as Southampton, Brighton, Newcastle or Liverpool could all attract some 30,000 or more. The small, socially-inferior meeting at Rochdale attracted an estimated 8,000 in 1848.[13] Crowd size was partly a function of the regional population density. The races at Newmarket had very low crowds, often less than a thousand, for much of the century. There were, however, large centres of population where racing was less attractive. Swansea and Cardiff never sustained major meetings.

The arrival of the railways consolidated numbers and by the 1860s race crowds of round 10,000 could be found even at smaller meetings well away from major population centres. At Scarborough, despite declining numbers of entries and moderate horses, estimates of over 25,000 present each day were common around 1850.[14]

Right through the century particularly interesting races were a specific attraction to a wider public. Unsubstantiated estimates of the crowd at the Epsom Derby were often as high as 200,000 or more, but crowds at the St. Leger could nearly rival this.[15] At York one of the earliest races to get huge attention was an 1804 match on the Knavesmire, between the youthful Alicia Meynell, the mistress of Colonel Thornton of Thornville Royal, Knaresborough, and Mr Flint, a one-time 'sporting' friend of Thornton's and her admirer. The combination of sexual rivalry and the underlying scandal drew about 100,000 spectators, who needed a detachment of the 6th Light Dragoons to keep the course clear.[16] In 1850 at Doncaster Voltigeur's victory over the Flying Dutchman in the Doncaster Cup, two days after Voltigeur's Leger win, generated great debate in Yorkshire about their relative standing and the owners agreed to a match the following year at the York spring meeting. The wide interest (and heavy betting) created its own momentum. All the railway companies with a connection with York ran special trains, 'extensive and extra accommodation had to be made for ladies', and the crowd was estimated at between 150,000 and 180,000.[17] The North Western Railway ran a cheap trip from Lancaster and 'a great number availed themselves'.[18]

While courses were unenclosed, crowd pictures in the *Illustrated London News* and in paintings such as Frith's 'Derby Day', indicate that women from all classes attended meetings in significant numbers. An analysis of a wide range of such sources showing crowds from 1838 to 1868 suggests a figure of around 10 per cent, although pictures such as these were often completed away from the course and their accuracy is open to question.[19] Newspaper reports singled out the presence of ladies for special attention only if there seemed to be more or fewer than usual. At Scarborough in 1851 a writer claimed that 'a richer display of ladies has rarely been witnessed'.[20] But most writers concentrated on the grandstand and, in fact, far more women were to be found on the raceground itself. While the course was free and open, the races were an attraction to both sexes because of the ancillary entertainments. Illustrations also show numbers of children present, a view supported by police court proceedings where mothers were victims of crime on the course, and by school log books which indicate that attendance was inevitably affected by meetings.[21]

D. Reid has argued that wakes and fairs were a part of the festive calendar which can be analysed in terms of the concept of carnival, a term also applied to the races by the press.[22] Racing also had a series of elements to which carnivalistic terms may be applied. These included not only the integral elements of sporting competition and uncertainty, but also institutionalized disorder, sexual licence, over-indulgence in food and drink, loud music, folly, festivity, carnival madness and the breaking of convention by gambling, betting and fighting. Some of those present went only for the spectacle, its show and entertainment; others were more active participants in the ludic behaviour, the betting and the drinking. For a minority the meeting provided an experience of what Geetz describes as deep play, risk- and chance-taking at the deepest level, characterized by a set of emotions dominated by uncertainty over outcome.[23]

Until the introduction of the enclosed park courses, courses had a wide range of money-making entertainments going on. Two examples from the upper and the lower end of racing around mid-century illustrate this. A full description of the Epsom Derby in 1858 by *The Times* referred to the grandstands and went on to describe the boxing booths, the 'daughters of Egypt' at work among the carriages, the 'card sharpers, organ grinders, nigger melodists – genuine and counterfeit, dancers upon stilts, acrobats, German bands, gentlemen, ladies, thieves and policemen ... performing dogs ... tender infants turning somersaults ... banjo men and tambourinists were numerous', while the newly-developed electricity was being exploited to stimulate the spirits of the crowd by men who used coil, machines and batteries to offer electric shocks for a penny.[24] An account of the small Hartlepool races in 1855 reflected the same carnival atmosphere. Starting with a description of the local elite in the wooden, temporary grandstand it then went on to the 'fast boys' and 'aged swells' occupying the centre and the immense number of 'nymphs of the pave' and hosts of light-fingered gentry and 'country blues' perambulating among the crowds of pedestrians crammed together like pens of sheep in front of the tents, grandstand and winning post, the carriages and other conveyances filled with the 'fairest of the fair', the prancing horses and gay dresses of the riders, the refreshment tents, boxing booths, shooting galleries, shows, exhibitions, cheap John's tents and stalls, the fire-eater, tumblers and itinerant musicians, and the innumerable crowds of amusements of one kind or another to captivate the senses.[25]

Those who wished could move fairly freely among the crowds. But it is also clear that alongside this apparent carnival atmosphere there was also an element of social zoning. Entrance to the grandstand was strictly controlled, weakening notions of true carnival. Carnival temporarily overturned status distinctions. Racing could too, but it could also preserve them for those who chose so to do. At the larger meetings grandstand accommodation increased through the century, allowing clearer social zoning. Beginning with a single grandstand in the 1820s, Doncaster later added a jockeys and trainers' stand, Lord Wharncliffe's subscription stand, a second-class stand, Lord Astley's Lincolnshire stand and other private stands and boxes.

The grandstand fulfilled a range of purposes. It provided shelter in case of poor weather. Grandstands were also used for betting and a number of courses had a stand described as a 'betting' stand.[26] Betting enclosures in front of the stands developed from the 1840s, when there were complaints about the noise and commotion of betting activity in the stand by non-betting spectators. Food and drink could usually be obtained from a kitchen area below and a band sometimes played there. Racing was a part of upper-class life and descriptions of the 'fair sex' in the grandstand are common through the period, sometimes with fashion notes appended – 'white coats and white hats ... muslins and latest Parisian novelty in bonnets'.[27] At irregularly held, small meetings, at beach meetings or alongside the permanent stands at larger meetings, wooden grandstands were assembled a few days before or were erected above innkeepers' booths. Usually these stood up to their task surprisingly well, although there were occasional collapses.[28]

The attendance of the leisured classes, the nobility and the gentry allowed for the exercise of patronage, a reiteration of their social standing in the area through their demonstration of conspicuous consumption, ritual and display. In the early part of the century, in particular, their arrival at the course by coach was an important part of this display. It was another feature which distinguished racing from true carnival. Carnival often entailed reverse ritual but in racing ceremonies followed convention. At Doncaster, for example, in the early nineteenth century there was a procession to the course of private carriages and coaches, with footmen, coachmen and outriders. Earl Fitzwilliam, the wealthiest of the Yorkshire aristocracy at the time, and his family, would arrive in two coaches, drawn by matched teams, piloted by postillions and preceded and followed by 20 liveried outriders and tenantry on horseback. But by the 1860s this was being discontinued.[29] At Ascot, however, the royal drive from Windsor on the Tuesday and the Thursday followed by a procession down the course was a major display of royal and aristocratic wealth and power from the late eighteenth century.[30]

The pomp and ceremony calculated to impress the status of local magnates on spectators was one form of display. Many of the old-established market-town meetings also had a range of other 'traditional' ceremonies leading up to the races which lasted until past mid-century. These seem to have died out once crowds from outside the area came specially for the races, presumably because such visitors had no understanding of the context of the ceremonies. A race cup was the chief focus, often paraded through the town on Cup day. At Richmond in the 1830s the procession started from the mayor's residence and perambulated three times round the market cross before making its way to the course. The

Gold Cup was decorated with ribbons, fixed to a pole and committed to the care of sergeants-at-arms dressed in 'full regalia of antique cloaks, lace cravats and cocked hats'.[31] At Ripon in the 1830s the cups were displayed around the town accompanied by a band, while in the 1850s the races were 'the great attraction' of a week of festivities centred round St. Wilfrid, with an effigy of the saint brought into the town and escorted around to drum and fife.[32]

Some of this display of status distinction was lost as the railways increasingly transported upper-class visitors. By the 1860s a former mayor of Doncaster was claiming that 'the general introduction of railways ... brought about an almost total discontinuance of the old custom of the nobility and gentry bringing their private carriages'.[33] It was replaced by the introduction of a more formal parade ring before the race, to begin with on the course opposite the grandstand and then later in an enclosed space near the grandstand. The Doncaster parade in front of the grandstand for the St. Leger, begun in 1826, was perhaps the earliest. From about 1840 saddling paddocks or enclosures were being introduced, usually adjacent to and only accessible from the grandstand, beginning at more exclusive courses such as Aintree and Goodwood. Manchester built one in 1841 'so that the visitors and the ladies on the stand will have an opportunity of seeing [the horses] before they go on the course to contend for the race and again when the jockeys come to be weighed'.[34]

While the railway reduced some of the coach traffic, many spectators continued to travel in by coach or omnibus through the century. Courses tended to set an area aside for such vehicles. Gentry coaches were increasingly located together, sometimes adjacent to or opposite the stand or in the centre of the course. This again was part of the display, allowing a good view of course activities, though location and the accompanying servants contributed a measure of social distance. In the early twentieth century motor cars slowly began to replace carriages as a display focus. Ascot, as the most select meeting, was among the first courses to feel their effects. Motors were allowed on the heath in 1912, and by 1913 there were clearly identified enclosures. By 1914 *The Times* was giving helpful advice for chauffeurs about motor routes from London to the course, having just previously complained of the 'invasion' of the Epsom Derby by the more popular motor omnibus.[35]

Although the enclosing of courses might be seen as increasing attendance, in fact, the converse was true. The increasingly widespread enclosure of courses from the 1870s often actually led to a drop in numbers at first. Enclosed courses had fewer attractions other than the racing itself and many who were less interested in racing than other course activities were unwilling to pay. Before enclosure the estimates of attendance at Manchester were usually around 100,000. After enclosure Manchester could attract only some 50,000 spectators per day in 1875.[36] Rural Richmond, which had about 10,000 in pre-enclosure days, had only 4,000 in 1890. But the initial impact of enclosure and entry charges from the end of the 1870s appeared fairly limited to contemporary newspaper columnists and racing writers. Rising real incomes and increased prize money kept racing attractive to those who could afford grandstand prices, and the more select grandstands had a higher proportion of ladies than before. Some new enclosed park courses deliberately aimed at the select market. At the first of these, Sandown, founded in 1875, vetting of membership was socially rigorous and for the first time women could apply for membership in their own right while gentlemen were allowed two ladies' badges. At first few women joined, but the support and attendance of the Prince of Wales helped the growth in popularity over the following five years. New courses such as Kempton, Haydock and Newbury followed the same pattern. Control over the behaviour of members meant that women were able to move more freely. Newspaper reporters increasingly either focused on the races, the horses, the trainers and jockeys, or upon the attenders, especially from the upper-class fast set and their display, an interest reflected in the increased press coverage given to descriptions of upper-class female clothing at Goodwood, Royal Ascot and Doncaster from the 1880s. Improved facilities above and beyond the ladies' rooms provided in the stands were also becoming common.

But less noted was that, with the introduction of the enclosed course, far fewer working- or middle-class women or children were to be found on the course. After enclosure, expense limited the attendance of families and married couples and crowds were increasingly of working men. Soon it became part of the taken-for-granted view of racing that this was the natural order of things. Indeed, at Newcastle in 1883 the reporter commentated with some surprise that 'even though *of course* [author's italics] the vast majority of the spectators was composed of men, there was still a fair sprinkling of womankind.'[37]

Racing continued to play an important social role in the aristocratic season. At Doncaster, Newmarket, Ascot or Epsom the cream of aristocratic society displayed itself. Most stayed at house parties outside the town and travelled in each day. Some women, such as the Duchess of Manchester or the Marchioness of Londonderry, were extremely knowledgeable about racing. Certainly the trainer George Lambton, in his *Men and Horses I Have Known* (1924) believed the latter to be more knowledgeable than most of the men he knew. Many of these ladies bet, although few with the lack of restraint of Lady Jessica Sykes, whose husband by the end of 1896 was forced to put an announcement in *The Times* repudiating any more of her debts.[38] Some smaller races were still an important part of the aristocratic social calendar for local magnates. Lord Zetland, who owned land at Redcar, was a regular attender at the much more 'select' August meeting, but not the much more popular Whitsuntide meeting. His party would stay on in August at his country house for the subsequent Stockton meeting, where the party from the Wynyard Hall estate of Lord Londonderry would join them. He also attended the small Richmond meeting near his Aske estate.

Thus far the discussion has focused upon changes, but, as indicated earlier, there were also large measures of continuity, much of which was associated with excess – eating, drinking, gaming and other entertainment, prostitution and betting-related activities. Spending a day at the races necessitated food and drink. Those who came in carriages usually catered for themselves. Not all perhaps had the 'Fortnum and Mason's hampers, so much ice and champagne' which Dickens believed characterized the 1851 Derby,[39] but pies, chicken, ham, tongue, shellfish and wine were fairly characteristic. Larger grandstands such as those at Doncaster, York or Epsom had refreshment saloons with catering facilities attached. Increasingly this became a specialized occupation. By the 1850s at Epsom this required large amounts of equipment, including 1,200 wine glasses and 3,000 tumblers, a range of food including 400 lobsters, 65 lambs and whole crates of boiled tongues, and cooks, confectioners, kitchen maids and waiting staff.[40] By 1900 the Royal Enclosure Stand at Ascot had a series of private luncheon rooms and a large dining hall, both looked after by an 'exclusive on-course caterer'.[41] Sometimes crowds in the grandstand were also entertained by bands.

Various forms of booth catered for the needs of other spectators, partly supplying food, but with the selling of alcohol playing a more prominent part. The 1834 Select Committee on Inquiry into Drunkenness had showed a clear wish to reform all such 'customs of the people which lead to intemperate habits' and most especially 'where large numbers are congregated for business or pleasure'.[42] There was no such attempt at reform at race meetings, where descriptions of course life stress the amount of time spent in booths, even when the weather was fine, throughout the century. Tent booths were most common but at most meetings some booths were permanent, made of wood, as at Richmond, or more commonly large, brick buildings, with bars beneath and a view from the roof as at Manchester, which also had turf huts.[43] Doncaster had 50 permanent booths by 1891, varying in shape, the two largest measuring 50ft x 25ft (15m x

7.6m) and 60ft x 24ft (18m x 7.3m).[44] Newcastle had over a hundred booths by the 1840s, with publicans coming not just from the Newcastle and Gateshead area, but also from Morpeth and Seghill to the north and from Durham and Liverpool to the south.[45] In 1859 Richmond had 150 tents and a large number of stalls, selling a variety of goods.[46] The race reports often include reference to adverse weather, and in such circumstances the booths provided shelter as well as refreshment. Drunkenness was probably tolerated; press reports imply that most of the time behaviour was good. Certainly few cases were brought before the local benches.

Victorian reformist morality was also challenged by the many illegal gaming activities always going on. Such operations were usually run by groups of men who followed the race and fair circuit, at first on foot and later more commonly by train. Most activities relied on sleight of hand, and ranged from 'prick the garter', thimble-rigging and the three-card trick, to selling a purse apparently containing more money in it than the cost of the purse. Such activities were perennial, since each new racing season brought fresh dupes visiting the racecourse for the first time, anxious to show off to their partners or demonstrate their cleverness. Middle-class males visiting the racecourse were as susceptible as any. In 1856 the painter Frith was sure that he could spot the thimble-rigger's pea and was about to back heavily until prevented by a friend.[47]

In the early nineteenth century the thimble-riggers, with their collapsible tables, thimbles, pea and horny thumb nails, were a major force. Tables were specially made, costing half a crown in 1843.[48] Groups of three to seven usually worked the table, pretended to bet, encouraged punters, and dealt with complaining losers.[49] Even–odd (EO) tables, a type of primitive roulette, or later roulette itself were also to be found.

Prosecutions were rare, although many of the tricksters were well known to the course police and had previous convictions, largely because they were accepted as part of the race atmosphere. The police, as well as keeping order, sometimes attempted to ban dice, roulette and other gaming from the 1830s, usually in response to magistrates' instructions. The former chief detective of the Manchester division later remembered paying 'much attention to gaming' but with little success.[50] Indeed, the *Sporting Magazine* saw these attempts as just increasing the amount of working-class bookmaking and betting on the course.[51] The Vagrancy Amendment Act of 1873 made it illegal to use betting machines, and there are fewer prosecutions or descriptions of these on the course thereafter, although this may have also been due to changes in fashion since winning was based purely on chance with no element of rationality. It was more likely that they were more difficult to introduce on the newer enclosed courses, where they would have to be brought through the turnstile.

By this time the three-card trick, canasta, banker and other games had become popular with gamesters, partly because they were easily concealed. The three-card trick was being described as 'a new game' in 1851, when operators were being charged a shilling by York pasture masters to use a stand.[52] The cardsharpers came usually from particular towns, beginning 'work' on the way to the meeting and continuing on the course. They were well organized. The 'captain of the Sheffield gang of cardsharpers' was fined at Newcastle in 1874 and again at Stockton in 1875.[53]

A large crowd meant easy pickings for pickpockets and for the passing of counterfeit coins. The trade of pocket picking was a skilled one, and some of the organized groups, part of the 'swell mob', travelled to the major meetings to ply their trade. The term 'swell mob' was generally applied to the travelling London pickpocket group, although there are also examples of its being applied to other areas. In 1861 a number of 'travelling pickpockets', some said to be 'swell thieves' from Manchester, were arrested at York races and imprisoned.[54] London pickpockets are found being prosecuted even on northern courses once the railway allowed easier travelling.[55] Travelling race gangs were a feature throughout the century, but the railways allowed for more mobility. By the 1870s the most notorious was the Birmingham 'Boys' who operated mainly in the Midland and northern tracks, although Glasgow, Leeds, Newcastle and Mexborough 'boys' were also active on the northern circuit. Territorial disputes were not uncommon, when more than one gang arrived at the same meeting, while gangs relied on quickness, violence, brute strength, terrorism and reputation for their success in achieving the pocket picking, blackmail, cardsharping, robbery or other criminal aims.

To an extent even they were part of the attraction. The element of ambiguity in the attitudes of racing regulars to such criminals was well caught in the writing of the northern owner, racing official and journalist Fairfax-Blakeborough, who admired their technique, the organizational skill, presence, self-confidence, racing knowledge and amusing conversation of their leaders, while recognizing their potential danger.[56] To an extent, gangs seem to have avoided the exploiting of regular race-goers, partly perhaps because they knew each other, although bookmakers, trainers or other racecourse habitués were occasionally their victims. The group which appears to have been safest was the wealthy, upper-class regulars, many of whom seemed to have gained some vicarious pleasure from their nodding acquaintance with the swell mob.[57] To prey on them would certainly, however, have been counterproductive, with the danger of finding courses closed or much firmer police control. When Sir John Astley had his watch stolen he was able to approach the 'head pickpocket' and have it returned with an apology, as having been stolen by a 'beginner'.[58]

By contrast, bookmakers were much more vulnerable to robbery or blackmail. Bookmakers were often tough individuals themselves; others employed bodyguards such as well-known pugilists, others paid tribute to the 'boys'. Bodyguards did not come cheap; they could cost from £5 to £10 a week by the late nineteenth century.[59]

Other itinerant individuals and groups were less dangerous, providing entertainment, sometimes on the course itself, some in the open ground beside it. At York and Carlisle in the 1820s balloon ascents were possible. At Manchester attractions between heats in the 1830s included 'melodramatic exhibitions, monstrosities of nature, sparring exhibitions'.[60] The open courses had side-shows or separate pleasure fairs similar to contemporary fairground attractions. Strong men, acrobats, jugglers, beggars, ringing the bull, 'knock-em-downs' and other activities such as the wheel of fortune might all be seen. Ethnic minorities found meetings less restrictive in terms of making a living. Black boxers, tipsters and musicians occasionally figure in descriptions. Gypsies followed the races, selling 'lucky' heather or 'willing to depict the future career of any gentleman or lady for a trifle'.[61] At Leicester in 1880 a visitor to the races estimated that there were 89 gypsy caravans on the course.[62]

Descriptions of the races often made reference to the presence of prostitutes. These were generally tolerated by the police. Some were local but there was also a travelling population. Mid-century prosecutions at York races showed them coming from as far afield as Leeds, Bradford, Hull and Nottingham.[63] At Chester prostitutes were 'systematically imported into the town from Manchester and Liverpool'.[64] London prostitutes visited Doncaster.[65] Descriptions of races usually hinted broadly at their presence but avoided indelicate details.[66] The anti-race newspaper the *Doncaster Reporter* more explicitly referred to 'prostitutes in abundance, apparently a necessary part of the throng'.[67] The racecourse, with its large numbers of free-spending men, some of whom would be substantial winners, was an ideal place to solicit custom afterwards. Women could also be used as decoys to lure mug punters into a position where they handed over money or could be robbed with impunity.

Race-card sellers were also a colourful part of the entertainment. Sellers were evenly divided between male and female and travelled in groups which seem to have been fairly cohesive and mutually supportive, with a sense of their own relatively high status when compared with singers, acrobats and other entertainers and vendors.[68] Many were larger-than-life characters with idiosyncrasies that helped them sell. The African 'Black Jemmy' was famous for his support for Lord Eglinton's stud.[69] To begin with local printers produced race-cards. One enterprising local printer even set up two presses on the ground at Darlington, to give racing cards and results.[70] But the railways threw the trade open. Some printers, such as James Patrick of Manchester, were soon specializing in their production. Patrick produced both entrance and return lists, selling both to race-goers and to the list houses, and covering all races not just local ones.[71] An estimated floating population of about 400 card sellers could be found on the northern race circuit, with between 200 and 300 following the races week after week. Estimated sales of cards at Manchester were around 15,000 a day and at York around 8,000, and individuals averaged around six dozen cards sold each day. Given that cards cost about from 2/6d to a shilling a dozen to purchase and were usually sold for sixpence or more each, the income was quite significant.

Even more significant amounts of money could be generated from a gullible public desperate for inside information by tipsters. A reporter who observed one 'black Negro' at Redcar in 1880 reported that he sold over 200 envelopes containing tips in a day at up to sixpence each.[72]

In fact, betting on the horses at the beginning of the nineteenth century was an activity only for a minority. Crowds were packed, and most would not be able to see anything of the races. Bets were made and settled individually. Occasionally evidence surfaces, such as the 1825 action by a Lancaster draper against a Kendal bookkeeper for assault. The quarrel had arisen out of a bet at the Kendal races made by the draper and two separate assaults had taken place after his refusal to pay. A positive attitude to betting among the jury was indicated by the plaintiff's award of a farthing damages, implying that he had brought the assault on himself.[73]

Above this level, those gentry and other owners who wished to place bets initially formed a ring near an appropriate betting post before the start of a race in order to make their bets. Hence the term 'betting ring' for the bookmaking area and 'ante-post betting' for that betting taking place before the horses went to the starting post. This group consisted both of layers and backers, taking and making bets in this ring, or in the grandstand, before the race. Many of the betters were from the aristocracy and the gentry. Many bets were simply individual ones between a backer of an individual horse and someone willing to take the bet. This led to limited but very high betting. Mr Mellish, for example, rarely placed a bet of under £500. Even so, at Ascot in 1822 there was scarcely betting enough to ascertain the state of the odds on the individual races.[74]

Anyone from this group who backed or laid against a horse recorded the bet in a small notebook. Hence the term 'bookmaker', which has led to a great deal of confusion, since originally 'making a book' applied to all members of the ring, of whatever class. Many aristocratic bookmakers laid against numbers of horses in a race. But most rings increasingly also contained 'bookmakers' from other social backgrounds, ready to take bets and most often laying against the favourite and backing the rest of the horses collectively (the 'field'). Even by 1822 at Newmarket, it was already clear that the backers of 'the field' were 'generally the most numerous and most noisy among the betters'.[75] By then the terms 'bookmaker', 'blackleg' or 'fielder' were increasingly being applied to this more proletarian group, useful to the rest of the ring since they usually met their debts. In the betting ring most betting was on credit, entered in betting books and paid after the race or, much more commonly, on a subsequent settling day in the betting rooms. Many bets were laid at long odds before the race, so payments could be large. William Davis, ex-joiner, the first 'Leviathan' of the ring, paid out over £40,000 in ready money bets on Voltigeur's Derby and a further £10,000 on settling day, and, making a £100,000 book on West Australian's Derby, paid out £60,000. When settlement day arrived some wagerers might refuse to pay and some 'bookmakers', whose books were wrongly balanced, might 'welsh' or 'levant', either absenting themselves or turning up to take winning bets but not paying out. On every big race there were always a proportion of losing betters who could not or would not pay.

Of those more proletarian bookmakers travelling the national racing circuit, London, Manchester and Nottingham bookmakers composed the largest group. They carried substantial amounts of ready cash. Indeed, a Nottingham bookmaker robbed *en route* to a meeting in 1860 was robbed of £1,840 in cash as well as a watch and cheques, yet was still able to meet his engagements.[76] Such bookmakers were the elite of the racing circuit.

Increasingly through the century the racecourses' attempts to socially zone their clientele extended to the betting. At first most of the high-stake betting was done by the richer group in the grandstand but by the later 1830s the noise betting generated was itself generating complaints from some spectators. At Doncaster it was 'the fairer part, who testified by their looks and gestures that they are not a little annoyed by the uproar in the betting ring ... which is suffered in the principal floor of the building'.[77] Goodwood had railed in an enclosure in front of the stand by 1837, Liverpool soon after and by the early 1840s most courses were enclosing a separate ring adjacent to the stand where betting could take place, confined to those social groups who could afford the entrance fee, and where major bookmakers could be found. York, like other large courses, fenced its 1844 betting enclosure with iron palisades. Ascot, where the Jockey Club used the older betting stand, created a betting ring in front of the new stand only in 1847. Newmarket was a major exception for much of the century. Here betting continued to be carried out in the older way, meeting at betting rooms previously and then making an informal ring just before the race itself. Within the betting ring, however, where many bookmakers and backers knew each other, much betting continued to be on credit. Indeed, the exhibition of betting lists in enclosure and stand was usually banned, although bookmakers were able to quote odds easily enough.

But as the *Stockton Herald* indicated in 1870, 'from the large bookies in the ring and grandstand – where many of our principal townsmen and district may be seen laying their ponies and fifties, to the investors of a modest half crown outside the enclosure, there is a wide gap in the social scale',[78] and many such attenders could not afford entrance to the grandstand.

Early in the nineteenth century crowd betting was individual and informal, but by the 1850s laying and backing *outside* the ring was also becoming more formalized and professionalized. By the 1860s meetings were levying charges for 'betting booths' or 'betting boxes'.[79] Despite their illegality they provided a valuable service. Here again prosecutions were rare. In 1861 the Salford police arrested a number of course bookmakers who were using refreshment booths from which to bet. Three were from Manchester, two from Nottingham and one from Yorkshire. Two described themselves as 'travellers', one was a lacemaker and one a shoemaker. Two of them had paid £5 each to the keeper of a refreshment booth to carry out their business at a window of the booth. The others had the more common stand. This was a slight wooden framework with which one man could stand on a little elevation to receive money, while a bookkeeper and ticket man could be concealed behind some carpet or drapery. It was explained that such standings 'are made so as to be set up regularly by means of a few iron pins and will pack up in a small compass'. The bookmakers exhibited a list of horses before each race and called out the odds, any money being offered being received and the bets entered in a book opposite a number which corresponded to that of a ticket issued to the person with whom the odds were laid. The fines were substantial: £25 or six weeks. The money carried by the men varied, the largest amount being £107.[80]

The fact that they could afford to pay a £5 fee for a site and could meet the fines showed the potential profitability of bookmaking. The standard model of working-class course bookmaking had now emerged, based on cash rather than credit, with bets entered in books, tickets issued and money paid out after the race. Some of these bookmakers were of solid reliability, others less so. Some may have intended to pay but found themselves short thanks to the ill-judged offering of odds. Others may have never intended to pay out.

To be noticed they made themselves conspicuous, standing on stools, inverted barrels or improvised tables. Clothing such as white beaver hats or large check suits also helped. Some ticketed themselves with their own names and addresses displayed on their shirtfronts.[81] Following the 1853 Betting House Act, although it was believed that on-course betting was legal, there were occasional examples of prosecutions where bookmakers made any sort of a stand which could be construed as 'a house, office room or place opened, kept or used for the purpose of betting', since that fell within the Act. This was almost certainly why betting booths became less common. But most bookmakers used stands and the lack of prosecution reflects a police unwillingness to prosecute. Generally the police did not interfere with bookmaking unless there was some form of outside pressure. Recognizing the possible ambiguity of the laws about betting, courses posted notices banning displays of betting lists, placards, colours, badges, stools, clogs or other ways of calling attention to bookmakers, but to actually act on this was much less common. Indeed, most courses charged bookmakers to bring in the equipment they needed to break the law. Some even provided it. At York in 1876 the freemen's accounts show that they raised revenue from the hire of stools for bookmakers to stand on.[82]

When Manchester bookmakers were 'forced to do without their paraphernalia' in 1876 it was back the next year.[83] Prosecutions everywhere were few, merely token and haphazard. Sometimes there was an element of a game about them. When the Newcastle police gave out an 'order against the use of blocks, cards and umbrellas so as to suppress the broader features of the betting man' the bookmakers countered by wearing 'Aminadab sleek hats with terrific brims'.[84]

Outside the reformist group few were prepared to act against course bookmakers. At Stockton the police posted notices in 1880 forbidding stands, but when they prosecuted bookmakers who used them the *Stockton Herald* described it as 'inconsistent and ridiculous' and asked, 'Why should the race committee charge the bookmakers 2/6d each for taking their instruments on to the course if the law forbids the use of them?' The police tried again in 1895, ordering bookmakers to 'dispense with satchel, book and every other thing by which they could be recognized'. But even the anti-racing *Northern Echo* commented that 'it was hampering the general public in a most irritable manner and does not afford the slightest protection against wrong-uns'.[85] The Home Office and the local magistracy were also ambiguous. At Doncaster the Corporation's race committee regularly let 'betting boxes' to raise money. In 1875 James Spencer, the editor and publisher of the *Doncaster Reporter*, began a campaign against 'illegal acts perpetrated annually at Doncaster races by permission of the authorities... the practice of betting and exposing lists' on ground let by the Corporation.

He claimed that 'a man from Bradford pays £800 for a small piece of ground to the Corporation, and he sublets it to betting men who expose lists at the rent of £15 per lineal yard'. He also claimed that the superintendent of police had been told by the race committee (whose membership overlapped with the watch committee) not to interfere. Spencer claimed the support of a minority of local magistrates and brought the matter to the attention of the Home Office. A letter from one of his supporters alleged that 'there are numerous complaints' against the betting, which was 'an almost intolerable nuisance as the language used is frequently abominable'.

The Home Office simply referred the entire correspondence back to the Corporation, questioning whether they adhered to the legal conditions applying to the letting of ground for temporary booths. These stated that such ground 'shall not be devoted to Public Betting and the Exhibition of any List will under no circumstances be permitted'. The mayor made a number of carefully worded points in response, confirmed that they adhered to the conditions and stated that it was the intention of the magistrates to suppress illegal gaming; constables were ordered to suppress all illegal gaming on the racecourse and on the roads leading thereto; any person erecting temporary stands knew that he was subject to conditions; handbills had been widely distributed in the town making this clear; and the superintendent had been given instructions to suppress all known breaches of the law. This sufficed to satisfy the Home Office. Racecourse betting at Doncaster, however, went on as before.[86] Despite later attempts (one as late as 1893) to raise the issue of 'disorder' with the Home Office by Spencer, his efforts were unavailing.[87]

Dishonest 'welshers' – bookmakers who could not or would not pay – were a recognized feature throughout the period. At Stockton racecourse in 1880 the local paper reported gleefully that on the Tuesday 'welching was much less rife than at Redcar'. Unfortunately, by Thursday 'welchers were present in strong force ... and from beginning to end unsuspecting backers who knew not good men from bad among the pencillers were continually done'.[88] Some welshers were not regular bookmakers but individuals trying their hand at bookmaking, with the hope of making a profit and of getting away quickly if they did not. Others were professionally organized gangs. According to *Baily's Magazine*, these were easy to identify: they were likely to offer better odds; worked usually in a group of three to six; had new pencils and betting books; sometimes used two betting books, one fraudulent; would tell punters that they had backed a different horse if they claimed to have won; or would accuse the backer of being a welsher himself.[89] They were skilled at organizing distractions. If arrested there was always the chance of squaring the prosecuting witness or, if they were middle-class, to threaten exposure.[90] Individual or outnumbered welshers were often roughly handled by the crowds. At some courses the clerk of the course had several able-bodied labourers with a barrel of tar and a sack of feathers.[91] At courses near rivers they were likely to be thrown in. Everywhere they were likely to be beaten up – if they were caught.[92] The police were firm with welshers who were brought to their attention. These they did prosecute regularly.

Given the large crowds often attending race meetings there was relatively little violence. Meetings were relatively orderly and good humoured. It was the normal peacefulness of the crowds which most struck onlookers. The Peterloo riots in Manchester in 1819 were followed closely by the races, yet Lord Strafford, who attended them, saw 'nothing in the shape of bad feeling', instead the meeting was 'quiet and good-humoured'. He felt that it would have been more dangerous to have stopped the meeting.[93] Most reports of country meetings describe them as maintaining a good 'standard of respectability' and a 'very small' amount of rowdiness.[94] At Kendal in 1820, despite the deep political divisions that then prevailed, which had led to disturbances, it was reported that the 'party spirit had been left at home and all was harmony during the races'.[95]

Despite the institutionalized over-indulgence, non-repressive and criminal behaviour the races were not seen as a social problem. Crowds probably accepted some of this as part of the attraction and risk. The internalization of underground codes of behaviour may be one explanation. Or it may be that races functioned as a place of social self-regulation. Major disturbances on courses were extremely uncommon. Sports-crowd disorders in the past have been most extensively studied in the case of football, where both Vamplew's and Mason's categorizations, covering the period from 1870, divided disorders into frustration (where spectators were thwarted), outlawry (where violence-prone spectators acted out anti-social feelings), remonstrance (where sport was used for political protest), confrontation between rival religious or ethnic groups, and expressive disorder due to emotional arousal.[96] All can be found in racing crowd disturbances up to 1914. However, the pattern in racing is more complex. Crowds were larger and a certain level of disorder may have been expected and unreported.

Early in the nineteenth century disorders were sometimes caused by resistance to middle-class or aristocratic attempts at social control through firmer policing of course activities. A chief focus in the period 1820–40 was the gaming tables, especially the thimble-riggers, a well-organized and powerful itinerant group. At Doncaster in 1825 complaints at the ever increasing numbers of thimble-riggers, belt-prickers and EO table operators led to an initial vain attempt to ban or control them by the magistracy. Subsequent attempts were also unavailing, and in 1829 a troop of the 3rd Dragoon Guards was called in and the ringleaders arrested.[97] Several days before their arrival the next year the *York Chronicle* announced that the magistrates were intending to suppress all gaming tables and that extra special constables were being sworn in.[98] An assemblage of thimble-riggers on the course was temporarily broken up by mounted men but the dragoons, the local militia – the Doncaster Yeomanry – and special constables were also called upon. The thimblemen barricaded themselves on the town moor, collected stones and used the legs of chairs in an attempt to avoid being driven off their traditional site. Local magnates mounted, and with the assistance of their grooms and hunt servants, assisted in driving them off. Some 150 were arrested.

Pickpockets too were organized. At Brighton in 1822 they mustered 'about 200 strong', and when one was arrested the officers were attacked with mud and missiles. A riot ensued and a crowd estimated at 3,000 stoned the magistrate who tried to restore order.[99] There were occasional minor incidents of the same type elsewhere.

Travelling semi-criminal groups such as the thimble-riggers sometimes found their victims organizing in return. At Lancaster they were attacked and driven off by the crowd in 1831 and again in 1836. By contrast, an attempt to control the gambling tables by the new rural police in 1840 led to fierce popular resistance and two days of disturbances, ending with the breaking of the town hall windows.[100] This was also seen locally as an attack on the Liberal policies of the council. It was not strongly pro-racing and was shortly afterwards replaced by a Tory one. Confrontation here was clearly seen as part of a broader social and political conflict not tied to any particular class. Violence by the crowd against perceived criminals such as welshing bookmakers or pickpockets could be found throughout the period. In 1913 a hostile crowd attacked the owners of a crooked marquee on Epsom Downs and it took 200 police nearly ten minutes to restore order.[101]

After mid-century urban expansion brought increasing numbers of migrants to the larger industrialized towns. Tension between social or ethnic groups sometimes broke out into violence, with the local races providing the locus rather than the cause. At Lancaster in 1855 there was a brawl between 'navvies' and members of the local militia.[102] In 1866 antagonisms between the Tyneside Irish and local workmen erupted at Newcastle races. Here political protest was also involved. A body of several hundred Irishmen, 'supposed Fenians', armed with railings and shillelaghs, marched in procession round the tents before being dispersed. After the races disturbances broke out, the Irish began striking out at all and sundry, but received 'a fearful thrashing' from the crowd before 40 policemen broke up the melee. Of the 15 Irishmen identified as injured, most were labourers from the shipyards at Jarrow, Hebburn and Gateshead, with an average age of just over 30.[103] Crowds and alcohol were always a potent mixture. In 1868 drunken Irishmen and Welshmen from the local works clashed in a Stockton refreshment booth. The riot escalated and the police had to work hard to get the matter under control.[104] The introduction of gate-money events and queuing at turnstiles also generated problems at first, especially at the smaller, less well policed grounds. At Streatham in 1878, for example, only an estimated one-third of the 13,000 attenders paid for admission while the rest broke into the course, damaging neighbouring property in the process.[105]

It was only rarely that political differences surfaced at the races. For the suffragist movement, however, attacks on the meetings provided a chance to strike at the male establishment and generate publicity. By 1913 women's suffrage agitation included attempts at arson at the grandstands at Ely, Kelso and Aintree and the well-known action of Emily Davidson, who brought down the King's horse Anmer at Epsom. Courses were in consequence forced to take special anti-suffragist measures.[106]

On all courses some of the crowd were part of a vast, floating, criminal population, and by the 1870s there were occasional orchestrated disturbances at the smaller, less well policed courses, joint attempts to rob with impunity. Such outlawry disorders were relatively uncommon. There was a serious disturbance, headed by well-known London and Birmingham thieves, at Shrewsbury in 1878 where they broke into the grandstand. Some time later, at Scarborough, 'dozens of villains' robbed the turnstiles, held up bookmakers and stole watches and money from those in the enclosure. Local opinion saw it as caused by 'south country welshers' and 'roughs'.[107]

Drink and excitement or the discovery of welshing bookmakers also caused isolated flare-ups. At Aintree the anti-racing journalist H. Shimmin saw 'two men, drunk and cursing each other's eyes ... pulling off their clothes to fight, while the friends of each support their man and back him'.[108] As an 1830s Newcastle songwriter recognized, part of the 'mirth and fun' of race week was an acceptance that 'sum had black eyes an' broken shins; and sum lay drunk among the whins i' cummin frae the races.'[109] Such activity was taken for granted and did not form a feature of police prosecutions or of most descriptions of meetings. An exception was London, where the government, always more ready to respond to metropolitan complaints, used legislation to suppress some meetings in 1879 on the claimed grounds of their ruffianism.

The potential for aggression may also have been reduced by the organized pugilism found on the early nineteenth-century courses, or by the pugilist or boxing booths which replaced them and which offered a more acceptable and potentially lucrative avenue. Other violence was the product of frustration, especially where money was involved. Jockeys or trainers whose activities had lost backers their money were prime targets, especially where their running in a particular race appeared problematic. When Lord Derby's horse Acrobat did nothing in the 1854 St. Leger and then won the Doncaster Stakes against a strong field two days later, well-backed by the stable, only the holding of the weighing enclosure by two previously-hired pugilists saved jockey and trainer from injury. Another horse, the I'Anson-owned and trained Blink Bonny, failed to win the St. Leger in 1857, despite previous outstanding form, and her infuriated backers tried to tear her trainer limb from limb and tried again when the horse won the Park Hill stakes in a canter two days later.[110] Perceived injustice was an important cause of much sports violence, through the frustration caused through the discrepancy between what should have happened and what actually did.[111] In the 1857 case *The Times* claimed that 'such a scene ... is of rare occurrence on a racecourse'.[112] It was, but only in the extent to which physical violence was used. Most crowds were very vociferous and could be threatening in such instances. This type of disorder was almost certainly underplayed in the press, since a judge's views were rarely shared by those who had not backed a winner in a close finish and crowd anger was expected.

The racing authorities attempted to respond to potential disorder and criminal activity through a range of policing strategies. Early in the nineteenth century the main focus of policing was simply to clear the course for each race. On the signal of a bell, course clearance would be enforced by a few horsemen and men on foot with long poles. But thereafter, from the Bow Street runners at Epsom in the early nineteenth century, through the arrival of the 'new police' from the late 1820s, to the hiring of county police and specials to supplement the local forces in the second half of the century, there was a great deal of continuity of police presence, often quite large, on the course itself. Epsom had nearly 300 by the 1840s. Most courses had police cells or police tents. In part police were there to keep the course clear and regulate horse traffic, and their presence no doubt also deterred some criminals.

But just as today, with the arguments over the effectiveness of officers on the beat, there was little evidence that local police were effective with more organized and expert criminals or, indeed, that they had the will to be so, especially where there was public opposition to their actions. This was especially true in dealing with petty gambling, to which a blind eye was often turned, although some police were sometimes bribed to do so.[113] Police had a difficult balance to achieve. Sometimes they were praised for achieving it. At Epsom in 1840 'police displayed a union of forbearance and firmness in the highest degree'.[114] Courses soon employed specialist detectives who knew names and faces. At Manchester in 1848 the county force kept the course, while detectives were spread across it to catch pickpockets.[115] The enclosing of courses actually made this process easier and urban detectives from London, Manchester, Leeds and other homes of the 'swell mob' were being recruited by the 1870s to check railway-station arrivals. Police detectives specialized in the recognition of the defaulters, thieves and sharpers who turned up on the course.[116] They were supported by specialist, travelling gatemen drawn from other racing places. This supposedly ensured that objectionable characters could be stopped at the gates. Some railway stations *en route* to a meeting were sometimes also patrolled by specialist police. Sometimes known criminals were put back on the train. Head-marked pickpockets could be taken up on suspicion and put temporarily out of harm's way. Others were given custodial sentences for 'acting suspiciously' as a way of deterring those who may not actually have been caught in a criminal act.

Despite such police activity there is no evidence of any major changes in the types or numbers of police prosecution, except for some hints of a reduction in physical violence from the 1890s. Prosecutions were fairly selective, almost forced upon the police. From the 1830s to 1914 pocket-picking, welshing on bets, drunk and disorderly behaviour, purse stealing and the issuing of counterfeit coins were the chief targets of police action, while there is no discernible, overall, pattern of crime, with any significant yearly divergence. Police reports need to be treated with caution, given the variations in the intensity of policing and the definitions of crime stressed by the authorities. Nevertheless, the relatively few convictions associated with individual meetings, usually amounting to no more than four or five, show a clear tolerance of behaviour.

This suggests that the racecourse may be seen as a liminal area where petty crime was tolerated by both by the racing and the urban authorities, where a range of popular cultural forms were able to shelter and survive. It provided a pretext for social gathering and cross-class mixing which undermined many reformist mores and fed a climate of anti-bourgeois behaviour.

This is an important finding. Much previous work has concentrated on examples of working-class leisure defeats in the urban context. Historians have analysed in some detail the abolition or slow decay of cockfighting, the fairs and wakes, the control of prostitution, and of drinking and street gambling, and suggested that the hegemonic power of urban middle-class elites constrained and controlled working-class life in a range of powerful ways. Yet in racing we find an example where control was both spasmodic and relatively ineffective. This suggests that there was a significant gap between the public expression of respectable middle-class ideology and power and its working out in practice. A number of historians have already argued that at times the working classes were active in the making of their own leisure despite the processes of industrialization and urbanization, and that they varied their behaviour significantly in different cultural contexts.[117] This analysis of racecourse life suggests not only that there was such an adoption of less-respectable behaviour in the particular context of the course but that it was not confined just to the working classes.

NOTES

1. 1862 Children's Employment Commission, quoted by G.J. Barnby, *Social Conditions in the Black Country 1800-1900* (Wolverhampton, 1980) p.219.
2. G. Jobey, 'Cock-fighting in Northumberland and Durham during the eighteenth and nineteenth centuries', *Archaeologia Aeliana*, Vol.20, Ser.5, 1992, p.2.
3. *Sporting Magazine,* June 1828, p.179.
4. Ibid., April 1822, p.48.
5. J. Fairfax-Blakeborough, *Northern Turf History,* Vol.11. *Extinct Race Meetings* (1949), pp.115, 242.
6. *Carlisle Journal*, 6 July 1839.
7. R.A. Hale, 'Horse Racing in Cumbria', unpublished BA dissertation Lancaster University, 1989.
8. R.J. Charlton, *Newcastle Town* (1885), p.356.
9. *Manchester Courier*, 29 May 1847.
10. *Yorkshire Herald*, 13 June 1846.
11. *Doncaster Gazette*, 7 September 1839.
12. A recent study of the Kentucky Derby shows similar features. See J. Harrah-Conforth, 'The Landscape of Possibility: an Ethnography of the Kentucky Derby', Indiana University PhD thesis, 1992.
13. Love and Barnton, *Manchester as It Is* (Manchester, 1839). F. Engels, *Condition of the Working Class in England* (1969 edn), p.78.
14. *Manchester and Salford Advertiser*, 22 June 1848.
15. *Yorkshire Herald*, 30 August 1851.
16. The *Westmorland Gazette*, 9 March 1839 quoted Mr Grant's *Travels in Town* as estimating 250,000 at Epsom, coming from a circuit of some 30 miles around and including 'vast numbers' of ladies.
17. Although she lost after her horse fell lame, she rode another match the following year against the Newmarket jockey Frank Buckle over two miles. Buckle carried four stones more but Alicia rode side-saddle and won. *York Herald*, 25 August 1804, 1 September 1804, 24 August 1805 gives details. R. Orton, *Turf Annals of York and Doncaster* (1844), p.277.
18. *York Herald*, 19 April 1851, 26 April 1851, 3 May 1851.
19. *Kendal Mercury*, 17 May 1851.
20. For examples see *Illustrated London News*, 17 June 1843; Supplement to the *Illustrated London News*, 23 May 1863, Derby Day; O. Beckett, *J.F. Herring and Sons* (1981), prints 89–92.
21. *York Herald*, 6 September 1851.
22. J. Crump, 'The great carnival of the year: Leicester races in the nineteenth century', *Transactions, Leicestershire History & Archaeological Society*, Vol.58, 1982–83, p.62. For a school log book example see 'low attendance ... due to the races' in 1884 at New Marske Primary School, Redcar, Cleveland. Log book held in school.

23. D. Reid, 'Interpreting the festival calendar; wakes and fairs as carnivals', in D. Storch (ed.), *Popular Culture and Custom in Nineteenth Century England* (1982). For examples of the use of the term 'carnival' see, *inter alia*, *Ripon and Richmond Chronicle*, 26 July 1856; *Salford Weekly News*, 10 June 1876; *Beverley Guardian*, 7 June 1884. R.W. Malcolmson, *Popular Recreations in English Society 1700-1850* (Cambridge, 1973), p.75, sees carnival as a key social function of much popular recreation at that time.
24. *The Times*, 20 May 1858. For a relatively contemporary American view of the Derby see R. Taine, *Notes on England* (New Jersey, 1958 edn), pp.32ff.
25. *Hartlepool Free Press*, 8 September 1855.
26. *Sporting Magazine*, June 1822, p.133.
27. *Newcastle Daily Chronicle*, 28 June 1865.
28. *Yorkshireman*, 29 June 1844; *Leicester Journal*, 21 September 1855; *Cleveland News*, 27 November 1880.
29. J. Fairfax-Blakeborough, *Northern Turf History*. Vol. III. *York and Doncaster* (1950), p.214.
30. D. Laird, *Royal Ascot* (1976), p.46.
31. W. Wise, *Richmond Yorkshire in the 1830s*, ed. L.P. Wenham (Richmond, 1977).
32. *Yorkshireman*, 24 August 1839; *Ripon and Richmond Chronicle*, 9 June 1856, 31 July 1858.
33. Fairfax-Blakeborough, *Extinct Racemeetings*, p.242.
34. *York Herald*, 8 May 1841.
35. *The Times*, 27 May 1912, 18 June 1913, 28 May 1914, 16 June 1914.
36. *Salford Weekly Mail*, 22 May 1875.
37. *Newcastle Daily Chronicle*, 28 June 1883.
38. G. Plumtre, *The Fast Set: the World of Edwardian Racing* (1985), pp.154–5.
39. C. Dickens, 'Epsom', *Household Words*, Vol.3, No.63, 7 June 1851.
40. Ibid.
41. See Plumtre, *Fast Set*, p.138.
42. Report and Minutes of Evidence of the Select Committee on Inquiry into Drunkenness, 1834 (4) XII, Recommendation 42.
43. *Manchester Guardian*, 7 May 1836.
44. *Doncaster Gazette*, 12 June 1891.
45. *Yorkshireman*, 29 June 1839. Newcastle Central Reference Library, The Herbage Committee, Lists of Tents and Stands at Newcastle Races 1847.
46. *Ripon Chronicle*, 8 October 1859.
47. A. Noakes, *William Frith: Extraordinary Victorian Painter* (1978), pp.60–1.
48. *Carlisle Patriot*, 16 June 1843.
49. At Goodwood in 1851 a correspondent suggested that each table was worked by no fewer than seven 'bonnets' besides the operator. *Doncaster Gazette*, 8 August 1851.
50. S. Bent, *Criminal Life; Reminiscences of Forty Years* (Manchester, n.d.), Ch.2.
51. *Sporting Magazine*, July 1848, p.7.
52. *York Herald*, 3 May 1851.
53. *North Eastern Daily Gazette*, 20 August 1875.
54. *Yorkshire Gazette*, 31 August 1861.
55. *Newcastle Courant*, 22 June 1866.
56. N. Fairfax-Blakeborough (ed.), *'J.F-B': the Memoirs of Jack Fairfax-Blakeborough, OBE, MC* (London, 1978), Ch.6.
57. H. Cox, *Chasing and Racing: Some Sporting Reminiscences* (1922), p.7 claimed that he had never had his person or property interfered with at a flat meeting.
58. Lord Rossmore, *Things I Can Tell* (1912), p.173.
59. A. Scott, *Turf Memories of Sixty Years* (1925), p.238.
60. *Manchester Courier*, 29 May 1847.
61. *Newcastle Courant*, 29 June 1866.
62. Crump, 'The great carnival of the year', p.64.
63. F. Finnegan, *Poverty and Prostitution: A Study of Victorian Prostitutes in York* (Cambridge, 1979), p.25.
64. W. Wilson, *Chester Races* (Chester, 1856), p.5.
65. Craven, 'The racing in September', *Sporting Magazine*, October 1851, p.218.
66. E.g., *Manchester Free Lance*, 15 June 1867.

67. *Doncaster Reporter*, 18 September 1867.
68. *The Yorkshireman*, 6 September 1845.
69. R.W. Proctor, *Memorials of Byegone Manchester* (Manchester, 1880), p.87.
70. The Druid, *The Post and the Paddock* (1856), pp.184–9.
71. Ibid., p.187.
72. *Cleveland News*, 22 May 1880.
73. *Westmorland Gazette*, 19 March 1825.
74. *Sporting Magazine*, June 1822 p.151.
75. Ibid., May 1822, p.61.
76. *Yorkshire Gazette,* 3 November 1860.
77. *The Times*, 21 September 1837.
78. *Stockton Herald*, 20 August 1870.
79. For examples see Newcastle Central Library, Minutes of the Herbage Committee, Newcastle Races 1866–67; Doncaster Record Office, Doncaster Race Committee Minutes 30 August 1866.
80. *Yorkshire Gazette*, 5 October 1861.
81. *The Free Lance*, 9 February 1867.
82. G. Benson, 'The Freemen of York and their connection with the Strays, 1912', quoted by Fairfax-Blakeborough, *Northern Turf History*, Vol. III, p.36.
83. *Salford Weekly News*, 10 June 1876.
84. *Morpeth Herald*, 25 June 1870.
85. *Northern Echo*, 14 August 1895.
86. Copies of the correspondence on this case are in the Doncaster Record Office D2/MD/14.
87. Letter of J. Spencer, 30 August 1893, Home Office/45/10005/A50014/41.
88. *Middlesbrough News*, 21 August 1880.
89. 'Rogues and Vagabonds – Welchers', *Baily's Magazine of Sport and Pastimes*, December 1870.
90. 1902 Select Committee on Betting, Evidence of C. Gould, JP, Q.1471–2.
91. E.g., at Catterick, *Bell's Life in London*, 6 April 1856; at Shrewsbury, *Sporting Life*, 19 November 1859.
92. For examples of such treatment at the Epsom Derby see *The Times*, 19 May 1866, 25 May 1867.
93. Select Committee of the House of Lords on Gaming 1844, evidence of Lord Strafford.
94. *Durham County Advertiser*, 14 October 1887.
95. J. Briggs (ed.), *Lonsdale Magazine*, Vol.1 (Kirkby Lonsdale, 1820), p.465.
96. For recent discussion on football violence see R.W. Lewis, 'Football hooliganism in England before 1914: a critique of the Dunning thesis', in *International Journal of the History of Sport*, Vol.13, 1996, pp.310–39. See also T. Mason, *Association Football and English Society 1863–1915* (Brighton, 1980), p.167; W. Vamplew, 'Ungentlemanly conduct: the control of soccer crowd behaviour in England 1888–1914', in T.C. Smout (ed.), *The Search for Wealth and Stability* (1979), pp.139–55.
97. *York Chronicle*, 17 September 1829.
98. Ibid., 16 September 1830.
99. *Sporting Magazine*, August 1822, p.261.
100. Anon., *Lancaster Records 1801–1850* (Lancaster, 1869); *Lancaster Guardian*, 25 July 1840; R.D. Storch, 'The plague of blue locusts: police reform and popular resistance in northern England 1840–57', *International Review of Social History*, Vol.20, 1975, p.79.
101. *The Times*, 6 June 1913.
102. *Lancaster Guardian*, 27 August 1855.
103. *Newcastle Courant*, 29 June 1866.
104. *North Star*, 14 August 1868.
105. Racecourses (Metropolitan) Bill, 1st reading, Mr Benett-Stanford.
106. *The Times*, 7 April 1913, 8 April 1913, 5 June 1913, 8 December 1913.
107. *Scarborough Gazette*, 16 September 1886; C. Richardson, *The English Turf* (1901), p.121.
108. J.K. Walton and A. Wilcox (eds), *Low Life and Moral Improvement in Mid-Victorian England: Liverpool through the Journalism of H. Shimmin* (1991), p.82.
109. K. Gregson, 'Songs of horseracing on Tyneside', *North East Labour History*, Vol.17, 1983, p.13.

110. See Fairfax-Blakeborough, *Northern Turf History,* Vol. III, pp.362, 366.
111. M.M. Mark *et al.*, 'Perceived injustice and sports violence', in J. Goldstein (ed.), *Sports Violence* (New York, 1983), pp.83–9.
112. *The Times*, 18 September 1857, 19 September 1857.
113. Gambling games could be hidden on the approach of police. See, for example, *Middlesbrough Weekly News and Cleveland Advertiser*, 27 August 1859. For bribery of officers see R. Samuel (ed.), *East End Underworld: Chapters in the Life of Arthur Harding* (London, 1981).
114. *Kendal Mercury*, 5 June 1840.
115. *Manchester and Salford Advertiser*, 17 June 1848,
116. See J. Caminada, *Twenty-five Years of Detective Work in Victorian Manchester,* Vol.II (1983) (first published 1893), p.7.
117. E.g., H. Cunningham, *Leisure in the Industrial Revolution* (1980), Ch.6. P. Bailey has argued that working-class roles were flexible and fluid and that role players modified their behaviour instrumentally to take advantage of opportunities.

6

Mingled Pleasure and Speculation: The Commercialization of Racing

A perennial theme running through nineteenth-century commentary was that racing was not just a leisure activity but also a world of money-making. Each new generation bemoaned the believed increase in the number of owners who saw racing as a trade or business.[1] The *Sporting Magazine* admitted as early as 1830 that racing was 'one of the commercial speculations of England' and that sums of money employed amounted to 'many millions'.[2] As racing became subject to statistical analysis and sporting journalism made explicit its links with other more work-related aspects of Victorian life, tables of the top sires, jockeys, winning owners and auction prices of stallions were all assembled to make betting, racehorse ownership and breeding information more widely available. Betting was an 'investment', winning was 'remuneration', the odds at Tattersall's were given 'as regularly and methodically as the price of corn and consols'. There had been a transition 'from sport to speculation' and a move to 'sordid gain'.[3]

This chapter attempts to establish the ways in which racing was commercialized at different stages and what the significance of this was. How should we read the place of commercial imperatives within racing? Were they just a question of profit, or were other factors involved? Did changing forms of commercialization erode the carnival atmosphere of the course and bring racing more into line with ideas of capitalization and moral hegemonies?

I

In the period 1800–60 the vast majority of courses had a single meeting a year and did not charge for entry. This made sound commercial sense. Meetings drew predominantly on local support and regional entries. A move to charge even a modest entry fee would have deterred spectators and in the long run collected less than could be raised by other means.[4] Working people could not afford to attend two meetings nor would subscribers and patrons give more than once, and the challenges of raising sufficient money to cover a meeting's costs and attract horses and spectators were considerable. This mattered little at elite Newmarket. There regular meetings were held each year by and for the upper classes and owners ran for their own money. It was more important at meetings such as Doncaster, and even more challenging at small local meetings such as Durham or Bath, where owners would not enter without reasonable prize money.

To attract entries, towns provided added money, although they tried to reduce overheads by clawing back money paid to winners in a variety of ways, including fees or presents for officials.[5] Few races away from large centres of population could be made profitable by direct means. Potential profits came by grandstand revenue or the spending of visitors on accommodation, subsistence, transport, gambling, entertainment and consumer goods. Local corporations, publicans, politicians, landowners, shopkeepers, those offering accommodation or subsistence, as well as those with shares in the grandstand could all therefore profit.

In 1856 Doncaster Corporation accounts showed that they made a direct profit of over £1,600 from the races while Rous claimed that the races put '£50,000 into the Doncaster pockets' indirectly.[6] By 1866 the Corporation derived a fifth of its income from the races.[7] Most places perceived that the races added 'largely to the business of the town'.[8] In Carlisle, one justification for the meeting was that it was 'of great importance to the town and cause[d] the legitimate expenditure of vast sums of money among our tradesmen'.[9] Different groups benefited, depending upon a range of factors including the date of and the status of the meeting and its attraction to distant visitors, especially the aristocracy and the gentry. At Durham, as the chairman of the Durham Grandstand Company admitted, most of the estimated £1,000 spent on each of the race days went to innkeepers and other refreshment-house keepers.[10] Those most likely to benefit directly were stand proprietors, the owners of hotels and other accommodation, licensed victuallers, keepers of refreshment rooms, cab proprietors and some tradesmen. Local landowners or the corporation often received ground rent for the course. On corporation courses careful control was exercised over the race meeting to ensure revenue and that a meeting would attract interest.

As crowds grew at major courses at the end of the nineteenth century income rose further. In Doncaster the Corporation were receiving by 1887 an income of approximately £10,000 per annum after paying out all expenses.[11] At Chester by 1898 the town received one-eighth of the race revenues in rent.[12] Such incomes led to reductions in local rates, a difficult argument to counter.

1. The finish of the 1827 Doncaster Cup, by J.F. Herring, Senior. Much sporting art omits the crowd, in favour of a more rural, idyllic context.

My Lord

Your filley ran away with the boy as I expected but made very good running for 3 miles she was beat a good way at last but beat some of the hors a long way — I shall take her to Penreth if I hear no more from Your Lordship —

I am
My Lord with all respect
Your Obed^t Ser^t
& commands
Thomas Pierse

2. Owners expected regular reports on the success of their horses. Thomas Pierse, a Richmond trainer, sent back regular letters to the Earl of Strathmore as he walked his horses from meeting to meeting.

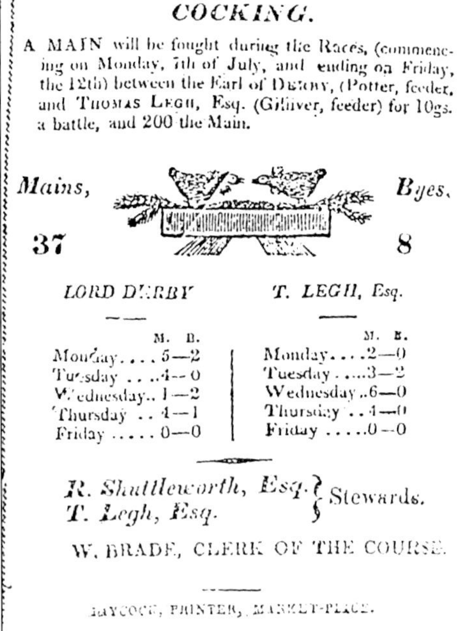

COCKING.

A MAIN will be fought during the Races, (commencing on Monday, 7th of July, and ending on Friday, the 12th) between the Earl of DERBY, (Potter, feeder, and THOMAS LEGH, Esq. (Gilliver, feeder) for 10gs. a battle, and 200 the Main.

Mains, 37 — Byes, 8

LORD DERBY	M. B.	T. LEGH, Esq.	M. B.
Monday	5—2	Monday	2—0
Tuesday	4—0	Tuesday	3—2
Wednesday	1—2	Wednesday	6—0
Thursday	4—1	Thursday	4—0
Friday	0—0	Friday	0—0

R. Shuttleworth, Esq. } Stewards.
T. Legh, Esq. }

W. BRADE, CLERK OF THE COURSE.

HAYCOCK, PRINTER, MARKET-PLACE.

3. Before the availability of cheap newspapers, local interest in results was met by printed bills sold at the end of the meeting. At Preston, cockfighting was still a part of the entertainment until the 1820s. Author's collection.

4. The former pugilist and butcher John Gully made a fortune on the turf as a bookmaker and backer on a large scale. Together with his confederate Robert Risdale they cleared over £60,000 in 1832 alone. He was MP for Pontefract from 1832 to 1837. Wildrake, *Cracks of the Day* (Ackermann, 1843).

5. Before the advent of the electric telegraph, results of major races were sent to betting men by carrier pigeon. *Illustrated London News,* 12 June 1843.

6. Doncaster during St. Leger week was a major blood stock auction venue from the 1820s, when Tattersalls began auctioning there. *Illustrated London News*, 21 September 1844.

7. Crowds across the social scale bent on profit as well as pleasure arrive at Epsom. *Illustrated London News*, 22 May 1847.

8. Lord George Bentinck, a dominating owner and bettor on the English turf between 1836 and 1846. Thormanby, *Kings of the Turf* (Hutchinson, 1894).

9. For the wealthier racegoer, eating, drinking and socializing were all important aspects of a day at the races. *Illustrated London News*, 1844.

10. In 1838 the huge response to the new Kingston line special trains to the Derby caused chaos at London stations. Even in 1847 there were still struggles to obtain a ticket. *Illustrated London News*, 22 May 1847.

11. Although betting rings were developed in front of the grandstand in the later 1840s, the traditional betting post was still being used at Epsom in 1844. *Illustrated London News*, 25 May 1844.

12. The varied social class, gender and age mix of the crowd is clearly illustrated in this splendid Punch cartoon. *Punch*, 1849.

13. The Derby was an opportunity for members of the Stock Exchange to socialize in a context where a very different form of gambling occurred. *Punch*, January–June 1847.

THE SETTLING DAY OF THE "BETTING OFFICE" FREQUENTER.

(Sporting Youth is Supposed to have "Borrowed" his Master's Cash Box to pay his Bets.)

14. By the early 1850s concern was growing about the supposed pernicious effects of betting offices. *Punch*, 19 June 1852.

15. The social elite were able to distance themselves in the relative security of the grandstand. *Illustrated London News*.

16. Even after the availability of cheap and rapid rail travel, many still went to the races by other means, as this Great Western Railway poster shows.

17. Siting electric telegraph offices on courses provided a rapid results service which played a major role in the growth of working-class betting.

SEASON, 1869.

THAT THOROUGH-BRED HORSE

SHARPSHOOTER,

BRED BY SIR TATTON SYKES,

The Property of Mr. Wm. Croasdale, of CHATBURN, NEAR CLITHEROE,

Will serve Mares this Season, 1869,

Thorough-bred Mares, Seven Guineas each, Half-bred Mares, three Guineas each, and Five Shillings the Groom.

"SHARPSHOOTER" is a Bay Horse, with short black legs, stands sixteen hands high, is of fine symmetry, has great muscular power, and very superior action. He was got by Rifleman, Rifleman by Touchstone, Dam, own sister to Jack Frost. Jack Frost was got by Sleight of Hand, Dam by Hampton, out of Emma.

"SHARPSHOOTER" won the following Races in 1861—The Claret Stakes of £130 at the Hoo, beating three others; the Berkshire Stakes of £202 at Hungerford, two miles and a distance, running a dead heat with Ipswich – SHARPSHOOTER made all the running and won cleverly by a length and a half; the Welter plate of £185 at Ascot, carrying 10 stone 7lbs. beating six others; he also ran third for the Durdans Plate at Epsom, when eleven started; and third for Her Majesty's plate of £105 at Hampton, when ten started.

Rifleman won the Great Yorkshire Stakes at York, in 1855. Touchstone won the Doncaster St. Leger in 1834, the Doncaster Gold Cup, in 1835 and 1836; and the Ascot Gold Cup in 1836 and 1837. Jack Frost won the Borough Handicap of £195 at Warwick, in 1853, beating eight others. Sleight of Hand won the Liverpool Cup in July 1840, and the Cleveland Stakes at Doncaster the same year. He was the Sire of Odd Trick, the winner of the Cambridgeshire Stakes, value £1810, beating a field of 29, he also won eight other Races the same year:—For particulars see Racing Calendar.

ROUTE.—*Friday*—Thro' East & West Martin, to Swan Inn, Gargrave, to Red Lion, Skipton, all night. *Saturday*—by rail to Colne, Crown Inn, till two o'clock, thence to Boot Inn, Burnley, till four o'clock, thence to the Prince of Wales Inn, Accrington, all night. *Sunday*—through Haslingden to the Wool Pack until two o'clock, thence to the Rawstron's Arms, Edenfield, till three o'clock, thence to the Derby Hotel, Bury, at five o'clock, to Mr. Place's Fish Pool all night. *Monday*—by Ratcliffe Bridge, to the Nag's Head, Bolton, until three o'clock, thence to Robt. Lee, the Crown Inn, Horwich, all night. *Tuesday*—to the Royal Oak, Chorley until twelve o'clock, to Mr. Howard's, Unicorn Inn, Walton, all night. *Wednesday*—through Brindle, to the Golden Lion, Blackburn, till three o'clock, thence to Mr. Croasdale's, Whalley Arms Inn, Whalley, 1 hour, thence to Spread Eagle, Lamb Roe, all night. *Thursday*—To Rose and Crown, Clitheroe, until ten o'clock, to Brown Cow, Chatburn, until one o'clock, to Sawley, until two o'clock, to Bolton-by-Bowland, until 3 o'clock, to William Bulcock's, White Bull, Gisburn, all night.

Any Mare tried by this Horse and afterwards served by another will be charged the full season price; or any Mare tried by this Horse and not coming forward to be served, but afterwards served by another, will also be charged the season price.

Sharpshooter got a PRIZE at Accrington, Skipton, and Burnley in 1864, and in 1865 at Haslingden, Accrington, Burnley & Skipton, and at Skipton in 1866.

All Accounts not paid on or before the 24th June, 1869, will be charged 5s. extra for collecting.

WILLIAM SHEPHERD Groom.

C. Tiplady, Printer, 53, Church Street Blackburn,

18. Stallions which had been successful on the turf could be advertised for breeding, providing the owner with additional income. Author's collection.

John Bowes Esq ____________ Dr.

____ To John Scott ____

		£	s.	d.
1853	To Nelson &c ---- Saddlers ---- £	56	10	.
	.. T. Oldaker ------ do. -------	12	18	.
	.. Wm. Maw ---- Vety. Surgeon ----	16	10	6
	.. Jos. Moon --- for Boys Liveries ---	33	.	.
	.. T. Swalwell --- Livery Hats -----	3	.	.
	.. Thos. Oxley ----- repg. Van &c. -----	9	7	6
	.. Mr Scott's Exps. to & from Streatlam twice ..	6	10	.
	.. Paid Mr Fitzroy, Cash lost in Sweepstakes ..	25	.	.
	.. Jno. Cartwright, share of Engt. & Exps. for Derby	10	.	.
	.. Flatman, Exps. to Malton for Trial, but prevented	5	.	.

____ Daniel O'Rourke ____

		£	s.	d.
To One Year's Assessed Taxes to Apl. 6th. — 3.17.–				
.. Exercising in Wolds 42/. Sainfallow 21/ — 3.3.–				
.. S. Templeman, riding a Trial ---- 2.2.–				
.. Exps. from Malton to Leatherhead .. 7.16.6				
.. Bill at Leatherhead -------- 22.10.–				
.. Exercising at do ---------- 1.1.–				
.. Clift riding a Trial at do ---- 2.2.–				
.. Exps. from Leatherhead to Malton .. 7.16.6				
.. Jno. Holmes, riding trial twice — 4.4.–				
.. Exps. from Malton to Goodwood 8.5.–				
.. Bill at Goodwood, Plating &c 11.15.–				
.. Exercising, Starting &c. at do ------ –.15.–				
.. Exps. from Goodwood to Malton 8.5.–				
.. Keep &c. One Year (Exp absences) 49 · 0 @ 40/. 98.–.–				
.. Boys Wages ---------- 52 · 0 @ 4/6 – 11.14.–				
.. Blacksmith, Druggist &c ------- 6.10.–				
.. Propn. of J. Scott's travelling Exps. ----- 3.10.–		203	6	..

Contd. £ 381 2 .

19. Costs of training a racehorse were high. John Bowes' horse Daniel O'Rourke, winner of the Derby in 1852, cost £203 in training fees with John Scott, whose bill is shown here.

20. Fred Archer was the outstanding jockey of the nineteenth century. He captured the public imagination as no other jockey had done. The death of his wife, pictured here at their wedding on 31 January 1883, contributed to his suicide in 1886.

21. The trainer William I’Anson owned much property, including this substantial house, at the time of his death at Malton in 1881.

22. Owner, trainer and trainer's family celebrate winning the Watt Memorial Plate at Beverley in 1897. Four bottles of champagne still to go. Author's collection.

23. Mr John Corlett, the editor of the *Sporting Times*, among the most influential of late nineteenth-century racing papers. *Baily's Magazine*, 1895.

October 16th, 17th, and 18th, will be produced the Great Racing Drama of THE

FLYING COLT!

Or, A RACE TOR THE DERBY!

Joey Jones .... (an old Jockey) .... Mr Horace Butler
Capt Clifton .... Mr Edwin Harris
Levi Moses .... (Men upon the Turf) .... Mr Alfred Leslie
Sam Slair .... Mr George Norton
Mr Danson .... Mr W. H. Woodville
Arthur Merton .... Mr Thomas Sennett
Tom Langey .... Mr Charles M'Laughlan
Sammy Jones .... Miss H. Temple
Lottie Jones .... Miss Annie Sinclair
Mr Arthur Merton's Flying Colt, by Blair Athol, out of Miss Hawthorn .... by a Real Horse
Tom Mayton .... (a Jockey) .... Master Woodville

ACT 1.—The FIELD and the FAVOURITE—Joey Jones gives the Squire a straight tip—the Exterior of the Stables—A glance at the Flyer—sending out the Commission against the Colt—the keys of the Stable—dismissal of the Trainer—the late Squire's Will—a sudden turn up—how young Merton comes into a fortune and the Flying Colt.

ACT 2.—The Clever Division in the Hole—Forging the Cheque—Cutting the Cards—The KING, QUEEN, and the KNAVE—How they Nobble the Flying Colt—Sammy Jones in the Sharpers' Den—A Clever Trick—Sammy Signs the Forged Cheque

SCENE SECOND.

INTERIOR OF THE STABLE.

The Flying Colt and the Old Jockey—A Midnight Visitor—Joey Makes a Mistake—The Colt must be made safe for the Derby—Despair of the Old Jockey.

GRAND TABLEAU.

ACT 3.—Plot and Counterplot—The Nobbling of the wrong Horse—Win now if you can—That's a Bargain—The Colt will be in the Ruck—Will he—The Road to the Downs—The state of the Betting

THE DERBY DAY!

Painted and designed by Mr William Channing.

A sudden turn up of the nobbled horse—the clever men outwitted—a last chance for life—drugging the Jock—Who will ride now?"—"I will!"

THE FLYING COLT WINS THE DERBY!

GRAND AND EXCITING TABLEAU.

24. The drama of racing, brought to Middlesbrough's Theatre Royal in October 1871.

THE ALEXANDRA PARK RACES, MUSWELL HILL.—SEE PAGE 36.

25. London's first enclosed course, the Hippodrome in Bayswater (1827), was not a financial success. Alexandra Park, shown here during its opening 1868 meeting, was, with six meetings a year by 1880. *Illustrated London News*, 1 July 1868.

Money was made also by the provision of accommodation. At the beginning of the century many gentry still used their houses in county towns for the races, but this became less common as the gentry vacated the county towns and withdrew some of their support for local meetings.[13] But up to and beyond the mid-nineteenth century at larger, more prestigious meetings, some magnates rented a fully-furnished house for the week and locally prominent residents would vacate their premises for the sake of the high rents.[14] Between 1800 and 1827 Earl Fitzwilliam paid between £20 and £54 a year per meeting for the use of a house at Doncaster or York, and with provisions, stabling and other sundries his weekly costs were usually £100–£150.[15] A foreign visitor to Doncaster in 1827 paid ten guineas for a lodging in a 'miserable chamber'.[16] By 1844 it was claimed that in Doncaster every house available could be let at a price that would cover nearly a whole year's rent, and at Epsom 25 guineas rent was being demanded for Derby Week in 1849.[17]

Other wealthy turfites stayed in hotels or lodging houses. At Chester in the 1830s the two major hotels each contributed £50 towards the meeting because of its benefit to their trade. Later in the century it was estimated that those who took lodgings for the week at Chester spent some £40,000 per annum.[18] But prices that were judged too high could deter visitors. At Bristol and Clifton hotel-keepers' increased tariffs was one of the reasons put forward for Bristol's struggles in the 1870s.[19]

Revenue from the grandstand receipts went sometimes to the municipality and sometimes in the form of dividends to shareholders, many of whom were local. Profit could also be made through catering. Grandstands often had catering facilities attached. Up to the 1840s local inns provided an 'ordinary'. Excursionists often sought sustenance in the town. At Doncaster in 1860 it was said that at almost every house banners were hung out bearing the inscription 'refreshments may be had here', while the 'linen draper vied with the saddler and the paper hanger' in providing for the wants of the hungry and thirsty visitors.[20] Food and liquid refreshment were also sold at the booths on the course by innkeepers. Such gains mirrored those of certain seaside occupations, although over a shorter season. Cab prices were high, tempting costermongers and donkey-cart owners into the business temporarily, and the provision of stabling for racehorses and visitors was a further source of revenue to innkeepers.[21] Shopkeepers too could sometimes benefit, especially if they were selling goods relevant to the needs of race-goers and some 'stuck to their counters with redoubled tenacity to make hay'.[22]

Theatres almost inevitably opened for at least part of the race week, although not always profitably given the late finish of many races early in the nineteenth century and their reliance on upper-class patrons.[23] But from mid-century theatres in large towns were laying on and profiting from attractions.[24]

II

These profiting groups were often involved directly in meetings through the raising of prize money to attract horses, owners and spectators. Most owners were interested in prize money, if only to reduce their contributions. Lord Derby was praised in 1869 for eschewing the 'small plates and chicken sweepstakes', prizes which some of his class appeared 'delighted to secure'.[25] Owners sometimes even pressed the organizers to raise the level of added money. At Doncaster in 1841 some 30 noblemen and gentlemen forced the Corporation to guarantee an increase in added money from £400 to £1,000, threatening that they would not otherwise enter for stakes the following year. The Aintree meeting's proprietor had offered £1,635 added money in 1840, and other courses such as Newcastle, Chester and Ascot were outstripping Doncaster.[26] York found itself losing prestige because of poor prize money, forcing a committee to increase added money to £1,000 in 1843.[27] As a result prize money reflected status (see Table 10).

TABLE 10
PRIZE MONEY IN 1862

	Total prize money	Prize money per runner	Prize money per winner
Races throughout Britain	£280,406	n.a.	£129
Doncaster	£16,272	£51	£378
York	£10,185	£43	£242
Ascot	£11,431	£36	£336

Source: Anon., *Horse Racing: Its History* (1863), p.325.

Competition drove it up. Leicester prize money was £810 in 1872, but in 1879, when enclosed courses were offering higher prize money, Leicester's committee, following a vigorous local canvas, increased the added money to £2,110.[28]

These local race committees managed the accounts, appointed the officials and other staff, maintained the fabric, instituted changes to the course, raised money through a variety of means and defended the races. Although there was sometimes a separate grandstand committee to manage the stand, as at Carlisle in the 1840s, the race committee and the grandstand committee probably acted together.[29] They met regularly. Most were self-perpetuating bodies, composed of local businessmen. Among the earliest surviving records are those of Preston, which begin in 1791. These show careful financial management, plus attention to the safety of the stands and other impermanent erections.[30] Committees themselves were accountable through annual meetings where the treasurer would report progress.[31]

Although membership of race committees was generally not directly profitable, it was usually socially or financially useful in other ways: members of the drink trade, for example, could often profit indirectly by increased sales during race week. The key semi-professional was the clerk of the course, with his personal contacts with owners, who was the key to a meeting's organization and success. At Carlisle in the 1860s, but for the clerk 'the meeting would be a mere matter of history long ago'.[32] At Leicester the acquisition of a new clerk in 1852 led to the revival of the meeting after a long period of moribundity.

Some courses, such as Aintree, which drew on larger crowds, made more direct profit, but even here indirect profit was important and the founder, a local publican, offered big prize money from the first.[33] The prize money necessary was at first raised through donations and subscriptions from those in the locality.[34] Collectors were usually appointed to manage this process. At the small Knutsford meeting 17 were appointed, including nine locals, receiving a contribution of 5 per cent of the sum collected.[35] Here subscriptions were collected quite early in the year, but many elsewhere were collected not long before the races. At Doncaster the mayor organized a committee to canvas each ward in 1841, and at Carlisle a sub-committee collected subscriptions.[36]

Subscriptions were raised from two groups: supporters of racing and those who profited from it. The *Racing Calendar* refers to innkeepers' plates, railway stakes, tradesmen's or corporation cups, ladies' purses and members' plates. It has been claimed that 'the titles of races indicate quite clearly who the turf's sponsors were'. But such information is not always reliable.[37] The title of the race was not always a reference to its true sponsor. Ladies' plates or purses were a feature of about one-sixth of all meetings in the 1830s. In 1839 at some meetings, such as Southampton or York, they were clearly collected from women. But at Leominster the ladies' plate of £50 was 'given by C. Greenaway, Esq., MP', while at Lee and Eltham the ladies' stakes had £20 added 'from the fund'. Equally, railways sometimes gave money, yet the Railway Stakes at the York Union Hunt Club meeting in October 1846 was funded by George Hudson, a railway shareholder certainly, but given in his capacity as a Member of Parliament.

Nevertheless, the titles provide some indication of the turf's key supporters. A study of such *Racing Calendar* descriptors for 1839 (see below) suggests that MPs, the local aristocracy and gentry, local town subscribers, innkeepers and tradesmen and the government were the main contributors. County and borough members were important in providing funding. This allowed the local MPs to demonstrate their generosity and concern for a popular local event and to profit politically by their support. Tory MPs were perhaps more consistent in their support, but many Liberal Members also gave money. Where political loyalties were split, both gave, although where both MPs were Liberal this was less common. At Leicester when both MPs were Liberal in 1847, they stopped subscribing and no further Liberal Members did so although the Tories continued.[38] But local MPs usually gave from £25 to £50, depending upon the meeting, and aspiring MPs would also sometimes endow stakes (see Table 11).

TABLE 11
NUMBER OF MEETINGS MENTIONING SPECIFIC FUNDING IN 1839*

Added fund (unspecified)	132
Members of parliament	70
Aristocracy and gentry	61
The town	56
Queen's plates	34
Ladies' cups, plates and purses	29
Innkeepers and tradesmen	23
Racing or hunt clubs	10
Grandstand or course proprietors	9
Corporation	7
Yeomanry or other military	6
Stewards	5
Railways and other sources	3
Total number of meetings	150

* Some meetings mention several forms of funding.

Direct support or subsidy from the upper classes appeared in most race-meeting records, often solicited by letter.[39] Upper-class hunt clubs and military garrisons also regularly subscribed. The office of steward, the ultimate adjudicator of the meeting, was an acknowledgment of social position as much as of racing expertise, and it was often expected that stewards would contribute financial support. Race meetings organized at seaside resorts could often rely on further subscriptions from upper- and middle-class visitors.

References to 'town' subscriptions are problematical since these could include subscriptions from local inhabitants generally, the corporation or innkeepers and tradesmen. As has been seen in terms of middle-class support for racing, corporations in a number of towns gave significant contributions, especially before the Municipal Corporation Act of 1835. At Chester the Corporation gave £50 towards the city plate from 1803, a figure increased to £63 in 1808.[40] By the 1820s many corporations subscribed some £50 to £60 per year for a cup or plate.[41] At Doncaster £400 in the 1830s had increased to £1,000 by the 1840s, and reached £1,200 by 1852.[42]

Support for races from local tradesmen, in the hope of stimulating trade, was already common in the eighteenth century. The tradesmen of Newmarket provided two plates of £50 in 1744 to stimulate racing there and at Chester the city guilds and companies subscribed.[43] Innkeepers were major contributors. At Chester the liquor trade represented between 42 and 46 per cent of subscriptions between 1854 and 1869.[44]

Limited contributions to racing were given by the Crown in the form of Royal Plates of 100 guineas. These longer-distance races for older horses to encourage horse quality were run at two Scottish courses, Newmarket and a number of other English ones, usually county towns. By the late 1860s these were attracting little betting interest since they were run at weight-for-age over two miles and there was plenty of published information on potential form. They attracted few runners. So in November 1875 the numbers of English plates were reduced and the prizes were increased in the hope of attracting more and better entries. Even this had little success and Royal Plates were finally abolished in 1887.

Coach services, which gained from the increased traffic, gave some support to meetings. At Liverpool, for example, the Coach and Car Proprietors gave a £70 plate to the May 1836 races, while at Newcastle guards and coachmen gave contributions between 1840 and 1846. The railways then took over. Vamplew has argued that they helped to raise the level of prize money through the sponsorship of races.[45] However, more recent research by J. Tolson has revealed that railway sponsorship was relatively insignificant, especially in Scotland and northern England.[46] The total amount contributed by all the railways in Great Britain peaked at £1,142 in 1861, when 22 courses appear to have had railway sponsorship, and declined quickly thereafter. Most railway donations were relatively small[47] and most support from the railways was irregular, although the London and South-Western Railway sponsored races at a number of courses over much longer periods of time. The proportion of railway sponsorship to total prize money was always less than 1 per cent.[48] By 1874 it was some £350 out of £315,275 (0.1 per cent). This is a surprising finding, since the railways certainly profited from meetings and often tried to attract race-goers by offering reduced fares to them.

III

Subscriptions, however, were rarely enough to make a meeting successful, and even early in the nineteenth century a range of other ways of raising added money were in place, most commonly by building a grandstand, and under terms which allowed a proportion of the entrance revenue to go to the race fund. Ascot's permanent grandstand of 1837 was built by a company with capital of £10,000, and a dividend of 5 per cent with £500 used each year to purchase shares; of the money left two-thirds was to go to the prize fund.[49] This was a good investment, since by 1858 surviving £100 shares were worth £175 with bonuses and the grandstand was free of debt.[50]

As well as profit early shareholders also got a free view of the races from the stand, with transferable tickets. The shareholders of mid-century joint-stock grandstand companies partly subscribed in the hope of profits, but a majority of companies were set up with shares that had to be redeemed as soon as possible, after which profits were to be applied to the benefit of the races. At almost all courses interest on shares had not to exceed 5 per cent, with any excess ploughed back, so purchase was in part simply a gesture of support.

Grandstand building occurred in every decade of the century and was both a major and a necessary part of wealthier spectatorship, and a key revenue raiser. Size varied even in the pre-railway period from stands accommodating up to 500 to much larger ones such as the 1830 Epsom grandstand, which could accommodate 5,000.[51] Investment costs varied as a result. Carlisle Race Stand Company had a capital of under £2,000; the later 1864 Newcastle Grandstand Company had a share capital of £10,000.[52]

Early nineteenth-century stands were rarely full. But at Doncaster the growing national importance of the St. Leger in the early 1820s led to a rapid growth in stand revenue from around £1,000 in 1820 to nearly £2,200 in 1825. By 1853 St. Leger day alone raised £2,000 at the grandstand; in 1860 income from the grandstand enclosure was £4,363 and by 1890 it was £12,324.[53] By contrast, Chester grandstand raised only £700 over the five days in 1830.[54] Prices varied from a pound or more for the race week at Ascot, Doncaster or Epsom in the 1850s to less than half that at small meetings such as Malton or Richmond. Daily tickets were also expensive, up to 10 shillings at Ascot for cup day, 3 shillings at Malton.[55] Revenues relied on the honesty of gatekeepers. At Doncaster in 1851 they let their acquaintances in without paying and sold off cheap tickets illegally.[56]

Many grandstands had ground-floor catering and facilities for the selling of alcohol, and doubled as turf taverns. This was another way of making money, direct or by auctioning the concession. At Ascot the catering revenue from the stand in 1839 went up from £50 in 1839 to £100 by 1851.[57] Leicester's stand raised £40 in 1850, while at Doncaster tenders for the grandstand concession raised £400 in 1867.[58]

Some grandstands were built privately as speculative ventures.[59] At Chester the Dee stands, built in 1840 and paying an annual ground rent of £20, were getting receipts of between £1,000 and £1,500 by 1870.[60] This meant a revenue loss to the race fund. Increasingly, however, race committees were alert to this and private stands or boxes were forced to contribute.[61] Doncaster derived a considerable revenue from private stands and boxes by the 1860s, and when a new subscription stand was built and its subscribers got in free, additional entrance tickets had to be purchased from the Corporation, giving the latter additional funds.[62] Further revenue was sometimes raised through animal grazing or the renting out of stands for county agricultural shows, other sports or military reviews.

A second way of raising money was through the auctioning of permanent and temporary booths and tents or the making of them available dependent on subscription. The latter was the common pattern in the early nineteenth century but the former was already to be found at more commercially-oriented meetings by the 1820s.[63] Ascot began auctioning booths when a new clerk took over in 1836.[64] Speculators soon recognized meetings as having potential for money-making. At Epsom Mr Barnard paid £700 to manage the booth rentals on the race committee's behalf, maximizing his profit by charging even thimblemen and three-card-tricksmen to use the course.[65] By mid-century the direct pricing of booths was also coming in, with the charges related to frontage or acreage.[66]

By the late 1830s another way of increasing revenue was through selling races: races where the winner had to be sold or auctioned for a minimum sum if demanded, with any excess split between the race fund and the second horse. These events rapidly became popular, and amounted to over one-fifth of all races by the 1860s; this indicates how courses responded to changes in demand from owners, allowing even poorer horses to succeed.

Up to the late 1820s gaming booths were a common source of revenue, but reformist opposition led to their virtual disappearance in the 1830s. They were soon replaced by (illegal) betting booths used by professional bookmakers who were, nevertheless, increasingly expected to contribute to the race fund. In Newcastle the first explicit reference to 'payment from betting men' for booths came in 1865–66, and by 1869–70 payment from 'betting men' was contributing £52.17s.4d.[67] As telegraph companies increasingly set up lines to the major courses in the 1850s to service the demands of newspapers, they too were expected to contribute and were charged a rental to install their services.[68]

As the income raised by grandstand enclosures became clearer, many courses began to charge entrance fees to carriages. By the 1850s this was common. At Doncaster in 1866 a space was ruled off in front of the grandstand for carriages, at a charge of 2 guineas for the front row and one for the second. Other vehicles (5 to 10 shillings) and horses (2/6d) were also charged.

Entrance fees, first charged for the grandstand, were slowly extended to areas of the course which could be cheaply enclosed. Betting rings in front of the grandstand were enclosed from the 1830s and a saddling enclosure or paddock was first created at Epsom, where a saddling enclosure cost a shilling to enter in the 1830s.

The first, early nineteenth-century enclosed park courses, including Croxton Park, and Stapleton Park (Pontefract), were enclosed not to raise money but for the amusement of their upper-class owners and to give opportunities for gentlemen riders, while trying to keep out the rougher element. Even then some clearly aimed at profit. Haigh Park in Leeds, developed in 1823 and continuing into the early 1830s on a profit-making basis, was unable regularly to attract large enough crowds to offer attractive prize money, although some 200,000 were estimated as having come on foot at 2d a head over the four days of 1825.[69] In 1837 John Whyte enclosed the Hippodrome circuit in London, and charged for admission, but even with a large population within easy travelling distance it did not generate sufficient spectators to be profitable.[70] As the standard of living rose some mid-century courses were enclosed, especially when a river surrounded much of the course, thus saving on fencing costs. Lanark was being run by an innkeeper syndicate, with an entrance charge of 'a copper or two' for a ticket by 1854.[71] Stockton charged a penny to everyone entering the course by 1859, as did Blaydon at about the same time.[72] But courses still had to largely rely on other sources of funding, and 1860s *Racing Calendars* still had references to members', stewards', ladies', licensed victuallers', tradesmen's or innkeepers' and stand plates, cups or purses and many references to town or gentry names, although these are becoming fewer and more unreliable. Certainly the support given by MPs was declining by the 1860s.

However, entrance charges were more successfully and regularly exploited in courses close to the major centres of population, especially Manchester, London and Liverpool. Manchester charged a penny toll on all who entered from 1847.[73] When its new course opened in 1868 it had a 13ft drainage ditch and stockade to ensure that everyone paid the 3d entrance fee.[74] In the same year Alexandra Palace was charging a shilling per head, although this was excessive.[75] By the 1880s enclosure was common even at provincial courses. Many smaller ones initially charged 6d but some were moving to a shilling by the 1890s, especially for major race days.[76] New, exclusive racing clubs, such as that at Sandown in 1875, also made racing more attractive to the upper classes once again.

Enclosure at first led to increases in the prize money as enclosed courses aimed to attract large crowds by well-publicized, big-money races of £1,000 or more. In 1889 there were races at Sandown, Manchester and Leicester worth £10,000 or more. But such courses proved unable to maintain this level of prize money. The Manchester Lancashire Plate, worth £10,131 in 1889, was worth only £7,930 by 1893. Even in 1913 there were only two races in Britain worth over £10,000.[77]

Increased commercialism can, however, be overstressed. There was no attempt to maximize income by running races on days which would maximize attendance. Right through the nineteenth century and into the twentieth there were few meetings on Mondays or Saturdays. Sunday was the chief day for racing in France. In Britain no recognized race meeting used Sundays, despite its clear potential for raising revenue, and the limited grass-root support of the Sabbatarian movement.[78] For the Jockey Club and for the directors of many recognized courses who were often of an upper-class background profit maximization, while important, was clearly not central. Even Saturday racing was found only at metropolitan courses such as Alexandra Park, Hurst Park or Sandown and provincial courses such as Manchester, Liverpool and Hamilton Park with large working-class populations to draw upon. At unrecognized courses there were far more Saturday single-day meetings.

For those meetings controlled by the Jockey Club the social aspects were important. Nevertheless, although the key meetings favoured by the Club at Ascot, Bibury, Doncaster, Epsom, Goodwood and Newmarket all survived unenclosed into the 1900s, all enclosed significant parts of the course. The shift to enclosed courses was almost complete by the early twentieth century. Committees were still as interested in racing as before, but, instead of getting profit indirectly out of the money spent by visiting turfites, their objective was increasingly to make profit direct. When in 1902 York Committee paid many of the incidental expenses of the meeting out of their own pockets, it was described in *Baily's Magazine* as 'almost alone in being a meeting run on the old, old lines; so old as to seem quite strange in these days when the main object is dividends.'[79]

At these larger, more famous, unenclosed courses revenue from the stands and enclosures was quite significant, as was that from the booths. All such major meetings had a range of stands catering for the varying needs of spectators. This may be seen from Table 12 which gives Doncaster's non-racing revenue for 1896.

TABLE 12
REVENUE FROM NON-RACING SOURCES AT DONCASTER, 1896

Grandstand tickets	£9,415.10s
Stand and 2nd-class stand tickets	£1,195
Private stand	£55
Lincolnshire Stand let to C. Charleworth, Esq.	£400
County stand	£868
Private boxes	£220.10s
Paddock	£1,939
Tattersall's enclosure	£1,160
Carriage stands	£ 577.7s.6d
Publicans' booths	£414.6s.0d
Temporary booths, tents, carts and wagons	£1,612.18s.6d
Refreshment rooms (let to Bradford firm)	£800
Race cards	£325
Fruit stalls (let to Salford firm)	£25

Source: Doncaster Record Office, Doncaster Borough Corporation Race Account 1896.

And revenue was rising: at Doncaster Sir John Astley had leased the Lincolnshire stand at an annual rent of £315 in 1886, but by 1896 it was £400.[80] Major unenclosed courses such as Ascot were soon charging £2 or more for weekly tickets.[81] In the later nineteenth century booths, tents and stalls raised ever larger sums. At Doncaster revenue raised from the booths alone was higher than the total from most meetings before mid-century. The revenue raised depended on a booth's position and size. At Newcastle in 1893 wooden booths raised £72 each, larger tents £36 to £38, other booths £20 to £33, while bids for stalls ranged from £2.15s to £7.15s.[82] Catering in the grandstands was by now raising substantial amounts, and even printers were expected to contribute significant sums if they wished to print race cards. The provision of stabling and accommodation for stableboys on the course, instead of relying on local inns, attracted more entries, and charges could be made for food and other costs.[83]

Nevertheless, while such courses had several meetings a year, the profits varied. At Newmarket the Jockey Club had lived from hand-to-mouth for much of the century, devoting the whole of its income to racing in the shape of added money, maintenance and the rent of gallops and courses, and payment of salaries to racing officials. However, its attitude was changing.

The 1870s saw a change of policy and it rapidly moved to increase revenue thereafter. Even so, some Newmarket meetings each year lost money while others made substantial profit. Revenue varied substantially from meeting to meeting, with the Second October meeting having more than twice that of the Craven meeting. When added money given as prizes is taken into account, the Craven meeting clearly lost money (see Table 13).

TABLE 13
JOCKEY CLUB INCOME (£) FROM MEETINGS IN 1897

	Craven	1st Spring	2nd Spring	1st July	2nd July	1st October	2nd October	Houghton meeting
Tattersall's	851	1,786	1,102	1,260	803	1,135	2,231	2,211
Grandstand	247	811	417	500	314	440	1,166	1,069
Private stand	70	269	113	192	99	128	331	328
Ring	138	410	210	245	140	223	607	522
Carriages	9	45	15	30	22	22	49	36
Saddling enclosure	139	403	191	230	203	171	416	399
Tolls	62	240	134	134	108	135	307	300
Half surplus sales	438	334	443	642	379	534	262	781
Entry forfeits	2,749	2,412	6,200	2,725	2,305	3,963	5,596	3,785
Totals	4,703	6,710	8,825	5,958	4,373	6,751	10,965	9,431
Added money paid	4,768	5,127	9,719	5,922	4,468	7,309	7,842	6,312

Source: Annual Accounts of the Jockey Club, 1897.
An estimated further income of about £2,000 was gained through annual payments for the Jockey Club stand and yearly tolls.

Where meetings were run for more than one day, there were significant differences in the revenue raised on particular days. The ratio of the receipts from the most popular days to those from the least popular varied from meeting to meeting, but was usually between 5:1 and 12:1. This implies that direct profit was not the only motive. Had it been, shorter meetings would have been held. Owners and race-meeting organizers enjoyed racing days out and the social side for such key supporters was important too.

The move to gate-money revenue acted against subscription revenue, even at Newmarket. Enclosed courses attracted smaller crowds, so some of those who had previously benefited from the races withdrew subscription. At unenclosed courses locals resented having to contribute when they no longer needed to at enclosed courses elsewhere. Only £100 was given by the residents of Beverley in 1875.[84] This was a vicious circle for some smaller courses. With fewer subscriptions they were forced to enclose, but then the crowds were smaller and then subscriptions dropped even further. At Richmond after enclosure some leading gentry and aristocratic patrons continued to subscribe, but local subscriptions dropped rapidly. In 1890 only £200 was raised through the turnstiles and £225 from the grandstand, insufficient without subscriptions, which by 1892 amounted to only £62.[85]

IV

Race meetings generated income, but their potential profit was limited by high and ever-increasing setting up and running costs. As we shall see, given the financial obstacles in the way of making a profit, it is unsurprising that many meetings were unable to sustain themselves in the face of constantly rising expectations.

Early courses were cheap to build; the 1810 Lancaster course cost about £1,000.[86] But costs soon rose. At Manchester the 1847 Castle Irwell site had a rent of £500 a year and it cost over £10,000 to build three stands, lay out the track and roads, while in 1867 New Barns cost its proprietors around £45,000 to buy land, lay out the course and construct the stands and other buildings.[87]

There were then further and regular additional costs. Few meetings owned land outright and, although initially ground rents were low, by the late nineteenth century leasing costs were rising rapidly as landowners placed both restrictions and higher financial demands on the race companies.[88] Rents escalated rapidly in the period from 1875 to 1900. At Pontefract the annual rent jumped from £50 to £500, and at York from £250 to more than £1,000.

Drainage was a further problem. At York the freemen who owned the rights of pasturage and revenue on the Knavesmire course were unwilling to spend money, generally looking to contributions to defray course development costs. In 1853–54 £230 was paid towards improved drainage and the building of new roads, altogether costing nearly £1,000, at a time when only £145 was being received in revenue from the rents from tents and booths. However, in the same year the old wooden booths were demolished and rebuilt in brick at a cost of £745, which raised a further annual income of £80, a substantial return on investment. Despite the work on drainage, another £2,700 had to be spent on it in 1861.[89]

All courses had regular maintenance costs, including painting, decoration and repairs to the rails, grandstands, judges' stands, booths and other buildings, and alterations and maintenance to the course itself, to straighten it, level it, mow it or smooth out curves and mend fences. Smaller courses found the raising of such money difficult. Durham struggled to raise the £250 for much-needed improvements in 1864.[90] As crowds grew through the century, additional stands were regularly needed at most courses, as were urinals. Neither were cheap. Building a new lunch room and stand in 1880 at Doncaster cost £2,500, and in 1885 a new county stand and further lavatories cost even more.[91]

Everywhere there was constant pressure from the press for

improvements. Changes elsewhere always caused demands for similar facilities. Grandstand betting rings, saddling enclosures and parade rings were being demanded from the 1840s, although some courses were slow to respond. Beverley built the latter only in the 1870s.[92] In 1883 the *Newcastle Daily Chronicle* was suggesting that 'a new stand for owners, trainers and the press would be a boon'.[93]

As well as the key racing officials, all earning significant sums (see below) a range of temporary staff were needed. At Ascot grandstand in 1851 there was a superintendent receiving £25, plus five money-takers and 13 money-checkers each receiving £3.10s.[94] Larger open courses required large numbers of staff. At York in 1875 these included superintendents of the paddock, enclosure, subscribers stand and cheques, several ticket salesmen, ten or more ticket-takers, a deputy starter, two telegraph operators (for the jockeys' telegraph showing riders), three scalesmen in the jockeys' weighing room, a bell ringer, ten or more enclosure guards, a toilet superintendent, and men on the gravel road around the course.

Only those police actually on the course itself, some of whom would be mounted to clear the course and control crowds, were normally paid by the race committee, and the town itself met the bill needed to control the extra numbers outside.[95] Early balance sheets often make no mention of police, so they may have been provided free of charge.[96] By the 1860s police costs related directly to the numbers attending. These were higher at unenclosed courses and were increasing at the popular ones. Newcastle had about 90 men on the course in 1864.[97] The York Race Committee, which had paid two detectives and 50 policemen at the summer meeting in 1885 was using from 60 to 80 policemen, depending on the day, by 1893, at a cost of some £60.[98] Leicester paid a similar figure in 1879.[99]

Advertising costs were also substantial. To begin with this had been a matter only of advertising the meeting in the sheet version of the *Racing Calendar* and in the local press. With the advent of rail travel and a cheap press wider national and regional coverage was expected.

With such a range of costs to meet, many new mid-nineteenth-century meetings were unable to establish themselves consistently, since subscriptions were initially difficult to raise. Even well-established courses sometimes lost money. Dates were all-important and a clear date was very helpful.[100] Attendance varied with the weather and with wider economic and political shifts. At Liverpool in 1852, before an election, the meeting was affected by 'the political movement over the length and breadth of the land'.[101] Agitation and unrest in the Durham coalfield and a slump in heavy industries during the mid-1880s affected Durham and Stockton up to and beyond 1887.[102] Poor attendance could be due to a combination of circumstances. The difficulties experienced by Bristol in the 1870s included the weather, competition from other places, distance from the training stables, lack of rich local patrons, local apathy, a bad date in the calendar, and the prices charged for local accommodation.[103] By the 1880s the Jockey Club itself was encouraging some courses at the expense of others. The enclosed Gosforth Park course near Newcastle was allowed by the Jockey Club to take nearby Durham's traditional Easter date in 1881.

But many courses were profitable. At Ascot in 1851 it was estimated that about £5,000 was raised through grandstand and other receipts, while only £777 was paid out in added money. The period around the mid-century saw meetings such as Hampton or Shrewsbury being privately organized by lessees aiming to profit.[104] In 1848 the *Sporting Magazine* claimed that meetings had become private speculations of great magnitude. Citing Dorling at Epsom, it claimed that 'his model will find plenty of the enterprising to adopt it, for it pays'.[105] Sometimes described as 'got-up' races, they were disliked by traditionalists, since they charged not only for booths, riders and carriages and grandstand, but for a range of additional costs. Some were accused of making 'sport subservient to business'.[106] At Hampton the lessees apparently made a 'small fortune' out of the speculation in 1859.[107] Manchester was seen as 'a highly profitable investment of money' in the mid-1860s, with 9 to 10 per cent average interest on shares.[108] But not all lessees regularly made a profit. The Liverpool lessee in 1851 failed to do so despite the large crowds because the increased prize money had not been covered by increased revenue.[109]

The new gate-money courses of the 1880s and 1890s, which required significant investment, also increasingly emphasized profit.[110] Some certainly made money. Gosforth Park declared a 10 per cent dividend as early as 1883, and by 1893 the shares had tripled in value.[111] Although profits were limited to 10 per cent by Jockey Club legislation from the 1880s, this was still a good level of return, and although the average dividend was only 7.5 per cent in 1913 this was higher than from many alternatives.[112] But such profit was more a feature of the larger courses close to major conurbations with a history of race-going. As we have seen, enclosure proved disastrous at many of the smaller meetings.

Attempts to found new enclosed meetings in highly-populated urban areas often failed. The Jockey Club was unhelpful about dates, there was often local opposition, and it was difficult to raise capital because of the risks and uncertainty involved. In many areas insufficient working-class spectators could either afford or chose to take time off for a meeting more than once a year. Few spectators, for example, attended the August meeting at Redcar; they kept their money for the Whit meeting.[113] The Sheffield and

Rotherham area had four separate, failed attempts at founding racecourse companies between 1874 and 1898, while there were other failed attempts at Bristol, Hull and Leeds.[114] A number of enclosed courses which were set up in heavily populated areas, such as Halifax, Four Oaks Park Birmingham or Portsmouth, at significant expense lasted for only a few years before going under.[115]

V

Clear evidence of early commercialization may also be seen in the emergence of paid professionals: jockeys, trainers and the semi-professional corps of racing officials and other staff. Although in the eighteenth century each course may have had its own clerk of the course or judge, by the early nineteenth century such jobs were already increasingly held by travelling officials, doing duty at more than one meeting, as well as their usual jobs. John Lockwood, the clerk at Doncaster, also held the post at York and Beverley early in the second decade.

Clerks, whose main job was to attract entries and subscriptions and arrange the meetings, worked for a salary and commission at most unenclosed courses.[116] Many charged each entry a fee, usually of 5 shillings.[117] Occasionally money was deducted from subscriptions.[118] Alternative or extra income was gained by subtracting a fee of a pound or more from the stakes before giving it to winners, although this was dying out after mid-century.[119] Before this clerks had sometimes also received presents from successful owners.[120] This could lead to dishonesty. The clerk at Ascot in 1860 confessed to having embezzled large sums of money from the Ascot Race fund since it was set up and had received money from owners for unspecified services.[121] Clerks working for several meetings were common by the 1840s and could earn significant sums.

Other racing officials were also paid by the meeting. Even by the 1830s it was only at the smallest of meetings that officials were local men of little experience. At nearly all the larger meetings the same names appear again and again.[122] The majority were highly professionalized. Dynasties sprang up taking on the roles of judge, clerk of scales, starter or handicapper together or separately at several meetings. The Clarks at Newmarket and elsewhere from 1805 to 1889 or the Ford family in the Midlands and the north in the later nineteenth century were good examples.[123]

The office of judge was also lucrative. Judges had received 'presents' or deductions from the stakes won by the winners of certain important races in the first half of the century. In 1848 this was fixed at £50 for the Derby and £30 for the Oaks, the Cesarewitch and the Cambridgeshire by the Jockey Club.[124] Judges' pay related to the number of races and status of the meeting. At smaller meetings fees ranged from £10 to £25, although this sometimes included limited handicapping. Larger meetings could double this.[125]

Handicapping was another lucrative occupation, especially at the larger meetings. By the 1880s and the 1890s the Doncaster handicapper earned up to £105 annually. Smaller meetings would have less than half this sum. Starters were generally less well paid. Up to and beyond the 1870s few earned more than £10 at most meetings and £5 was a more common sum.[126] By this time some major courses were also appointing full-time course managers. The York manager was receiving £80 annually by 1895.[127]

The professionalization of jockeys and trainers began somewhat earlier. Private trainers worked for a single owner, sometimes on his estate, while public trainers working in one of the major training areas scattered throughout the country trained for several owners at one time. Public trainers were already common in Yorkshire and at Newmarket at the beginning of the nineteenth century and were soon also found elsewhere, which reflects the early commercialization of racing. The horse owners could co-operate, increasing the chances of betting coups and sound placement of horses.

Private trainers were fewer, around 20 per cent of the total, and often earned less. John Smith, Lord Strathmore's trainer at Streathlam up to 1811, never received more than £30 a year in wages although he also received 'board wages' and generous clothing and living expenses while accompanying horses to meetings, and was treated as a senior and important servant.[128] But by the 1830s it was being recognized that exclusive use of a top trainer could be a betting advantage, or a means to success in top races, and more generous salaries were supplemented by non-contractual productivity bonuses in the form of presents for big wins. In the 1830s Fobert was training Lord Eglinton's horses for a salary of £200, supplemented by presents of £100 when any of his horses won an important race and sometimes also received further presents from friends of the owner.[129]

Some public trainers had the income, status and lifestyle of 'gentlemen' in their own area even in the early nineteenth century, when the wills of successful trainers sometimes show four-figure sums on probate. By 1841 census data show their high standard of living, often with two or three servants.[130] After the 1860s five-figure incomes are common, although unsuccessful trainers and those who failed to save often died in poverty. Sometimes this was partly due to the trainers' weaknesses in terms of financial management.[131] It could also be a problem of cash flow or of owners' debts.[132]

Top jockeys were hiring out their services to a range of owners from before 1800, earning money from four main sources: fees for riding races and trials, retainers, presents and bets. Frank Buckle was already earning an estimated £1,200 per annum in the early 1820s.[133]

Basic fees for riding stood at 5 guineas for winning non-classic races, 3 guineas for losing races and 2 guineas for trials from early in the century.[134] Extra fees were often paid for classic races. Jem Robinson apparently received 100 guineas for his ride on Ephesus in the 1851 St. Leger.[135] The best jockeys got both a disproportionate number of rides and of winning horses, especially if they lived at Newmarket or in the south where there were opportunities for more rides.[136] However, fees could be difficult to obtain. Poor Jem Snowden once confessed to a friend at Carlisle races that 'the owner of this horse ... owes me three times as much in riding fees as the d—d stake is worth', and on another occasion he rode seven winners at Ayr and received only seven promises to pay.[137] Only in 1880 was a rule introduced enforcing the payment to the stakeholder of all fees to which jockeys were entitled.[138]

Top jockeys could also obtain a retaining fee or salary, related to their ability and reliability and fashionable demand for their services. Sam Chifney, first jockey to the Prince of Wales, received 200 guineas a year as early as 1790, but this was exceptional.[139] From the 1820s to the 1840s most retainer fees were rarely more than £50 and sometimes this included expenses.[140] By the 1850s the best riders' retainers were rising. Frank Butler, who rode for the powerful Scott stable at Malton, had General Anson as first master, followed in turn by John Bowes, Lord Chesterfield, Lord Derby, the Duke of Bedford, Baron Rothschild, Mr R. Nevill and Lord Glasgow.[141] In 1861 a top lightweight was receiving £600 and expenses.[142] Twenty years later Fred Archer was collecting £1,000 in individual retainers; indeed, in 1886 the Inland Revenue assessed his previous year's total income as £10,000.[143]

Commercialization of sport often leads to a heavy emphasis on the need to win. Presents to winning jockeys were becoming common as further inducements by the 1820s. *The Times* reporter in 1825 claimed that, although he 'had repeatedly heard of gentleman proprietors making scarcely any addition to their jockies' demand of £5 for riding a winning horse', he had also heard 'of very handsome complements, even amounting to hundreds by the more liberal.'[144] Classic races, especially the St. Leger, were particularly good sources for presents. Ben Smith received £1,500 from 'several distinguished supporters of the Turf' in 1824. In 1827 Jem

Robinson had presents made to him of £1,200 from the owner and grateful backers, and £1,500 was given on the 1830 St. Leger.[145]

Southern owners were somewhat slower to respond, although Connolly reputedly received nearly £1,000 for winning the 1834 Derby. Sim Templeman allegedly received £2,000 for winning the 1848 Derby and Job Marson £5,000 in 1850. These presumably were noteworthy because excessive. The most quoted figures up to the 1850s were between £300 and £1000.[146] Some, at least, of these 'presents' may, in fact, have been winnings as owners often placed bets for jockeys. Presents for non-classic winners were usually associated with a betting success, as when Mr Allen of Malton won a good stake in bets on the July Liverpool Cup and gave the little-known jockey Dodgson 50 sovereigns.[147]

From the late 1840s presents began rising more dramatically. By 1862 one racing insider believed that presents were given 'without exception in all great races'.[148] This was an exaggeration. Henry Custance's £100 received from the Scottish ironmaster James Merry for winning the 1860 Derby was the only present he received during the three years he rode for him. But by later in the century it was generally believed that income from presents was greater than the riding fees.[149]

Breeding for sale was another relatively commercial activity already found at the beginning of the nineteenth century. Over the century it changed from the predominantly part-time activity of gentry breeders, innkeepers, farmers and trainers to the dominance of the specialized stud farm and stud company, and from private contract selling to selling by auction.[150]

At the heart of most commercial breeding lay the the utilization of stallions. Only the most successful stallions went to stud and not all of these proved potent, but provided that some offspring proved to be winners, a stallion could earn money if marketed correctly.[151] Untried stallions had a more difficult job and advertisements would often offer coverage of 'dams of winners half price' as sweeteners. Stud fees rose steeply after mid-century (see Table 14).

In the 1840s a fashionable stallion covering about 40 mares a year would earn nearly £1,000, including costs.[152] In the 1890s the owner of a fashionable stallion could be obtaining a much higher profit. Over the years 1886–1905 the stallion St. Simon returned £228,693 in stud fees.[153] Fashion depended on the ability to breed winners, and up to the end of 1904 St. Simon had bred 271 winners of 506 races, worth over £510,000. The most lucrative stallions tended to stay in the hands of private breeders; breeding companies were often forced to charge lower fees. The value of top stallions shot up with stud fees. In 1836 Bay Middleton was sold for

TABLE 14
DISTRIBUTION OF STALLION STUD FEES 1809–99 BY PERCENTAGES

Date	0–10g	11–20g	21–30g	31–50g	51–75g	76–100g	More than 100g	Number of stallions in sample
1809	80	19	1	–	–			80
1839	65	28	6	1	–			80
1869	24	39	27	7	–	3		59
1899	32	25	18	13	–	6	5	294

Sources: *Racing Calendar*, 1809, 1839, 1869; *Ruff's Guide*, 1899.

£4,000, by 1873 Blair Atholl sold for £13,125 and Doncaster for £14,500 and by 1900 Flying Fox was sold for over £39,000.

Breeding from brood mares was less profitable, although their numbers expanded. The 735 brood mares of 1822 had reached 2,593 by 1872 and by 1900 the figure had reached 5,890.[154] Despite the constant demand of the foreign market, many writers accepted that breeding was 'a lottery',[155] and in reality many breeders bred at a loss.[156] The use of mathematical mean prices for bloodstock sales concealed the real risks of breeding, since very high prices for some fashionable studs significantly pushed up figures. Debates in the nineteenth century on the profit and loss of breeding were therefore often 'discussed in an unreliable spirit, owing to the ignorance prevailing on the subject'.[157]

Shifts upwards in the price of yearlings due to increased demand led to short-lived breeding studs being set up, which soon struggled once prices fell, although it was believed that a stud farm, judiciously run, could combine business with pleasure and occupation with profit, and at least 'minimize the chances of failure'.[158] Attempts to calculate the costs were made. *The Times* in 1874 claimed that yearlings then realized a profit if sold for over 100 guineas.[159] If that were so, then many small breeders and some large ones were certainly making a loss if selling at public auctions. During the 1887 season, when the mean auction price per foal or yearling reached just over £200 a head, apparently giving breeders a good profit, in reality 65 per cent of the foals and yearlings recorded in the auction figures in *Ruff's Guide* were sold for less than 100 guineas. Of all the breeding lots (all the horses sold by a breeder) sold, of various sizes, 28 per cent reached less than 50 guineas per head and a further 24 per cent went for less than a hundred guineas. So more than half of the breeders lost money at public sales, although they may have sold their best stock privately. However, in 1887 some 22 per cent of breeders sold their stock at an average of over 200 guineas a head so there were profits to be made for the minority of breeders lucky enough to have currently 'fashionable' stock.

TABLE 15
SALES AT AUCTION 1887–99

Date	Numbers of foals and yearlings auctioned	Different sires	Average price	Total
1887	639	192	199g	127,403g
1893	624	191	218g	136,078g
1895	636	192	263g	167,017g
1897	716	211	198g	141,600g
1899	811	234	181g	146,321g

Source: *Ruff's Guide.*

Although the prices of bloodstock rose over the period, the trends overall concealed significant short-term fluctuations. Fluctuations in the late-nineteenth-century auction market are illustrated in Table 15.

The group most vulnerable to fluctuation were the large-scale breeding companies, which rarely survived long-term. The first, the Rawcliffe Stud company, founded in 1851–52, adopted a business mode and marketed aggressively, but by 1862 the company was failing.[160] Further large-scale breeders entered in the 1870s, when the Middle Park stud sold up to 90 lots annually. But it experienced severe annual average price variation: as low as £105 per lot in 1858, an average of over £400 in 1866 and 1867, then dropping in the early 1870s to prices of £200 to £250 before rising again. Most joint-stock studs suffered difficulties in capitalization and were not attractive to the public.[161] Others, such as the Cobham stud, were badly managed.[162]

That some owners were also motivated by economic considerations is suggested by the increase in two-year-old racing after the 1840s. In 1829 the ratio of two- to three-year-old horses racing was 2:7, by 1859 it was 8:7, probably indicating a wish by owners to capitalize on their investment in horseflesh more quickly. While some, and not just the wealthier owners, treated racing as a hobby and others entered as part of inter-generational social mobility, other owners always clearly responded to the attraction of prize money. Unfortunately for owners, however, prize money fluctuated, and few could win more than they spent. Any rises in total prize money were followed by an increase in racehorse ownership and the number of horses racing, reducing averages (see Table 16).

Dividing the total prize money by the total numbers of competing horses shows a similar pattern. Between 1881 and 1890 mean prize money per horse was at its peak, nearly £207, but it then fell again. In 1892 the total prize money of £486,556 was shared among 2,559 competing horses. In 1913 prize money of £573,188 was shared among 4,021 horses.[163] Between

TABLE 16
PRIZE MONEY PER RACE 1802–62

Date	Number of races	Total prize money	Average prize money
1802	537	£71,780	£134
1822	883	£140,960	£160
1842	1,146	£182,910	£160
1862	2,171	£280,406	£129

Source: Anon., *Horse Racing: Early History* (1863), p.323.
These figures appear to have involved an estimated value for some of the cups which were commonly offered as prizes.

1891 and 1900 it was only £160 per horse and between 1901 and 1910 only £147.[164] Such figures were substantially below the annual costs of having a horse in training, some £366 in 1905.[165]

Owners could only reduce their costs by effective gambling, and the great majority gambled to a greater or lesser degree, although whether or not they succeeded is another matter.[166] Betters needed information and touts were employed to obtain it about other owners' horses. They were to be found in all major training areas even at the start of the nineteenth century. Later a more widespread interest in betting and the increase in the number of newspapers giving training information probably increased their numbers. By 1884 there were about 50 touts at Newmarket alone, and a social hierarchy was beginning to emerge, with the top touts earning up to £1,000 per annum.[167] A top tout was believed to be 'frequently a man of substance, wallowing in house property'.[168]

VI

This chapter has concentrated on the central commercial aspects, and certainly racing gave direct employment to many thousands of people. The evidence of *Ruff's Guide* suggests that in spring 1900 there were about 1,300 owners, 164 trainers, 95 jockeys and 92 apprentices. Sixty-four judges, starters and other licensed officials and 34 secretaries were employed by the racecourses. The training stables would have needed about 1,500 stable lads and the breeding studs would have required a similar number of lads and stud grooms.[169] An unknown further number would be involved to support the 'flapping' meetings which remain less well documented. Historians of betting have shrunk from estimating the numbers of bookmakers and tipsters. If McKibbin is correct in suggesting that up to four million people were betting more or less regularly by 1914, many thousands would have been needed. In the mid-nineteenth century *Ruff's Guide* has a figure of around a hundred trainers, and over 200 jockeys and apprentices, so the totals involved direct in racing were probably around two-thirds of the 1900 figure.

Nothing illustrates the commercial importance of racing more than the range of organizations from within the sport which emerged from the late nineteenth century when it was under attack by the National Anti-Gambling League. *The Sportsman* set up the Sporting League in 1894 and the similar Anti-Puritan League was formed in 1897. In 1902 the *Sporting Life,* concerned to counter the possibility of anti-gambling legislation affecting its revenue, threw its weight behind first the National Sporting League, founded around 1900, and then in 1907 the Turf Guardian Society. The Racing Correspondents Association, representing tipsters, was in existence by 1902. Two other key associations were the Racecourse Association and the Racehorse Owners' Association.

Bookmaker bodies also emerged. The Commission Agents Guarantee Association was formed in 1901 with objectives which included the legalization of betting and the licensing of bookmakers, registration of defaulting clients, and the formation of branches to secure the return of municipal election candidates pledged to support this.[170] Its 500 to 600 members were concentrated in the north-east, the West Riding, London, Manchester, Liverpool and Birmingham. The Bookmakers' Protection Association and the Society for the Suppression of Street Betting and Compulsory Registration of Bookmakers (created about 1906) were national associations with strong regional links. There were also regional groups such as the Leeds and Bradford Association of Bookmakers (*c.*1901) which had some 50 members in 1902.[171]

Significant indirect employment was also created by racing. This included gatesmen and other racecourse employees, racing journalists and newspaper publishers, blacksmiths, saddlers, veterinary surgeons, cab and omnibus drivers, telegraphists, publicans, gold and silversmiths, sporting artists, auctioneers, hotel keepers, prostitutes, touts, policemen, race detectives, bookies' runners and others. Printers, for example, produced race cards, betting books and judges' books, as well as sporting prints. A whole genre of sporting art centred around the racing and breeding world.[172]

This chapter has argued that racing was among the first highly commercialized sports industries to emerge. Profits were initially made by race organizers by indirect means, through the supply of food, drink and other services. By the mid-nineteenth century the nature of commercialization was changing, with profits made by shareholders in grandstand companies and by course lessees, as well as through the supply of goods and services. At the same time, however, the costs of putting on meetings were rising.

After the 1870s profits at many courses were increasingly made through the turnstiles direct, but costs were now higher still. This change in the commercial approach, increasing specialization, had a number of consequences for racing. First, it led to a much less integrated sense of racing's links to the wider communities which the meetings served. Secondly, it affected the nature of the meetings themselves. They became less carnivalistic, less prone to excess and there was more focus on the racing and betting itself, as more limits were placed on access. Thirdly, it made it much more difficult for new meetings to set up and offer the level of prize money necessary to attract the best horses, while making it almost impossible for many older meetings to survive. Finally, and this links to the following chapter, the changing economic imperatives and new kinds of investment in racing aided the rise of the Jockey Club.

NOTES

1. H. Strutfield, 'Racing in 1890', *Nineteenth Century*, Vol.27 (1890), p.925.
2. *Sporting Magazine*, September 1831, p.361. *Victoria County History of Sussex*, Vol.II, p.457.
3. Based on a survey of the *Sporting Magazine* and local newspapers from 1840 to 1850.
4. W. Vamplew, *The Turf* (1976), pp.19–20.
5. See Vamplew, *The Turf*, pp.35–6.
6. A. Rous, 'Horse Racing 1866', quoted in J. Fairfax-Blakeborough, *Northern Turf History*, Vol.III, *York and Doncaster* (1950), p.11. *Sporting Magazine*, December 1856, p.387.
7. 'Doncaster Races; a safe investment', *The Times*, 15 February 1866.
8. *South Durham Herald*, 12 August 1871.
9. *Carlisle Journal*, 15 September 1838.
10. *Durham County Advertiser*, 8 June 1888.
11. 'Doncaster', *Bailey's Magazine*, October 1887, p.130.
12. York Archives, Copy to York Town Clerk of the agreement between the Mayor, Aldermen and citizens of Chester and the Chester Race Company (1891).
13. See R. Hale, 'The Demise of Horse-Racing in Lancaster and Preston', Undergraduate Dissertation, Lancaster University 1991, pp.22–3, 33–5 for examples adversely affecting local meetings.
14. *Doncaster Reporter*, 4 September 1867. Houses were still being taken for Ascot week in the early twentieth century, *The Times*, 6 June 1911.
15. Sheffield Record Office, WWM Racing Vouchers for Doncaster 1783–1827 and York 1783–1819.
16. Fairfax-Blakeborough, *York and Doncaster*, p.297.
17. Minutes of Evidence given before the Select Committee on Gambling, 1844, Q.1030. 'Clubs as accessories of the national sports', *Sporting Magazine*, March 1853, p.169. In 1841 the mayor argued that property would not be of so much value were it not for the races. See *Doncaster Gazette*, 3 September 1841.
18. F. Simpson, *Chester Races: Their Early History* (Chester, 1925); A Chester Tradesman, *Chester Races: Do They Pay?* (Chester, n.d.), p.7; J.S. Howson (Dean of Chester), *Chester Races* (Chester, 1870), p.6.
19. Our Van, *Baily's Magazine*, April 1876, p.297.
20. *The Times*, 13 September 1860.
21. In Newcastle in 1865 cab drivers and omnibus drivers were not only busy cleaning their best-

looking machines but also 'patching up crazy old shandridians' to cash in on the chance of profit; *Newcastle Daily Journal*, 28 June 1865. At Ripon the Crown and Anchor and the Black Bull were used for stabling; *Ripon Chronicle*, 8 August 1857.

22. *Stockton Herald*, 21 August 1880.
23. An Octogenarian, *Reminiscences of Old Manchester and Salford* (Manchester, 1887), p.27 believed race week there was 'not a good one for managers'.
24. Newcastle Theatre Royal advertised 'Great Attractions for the Race Week' in 1865 and got full houses; *Newcastle Daily Journal*, 27 June 1865.
25. 'Vandriver', *Baily's Magazine*, November 1869, p.270.
26. *Doncaster Gazette*, 17 September 1841.
27. Fairfax-Blakeborough, *York and Doncaster*, p.128.
28. J. Crump, 'The great carnival of the year: Leicester races in the nineteenth century', *Transactions, Leicestershire History & Archaeological Society*, Vol.58, 1982–83, p.61.
29. *Yorkshireman,* 1 February 1845.
30. Lancashire Record Office, Preston, DDX 103/4, Record of meetings of proprietors of Preston Races, Minutes of 9 July 1829.
31. At Beverley a race audit dinner attended by some 30 or 40 supporters was held each September in the grandstand, run by one of the local landlords who catered at the course; *Beverley Guardian*, 17 September 1864.
32. *Newcastle Daily Chronicle*, 9 May 1864.
33. *Sporting Magazine*, July 1838, p.255.
34. Ibid., October 1851, p.225.
35. Cheshire County Record Office, D4222/24, Knutsford Race Committee Minutes 1849–52.
36. *Doncaster Gazette*, 3 September 1841; *Carlisle Journal*, 15 September 1838.
37. D. Brailsford, *British Sport: a Social History* (Cambridge, 1992).
38. Crump, 'The great carnival', p.66.
39. A letter to one East Riding landed proprietor from the Beverley committee claimed that a few of the gentry of the Riding were being approached to maintain the meeting's good character and prestige, and named the high-status aristocracy and gentry who had already subscribed; Hull University Archives, DDBC/4/8, letter from E. Crosskill, chairman of the race committee to T. Sykes, 28 May 1880.
40. Simpson, *Chester Races*.
41. Richmond Corporation were subscribing £60 to the cup in 1821; Northallerton Record Office, Richmond Racing papers, DC/RMB.
42. 'Turf pencillings', *Sporting Magazine*, October 1853, p.271.
43. Simpson, *Chester Races*, pp.10–11.
44. See Howson, *Chester Races*, p.5.
45. Vamplew, *The Turf*, p.32.
46. J. Tolson, 'The Railways and Racing', PhD thesis, De Montfort University Leicester, forthcoming.
47. In 1847, for example, the Newcastle and Carlisle railway gave 'the usual contribution of 10g[uineas] to the race fund' at Newcastle; *Newcastle Journal*, 17 June 1847.
48. Nevertheless, race committees sought funding from railways. At Ascot in 1853 the Great Western Railway gave £100 towards the race fund, but the South Western Railway refused; *The Times*, 6 June 1853. When the new Manchester Castle Irwell course was opened, one of the first actions of the company was to write to two important railway companies asking both for special transport facilities and whether they would 'give a sum of money to be run for as a stake'; Salford Archives, Minutes of the Manchester Racecourse Company Ltd, 18 February 1868.
49. G.J. Cawthorne and R.S. Herod, *Royal Ascot: Its History and Associations* (1902), p.72.
50. D. Laird, *Royal Ascot* (1976), p.100.
51. S. Lewis, *A Topographical Dictionary of England*, Vol.II (1849), p.180.
52. Public Record Office, BT 31/1946/8150, Carlisle Grandstand Company; BT 31/996/1533, Newcastle Grand Stand Company.
53. Fairfax-Blakeborough, *York and Doncaster*, pp.268, 280; *The Times*, 22 September 1825, 15 September 1853; *Doncaster Gazette*, 11 September 1891.
54. J. Fairfax-Blakeborough, *Chester Races* (1951), p.13.
55. Cawthorne and Herod, *Royal Ascot*, p.72; *York Herald*, 12 April 1851.

56. Doncaster Record Office, AB/2/2/29, Minutes of the Race Committee, 14 November 1851, 20 November 1851.
57. See Laird, *Royal Ascot*, p.102.
58. Doncaster Record office, AB/2/2/29, Minutes of the Race Committee 1867; Crump, 'The great carnival', p.62.
59. Early examples include the betting stand at Ascot, the Dee stand at Chester and Maw's stand at Doncaster.
60. See Howson, *Chester Races*, p.4.
61. Vamplew, *The Turf*, p.21.
62. Doncaster Record Office, AB/2/2/29, Minutes of the Race Committee, 2 July 1866.
63. At Durham innkeepers subscribing to the Subscription Plate could erect booths on 'the usual terms' in 1795; Fairfax-Blakeborough, *Northern Turf History*, Vol.II. *Extinct Race Meetings* (1949), p.87. At Richmond booths were dependent on subscription; North Yorkshire Record Office, DC/RMB, Richmond racing papers. At Manchester booths were auctioned; *Manchester Guardian*, 8 May 1824, 14 May 1831.
64. See Cawthorne and Herod, *Royal Ascot*, p.72.
65. Select Committee on Gaming, 1844, VI Q.1388–93.
66. At some courses at the mid-century tents were charged the appropriate fraction of £100 per acre per day; 'Clubs as accessories of the national sports', *Sporting Magazine*, March 1853, p.166.
67. Newcastle Herbage Committee, 'Newcastle Races: Lists of Tents and Standage', held at Newcastle Reference Library.
68. Doncaster Record Office, AB/2/2/29, Minutes of the Race Committee, 1858 show that Doncaster charged rent to the telegraph company and even charged its clerks a shilling for entrance to the enclosure.
69. *Sporting Magazine*, June 1825, quoted by Fairfax-Blakeborough, *Extinct Race Meetings*, pp.157–60.
70. Vamplew, *The Turf*, p.27.
71. J. Fairfax-Blakeborough, *Horseracing in Scotland*, pp.75ff ; *Racing Calendar*, 1857.
72. J. Gale, *The Blaydon Races* (Newcastle, 1970), p.18.
73. *Manchester Courier*, 15 May 1847.
74. 'The Omnibus', *Sporting Magazine*, July 1868, p.5.
75. Ibid., August 1868, p.76.
76. Richmond was charging a shilling by 1889 in an attempt to break even, *Darlington and Stockton Times*, 19 July 1889. Durham began by charging 6d in 1881 but crowds were down; *Durham Chronicle*, 3 April 1881.
77. *The Times*, 25 November 1913.
78. J. Wigley, *The Rise and Fall of the Victorian Sunday* (Manchester, 1980), shows that, despite the sound and fury of the move to keep Sunday free from some leisure activities, its influence was limited.
79. Quoted in Fairfax-Blakeborough, *York and Doncaster*, p.156.
80. Doncaster Record Office, AB/2/2/5/1, Minutes of the Race Committee, 10 November 1886. By this point the Committee was maintaining full registers of, for instance, private boxes and county stand ticket-holders, details of booth rentals, and general cashbooks which provide an excellent insight into course management at this period.
81. See Cawthorne and Herod, *Royal Ascot*, pp.191–3.
82. *Newcastle Daily Chronicle*, 9 June 1893. In 1882 Stockton booths raised from £47 to £8 depending on the site; *North Star*, 4 August 1882. At Doncaster booths raised from £350 for the largest permanent booth to £70 for a temporary one; *Doncaster Gazette*, 12 June 1891.
83. This had been done at Aintree in Liverpool from its development in the 1830s and was found at Stockton by 1841; *York Herald*, 10 July 1841. At Manchester they charged 30 shillings the box or 40 shillings a double stable, plus provender at 5 shillings a day in 1868; 'The Omnibus', *Sporting Magazine*, July 1868, p.5. By the twentieth century stabling was being provided free.
84. *Beverley Guardian*, 19 June 1875.
85. *Darlington and Stockton Times*, 19 July 1890, 15 May 1892. At Durham the decline in subscriptions had forced enclosure on the committee, but most remaining subscribers discontinued their subscription at that point; *Newcastle Daily Chronicle*, 22 March 1883; *Durham County Advertiser*, 8 June 1888.

86. Building the course cost £700, plus the cost of the grandstand, built by a race committee for £300. Here corporation support meant that a ground rent of only one shilling a year was paid; *Lonsdale Magazine*, Vol.1, 1820, p.471.
87. C. Ramsden, *Farewell Manchester* (1966), pp.8–17; *Sporting Magazine*, July 1868, p.5. Salford Library holds Manchester Racecourse Association Minutes from 1867 to 1880, Deed of Manchester Racecourse.
88. The agreement between the Chester Race Company and the Corporation and citizens of Chester in 1898 laid out detailed requirements for the 21-year lease, focusing particularly on the use to which receipts were put. One-eighth of the receipts were to be paid as rent, with a minimum figure of £500 imposed. Half of the remainder was for expenses, debts, dividends and other financial issues such as the appointment of directors, building regulations and payment for extra police at the meeting and in the city. The other half had to be used 'for racing purposes'. There was to be only one meeting a year. The course was to be enclosed ten days before and stands, refreshment tents and temporary urinals erected. Regulations were laid down both about the times of opening and closing of places of refreshment, and the prohibition of gambling. An entrance charge was to be levied. Those riding on the course had to be controlled and there were to be no shooting galleries, swing boats, etc.; York Archives, copy of Chester Agreement sent to York Town Clerk in 1901.
89. G. Benson, *The Freemen of York and their Connection with the Strays* (1912 edn), quoted by Fairfax-Blakeborough, *York and Doncaster*, pp.35–6.
90. *Newcastle Chronicle*, 2 April 1864.
91. Doncaster Record Office, AB/2/2/29, Race Committee Records.
92. *Beverley Guardian*, 19 June 1875. Stockton got a paddock only in 1882; *North Star*, 16 August 1882.
93. *Newcastle Daily Chronicle*, 15 June 1883.
94. See Laird, *Royal Ascot*, p.101.
95. At York the local Watch Committee had to recruit extra police to supplement its own hard-pressed force, and the cost of this doubled between 1871 and 1891. York Archives, Watch Committee Minutes, 7 August and 9 November 1871, 10 August and 9 November 1891.
96. A Durham balance sheet of 1859 has a charge for 'County Policemen Refreshment'. Fairfax-Blakeborough, *Extinct Race Meetings*, p.95.
97. *Newcastle Courant*, 29 June 1866.
98. York Archives, Minutes of York Race Committee, August 1893. Manchester had similar costs at this time; see Salford Archives, U322/AM1, Manchester Race Committee Minutes, 1880–1902.
99. Crump, 'The great carnival', p.71. As crowds grew at the unenclosed courses in the 1890s such costs were dwarfed by those at Doncaster, where in 1891 the Corporation paid £656.2s.4d. for police, special constables and detectives, a figure which rose to over £800 by 1896. *Doncaster Gazette*, 4 September 1891, 11 September 1891. By contrast the small Blaydon meeting needed police costs of only about £20 to cope with fewer than 10,000 people in 1894.
100. Beverley's clear date in 1883 encouraged good entries and the funds benefited far more than in the subsequent year when it clashed with Ascot; *Beverley Guardian*, 7 June 1884.
101. *The Sporting Magazine*, July 1852, p 78. The 'disturbances in India' deprived Doncaster of 'many of its influential supporters' in 1857; *The Times*, 15 September 1857.
102. *Durham Chronicle*, 22 July 1887.
103. *Baily's Magazine*, April 1876, p.297.
104. For Shrewbury see *Sporting Life*, 19 November 1859.
105. *The Sporting Magazine*, July 1848, p.3.
106. Ibid., March 1853, pp.166–7.
107. *Sporting Life*, 25 June 1859.
108. P. Fitzgerald, MP, 'A letter addressed to a member of the Manchester Racing Association giving reasons for refusing to renew the lease of the present race course'. Salford Public Reference Library.
109. *Sporting Magazine*, July 1851, p.78.
110. Costs of setting up varied: Manchester, 1868 (£40,000), Gosforth Park, 1881 (£60,000), Sandown Park, 1885 (£26,000), Haydock, 1898 (£34,000), Newbury racecourse, 1906 (£80,000); W. Vamplew, *Pay up and Play the Game*, p.57; Public Record Office,

BT31/1385/3874, Manchester Racecourse Company; M. Kirkup, *The Pitman's Derby: A History of the Northumberland Plate* (Newcastle, 1990), p.16, and C. F. Moffat, *For a Purse of Gold (Newcastle*, 1986), pp.12–13.

111. *Newcastle Daily Chronicle*, 6 March 1883; *Newcastle Daily Journal*, 9 June 1893.
112. See Vamplew, *Pay Up*, p.101.
113. M.J. Huggins, 'Mingled pleasure and speculation; the survival of the enclosed racecourses on Teesside 1855–1902', *International Journal of the History of Sport*, Vol.3, No.2 (1986), pp.158–72.
114. Public Record Office, BT31/2051/8990; BT31 3128/18026; BT31 3252/19096; BT31 3389/20285; BT31/3624/22327; BT31/4406/28648; BT31/ 4883/32466.
115. See Vamplew, *Pay Up*, p.57. Fairfax-Blakeborough, *Extinct Race Meetings*, examines a number of northern examples.
116. Earl of Suffolk and Berkshire and W.G. Craven, *Badminton Library: Racing and Steeplechasing* (1886), p.62. He saw the job as 'withal not an unprofitable berth'.
117. E.g., at Northallerton, *York Herald*, 4 September 1813; Newcastle, *York Herald*, 4 June 1831. Even after enclosure the clerk at Catterick Bridge was still earning money by this means. See North Yorkshire Record Office, ZRL 4/7/1, Records of the meeting for 1886.
118. *Yorkshireman,* 12 October 1839.
119. The Richmond clerk in 1825 charged a guinea. North Riding Record Office, DC/RMB, Richmond Racing Papers, 1825.
120. Sheffield Record Office, WWM F130, shows that Fitzwilliam gave presents to the York clerk of £15 in 1812 and £21 in 1815.
121. *Sporting Magazine*, October 1860, p.374.
122. John Orton, 1802–45, the York bookseller, racing writer and coffee-house owner, was also judge there and at 15 or more Scottish and northern courses in the 1830s. See *York Herald*, 12 October 1839. His successor R. Johnson, originally a sporting sub-editor and reporter, was initially only judge at York and Ripon, but by 1846 he was judge at nine northern meetings, *York Herald*, 29 August 1846. See also J. Osborne, *The Horsebreeder's Handbook* (1898), p.xc.
123. For a biography of J.F. Clark see *Baily's Magazine*, June 1876, pp.385ff. W.J. Ford earned £86 at York as judge, handicapper and clerk of scales in 1886 and received £110 the following year; York Archives, Minutes of York Racing Committee, 3 January 1887.
124. See C.M. Prior, *The History of the Racing Calendar and Stud Book* (1926), pp.217, 227.
125. J. Fairfax-Blakeborough, *The Analysis of the Turf* (1927), Ch.10; Doncaster Record Office, AB 2/2/5/1 and AB/2/2/29 Race Committee Records show fees rising through the century.
126. York Archives, Minutes of York Racing Committee, 10 March 1854; Northallerton Record Office, ZRL 4/7/1, Catterick Meeting 1886; Fairfax-Blakeborough, *Extinct Race Meetings*, p.95. As late as 1896 the Hamilton Park starter earned only 2 guineas at one meeting, although at Doncaster even the spring meeting then paid £30, while clerks of the scales equally rarely earned more than £10 as late as the 1890s; Fairfax-Blakeborough, p.x.
127. York Archives, Minutes of York Racing Committee, 6 January 1895; Durham County Record Office, D/ST/C1/10/58–61.
128. Durham County Record Office, D/ST/C1/10/58–61.
129. M.J. Huggins, *Kings of the Moor: North Yorkshire Racecourse Trainers 1760–1900* (Middlesbrough, 1991), p.19.
130. Ibid., p.29.
131. Job Marson, a successful Beverley jockey and subsequent trainer, spent most of his training career in the 1830s in debt before his final bankruptcy in the 1840s; North Riding Record Office, ZPB III 6/4, accounts between William Allen and Job Marson.
132. Will Chifney went bankrupt in 1845, owed £15,000 by 'noblemen and others' but 'had no hope of getting it'; *Bell's Life*, 19 January 1845.
133. *Sporting Magazine*, June 1824, p.128.
134. Durham Record Office, D/St/C1/10/6, account of John Smith's receipts and expenditure as trainer 1808–11.
135. *Doncaster Gazette*, 19 September 1851.
136. When Tom Aldcroft, the Middleham jockey, was featured in *Baily's Magazine* in 1862 it was said of him, 'if he were to shift his quarters from Middleham to Newmarket ... his income tax would be trebled'; *Baily's Magazine*, January 1862.

137. A. Scott, *Turf Memories of Sixty Years* (1925), p.70.
138. Earl of Suffolk and Berkshire and W.G. Craven, *Racing and Steeplechasing Racing*, p.106.
139. R. Onslow, *Headquarters: A History of Newmarket and its Racing* (1983), p.69. Ben Smith had a retaining fee from the Earl of Strathmore of £52.10s, plus his 'expenses and disbursements' in 1805. Durham Record Office, D/St/C1/ 10/60, Accounts of receipts and expenditure of Lord Strathmore's stud.
140. The Middleham jockey John Cartwright signed a contract agreeing 'to ride the racehorses of Mr Orde of Nunnykirk for the year 1838 he receiving for such riding the sum of 50 guineas which sum is to include every expense whatever' and had received £60 the previous year without a retainer. Northumberland Record Office, NRO 1356 D2, Letter to Orde from J. Cartwright, 20 December 1838. NRO 1356/D/15, Training bill for 1837.
141. Over the period 1843–55 he received from Bowes alone an average of just under £106 annually made up of fees and a £35 retainer. Durham Record Office, Strathmore Box 162, Bowes training costs.
142. Harry Grimshaw was receiving this from Lord Hastings, his first master; *Newcastle Courant*, 30 March 1866. The same year Mr Eastwood was writing to his trainer William Oates at Richmond, saying 'you must try to engage some good sporting jockey, even if you give him £300 or upwards per season'. J. Fairfax-Blakeborough, *Northern Turf History Vol.1: Hambleton and Richmond* (1948), p.317.
143. J. Welcome, *Fred Archer: His Life and Times* (1967), pp.34ff; *Newcastle Daily Chronicle*, 8 February 1886. By 1891 Jamie Woodburn, another lightweight, was receiving £1,000 from Falmouth House; *The Racing World and Newmarket Sportsman*, 25 April 1891.
144. *The Times*, 23 September 1825.
145. Orton, *Turf Annals of York and Doncaster*, p.685; *York Chronicle*, 27 September 1827; *The Times*, 24 September 1830; Vamplew, *The Turf: a Social and Economic History of Horse Racing* (1976), p.146.
146. For examples of presents, see *Yorkshire Gazette*, 7 June 1834, 16 June 1849, *Bell's Life*, 22 September 1850; *York Herald*, 20 September 1851; *Doncaster Gazette*, 29 August 1851.
147. *York Herald*, 24 July 1841.
148. Anon., *Horse Racing: Its History and Early Records* (1863), p.327.
149. Fairfax-Blakeborough, *Analysis of the Turf*, pp.26–7.
150. Auctioneers were already active in sales of studs and thoroughbreds generally by the late eighteenth century, normally taking 5 per cent commission on sales. They were active across the country in the early nineteenth century, but as private-contract sales disappeared, Tattersall's came to dominate the thoroughbred trade across most of the country. R. Orchard, *Tattersalls: 200 Years of Sporting History* (1953), provides an overview.
151. Early nineteenth-century advertisements may be found in a wide range of local and regional newspapers, although printed cards and larger sheets were also used. Later in the century free publicity could be obtained from sports writers' descriptions of stud visits.
152. See Vamplew, *Pay Up*, p.110. Forty mares was a traditionally accepted maximum. Mat Dawson argued that 40 mares was the 'proper number' to be put to a stallion in his evidence to the 1890 Royal Commission on Horse-Breeding, 3rd Report, Minutes of Evidence 1890 [C.6034], XXVII.
153. T.A. Cook, *A History of the English Turf* (1905), pp.xxi–ii.
154. C.M. Prior, *The Early History of the Thoroughbred Horse* (1926), pp.21–36. Not all of these would be covered, however.
155. E.g., letter from Admiral Rous, quoted in *Manchester Courier*, 4 June 1869; 'Is racehorse breeding a lottery?', *Baily's Magazine*, Vol.62, October 1894, p.218.
156. See M.J. Huggins, 'Thoroughbred breeding in the North and East Ridings of Yorkshire in the nineteenth century', *Agricultural History Review*, Vol.42 (1994), pp.115–25.
157. 'The stud company', *Baily's Magazine*, Vol.22 (1872), p.131.
158. Ibid., Vol.29 (1876–77), p.387, Vol.62 (October 1894), p.220.
159. *The Times*, 22 June 1874.
160. Public Record Ofice, BT 31/58/226.
161. 'Stud Gossip', *Baily's Magazine*, Vol.29 (1877), p.378. For examples, see Public Record Office, BT31/1323/3448, Low Field Stud Farm, 1867; BT31/2265/10835, The National Stud Ltd, 1876; BT31/2357/11588, Enfield Stud Ltd, 1877.

162. W. Allison, *My Kingdom for a Horse* (1919), p.250. The stud was finally liquidated in 1887; Public Record Office, BT31/3581/13530. Its failure was blamed on 'bad management and tortuous finance'; *Country Life Illustrated*, 19 June 1897, p.675.
163. R. Black, *Horseracing in England: A Synoptic Review* (1893), p.266.
164. Calculated from data in *Ruff's Guide to the Turf*.
165. See Vamplew, *Pay Up*, pp.104–5.
166. Ibid., p.107.
167. 'About racing touts and tipsters', *Baily's Magazine*, Vol.42 (August 1884), p.414.
168. 'About touts', ibid., Vol.62 (1895), p.377.
169. Based on the number of horses in training in *Ruff's Guide*, 1899 and the number of brood mares and foals identified in *The Stud Book*, Vol.19 (1901).
170. For details of its objectives and membership, see 1902 Select Committee on Betting, Qs1120, 1231.
171. Ibid., Evidence of F. Spruce, Q1011.
172. Most of these have an unhistorical view of the wider social context. See *inter alia* O. Beckett, *J.F. Herring and Sons* (1981); J. Fairley, *Racing in Art* (New York, 1990); C. Lane, *Harry Hall's Classic Winners* (1990). An exception is C. Deuchar, *Sporting Art in Eighteenth Century England: a Social and Political History* (New Haven, CT, 1988).

7

The Jockey Club: Power and Control over the Sport

Changing economic imperatives, kinds of investment in racing and more commercialism gave an impetus to the rise of the Jockey Club in the later nineteenth century, and thus to the centralization of racing. Most modern sports historians have wrongly dated this rise much earlier, thus helping to contribute to the misreading of racing's more general, socio-historical significance.

Holt, for example, saw the Jockey Club emerging as a regulatory body before the formal creation of national governing bodies by the Victorians, while Beckett saw the 1840s as the time when the Club 'finally established itself as the sport's accepted governing body'.[1] Vamplew, in a more thoroughgoing review of the Club, saw it as 'making a bid for power' quite early in the century, going on 'the offensive' in the 1830s, instituting 'turf reform' and the imposition of order in the 1840s under Lord George Bentinck, by which time other courses recognized the 'supreme authority of the Club'. He then argued that, following an undermining of its authority between 1846 and 1855, Admiral Rous worked hard to regain the Club's authority and by the 1870s the Club had 'tightened its grip on racing', a grip which strengthened after the development of the enclosed course so that by the last decades of the century the Club was the undisputed authority.[2]

While Vamplew is correct about his assessment of the latter phase, the limitations of his sources have led to a misinterpretation of the earlier nineteenth-century Jockey Club role. This chapter argues that Club power was largely reactively defined rather than purposefully enforced for much of the period. In reality, up to and sometimes beyond the 1860s, outside Newmarket and a minority of elite courses, the Club was ineffective, with some influence but little actual power except in Parliament. The Club was then reluctant to enforce any rules which might adversely affect upper-class investment in the sport. But by the later nineteenth century the Jockey Club's response to changing economic imperatives gave it much more influence over major 'recognized' meetings (although not over more local ones). The journalistic, secondary racing literature written at that time tended to read that influence back into the past, thus influencing later historians.[3] By contrast, the Club's ability to influence parliamentary legislation had declined, and it had withdrawn from any attempt to control the majority of smaller, 'unrecognized' flat races.

Previous historians have largely relied on material produced after 1890, usually synthesizing existing secondary sources and have been highly dependent on the views of several earlier historians of the Club itself and its supposed leaders Bentinck and Rous.[4] Club historians were selective in their use of material, which was interpreted from a pro-Club perspective, and were concerned with portraying a relatively unproblematic and progressive growth in its power.

The same could be said of some earlier nineteenth-century writers. Many of the books and magazine articles on racing produced during the century were by writers who associated with Club members or were more knowledgeable about the elite courses such as Newmarket, Ascot, Goodwood or Epsom.[5] Weatherby's *Racing Calendar*, much used as a source, was also biased. Its founder, James Weatherby, had been Keeper of the Matchbook at Newmarket in 1771, and when he began publishing the *Calendar* in 1773 it soon therefore became the *de facto* mouthpiece of the Club, and continued so under his successors (who acted as *de facto* clerks to the course at Newmarket and later elsewhere) until it was finally purchased by the Club in 1902. It published details of such matters as the Club wished to make known more generally, and not those it wished to keep dark.

This chapter therefore provides a critical reassessment of the role of the Club in the sport, using a wider range of material. It brings out more clearly how the Club extended its influence in particular ways and the separate chronology of different advances in its power. It addresses key questions. How important was its control over Newmarket? What might a body attempting to administer racing be expected to do in terms of managing appeals, rule making, control over meetings and betting, and to what extent did the Club attempt to do it? To what extent did it succeed? How and when were the several issues resolved? What was the relationship of the Club to the state and legislation? Such questions are valuable in illuminating the larger ones about the ways in which an over-concentration on the Jockey Club has led to a neglect of racing's wider socio-historical significance.

I

The 'Jockey Club', the sport's most important single body since the eighteenth century, was not a club in the modern sense nor were its members professional race riders. Members were 'jockeys' in the earlier sense of being people who managed or had to do with horses and were upper-class, while any club function was confined to the setting of the Newmarket races.

Most meetings had upper-class racing clubs associated with them, but at Newmarket royal associations and upper-class attendance led to the formation of a particularly select, self-elected, aristocratic, private club, the Jockey Club, in or before 1752.[6] By 1758 its order concerning the weighing-in of jockeys suggests that it was regulating all Newmarket racing. Its membership was drawn from those of aristocratic and gentry background, as it was when membership was first brought to public awareness in the *Racing Calendar* in 1835.

The Club's membership totals were small, less than a hundred, and the active membership was smaller still. At any time some members were aged, others were inexperienced; some were regular attenders at Newmarket and other race-meetings, others had ceased to attend even Newmarket meetings. Some were owners, others were more interested in breeding. Among the membership attitudes to and knowledge about both racing and betting could be anywhere on the continuum from deep to shallow. This meant that on many issues the membership was disunited and it spoke only rarely with one voice. On subjects such as betting, the racing of two-year-olds or the control of jockeys the membership was split.

Any original power the Club possessed lay almost entirely in the control it exercised over Newmarket, where seven lengthy meetings were held each year, far more than the single meetings held elsewhere before the railways came, and where a significant proportion of trainers and jockeys were therefore based. As the Heath slowly fell into the hands of the Jockey Club after 1808, when it first set about acquiring leaseholds and freeholds of land, it was able to raise revenue by imposing an annual heath tax on each horse racing or being trained there: one guinea in 1819, two in 1864. Further rises in 1873, 1880 and 1887 brought it to seven guineas. The Club was able to warn off the Heath those who flouted its rules, following the establishment of its legal right by the Duke of Portland in 1827, although this was rarely exercised.[7] From early in the nineteenth century Newmarket racing gave substantial employment to a majority of top southern trainers and jockeys and offered regular, high, prize money, so the Club was a critical definer of reality for many owners and their employees, even those not directly associated with it. It published a membership list in the *Calendar* in 1835, possibly to call attention to its members' status in a period when some upper-class support for racing was in temporary decline. For much of the century members owned a substantial proportion of all horses in training. As late as 1869 they still owned almost a quarter, many trained at Newmarket.[8]

Financially the Club struggled to maintain its local power during the years around the mid-century, as northern horses dominated the classic events. Fewer top trainers were to be found at Newmarket as a result; there were many empty yards, and many rich owners, including many Club members, had their horses trained elsewhere. Such a lack of Newmarket racing success is part of the explanation for the Club's weakness during this period. By 1855 it was in deficit, since few spectators attended Newmarket. Following 1856, however, when the finances were put in the charge of Rous, a steward and virtual president of the Club from 1859 to 1875, the accounts were in better shape, while renewed classic successes from 1863 onwards revived Newmarket racing.[9]

The Club's control over Newmarket training and racing, and hence indirectly over many of those involved in racing more generally, was a major factor in its growth in power after 1870. By 1883 some one thousand horses, almost half of those being trained, were being trained on Jockey Club land and all trainers there were required to be licensed. Licences had been refused to several trainers, putting others under more pressure to conform or lose their livelihood. Previously many Club members had had their horses trained in the north where the Club was less powerful. More recently, influential northern members such as Lord Durham, the Earl of Zetland and Sir James Lowther, had brought their horses to Newmarket. In the period from 1875 to 1914 horses trained at Newmarket were regularly successful in the major races, usually winning over half of the top 20 or 30. Indeed in 1883 19 of the most important 22 events were won by horses trained at Newmarket, and in 1903, a poor year, 15 of the top 32.[10] Over the period 1895–99 eight of the top 15 winning owners were Jockey Club members. At the same time Club income was increasing. The heath tax, control over Newmarket Heath and the rapid shift first to charges for carriages in 1866, then improvements to existing stands, the building of a large grandstand in 1875, further enclosures, the purchase of the Exning Estate in 1881 and yet other developments thereafter brought growing financial wealth.[11] From the 1890s the Club accounts show that income from racing, training, the Exning Estate, the Jockey Club Rooms and Chambers and Southfield Farm was under careful financial management.[12] The final confirmation of the Club's commercial attitude came in 1908 when it changed its attitude to the railway-excursion traffic outside the days of its three major betting races, and approached the Great Eastern Railway for excursions to be run from London on every day of every meeting.[13]

II

In examining the extent to which the writ of the Club ran beyond Newmarket the situation is more complex. Thus we now examine the Club's original role as a court of appeal, its use of rules to influence courses elsewhere, the modifications to its rules and the extent to which its jurisdiction was extended at several points.

One of the first ways in which the Club established a wider influence was through its arbitration on limited numbers of disputes elsewhere. An appeal was made from Preston 'to the Judgement of Newmarket' as early as 1731, before the founding of the Club, so it was not surprising that in 1757 a dispute at the Curragh was referred to it.[14] In 1807 the *Calendar* began publishing the results of the cases it had judged as a guide to stewards elsewhere. In 1816 the *Calendar* announced that 'persons who may be inclined to submit any matter in dispute to the decision of the senior steward of the Jockey Club' could do so. Vamplew suggests that this was 'a deliberate attempt to cast wider the net of influence'. If so it was a limited one, since the conditions made clear that this could be done only with the permission of local stewards and the parties had both to agree a statement of the case and to accept any subsequent ruling. Few appeals followed, and this suggests that other meetings disregarded any such attempt. Local stewards valued their independence. Most appeals came only when local stewards were unwilling to decide on a winner. When the Doncaster stewards referred the 1819 St. Leger to the Club it was due directly to pressure from upper-class Jockey Club members of the Doncaster Racing Club.[15]

In 1832 the Club limited such adjudication only to cases arising at those meetings elsewhere with printed articles making it clear that they used the rules and regulations of Newmarket. This may have been an attempt at extending its power by encouraging other courses to follow its rules, as Vamplew has suggested, but could equally be interpreted as the Club's attempting to reduce the tiresome necessity of responding to appeals.[16] The wording makes it clear that Jockey Club rules and orders applied to 'races run at and engagements made at Newmarket only' and that they had 'no authority to extend their influence'.[17] There were still few appeals, indeed, even Jockey Club members were forced to go to law in several notorious suits in the 1830s and the 1840s rather than rely on the Club for help.[18] But from the 1860s the stewards were handling more appeals. This was related to the Club's growing influence in terms of its rules, to which we now turn.

A key mark of any authoritative sport regulatory body is its ability to formulate rules and impose them on the sport as a whole. The Club had more regular meetings than the similar racing clubs found at other meetings and so issues of concern were likely to be addressed through rule making, not least because of the frequent association of Club members. The situation is made more complicated because of the two types of rule found in Weatherby's *Calendar*: General and Club rules. Before the Club's founding, Cheny, in his 1732 *Calendar*, had promised to provide a standard set of rules or 'Articles' for racing, and Pond's *Racing Calendars* for 1751–57 contained a detailed set of 'Rules Concerning Horse-Racing in General', so known, general rules for racing already existed. Up to 1797 Weatherby's *Racing Calendar* contained only the Rules and Orders of the Club itself, which mainly concerned betting matters. The Club could publish and enforce its rules only at Newmarket.

From 1797 a copy of Pond's general rules was also provided for public use and these continued almost unaltered to 1858. This suggests an unwillingness to impose a Club view on the more general rules which had long been in force elsewhere.

The rules and orders of the Jockey Club applied only to Newmarket, just as London's Marylebone Cricket Club rules originally controlled only Lord's, the cricket equivalent, and as such were regularly modified. There were, for example, additions in six of the ten years 1815–24 and a major revision in 1828. With seven or eight meetings a year at Newmarket and regular attendance by members, it was relatively easy to create rules of racing and good organizational practice in a systematic way. Members attended race meetings all over Britain and, while the Jockey Club was by no means an innovator, it took up and popularized useful rules or practices originally introduced elsewhere. While the Club could not enforce its rules except at Newmarket its resolutions did 'recommend' their general use.

At this time, however, most stewards elsewhere took little notice and wanted only to control their own meetings. Punishments were limited to the meeting itself. When the Doncaster races were marred by regular false starts by the jockeys in 1831, the heaviest sanction the steward Sir David Baird could exercise was the threat that 'if anything unfair was proved against a jockey he would not be allowed to ride any more at Doncaster'.[19] As the *Sporting Magazine* observed in 1838, 'one of the most striking features in racing is its locality', and stewards from the local nobility and gentry were able to arrange stakes, dates of meetings and the general rules and routines of the sport without reference to other courses.[20]

Once new rules were introduced by the Jockey Club other meetings did often follow suit. But this was a slow process and took place by osmosis rather than diktat. The Jockey Club change in 1833 to take horses' age from 1 January rather than from the customary 1 May, for example, was still explicitly ignored at major meetings at Coventry and Warwick in 1839 and took a long time to be generally accepted.[21]

What wider influence there was was gained by individual Club members. By the 1830s Jockey Club stewards were also acting as stewards at Ascot and Epsom, where the Newmarket starter Clark officiated. When the royal meeting at Ascot languished during William IV's reign, a Jockey Club dinner was given over to the issue. It was pointed out that entries were low because of insufficient prize money and the Club appointed new officials to raise income. As a result the Ascot prize fund swelled to over £1,000. The innovations introduced by Lord George Bentinck in the 1830s and the early 1840s were largely introduced first at Goodwood, where his close relative the Duke of Richmond gave him a free hand, and only later taken up at Newmarket and elsewhere. He was a dominant figure in the Club only in the mid-1840s.[22] His exposure of the frauds associated with the 1844 Derby brought him and the Club positive publicity.[23] The Duke of Richmond issued a notice that no horse which had been fraudulently entered would be allowed to run at Goodwood in 1845 following the Club's action.[24] York followed its lead in expelling defaulters and in demanding to have horses' mouths examined if objections were made.

Many of the Club's apparent innovations at Newmarket had actually been copied from those at courses elsewhere in Britain. The shift from fining jockeys who were disorderly at the starts to suspending them for the rest of the meeting, for example, later made general, was originally introduced by the Liverpool clerk and stewards in 1853 and only later taken up at Newmarket.[25]

By the 1850s Admiral Rous, often seen as the next and most famous turf reformer after Bentinck, was a dominant figure, although in fact he owed his fame primarily to his constant letters to the press on turf matters, his maintainance of a high standard of conscientiousness and efficiency as a handicapper, and to the weakness of the Club itself, which had, as the authoritative Badminton Library book on racing admitted in 1886, a 'lack of energy' during his reign.[26] Rous was an opponent of much change. For much of the 1850s the duties of the Jockey Club stewards were, as Rous himself explained, to 'superintend the races run and engagements made at Newmarket only', although its stewards also officiated at other principal courses.[27] There were regular complaints that the turf was in major need of reform. Its honesty was open to question, while among more socially-elite writers there was a concern that turf betting had been taken over from the aristocracy by commercially-oriented, middle-class bookmakers – 'the trading blackleg, whether patientless doctor, or briefless attorney'.[28] But there was real debate about whether the Jockey Club was the right group to provide leadership.

As a result, many inside the turf felt that what was needed was reform at the local level. Craven, the *Sporting Magazine* racing writer, argued that while racing needed reform, the Jockey Club, although a 'distinguished oligarchy', was not capable of doing so. Turf law was of 'intrinsically-local nature', so reform had to be local and the rules of racing offered by the Club were at best suggestive. He argued for local control, 'effective local arrangements and regulations ... for the organization of a more general and definite system in reference to its operative agency, exchequer, charges, provisions for cases of default and malpractice – and, above all, for rescuing it from the grip of private mercenaries'. He believed that racing was too commercialized and corrupt for the 'amateur' and 'honour'-based rule of the Jockey Club.[29]

Jockey Club punishments still formally applied only to Newmarket in 1857. When the horse of the Hon. Frank Villiers, who had been declared a defaulter there, ran at Doncaster that September in Lord Clifton's name, an attempt to argue that the Newmarket rules about defaulters applied to Doncaster was dismissed by the three stewards.[30]

Even some members felt the Club was too weak, wanting more action to be taken against dishonest gamblers and a toughening of the rules. The Earl of Derby, one of the few members known as a non-gambler, wrote to the Club in June 1857 claiming that increasing numbers of horses were owned by men of inferior position who used them as 'mere instruments of gambling' and called attention to the censurable inactivity of the Club in failing to warn-off publicly known wrongdoers. He was referring to a well-known case: that of a gambling hell and racehorse owner James Adkins, who had been found guilty of defrauding a Manchester man of £25,000 but continued to race and bet. His action forced the Club to act and Adkins was warned-off Newmarket. *The Times* concluded that the action simply proved that other reprobates were 'deliberately tolerated' by the Club.[31]

Lord Derby's action provided the impetus for a Club committee to be formed in December 1857 to draw up a new code for the regulation of racing. After over a hundred years new rules of racing were produced for the Craven meeting, coming into operation in April 1858. The 'Rules Concerning Horse Racing in General' were intended to apply to all the meetings which adopted them; 'Orders of the Jockey Club' still applied to Newmarket only. Most meetings still took only limited notice of the new rules to begin with. In selling races, for example, where the principle of claiming the winner if demanded was in general use, winning horses were claimed by other owners in the race, in place order, at the price at which the horse was entered to be sold, or were auctioned for the race fund. Jockey Club practice at Newmarket since 1850 had been to forbid sales by auction. This rule, now intended to apply to all courses, would have lost committees the extra revenue which came to the race fund and was generally ignored. Rous admitted in 1866 that at York 'they have illegally received in two years £2,138 for sales by auction'.[32] Other more aristocratic utterances lend support to the view that the Club's power was still relatively limited. In 1860 Earl Granville accepted that the Club had 'no power whatever' over other racecourses, and the adoption of their regulations was 'an entirely voluntary act', while Lord Redesdale accepted that 'any steps it took [with regard to lightweight jockeys] would not be universally accepted'.[33]

In the 1860s the Club was still ineffective outside Newmarket and its influence was diminished by the attitudes and behaviour of some of its members. Most meetings of the Club were poorly attended at this time. The AGM in 1865 attracted only 12 members.[34] The Bentinck Benevolent Fund, set up in 1844 and a benchmark of the Club's care for the dependants of honest trainers and jockeys who had fallen on hard times, then consisted of only £5,800 in consols and had received only £50 in subscriptions from members that year, so that it could have helped relatively few.[35] At most meetings local control was still valued. In 1863 it was claimed that horseracing was popular partly because it was a cross-class enjoyment in which 'the people themselves originate the amusement, fix the time and place, issue the regulations, and have sole control and rule over the proceedings'.[36] The 'people' concerned were local committees of predominantly middle-class membership, who took little notice of Jockey Club rule changes.

The first truly effective move to extend the Club's power beyond Newmarket came in 1870, when new rules were introduced and more attempt was made to ensure that the majority of major courses would use them. Flat racing was limited to a period between the week including 25 March and that including 15 November. The programmes and results of meetings would be published in the *Racing Calendar* only if the course concerned was advertised to be subject to the published 'Rules Concerning Horse Racing in General', and horses running in flat races not subject to such rules would be disqualified from entering at meetings where 'the established rules of racing are in force' (rule 73). This was a more powerful and increasingly coercive control, although there was still no way of ensuring that meetings claiming to be subject to such rules actually observed them. Any fraudulent entry would result in the perpetrator being warned-off Newmarket Heath and the horse disqualified from all public races thereafter (rule 18).

The effect of this may be seen in the reduction in meetings reported in the *Calendar*. In 1869 there were 144 reported meetings in Britain but by 1876 only 104. Other meetings had found the new rules too stringent. A new and more effective strategy for the Club was emerging. The Club had always been distant from the smaller meetings; these small meetings took little notice of the Club and were a law unto themselves. There 'the local officials constituted themselves in to a self-contained Jockey Club and a Messrs. Weatherby's of their own. It was their meeting, and what had anyone in London or anywhere else to do with it.'[37] Those smaller meetings where the Club rules were not enforced or dishonesty was too overt were to be ignored by the *Calendar* and control was to be exercised over those larger, wealthier meetings where Jockey Club members, and the upper-class generally, were more involved and ran their horses.

The increasing number of enclosed courses also led the Club to a recognition that there was less need for the upper-class provision of subscriptions to meetings; prize money should come from a combination of gate money and owners' entrance fees. So the Club next moved both to strengthen its hold over wealthier meetings and push for more prize money for owners.

The new code of rules it introduced in January 1877 were now described as 'Rules of Racing, made by the Jockey Club at Newmarket' and included a new rule that no meeting should be included in the Calendar unless having added money of at least £300 per day, with at least £150 added to races of a mile or more. The power of the stewards was extended and they were encouraged to report to the Jockey Club stewards any official or jockey needing punishment beyond that imposed at a meeting. It was made clear that all meetings should also exclude persons warned-off Newmarket Heath for corrupt practices, making sanctions more effective. Club stewards' decisions were final and could not be questioned in any court. Weatherby's was made the Club's registry office.

The Club now began exercising more control over an increasingly smaller but wealthy group of major meetings. The pace of rule making increased. In 1876 there were 56 rules; by 1890 there were 184. There were further demands for prize money in 1878, with the introduction of the rule that every plate or sweepstakes had to be worth £100 to the winner, and the barring of defaulters from ownership or training.

In 1883 the stewards announced that applications for new courses would be considered only under exceptional circumstances. New courses also had to have a straight mile and provision for distance races, no bonus or dividend of over 10 per cent was allowed to their shareholders and finances were subject to inspection. This increasing power through the licensing of courses may be interpreted simply as an attempt to improve the quality of racing. But it also ensured a manageable number of major meetings and kept down competition. Essentially it was a process of cartelization. Many new Club members were financially or otherwise linked to the new enclosed courses, defending them and driving out the old traditional open meetings which they were replacing. Sandown Park was opened in 1875 and by 1880 was running five meetings. Its founder, General Owen Williams, was elected to the Club in 1881. At Leicester a new gate-money consortium, the Leicestershire Club and County Racecourse Company Ltd, opened on a course just outside the town, a rival to the flourishing traditional Leicester meeting which was still supported by the Duke of Rutland (a long-standing, but inactive Club member) and in the town at large. Although the two could have co-existed, the Jockey Club transferred recognition to the new course and the central figure involved was Earl Howe, a newly-appointed member of the Club and a director of the new company. The London magazine *Truth* claimed that this was apparent reform but in reality 'the cloven hoof of the jobber', while *The Sporting Life* claimed that the Jockey Club now 'look as much after the £.s.d. business as any running ground in the country'.[38] At Hamilton Park, another member, Sir John Astley, was involved with the course at its revival in 1887–88.[39] Meetings without such support were not allowed into the charmed circle. Attempts to resurrect the Leeds meeting by a consortium of trademen, brewers and innkeepers on a highly commercial basis in 1883 failed when they were unable to get a licence from the Jockey Club. In 1896 the Club even began charging a 'fixture fee' of £5 per racing day on all recognized meetings.[40]

By the 1890s it was believed that the Club had achieved a 'complete ascendancy'.[41] By 1900 most of those in racing accepted that it had achieved power over elite British flat racing. Even so, its power to enforce its rules was limited. The sporting editor John Corlett, a regular critic, accepted that the Club had become a powerful body, even though he saw its power as 'moral ... but not legal power', with the consequent risk of vexatious litigation in attempting to enforce its regulations.[42] Giving evidence to the 1902 Select Committee on Betting, one member, the Duke of Devonshire, claimed that the Club exercised more active supervision over the management of meetings than 20 years previously. How true this was is unclear, since the members' evidence showed that they held the local executive responsible for the observance of many of the details. The Jockey Club would inspect the course, but it was accepted that the Club would hesitate before it closed the course, and that the Jockey Club was 'a lenient body'.[43]

Although the Club controlled an elite of meetings, it did not now control the majority of races in Britain. Hurdle and steeplechase races were controlled by the National Hunt Committee, and a study of such races lies outside the scope of the present work. Many small, local meetings continued, offering a mixture of flat racing, hurdles and steeplechasing, with horses whose owners were unconcerned by being outside the Jockey Club's purview, ridden by jockeys of less skill and opening on Saturdays or holidays. The West Hartlepool meeting in 1889 had two sweepstakes, a hurdle race and races for ponies and harness horses, all with prizes of under £10.[44] Such meetings were looked down upon by the Club. The usual name applied to them was 'flapping' or 'leatherflapping' events. Their honesty was more open to question than that of major events. These meetings still needed rules, some of which were locally made. In the 1860s Blaydon race lists show that it was apparently being run under British Racing Club rules, although nothing is known of this organization. In 1884 a group was formed at Edinburgh, also called the British Racing Club, to 'promote measures and frame rules for the better regulation of all race meetings that have found it necessary to join the British Racing Club owing to the observance of the Jockey Club and National Hunt rules (through their stringency) being found impossible'. It was based in Scotland and most of its members were Scots, with a minority of northern English courses.[45] Towards the end of the century its membership was increasingly from north-east England. It included enclosed courses at Chesterfield, Hawick, Hartlepool, Blaydon, Boldon, Byker, Houghton-le-Spring and Newcastle.[46] The majority of the horses running at such races were cast-offs from the principal training stables. Courses were enclosed but small. The Newcastle course, set up by two innkeepers, was only 25 acres (10 ha) in size, had four turnstiles and a grandstand for a thousand.[47]

III

The slow pace at which the Club moved to control and regulate may be partly explained by the nature of the membership. Many showed a lack of ability and concern about racing, and social position, not ability, determined election. The Jockey Club was characterized by apathy or inertia in tackling some of the key issues of racing. This may be illustrated by looking at four key themes, chosen from across the period: betting, the racing of two-year-olds, control over jockeys, and the doping of horses.

What bound much of the membership together for much of the period, but most particularly up to and beyond the 1870s, was the manipulation of the betting market and a study of the Club's approach to betting is revealing in explaining why its power was limited up to that time. Financial betting considerations and racing morality both acted against reform of thc turf.

Newmarket raccs were betting races. In the first half of the century there were 'no shows, no theatre, no balls, no breakfasts, no ordinaries, no ladies and very few gentlemen. Nothing but race, race, race and bet, bet, betting.'[48] Throughout the century most members bet. In 1857, for example, the *Daily Telegraph* claimed that betting and backing horses was 'common' among members. It could identify only three who did not bet.[49] Betting approaches ran on a continuum from those (relatively rare) members who had public trials, ran horses to win at all times, and never bet, to those who would employ a range of machinations which might have been considered dishonest outside their world to ensure that they made money from their racing and betting, and colluded with others of a different background in so doing. For most of the nineteenth century only a minority of members were reformist and wanted to stamp out dishonesty. A majority usually wished to maintain the status quo and look after their own interests.

The jurisdiction of the Club was always incomplete unless it accepted the responsibility of regulating betting and dealing with disputed bets. The stewards accepted appeals on disputed bets up to the 1830s, but rule-making was another matter. Most of the members, with their ownership of horses, access to training and betting information, and ability to run to win or not as it suited their betting book, might be adversely affected by any legislation, while the Club stewards would be involved in even more appeals. Nor were they necessarily keen to deal with 'defaulters' (those who might default on bets) since to ban them *sine die* usually meant that a bet remained permanently unpaid.

Before being hanged for poisoning Newmarket racehorses in 1812, the tout Dan Dawson talked freely but bitterly of the Club, claiming that 'there were not three upright betters among them' and, speaking of one noble lord, claimed that 'if his lordship had made a match with his creator he would cheat him if he could'.[50] While the claim may be exaggerated, the morality of Club members was no higher than that found elsewhere on the turf, much of which looked dishonest to the outsider. When one member was accused in 1837 of manipulating his horse in the betting market the Club response was to warn-off from the Heath the journalist who accused him.[51] When the same member was discovered betting against his horse in the 1842 Derby after he found it lame, he defended himself by claiming that everybody on the turf would have done so.

The stewards' declaration in the 1838 *Calendar* of 'their extreme disapprobation of horses being started for races, without the intention of their owners of trying to win with them' was thus public rhetoric. In reality, the withdrawing of horses or running them to avoid winning, if that were more appropriate, might suit betting needs. Even the Club stewards claimed the right to withdraw their horses if they could not get the odds they wanted, and were opposed to any rule that would prevent someone from laying against his own horse and withdrawing him at the post.[52] Running horses to lose was part of the turf morality of many owners and trainers, including some Club members. Indeed, one of the highly praised and more 'gentlemanly' conventions when an owner was running two horses in the same classic race was to 'declare to win' just before the start with one horse. This was fairer to the public betting on the course and showed which one had been backed by the owner, but it also showed that the other horse was not running to win and would be held back by the jockey, having often been previously exploited in the betting market by the owner. Even 'declaring' was often ignored. The 1838 announcement was not followed by any action against any owner. It was simply a pious platitude, ignored by many Club members, and sparked by the increasing number of owners of other social classes doing the same thing.

The turf writer Nimrod, also writing in 1838, saw 'noblemen and gentlemen of fortune' as standing back while racing was taken over by a 'horde of determined depredators', and was puzzled as to why the Jockey Club suffered offences 'to grow before their faces'.[53] But to stop others might have required a change of personal practice. Admiral Rous, writing in 1856, admitted that some Club members had no scruples in setting the resolution at defiance.[54]

The Club's unwillingness to decide on appropriate betting practice is seen in its split over betting debts owed on the 1841 Derby by a defaulter who could not pay until his creditors had settled with him. The three stewards, Rous, Anson and Greville, believed that his creditors should settle first. But one, a Mr Thornton, refused to pay and was supported by three other powerful members, Lord George Bentinck and the Dukes of Portland and Richmond. The stewards attempted to warn Thornton off the Heath, but Portland refused to warn-off Thornton from the part of Newmarket which he owned. Bentinck wrote to the *Morning Post,* arguing that if the Club continued to support the stewards' view it should be abolished, claiming that 'there is no good in such an assembly, in fact it is an absolute nuisance'.[55]

So the difficulties of judging betting cases were clear, with the ever-present and growing danger that Club members would be involved, not least because by 1842 prominent members of the Club were acting as modern bookmakers and betting round.[56]

The Club therefore decided to distance itself from further trouble. Recognizing that betting debts were not legally enforceable and the limitations of their own power, late in 1842 they decided to take no recognizance of disputes concerning betting in the future, referring them instead to Tattersall's committee and the Jockey Club rooms at Newmarket, and completely abdicated any possible responsibility for betting, even at Newmarket.[57] The Club's New Subscription Room at Newmarket, built in 1843, had a constitution which allowed for only 57 members in addition to Club members, and the Club membership dominated both committees, yet officially it would not rule on betting matters. This made the continued claim to be keen to warn-off defaulters somewhat paradoxical. Since the rules 'respecting stakes, forfeits and bets' continued in the *Racing Calendar*, it seems clear that the Club was simply trying to avoid involvement in too many appeals by outsiders. Defaulters now had to be posted by Tattersalls, and defaulters in the 1840s and the 1850s generally ignored any such prohibition.[58] Rous admitted in 1856 that even at Newmarket 'there is no defaulter of any notoriety who is not seen in the course on every interesting occasion although he may be formally warned off.'[59]

Bentinck, well known for his activities to rid the turf of abusers, was neither upright nor straightforward in his own betting dealings. As his one-time racing partner Charles Greville claimed, 'the same man who crusaded against the tricks and villainies of others did not scruple to do things quite as bad as the worst of the misdeeds which he so vigorously and unrelentingly attacked.'[60] Although he made a contribution to the smooth running of races, in order to increase public interest and hence bring in more money, many of his efforts were devoted to actions to help betting to be carried on effectively and campaigns to ensure that betting debts owed to him were paid. He felt that many of his fellow members were both incompetent and selfish. His most famous action, which gave him his high reputation for combating turf dishonesty, concerned the admittedly well-publicized 1844 Derby, although even here his motives were alleged to be 'vitiated by an intermixture of regard for his own and his friends' pecuniary interests', and some believed that he was motivated by his betting book.[61] The Derby had two substitutions, with the four-year-old horses Running Rein and Leander running as three-year-olds, and the former winning the race. This reflected badly on the Jockey Club whose stewards officiated at Epsom, since it was a matter of common knowledge beforehand in the racing press and resolute action would have boosted their reputation.[62] The stewards had had every opportunity of examining the horses beforehand, but did nothing despite the fact that both owners were notorious for fraud.[63] Wins for either horse may have suited some members' betting books. Legal action by the Jockey Club owner of the second-placed Orlando, using evidence assembled by Bentinck, was able to prove dishonesty. Before the race, Bentinck's own horse Ratan was nobbled and then held back by its jockey, to Bentinck's fury, and there were rumours here too that senior members of the Club rooms were involved. After pressure from Bentinck the Club held an enquiry, but in secret. Although the jockey was temporarily warned-off, the impression was left that there had been a cover up. Indeed, it was suggested that 'they could not have taken more efficacious means to have their honourable character impugned'.[64] Bentinck, who was not popular within the Club, was finally made a steward in 1845 as a result of his work. That same year the trainer William Day and two 'legs', Bloodsworth and Stebbings, were warned-off Newmarket Heath for attempting to nobble the Derby entrant Old England, although all three continued to be centrally involved in turf affairs thereafter. Stebbings, who lived for some time afterwards in Portland Place in London, was said to have been much liked by 'upper members of the turf, with whom he was on better terms than was generally imagined', and was, according to his obituarist, a close confidant of Rous.[65]

A usually well-informed *Sporting Magazine* contributor claimed in 1848 that there 'were peers who ran rogues, stopped, bolted, did everything but run straight'.[66] He particularly attacked 'play or pay' betting, a system commonly used within the Club and at Tattersall's, by which once a bet was laid the failure of the horse to run for whatever reason meant that the bet was lost, because it allowed owners to win bets by ensuring that their horse did not run. He felt that the rule should be that the animal had to start before a bet was valid. Others were still asking for this change 20 years later, but the rule suited all the 'knowing ones' (core turfites), peers as well as proletarians. The Club had several opportunities to ban the much-abused system, often used by owners who would take money against their own horse through a commissioner and then withdraw the horse claiming that it was unwell. At a meeting on 2 October 1855 there was a motion put to ban this practice but it was thrown out with little discussion. Indeed, in 1856 the Club actually agreed to adjudicate on play or pay disputes relating to the classics and major handicaps.[67]

So around mid-century the upper-class group to which the Club was linked were more concerned to profit from betting than to control the courses which they rarely attended. In 1848 another racing insider and Jockey Club member Charles Greville claimed that it was 'monstrous to see high born and bred gentlemen of honoured names and families, themselves marching through the world with their heads in the air ... mixed up in schemes that are neither more nor less a system of plunder'.[68] Rous admitted in 1869 that in his 50 years on the turf he had 'very rarely had the good fortune to find a man of high rank who did not run solely for profit'.[69] 'Vandriver', the *Baily's Magazine* turf writer, claimed as late as 1875 that 'things have been done by men of position and repute which if done in any other society than the Turf would have led to unpleasant consequences.'[70] When the Jockey Club steward Frank Villiers fled the country in 1855, when he was unable to meet his betting debts of some £100,000 and was declared a defaulter, it suggested again that dominant figures in the Club were keener on betting than on improving racing more generally.

Many in the Club continued to employ trainers or jockeys whose honesty was doubtful. They stayed at the same hotels, and sometimes mixed socially with notorious 'legs'. In Greville's diary he describes himself, while engaged on turf pursuits, as living with 'the merest wretches whose sole and perpetual occupation it is, jockeys, trainers, betters, blacklegs'.[71] According to *The Times*, 'aristocratic sporting men' consorted with 'blacklegs' and 'worthless fellows', claiming that 'they too often recognize them, encourage them, bet with them, make use of their sharp intellects and ill-gotten knowledge, employ them as touters, as bookmakers'.[72] For all their rhetoric about caring for racing, most members cared simply for their own pleasure and betting profit.

By the 1860s the racing press had expanded significantly to feed the needs of the nascent betting industry and this began to change attitudes. First there was bad publicity. Racing could no longer afford overt dishonesty, since the press demanded that control be exercised over meetings and betting so that they at least appeared fair and honest. The press often seized on examples of dubious attitudes to betting from Rous and others.[73] When the *Morning Post* turf correspondent ventured a few remarks on the character of the Club as a result of one such incident, he was warned-off Newmarket Heath by a majority vote, indicating a split in Club views about how to cope with press criticism.[74] Later in the decade the financial difficulties of a number of young aristocratic plungers, including Lord Hastings, the Earl of Jersey and the Duke of Newcastle, which received major publicity, seemed to reflect an excessive preoccupation with betting which also reflected badly on the Club.

As expansion of the telegraph system improved communications, the press began paying touts to provide training reports on the horses' progress. Tout reports on form prevented the Club from exploiting its horses for betting. As the *Sporting Magazine* explained, 'The object of the public is to know as much as possible of owners' horses and the object of owners is that they should know as little as possible. They seek to prey upon each other.'[75] The Club received a petition from trainers in 1876 complaining about touts, but since it was well known that many individuals 'holding a high position in the racing world and themselves lawmakers of the Turf' (that is, Club members) also employed touts for their personal betting advantage, it was difficult to ban it.[76] Indeed, in a revealing court case in 1869 one Club member, the Earl of Stamford, was shown to be employing a tout.[77]

Attitudes to high-stakes betting finally began to shift in the 1870s and the 1880s and, instead of the membership being dominated by those with betting interests, the majority of members of the next generation seem to have been more interested in breeding or success in major races. In 1899 Tattersall's and the Jockey Club Rooms committees merged, and only three out of the ten members were drawn from the Club.

Another issue which split the Club and revealed both its weakness and its emphasis on betting, was the increase in the racing of young, immature horses, which Rous strongly supported. Two-year-old racing allowed horses to be raced earlier and encouraged sprints, where betting outcomes were less certain. In 1869 Sir Joseph Hawley and the 2nd Earl of Durham proposed a range of reforms including the reduction of two-year-old racing. Although himself a better, Hawley believed that the Club was being run too much for the benefit of betting. His fellow member Lord Derby and much of the press and public supported him. Derby argued in a widely reprinted letter to the press that to run two-year-olds before May was premature, and was, like the multiplication of short races, or the practice, 'so common as hardly to be reprobated', of running horses to lose, a vice lowering the character of the turf, reflecting the large numbers of owners running horses for profit and betting purposes.[78] Rous, by contrast, perhaps more realistically, argued that betting was evil, but that racing had always been 'a gambling speculation' and that the 'prosperity of the turf' was secured by it.[79]

His own view was that young horses needed early training, as it weeded out the weak ones, and that it was only the over-running of two-year-old horses over a long season which was destructive.[80] His economic arguments against the proposed reform made clear the limits to Jockey Club power. It would ruin Newmarket, 'to which place the rules would be confined', since the stewards had 'no power to enforce them elsewhere'.[81] At a heavily attended meeting on the Monday of Derby week the Hawley motions were defeated, although the motion to prohibit two-year-old horses from running in a handicap only by 24 votes to 16. The only compromise was to limit two-year-old racing to after 1 May. Hawley came back to the attack in

January 1870, arguing for these and further reforms, claiming that the Club was too passive, that the turf needed reform since it now had nothing to do with improving the breed of horses but was a gambling speculation, and that the Club needed to set up a committee to reconstitute, revive and revise the Club. Rous responded by attacking Hawley, who was a heavy better himself.[82] He then ensured the setting up of a stewards' reform committee which eventually reported with no proposals for significant reform, although two-year-olds were not allowed to race until 1 May.[83] The Club reversed even this rule in 1873.[84] There was no move either to reverse the trend to sprint races for younger horses. Although Lord Coventry argued in 1874 that there was a deterioration of horses in terms of quality due to the increasing number of short races, his views were those of a minority within the Club.[85] The Club finally took action to curb the worst excesses of two-year-old racing and to encourage some longer races only in 1899.

In dealing with a majority of racing issues the Jockey Club was characterized by inertia or leniency even towards the end of the century. Two examples of this are control over jockeys and the doping of horses.

Leniency had always characterized most dealings with top jockeys. Outside Newmarket jockeys whose riding was doubtful would be warned-off only for the duration of the particular meeting. When a horse was clearly pulled at Malton in 1856, the jockey was suspended but continued to ride elsewhere.[86] Even Jockey Club suspensions were applied inconsistently, because of the self-interest of members. If a top jockey was banned then this often affected the potential racing success of those members whose horses he was due to ride.

Jockeys betting on their own horse might not be a problem, but jockeys might also bet against their horses and this could lead to conflicts of interest. The Club introduced the licensing of jockeys in 1879, but proposals to penalize jockeys who owned horses or betted were rejected in the face of threats from the top jockeys to retire if it were passed.[87] In 1882 the rules of racing were reviewed yet again, and the stewards were given 'discretion' to refuse licences to jockeys keeping racehorses without permission and betting 'notoriously', which suggested that it was acceptable if kept quiet.[88] It had little effect and by 1884 rumours of a jockey ring fixing races were rife.

Many believed that the best jockeys were *de facto* masters of the situation, since they were rarely pressed by the Club and their starting and other offences were regularly overlooked by Club stewards and starters. Here again there were differences of practice within the Club. The 3rd Earl of Durham, one of the few Club members consistently to oppose corruption, took public issue with another member and steward Lord

Chetwynd, over the running of his horses and his relationship with the stable jockey Charlie Wood. At first Durham was unspecific, claiming that there had been 'frequent insinuations in the public press and on courses about the running of certain horses and the conduct of owners', but at a special meeting of the Club in February 1888 he was more direct, accusing Wood of 'being in the habit of pulling horses' for the stable and Chetwynd of 'having connived at serious malpractices which are contrary to the rules of racing'. More generally, he claimed that some men 'equal to us in social position and in racing influence have failed to maintain the fair reputation of the turf', employing notorious jockeys because they rode well, because they needed the jockeys on their side, or because he could square other jockeys in a race. Another member, Harry Chaplin, pointed out that another jockey (Martin) who had admitted pulling horses had been employed by two other members that year.[89] Chetwynd denied the allegations and took the case to court, where he was proved to be a professional punter. Wood was warned-off, although he was back in five years. This was longer than for most. Warnings-off of top jockeys were seldom permanent, since influential employers, including Jockey Club members, were unwilling to lose them.[90] Accusations were still being made by the press that the irregularities of the leading jockeys were ignored at the end of the century.[91] This applied to the first successful American jockey Tod Sloan, who first came to England in 1897. He returned in 1898 at the invitation of Lord William Beresford, a Club member, who made Sloan a partner at Heath House, Newmarket.[92] Sloan was a great jockey, but he was a regular better, even though the rules of racing supposedly prevented this and he flouted these and other rules in a flagrant way for the next two years. Although he had been offered a big retainer to ride for Edward VII in 1901, which indicated that success was more important than rule-keeping on the turf, his tirade in front of the stewards at Newmarket against a jockey who had refused to pull his winning horse to allow Sloan to win a bet of some £60,000 on the Cambridgeshire forced the Club to act. He received a serious reprimand and was advised not to reapply for his licence.

Leniency was also certainly shown in the Club's attitude to horse doping, which from the late 1890s had become an increasing problem. Most writers agree that the Jockey Club either turned a blind eye to it or was reluctant to act.[93] British trainers had made limited use of stimulants previously – a bottle of old port was a favourite, with whisky for rogue horses, and more often used dope to retard a horse's running; indeed, Nimrod had referred to the use of 'opiate balls' for this purpose as early as 1838.[94] Americans were more scientific in their use of stimulants. Two American owners alone – William 'Betcha a Million' Gates and James

Drake – using their own trainer, probably took about £2 million out of the ring over four years by backing their doped horses, but British owners may well have followed their example. The Jockey Club was finally forced to act when the respected trainer the Hon. George Lambton demonstrated to his brother the Earl of Durham, a Club steward, that he too could achieve success with poor horses by using stimulants. In October 1903 it announced that rule 176 would be extended to make the use of drugs or stimulants administered by hypodermic or other methods to affect the speed of a horse a warning-off offence.[95] In the short run this had some effect, since the chief offenders moved to France where the practice was still legal. But increased awareness of it meant that it was not done away with, merely driven underground; it became a part of the repertoire of racing.[96]

Such apathy and leniency may be contrasted with the much quicker Club response when the breeding and racing success of members' horses was put at risk. With the continued entry into Britain of good quality, foreign-bred horses at the end of the nineteenth century the Jockey Club, after consultation with the major breeders, tried to reduce the flow by agreeing in 1901 that 'any animal claiming admission should be able to prove satisfactorily eight or nine crosses of pure blood, to trace back for at least a century, and to show such performances of its immediate family on the turf as to warrant the belief in the purity of its blood.'[97] But to try to stop the flow totally could have led to reciprocal action and the loss of the lucrative export sale of thoroughbreds.

In 1908 a series of anti-betting laws in the USA brought racing there almost to a halt. Many good American racehorses were sent to Britain. This caused great anxiety among British breeders and received an uncharacteristically quick response from the Club. In 1909 the *Stud Book* announced that 'no horse or mare can be admitted unless it can be traced to a strain already accepted in the earlier volumes'. The Jockey Club stewards endorsed this view, to the anger of the Americans. Further complaints from British breeders came as American bloodstock sales began increasingly to hit British thoroughbred exports, and at a meeting of the Club in May 1913 Lord Jersey pushed through a new rule which said that 'no horse or mare can, after this date, be considered as eligible for admission unless it can be traced without flaw on both sire's and dam's side of its pedigree to horses and mares themselves already accepted in earlier volumes'.[98] British writers claimed that the rule met with 'the hearty approbation of all breeders of any standing both at home and abroad' because it preserved the purity of thoroughbred stock. Some of the American press claimed, with some truth, that the 'Jersey Act' was directed against their stock to the direct advantage of the British breeders.[99]

IV

The upper-class, predominantly aristocratic membership of the Club was at first arguably more influential in Parliament than it was on the turf. As early as 1784 an attempt by the government to increase taxes on racehorses was withdrawn after a deputation from the Club met Pitt.[100]

The successive governments of the early nineteenth century also raised revenue direct from racing through assessed taxes on all racehorses, but returned some of it in the form of royal plates and financial support for a specified number of long-distance races. Earlier legislation regarding racing was generally unenforced. This changed in 1843–44 when, following attempts by Bentinck and the Duke of Richmond to bar from the Goodwood betting a number of defaulters whom they viewed as in 'want of principle and honour', a small group of Jockey Club members plus their working-class commissioners were legitimately sued by this group for substantial amounts, using early eighteenth-century legislation.[101] Where their pockets were involved Club members were clearly able to marshal substantial parliamentary pressure. The cases were delayed through legal manœuvring until the 'Manly Sports' Bill, which repealed this legislation, was got through Parliament by the Duke of Richmond, following pressure from Bentinck and other racing MPs. At the same time a Select Committee on Betting was set up to allay concern. A study of its membership, the questions it chose to ask and the people it chose to interview (or not to interview) suggests that it had been 'nobbled' by the wealthy, landed racing interests, anxious to argue that their gambling was legitimate and that only the poor needed protection. Subsequent action against betting focused upon working-class betting rather than that of the Jockey Club. In 1845 the Gaming Act rendered gambling (that is, betting) debts unenforceable by law, attempting to curb betting through the risk now supposedly involved in betting, and in the hope that money would bc invested in more rational and principled ways. Within the world of the turf it had no effect. Equally the 1853 Betting House Act was carefully directed against working-class gambling. It was framed so that its prohibitions did not apply to betting on credit by correspondence or to betting among members of a club, thus safeguarding upper-class credit bets made on the course, at Tattersall's or elsewhere.

The majority of Members of Parliament around mid-century supported racing. Parliament formally adjourned for Derby Day from 18 May 1847, originally by the motion of private members. In 1860 the government formally closed down for Derby Day, with Lord Palmerston declaring that to adjourn over that day was part of the unwritten law of Parliament. The

Jockey Club at this time held significant political power. It then contained 20 privy councillors, of whom seven had held cabinet and two prime-ministerial posts.

In that same year Lord Redesdale introduced a Light Weight Racing Bill into the Lords to raise the minimum weight carried by horses to 7 stones (44.5 kg).[102] He was opposed by Lord Derby, representing the Jockey Club, who argued that the regulation of racing was 'better entrusted to the authority which has hitherto made Rules', and that it was currently giving the matter consideration. Redesdale then sought to ensure a lower limit of 6 stones (38 kg) and was supported by a petition from 25 mainly Newmarket trainers. Derby then compromised, suggesting that the Club would probably accept 5½ stones (35 kg). Other peers also spoke against it and the Bill was then withdrawn. This incident shows that the Club's influence over Parliament was still great.

Aristocratic power had survived the partially reformed central political system of 1832 almost intact.[103] But from the 1870s the aristocracy was facing challenges and by the 1880s their political position was being seriously undermined.[104] This had its effect on the power of the Jockey Club in Parliament. A first sign of this came with the Club's failure to see off the Racecourses (Metropolis) Bill of 1878, which reveals also the limits to the Club's power over some courses.

In 1876–77 there was a range of actions by local magistrates, usually using the licensing laws, against small, suburban meetings around London, although many of these were steeplechases.[105] This led Mr Anderson, MP for Glasgow, to introduce a private member's Bill in 1877 to enable local magistrates to license annually all recently opened suburban racecourses within ten miles of London. When it came before the House in January 1878 such meetings were attacked. In reply, a prominent Jockey Club MP, Jim Lowther, claimed that the recent alterations to the rules of racing had materially strengthened the powers of the Club and that prohibition of a meeting in the *Racing Calendar* amounted to an absolute prohibition (an untruth, since many flat race meetings were already running unnoticed by the *Calendar*). He also claimed that the three stewards of the Club, all prominent MPs, had full authority within the Club and could better conduct racing affairs than local magistrates.

Anderson then suggested that at such meetings as Eltham, Kingsbury and Streatham the Club had 'no real power'. Racehorse owners there were not bothered about running their horses at more respectable meetings, while there were plenty of jockeys who would ride them, so 'the Jockey Club was utterly powerless to remedy the evil'.[106] The Bill received a first reading, although by only two votes. Despite a year in which to marshal opposition, the Jockey Club made little progress. On second reading Lowther had assured Parliament that the issue would be 'brought under the notice of the Jockey Club', claiming that the Club would deal with such issues. At a general meeting the Club decided to oppose the Bill and at a subsequent one they agreed to 'take cognisance of abuses which were brought to their attention'. They were very unhappy with any proposal to license racecourses.[107]

When the Bill was examined in Committee Lowther claimed that the Club had 'complete power' over such meetings, and that if the publication of the programme in the *Calendar* were prevented the meeting would come to an end. The Club had also published a notification requesting gentlemen not to act as stewards unless they had been assured that meetings were conducted properly. In reply, Anderson argued that the Jockey Club had done nothing to enforce its own rules at these meetings, while the fact that one important Club member and MP (Henry Chaplin) had withdrawn his opposition suggested that 'the Jockey Club could not deal with the matter'.[108] Although Club supporters continued to argue that the Club was better able to deal with racing, opponents pointed out that up to that time its actions had had no practical effect. The Club, it was suggested, looked after the great meetings well, but ignored the smaller ones.[109] These arguments had their effect and the Bill became law.

The period 1880–1914 saw concern over betting growing in Parliament and having an impact on attitudes to racing among members, who were now less favourably disposed towards racing. In the 1880s the motion to adjourn for the Derby was being left to private members, and the motion was finally rejected altogether from 1892. Even so, there were still sufficient influential Jockey Club members in Parliament to ensure that the attacks on betting and horseracing organized by the National Anti-Gambling League (see Chapter 8), which could have affected upper-class betting and Club-controlled racecourses, were deflected on to working-class betting issues. In 1901 a Select Committee of the House of Lords began an investigation of betting, in the context of growing public and press confusion and uncertainty about betting and its legislation, with its terms of reference to 'inquire into the increase of Public Betting among all classes, and whether any Legislative measures are possible and expedient for checking the abuses occasioned thereby'. As it was a controversial matter, the Committee included three racing peers, including the chairman, the Earl of Durham, four anti-gamblers and two neutrals. The original assumption of 'abuses' of betting existing 'across all classes' found little favour. The findings, carefully steered by the chairman, created what was to be the new political agenda – the perceived 'problem' of working-class betting and attempts to control it by increased legal action against street bookmakers and the prohibition of tipsters' advertisements and betting circulars.[110] Attempts by National Anti-Gambling League (NAGL) supporters who had given evidence before the Committee to have the publication of starting prices stopped, to stop credit betting by letter, telegram and telephone or to have betting on courses made illegal did not appear among the major proposals. The power of the upper-class racing supporters and the reluctance of the press and postal authorities to support such moves was too great. Licensing, registration and taxation of bookmakers by the state were also rejected. It could be seen as 'state complicity' amid wider concerns about state intervention, and would make betting debts recoverable by law, thus swamping the courts. Although supported by bookmakers' organizations (and later by Horatio Bottomley, who introduced a Bill for their licensing in 1906) it had no support whatsoever at this time in either House. The anti-betting group wanted suppression, not control.[111] This was a view shared by both the Home Office and the police. The Chief Constable of Manchester, Robert Peacock, in his evidence to the Committee, felt that if the trade of bookmaker and street betting were made illegal the law could be enforced.[112]

The Conservative government, although broadly in support of some anti-gambling measures, was well aware that any Bill attacking betting would be opposed by some of its own members, since there was now an increasingly obvious alignment of the upper classes behind the Conservative interest. The Street Betting Bills which emerged over the four years following the Select Committee's Report were all private members' Bills. The first in 1903, introduced by Lord Davey, a non-conformist Liberal lawyer, incorporated most of the Report's provisions, but was strongly opposed by Lord Durham, the Committee chairman, who argued that it attacked the racecourses and upper-class betting. Again this indicates the power that individual Club members still enjoyed. The House of Lords contained a number of Club members and the view there was clearly that any measure should focus on street betting. Two subsequent Bills for 'the better suppression of street betting' reached the Commons but proceeded no further, partly because of drafting problems.

The 1906 election saw a large Liberal majority, much more in favour of anti-gambling legislation. There was support among the leadership, while concerns surfacing in London over allegations of corruption and bribery of the police by bookmakers gave legislation some further impetus. Despite attempts by anti-gamblers to extend the 1903 Bill's scope and suppress racecourse and telegraph betting and criticisms from some MPs that it was a blatant piece of class discrimination, Lord Davey steered a redrafted Bill through Parliament and the Street Betting Act was passed in December 1906, with the support of Labour MPs, reflecting their non-conformist moralism and attitudes to self-improvement and self-discipline.[113] More importantly, the Jockey Club was now less anxious that it would affect them, and indeed the Bill depended on aristocratic support. This reflected a change in its attitude. Some members now shared the views about working-class gambling as a social and economic problem; others saw that to divert attention and criticism away from the racecourse towards the streets actually legitimated racing.

V

This chapter has drawn on a wider range of contemporary sources to demonstrate that the Club's path to power was slower and much more problematic than has been generally thought. Originally, any power was solely over Newmarket racing, although it was extended to Ascot and Epsom by the 1830s and at times to courses elsewhere where individual members had strong links. The Club began making changes to more general rules in the late 1850s and only really began attempting to extend its power to courses more broadly from 1870. With each new set of significant rule changes, the number of race meetings it recognized dropped. Many courses found the rules too stringent and either went out of business or turned to some other form of racing.

By 1914, although it had lost some of its influence in Parliament, the Jockey Club had established itself as the dominant power in terms of recognized meetings. The Club had established a clearer power base and a clearer sense of unity and direction. Previously, as we have seen, the Club was regularly split over many key issues such as betting and the running of two-year-olds. The path to power had taken a long time. For much of the nineteenth century the Club had some influence, but no actual power beyond Newmarket, and much of the membership had been either apathetic or motivated mainly by self-interest and financial gain. This is an important finding, which stands as a powerful corrective to earlier accounts. Further work, however, remains to be done in examining controls over racing. Although there have been studies of National Hunt racing, its committee and other racing bodies such as the British Racing Club still await more detailed work, while we still know little about the numbers, organization and control of the non-recognized racing events.

The Jockey Club's sanctioning of specific, 'elite' meetings and its deflection of accusations of moral turpitude towards more local and working-class meetings indicate that as it adapted to events and became a national body it became a moral agent of self-policing at the expense of some courses. In part this was a response to the contested nature of racing in public debate and it is to the opposition to racing that we now turn.

NOTES

1. R. Holt, *Sport and the British: a Modern History* (Oxford, 1989), p.29; J.V. Beckett, *The Aristocracy in England 1660–1914* (Oxford, 1986), p.359.
2. W. Vamplew, *The Turf* (1976), Ch.6.
3. Such as R. Mortimer, *The Jockey Club* (1958); See Vamplew, *The Turf*, Ch.6.
4. R. Black, *The Jockey Club and Its Founders* (1891); Mortimer, *Jockey Club* (1958); J. Kent, *The Racing Life of George Cavendish Bentinck* (1892); T.H. Bird, *Admiral Rous and the British Turf* (1939).
5. J.C. Whyte, *History of the British Turf*, Vols.1 and 2 (1840), for example, a commonly used source for later writers, dedicated to the Club. *The Sporting Magazine* and *Sporting Review* both gave much more attention to elite races. Writers such as Craven, the editor of the latter, portrayed an idealized Club, 'a body of gentlemen adopting one of the sports of their county for its better promotion and protection. In all its relations – its circumscribed dimensions – the scrupulous adaptation of its arrangement – the finish and elegance of its *materiel* – the Jockey Club may truly be denominated the model of a club.'; Craven, 'Clubs as accessories of the national sports', *Sporting Magazine*, March 1853, p.163. By contrast the *Sunday Times* in the 1840s and the *Era* or the *Licensed Victuallers' Gazette* a little later took a different view. Later still in the 1890s L.H. Curzon, *A Mirror of the Turf* (1892), p.371, agreed that the Club had in latter years been 'criticized by several sporting writers with unsparing severity', although he conceded that it had done 'useful work ... within the last ten or twelve years'.
6. The first mention of the Club in print was in Pond's *Sporting Kalendar* for 1752. Different writers suggest different dates for the founding of the Club. See Vamplew, *The Turf*, p.78 who suggests that it was probably in 1751 or 1752.
7. R. Black, *Horse Racing in England: a Synoptical View* (1893), p.118.
8. Letter from Rous, *The Times*, 13 February 1869.
9. See Vamplew, *The Turf*, pp.93–4; R. Onslow, *Headquarters: a History of Newmarket and Its Racing* (Cambridge, 1993), p.81.
10. *The Times*, 13 November 1883, 26 December 1903.
11. Curzon, *Mirror of the Turf*, p.364.
12. For the purchase of the Exning estate see *The Times*, 22 July 1881. For Jockey Club income from the 1890s to 1914 see the Club accounts held at the Jockey Club Rooms, Newmarket.
13. Railway Magazine, November 1908, p.373 quoted by A. and E. Jordan, *Away for the Day: the Railway Excursion in Britain 1830 to the Present Day* (Kettering, 1991), p.89.
14. C.M. Prior, *A History of the Racing Calendar and Stud Book* (1926), p.105.
15. *The Times*, 11 October 1819.
16. See Vamplew, *The Turf*, p.84.
17. Brailsford has claimed that it was 'an effective way of distancing and weakening the less reputable events'. If so, it is surprising how little discernible effect it had over the next two decades, when numbers of small, less reputable meetings recorded in the *Calendar* actually increased. See D. Brailsford, *British Sport: a Social History* (1992), p.72.
18. Examples include the 1839 Bloomsbury case, where Lord Lichfield took the matter out of the hands of the Ascot stewards, *Yorkshireman*, 24 August 1839 and the Running Rein case in 1844, where General Peel was not confident that the Club stewards would act decisively; M.J. Huggins, 'Lord Bentinck, the Jockey Club and racing morality in mid-nineteenth century England: the Running Rein Derby revisited', *International Journal of the History of Sport*, Vol.13, No.3, 1996, pp.432–44.
19. *Yorkshire Gazette*, 24 September 1831.
20. *Sporting Magazine*, August 1838, p.368.
21. *Racing Calendar*, 1839, pp.2, 4.

22. Introduction of fines for late starting, introduced at Newmarket in the 1840s, were introduced at York only in 1866; J. Fairfax-Blakeborough, *The Analysis of the Turf* (1927), p.162.
23. See Huggins, 'Lord Bentinck'.
24. *Bell's Life*, 7 June 1845.
25. Cecil, 'The Turf Exchange', *Sporting Magazine*, October 1853, p.253.
26. Earl of Suffolk and Berkshire and W.G. Craven, *Badminton Library: Racing* (1886), p.51.
27. Admiral Rous, 'On the past and present state of the turf', *Yorkshire Herald*, 29 December 1855.
28. *The Times*, 14 June 1856, quoting the *Doncaster Gazette*.
29. Craven, *The Sporting Magazine*, March 1853, p167.
30. All three stewards were Jockey Club members, but argued that 'the rules of that meeting [did not apply] to the cases on which decisions have been made elsewhere'; J. Fairfax-Blakeborough, *Northern Turf History*, Vol.III. *York and Doncaster* (1950), p.363.
31. Bird, *Admiral Rous*, p.169.
32. Admiral Rous, *Horse Racing* (1866), quoted by J. Fairfax-Blakeborough, *Northern Turf History*, Vol.III, p.11.
33. *The Times*, 13 June 1860.
34. Ibid., 21 April 1865.
35. *Sporting Magazine*, July 1868, p. 6.
36. Anon., *Horse Racing; its History and Early Records of the Principal and Other Race Meetings* (1863), p.2.
37. See Fairfax-Blakeborough, *The Analysis*, p.162.
38. J. Crump, 'The great carnival of the year: Leicester races in the nineteenth century', *Transactions, Leicestershire History & Archaeological Society*, Vol.58, 1982–83, p.69.
39. J. Fairfax-Blakeborough, *Horse Racing in Scotland* (1973), pp.101–2.
40. York Archives, Minutes of York Racing Committee, 2 April 1896.
41. See Vamplew, *The Turf*, p. 99.
42. 1902 Select Committee on Betting; Evidence of John Corlett, Qs3359–60.
43. 1902 Select Committee on Betting; Evidence of the Duke of Devonshire, Q3266; Sir James Lowther, Qs2495–504.
44. *South Durham and Cleveland Mercury*, 24 August 1889.
45. See Fairfax-Blakeborough, *Extinct Race Meetings* (J.A. Allen, 1949), p.9.
46. 'The Sporting Man', *Newcastle Evening* Telegraph, 6 July 1899 (noon edn).
47. Ibid.
48. 'A Yorkshireman at Newmarket', *Sporting Magazine*, December 1831, p.174.
49. *Daily Telegraph*, 20 October 1862.
50. *Sporting Magazine*, August 1812, p.200.
51. Ibid., December 1837, pp.66–71,
52. 'Betting on P.P. Races', *Sporting Magazine*, June 1838, p.122.
53. Nimrod, *The Chace, the Turf and the Road* (1852 edn), p.127.
54. A. Rous, 'On the past and present state of the turf', *Yorkshire Herald*, 29 December 1855.
55. He also claimed that Rous had had a financial interest in this and two other cases stewards had recently decided; M. Seth Smith, *Lord Paramount of the Turf* (1971), p.62.
56. 'A few hints on betting', *Sporting Magazine*, December 1842, p.650.
57. Mortimer, *The Jockey Club* (1968), p.105.
58. J.G. Dixon, a defaulter warned-off in 1843, gave evidence before the Select Committee on Gaming in 1844 that he had been to Newmarket since then and betted. Select Committee on Gaming, Appendix 1 and Index, 1844 (297), Vol.VI, Evidence of J.G. Dixon, 21 March 1844, Q.2127.
59. Rous, *Yorkshire Herald*, 29 December 1855.
60. H. Reeve (ed.), *The Greville Memoirs*, Vol.2 (1885), 28 September 1848.
61. Black, *Horse Racing in England*, p.177.
62. The two horses were described as the 'modern antiques' not just in London but also in the Yorkshire papers. See *Yorkshireman*, 18 May 1844.
63. Prior, *History of the Racing Calendar*, pp.199–206.
64. Anon., *Horse Racing: Its history and Early Records*, p.412.
65. See obituaries in *Newcastle Daily Journal*, 1 March 1869; Vandriver, *Baily's Magazine*, March 1869.

66. Craven, *The Sporting Magazine*, November 1848, pp.306ff.
67. *York Herald*, 27 October 1855, 13 January 1856.
68. Diary extract 7 November 1848 in P.W. Wilson (ed.), *The Greville Diaries*, Vol.1, 1927.
69. *The Times*, 3 June 1869, quoted by the *Manchester Courier*, 4 June 1869.
70. 'Our Van', *Baily's Magazine*, December 1875, p.62.
71. Diary extract, 10 May 1845 in P.W. Wilson (ed.), *The Greville Diaries*, Vol.1.
72. *The Times*, 14 June 1856.
73. In 1862 came the 'Reindeer/Raindeer' controversy, a case concerning a bet on the spelling of the word during an upper-class house party for the Exeter races. Although it was not commonly known that the then standard dictionary gave 'raindeer' similar bets on its spelling had been made at race clubs previously and there were suggestions of sharp practice by the original wagerers. Jockey Club members, including Rous, became involved in ruling on the dispute, which then reached the press, much to the Club's dismay. See letter to *The Times*, 15 November 1862.
74. See *Morning Post*, 20 October 1862; *The Times*, 6 November 1862.
75. 'The Omnibus', *Sporting Magazine*, July 1868, p.4.
76. 'The common sense of touting', *Baily's Magazine*, June 1876, p.400.
77. Mortimer, *The Jockey Club*, p.49.
78. Letter to the *Manchester Courier*, 1 June 1869.
79. *The Times*, 23 February 1874.
80. Letter to *The Times*, 9 February 1874.
81. Letter to *The Times*, quoted in Bird, *Admiral Rous*, p.265.
82. There were press allegations that he was so angered that some of the commission agents forestalled him in the betting market and shortened the odds on some of his horses before he had backed them that he used his influence to have them raided in 1869; *Sporting Life*, 23 June, 26 June, 30 June and 28 July 1869.
83. See R. Mortimer *et al.*, *Biographical Encyclopaedia of British Flat Racing* (1978), pp.523–5.
84. *The Times*, 27 October 1873; *Newmarket Monthly Illustrated Journal*, November 1873.
85. 'Our Van', *Baily's Magazine*, January 1876, p.123.
86. *Bell's Life*, 27 April 1856.
87. See Earl of Suffolk and Berkshire and Craven, *Racing*, p.105.
88. *The Times*, 4 July 1882.
89. Ibid., 8 February 1888.
90. See Vamplew *TheTurf*, p.106; idem, *Pay Up and Play the Game*, p.262.
91. *The Sporting Man*, 1 July 1899.
92. S. Menzies, *Lord William Beresford, VC* (1938), pp.283ff.
93. See Mortimer, *The Jockey Club*, pp.131–2.
94. Nimrod, *The Chace, the Turf and the Road*, p.133.
95. *Sporting Life*, 1 October 1903.
96. *The Times*, 21 November 1905.
97. Preface, *General Stud Book*, Vol.XIX (1901).
98. *General Stud Book*, Vol.XXI (1909), Vol.XXII (1913).
99. Prior, *The History of the Racing Calendar*, pp.39–40.
100. Ibid., pp.166–7.
101. At the time this caused great alarm among Club members since it was clear that their betting was illegal. For the correspondence between Bentinck and Bowes see C.E. Hardy, *John Bowes and the Bowes Museum* (Newcastle, 1970), pp.67–70.
102. *The Times*, 13 June 1860.
103. Beckett, *The Aristocracy in England*, pp.456–7.
104. Ibid., pp.460–1.
105. *The Times*, 20 December 1876, 3 January 1877, 26 January 1877, 30 January 1877, 6 July 1977, 14 December 1877.
106. See the comments of speakers during the discussion of the Racecourses (Licensing) Bill, *Hansard*, 29 January 1878, col.638–51 and comments in *The Times*, 8 February 1878.
107. Sir George Chetwynd, *Racing Reminiscences*, Vol.1 (1891), p.163; *The Times*, 8 February 1878.
108. *Hansard*, 10 June 1878, col.1483–9.

109. Ibid., 14 February 1879, col.1265–73.
110. See R. Munting, 'Social opposition to gambling in Britain: a historical overview', *International Journal of the History of Sport*, Vol.10, No.3 (1993), p.302.
111. See D. Dixon, *From Prohibition to Regulation* (1991), Ch.4.
112. 1902 Select Committee, Evidence of Peacock, p.19, Q.336.
113. See D. Dale, 'Class act: the Street Betting Act of 1906', *International Journal of the Sociology of Law*, Vol.8 (1980), pp.101–28, for a discussion of the Act.

8
'Last and Greatest of Social Evils': The Opposition to Racing and Betting

In 1859 Samuel Smiles published his famous *Self Help*, espousing the virtues of the Protestant work ethic, with its emphasis on hard work, deferred gratification, self-denial and saving, and the building of wealth associated with the building of character. In the same year, a well-educated, artistic and cultivated Ipswich farmer's wife, her husband, her brother, her sons and her relatives, all attended the local races.[1]

Such behaviour was fairly typical for the locality, indeed for the nation. Yet racing and betting aroused widespread opposition. Racing was a focus for competition between two contrasting, middle-class value systems, and was located on a major frontier of socio-cultural change, where there were struggles over the 'right' use of time, territory and income. The story of racing is partially an interplay between the attempts by those espousing middle-class or reformist leisure culture to close meetings and control betting, and the adaptable vitality of a cross-class cultural form. To understand the opposition to racing we need therefore to examine in some detail the nature of the arguments presented against racing and the way they shifted over time. By examining the language and modes of discourse in which such views were expressed and the various rhetorics used, we gain a deeper insight into how British society viewed racing. There is then a need to examine the practical ways in which such opposition was mounted, both in terms of the range of media penetrated by these views and in terms of the forms of action taken by anti-race and anti-betting campaigners, in order to assess the extent of its success.

I

Although the late nineteenth- and the early twentieth-century opposition to working-class betting has begun to receive more detailed attention, earlier anti-racing campaigns have been neglected.[2] In the eighteenth and for part of the nineteenth century opposition was not directed against the races themselves but against a number of activities associated with them, especially betting and gaming, drinking and prostitution. In the earlier nineteenth century, however, the argument was more often focused on apparently wasted time, and was concerned with the opportunity costs of involvement in attendance at the races and their associated activities. It came often from religious groups who detested racing as one of 'the devil's entertainments',[3] and, although stronger among some social groups, came from across the class system. William Wilberforce, for example, who had attended race meetings in his youth, refused the stewardship of York races as early as 1790 because of his views on racing. Opposition was strongest among nonconformists. The Church of England, whose priesthood was sometimes drawn from the upper classes, was less antagonistic. Indeed, the 1813 York August meeting was 'fashionably and genteelly attended' by at least ten named clergy.[4] When Sydney Smith preached at the training town of Malton against horseracing and coursing in 1809 his audience included the Archbishop of York and a number of the 'sporting clergy'.[5] Thereafter, however, the Anglican revival alongside the further growth of nonconformism led to a stiffening of religious opposition against gambling in general. The abolition of the state lottery was an early mark of its success and clerical involvement with racing was soon much less.[6] At Hartlepool the parish priest led a strenuous but unsuccessful protest against the races in 1823.[7] At Chester a combination of nonconformist and ecclesiastical antagonism from about 1824 led to unsuccessful attacks in the press, protest meetings and anti-race processions.[8] At Sheffield ministers led protests in 1830.[9]

Gaming tables, rather than the racing itself, became an initial target, both on courses themselves and in the smaller gaming houses in the towns, although the gaming at the more exclusive gaming houses frequented by the upper classes was left alone, implying a paternalistic concern that the lower orders were spending money inappropriately rather than concern about gaming *per se*. At Doncaster a local solicitor formed an anti-gambling association of 'neighbouring gentry' in the late 1820s, which the local MPs and Lord Fitzwilliam joined, in order to get the smaller gaming houses closed down. The movement was paralleled at courses elsewhere. Gaming houses and larger gaming booths disappeared from most meetings by the mid-1830s as a result, although at Epsom they held out until 1844.[10]

Even before this point a wider range of leisure activities were coming under attack from such groups, who were attracting a wider following and whose attitudes were linked to broader processes of urbanization and industrialization. Fairs, bear baiting, cockfighting and other popular pursuits suffered as a result, and this broader process might have had some limited effect, mainly on entries for meetings at towns where the local gentry had a political interest. Certainly the number of meetings, which had been rising up to 1828, dropped back until after the mid-1830s. Many courses suffered major drops in quality and popularity. Indeed, the *Sporting Magazine* felt that many country meetings were 'on their last legs'.[11]

The struggles of the courses in the early 1830s were due partly to the efforts of anti-race groups, but they need to be seen in a broader, socio-political context. In some towns where racing had had a longstanding hold as part of gentry leisure their economic power, political control and social prestige were being challenged by emerging, middle-class, urban elites. The gentry had used these towns as social centres, but were withdrawing from some political and social involvement by the late 1820s. The entering of horses at local meetings had been part of that activity and patronage. The 1830 election and the 1832 Reform Act were political watersheds, marking points when a number of towns attempted to cast off gentry support. Where there was a political balance both Whig and Tory gentry had often supported the races by contributing subscriptions and entries. A political defeat suffered by either side could lead to a withdrawal of funding from the races.[12] The problem for some northern courses was exacerbated by the death of some of their principal patrons and by the agricultural depression of the 1830s as corn prices fell.[13] In York many tradesmen struggled and many farmers were insolvent, leading to a significant fall in the numbers at its course through the 1830s into the early 1840s. However, few courses closed. The 1830s saw many reformed corporations outflank and defeat Tory elites who supported racing and the sport suffered incidentally as a result but had recovered by the 1840s.[14]

In general, the races proved remarkably resilient to the preaching of the anti-race campaigners and to press and political campaigns, even if they were simultaneously directed against aristocratic patrons, since there was usually underlying political and social support for the races which could be mobilized given time. Cheltenham races provide a useful example. There both secular and religious affairs were dominated from around 1826 to 1848 by the uncompromising evangelical the Reverend Francis Close, who extolled sobriety and sabbath observance and attacked both aristocratic decadence and popular leisure. In 1827 he called for the ending of the three-day races, an attraction for all social classes, which were supported by his opponents, the leading Whig family in Gloucestershire, the Berkeleys. He was supported by both the *Cheltenham Journal* and the *Cheltenham Chronicle* and attacked the evil consequences of attending the meeting, alongside a tirade of abuse directed against the Berkeleys for what he claimed was their bad example, wild orgies and escapades. He claimed that licentiousness, prostitution and drunkenness, betting and gaming were associated with the races.[15] His arguments may have had some effect since in 1831 temporary political pressures led to the relocation of the races to Tewkesbury, but they were back by 1835.[16] Similar examples may be found elsewhere. At Lancaster attacks on the races by dissenting ministers and Anglican clergy encouraged a refusal in 1832 by the Liberal town council to support races patronized by Lord Hamilton and they were cancelled for that year. Here again, however, the defeat was only a temporary one and the races were back the following year.[17] At Derby the gap was somewhat longer. Evangelical pressure in the press, the pulpit and at public meetings forced the abandonment of racing in 1835, but by 1845 a majority of the town council favoured their revival, although with efforts to police the course more effectively and attempts at the abolition of 'all low gambling'.[18] At Leith in 1846 a long petition signed by hundreds was presented to the town council complaining of the 'vice and profligacy' and the 'disgusting intemperance' which had ensnared the 'young, the innocent and the unwary'. It was unsuccessful.[19]

Opposition to the races by anti-race campaigners grew stronger in the years around the mid-century, despite the expansion of middle-class recreation and greater economic security. By then both evangelicals and high Anglicans were beginning to acquire positions of power and influence and were more active in opposition. Parish appointments reflected this pattern and priests' attitudes to racing came under scrutiny. The Bishop of Oxford, Samuel Wilberforce, reflected widespread clerical attitudes in his belief that 'a sporting clergyman is a great evil in a parish'.[20] Although there were a number of clerical owners and breeders around 1850 they raced under assumed names or the name of their trainer.[21] The later fate of one racehorse owner, the Reverend J.W. King, who had raced or bred under the pseudonym 'Mr Laune' for some 50 years and whose family had a history of involvement in racing and breeding, illustrated anti-racing feeling. In 1874 one of his horses was particularly successful. His name appeared in the press, forcing awareness upon his bishop, who wrote to him, telling him that this was 'a discredit to your sacred profession and inflicting injury on the Church'. He was offered the choice either to 'resign your pastoral cures or relinquish a course which seems to me altogether at variance with the sacred obligations [of] a clergyman.'[22] King, now seen in *The Times* as 'a painful anachronism', resigned, receiving an episcopal letter expressing gratitude for his willingness to 'sacrifice private interest to public principle'.[23]

By this period a range of pamphlets and articles were being directed against racing. The growth of a cheap regional and local press aimed in the main at a middle-class, 'respectable', urban audience gave the arguments against horseracing's associations a fuller rein, while for some anti-race protesters earlier 'victories' against forms of working-class leisure meant that racing could be demonized as 'the last and greatest of social evils'.[24]

This alarmist campaign misunderstood the reality of British working-class betting and much of such material took the view that, if only the pulpit and the press worked harder to inform people of the reality of racing and publicized its evils, the public would take away their support and racing would be abandoned. Many arguments were marshalled against the races, mixing social, moral, economic and humanitarian reasons. The chapter headings in Dr T. Houston's 1853 pamphlet on the 'evils' of racing refer to 'idleness', 'misspending of money', 'theft and dishonesty', 'sabbath profanation', 'drunkenness', 'cruelty to animals', 'loss of life to riders' and 'gambling'.[25] While off-course more regular betting was increasing, causing some public alarm, at this stage it was still the *local* races themselves and the betting associated with them which were most often seen as the evil, although the middle-class moral onslaught against betting was supported by industrial employers who saw it as conflicting with the work ethic.

As towns expanded and links with rural life became more tenuous, some urban dwellers, with no association with or love of horses, simply saw racing as irrelevant. Others, who did not benefit from the races, put forward economic arguments against them. This group often included industrialists, merchants or other large employers. Industrialists lost money because large-scale absenteeism forced the closing down of works and the loss of time which should have been spent on production. The Manchester Whitsuntide races caused absenteeism right through that week, not just on Whit Monday, and a majority of employers seem to have been powerless to enforce sanctions in the face of resistance involving a range of medium-sized meetings.[26] The economic cost of increased theft, pickpocketing and counterfeit coinage was also counted. A Leeds vicar was not alone in arguing that the races should be stopped because extra police had to be drafted in and paid for to supervise those race crowds, 'viewed with disgust by large numbers of respectable people'.[27]

In the early part of the century even anti-race groups had to concede that the presence of county families in a town contributed economically to the income of many tradesmen as well as of innkeepers, transport service providers and others. But once the railways ensured that county families could travel in daily, this was less obviously the case. By about 1860 in Chester an anti-race tradesman was arguing that shopkeepers were suffering diminishing trade and returns. He claimed that, having surveyed the leading thoroughfares of the town, the majority of tradesmen saw the races as a serious item of loss of up to 50 per cent.[28] The more respectable did not frequent the streets during race week, while money was not being spent on consumer goods but on betting. At Scarborough, which was anxious to maintain its select resort status, the dominant feeling on the town council by 1886 was that the races kept respectable visitors away and that only professional betting men really profited.[29]

Another set of arguments were social. The result of the races was 'gaols filled, characters lost and families embroiled and ruined'.[30] The races brought to the towns the 'worst of humanity, gamblers ... blacklegs ... and women of easy virtue'.[31] The press made much of increased criminal activity during race weeks, including the passing of counterfeit money, pickpocketing and other thefts.[32] They were often also keen to seize on apparent evidence that betting losses were often the cause of theft from employers to get money which was then wagered and lost in its turn. When the Attorney General introduced the Betting House Bill of 1853 he argued that lower-class betting became addictive and led servants and apprentices to be drawn into robbing their masters and employers. The press seized on any examples where betting was involved in such crimes throughout the century. Paternalistic concern for the less well-off and anxiety to protect the property of the wealthy combined.[33]

It was also argued that money earned through work was 'improvidently squandered' at the racecourse or in betting and so damaged family life. It was argued too that most money wagered left the area and took it out of local circulation, and that tradesmen were hit by the impecuniosity of their customers after race week.[34] There was no sense that workers won money as well as lost it and that money was in the main merely redistributed within the community. Most of betting's opponents betrayed a real ignorance of it and the circulation of money in the betting market and grossly exaggerated the bookmakers' profits. Bookmakers had bad debts, yet they had to pay out or go out of business. The winnings of successful 'Leviathan' bookmakers were regularly cited as showing how the general public lost money on the races; there was never any mention of failed bookmakers.

Working-class attendance at and betting on meetings was seen as a personal vice, a moral weakness, which could have tragic results: poverty and destitution for the gambler and his dependants. The Chester artisan spent his money on 'selfish rioting, drunkenness and debauchery, bringing misery on himself and his family'.[35] Not only that, since many works were forced to shut down for race week, all workers lost money whether they wanted to work or not. In Chester in the 1860s the loss of earnings was estimated as near to £4,000.[36] In the Stockton area by the early 1880s newspaper estimates ranged from £30,000 to £100,000 losses for the

August week.[37] Shopkeepers suggested that turnover was low as a result for two weeks after the races.[38] There was possibly also the rarely spoken, further fear that this would increase demands for charity and poor relief.

There was also anxiety about the effects of excessive middle-class gambling, especially by clerks. Embezzlement was a key theme, reflecting the hidden attraction of betting to the middle classes.[39] The 'Liverpool Bank case' of 1901–02, when a bank clerk embezzled £160,000 to feed his betting debts was perhaps the most notorious.[40] Another was bankruptcy of companies. Lord Hawke in his evidence to the House of Lords Select Committee on Betting in 1901 quoted accounts in the criminal court over five years of 80 suicides, 321 embezzlements and 191 bankruptcies, all allegedly due to betting and claimed that these were underestimates. But such evidence was selective. The press regularly referred to such cases, yet reading below the headlines often reveals a more complex situation in which betting was only a contributory factor. A young Burnley picket maker, who had taken over his father's business, claimed he had lost nearly £1,000 in betting at his bankruptcy hearing. But evidence also revealed that his bookkeeping had been bad since he had taken over and that he was already in debt before he turned to gambling.[41]

Some of Hawke's supporters saw profit as legitimate only if based on thrift, hard work and skill. Even insurance and investment on the Stock Exchange came under attack and gambling of any kind, since it was an unproductive activity, was seen as an illegitimate form of profit-making activity.[42] Betting was wrong because it took money from somebody without giving goods or a service in return. There was no possibility of mutual advantage. Furthermore, if one person had more inside knowledge about a horse than another, then betting was simply taking advantage of someone else's ignorance and was also morally wrong.

There was a particularly potent mixture of fear and disapproval attached to the behaviour so often to be found on or *en route* to the courses and to the equally visible blocking of urban streets by large numbers of betting men and bookmakers, often using foul language and failing to display the appropriate level of deference. Racing generated large crowds, associating in dangerous ways. The Dean of Chester, whose attacks on the Chester meetings were given national coverage in the early 1870s, saw them as attracting 'like an army of locusts' some of the 'vilest and most degraded' of characters.[43] Brawling and drunkenness at the races were also inappropriate forms of behaviour. Racing could therefore be seen as a territorial threat to the social order. Such objections could most particularly be found among church- and chapel-goers, of whatever class, but were also prevalent among some urban business and professional groups.

Pre-enclosure race meetings, like fairs, seem to have been an opportunity for meeting the opposite sex and a number of anti-race pamphlets saw the races as a setting for the loosening of sexual restraint. Chester races were argued to be characterized by 'fornication', and had 'robbed many ... an unguarded female of her purity' so that its closure would be 'in the interests of purity and virtue' as well as of sobriety.[44]

Economic and social arguments often emerged publicly as moral and religious ones, continuing the 'rational recreation' debate of the 1830s and the 1840s.[45] Racing's attractions could be dismissed as 'a love of amusement in the vulgar and the gross',[46] as unhealthy both in mind and body, both of which suffered through licence, excitement and excess. A fundamental shortcoming of such views was their lack of any understanding of racing. There is little evidence to support the view that objectors actually visited the races or associated with those who did.

Although off-course betting by the working classes on races beyond the local meeting was already significant by the 1860s in some areas, awareness of this took some time to come to wider recognition. In Manchester one of the reasons advanced by Mr P. FitzGerald, MP for his refusal to renew the racecourse lease in 1868 was that 'gambling was an immoral act' and that 'betting on the large and ruinous scale is spreading ... and great numbers of our workmen catch the frenzy'.[47] By the 1870s such activity was already being increasingly described as 'the betting nuisance' and as a large and growing social problem by some racing commentators, but often only as an aside while attacking the 'elements of chicanery' and 'seminaries of swindling' associated with racecourse betting manoeuvres.[48] Such complaints were from a minority, and the betting issue did not assume the scale of a moral panic until the 1880s. The reasons for this are unclear. D. Dixon argues that the 1880s were characterized by a concatenation of social, economic and political forces which brought working-class betting (and gambling more generally) to the attention to the public.[49] He suggests that it might be one of a number of concerns fuelled by the economic and social changes of the later nineteenth century; or it may have been the product of the apparent success of the temperance movement in changing attitudes and behaviour in relation to alcohol, and that by the late 1880s people of strong religious and social beliefs were looking for a new crusade, although drink was still a major moral and political issue at this time. Equally it may be that social investigations and the new theories of poverty emerging in the 1880s had made people more aware of the material conditions of working-class life and given a new understanding of the contribution of irresponsible expenditure on betting to secondary poverty, although there was also a humanistic concern for the misery caused as a result. Anti-urbanism, with its stress on betting as a symptom of the disease of city life, was also emerging during this period.[50] It is also possible that the move to highly-capitalized, enclosed courses and the lessening of any identification with local meetings that it entailed had some effect. There is currently insufficient information to be certain on this point; this is an area where further research is needed.

While, as we have seen in Chapter 4, betting among the working classes had been growing for many years before this, the debate on betting now afforded it a higher priority. Working-class betting was seen as a new phenomenon, one which had arrived during the last decade and was spreading rapidly. Books, pamphlets and press articles, sermons and church debates all provide evidence of widespread concern and demonstrate the range of the outlets into which anti-working-class gambling views spread, showing a deep penetration of the British power structure. Public figures such as judges, politicians, magistrates and councillors were soon leaping on the bandwagon to call for action and police prosecutions increased. The inadequacy and under-utilization of legal controls were blamed, and bookmakers and the commercialization of racing were scapegoated. Betting was seen as having disastrous effects on the individual. According to Seton Churchill, it:

> produces godliness and irreligion, deadens the moral sense, unfits man for the sterner duties of life, creates feverish excitement in the place of steady work and industry, lowers self-respect, degrades manhood, develops low cunning and selfishness, destroys domestic happiness and home life, unsettles the labour market and encourages crime and general recklessness.[51]

The shift from attacks on races to attacks on betting was accompanied by a change of emphasis in the argument. Much of the new campaign had a more strongly moralistic tone running along with many of the earlier arguments, stressing betting as inherently wrong, rather than (as previously) wrong because of its effects. Three interconnected assertions were constantly levelled against it.

First, betting was seen as in social-Darwinian terms as a ‘descent to a lower plane of thought and feeling’, something which was irrational, appealing to chance and rejecting reason.[52] Although the press were blamed for encouraging it, there was no recognition of the argument that the increased availability of news information had actually made betting more rational. Secondly, it was argued that betting was anti-social and selfish, rendering relationships between gamblers immoral. It was an attempt to gain at the expense of other people, leading to a deterioration of character and conduct.[53] Finally, there was a reiteration of the point that betting was an illegitimate method of dealing with wealth, which, it was argued, could be transferred only by gift, exchange of goods or as payment for work. Betting could therefore be seen as disturbing the equipoise of a society based on proper reward for labour and a major threat to the whole economic system of society and wage-labour. Money won by betting was morally debasing because it had not been earned.[54]

Changes in society and new social concerns had an impact on the arguments, and betting was increasingly attacked for its supposed contribution to industrial inefficiency and physical degeneration. Structural weaknesses in the British economy were causing anxiety by the turn of the century. Profits were falling. Earlier arguments from industrialists and other employers against absenteeism and betting were now reiterated against off-course betting as the cause of industrial inefficiency. Workers were supposedly over-excited by gambling and less able to take pains and concentrate upon their work. Economic concerns about competition from the USA and continental Europe were linked to betting arguments. In evidence given to the 1902 Select Committee, a Newcastle magistrate and former trade-union leader argued that 'if the betting craze goes unchecked, the sober youths of Germany will take the reins of the commercial world'. Employers giving evidence were unanimous in wanting to stop betting; one sacked those discovered to be gamblers.[55] City life was seen as particularly conducive to betting, providing stimulation and excitement at the expense of physical degeneration and mental weakness. It was linked to imperialist ideals with the suggestion that betting made men 'unfitted to defend their country' and face 'the harder and sterner duties of life', and that men were spectators of and betting on rather than participating in more 'manly' sports.[56] Contemporary medical debates about nervous illness were also called upon to bolster the argument that the artificial stimulation of the nervous excitement of gambling would cause mental instability among the working classes.[57] Sexual roles were also affected by betting, and gambling among women was cited to argue that betting was adversely affecting family life.[58] The Liberal writer Lady Bell, recognizing from her home visits in her husband's Teesside works the problems faced by working-class women, their vulnerability when they lacked resources, and inability to camouflage difficulties, felt 'sick at heart at seeing the disasters brought about ... by betting', and in her writing highlighted the insidious effects of small-scale gambling in their lives.[59]

This last point linked to political concerns among anti-gamblers about the need for social reform. Although there was agreement on the need for this, these concerns were approached from different and sometimes competing perspectives. By the late 1880s opposition to betting was coming from an ever-widening range of groups, which now included the Protestant churches, the administrative–professional middle classes, some employers and New Liberal thinkers attempting to construct and implement a progressive social programme. By the 1890s it was also attracting members of the increasingly powerful Labour leadership, many of whom retained their evangelistic beliefs. The political alliances between these groups were shifting, fragile and transitory, but their views on betting gave an illusory impression of unity. From the political right, Seton Churchill argued that gambling was linked to the rise of socialism and the dangers of revolution, and saw the control of betting as part of the legitimation of capitalism and the defence of the Empire.[60] In the churches, bishops were often more cautious about betting than the evangelical wing. The 'official' classes had more concern about the possible ruin of industry by betting than had many employers. The Liberals, espousing a philosophy of state action and moral reform within the existing socio-economic framework, wanted to protect the working classes from the exploitation of bookmakers, tipsters and the sporting press, in order to help to tackle the broader problems of secondary poverty identified by Booth, B.S. Rowntree and other social investigators. Rowntree, whose opposition to betting was both moral and practical, edited *Betting and Gambling, a National Evil* in 1905, arguing that even women and children were being drawn into gambling by an 'army of social parasites' – bookmakers and touts, and this particular concern for women and children is an interesting aspect of the moral position.[61] Many Labour leaders were also strong supporters of the anti-gambling movement, especially in the period around the 1889 dock strike, when they were trying to construct a labour movement. They, however, saw the real problems of working-class betting as being the part they played in distracting people from and being inimical to social and political progress. Time spent on betting and reliance on luck inhibited social change. They saw community self-discipline, self-respect and self-reliance as all potentially damaged by spending on betting. Ramsay MacDonald was speaking for much of the labour movement when he claimed that 'every labour leader I know recognizes the gambling spirit as a menace to any form of labour party'. He saw betting as a 'class disease', particularly attractive to those on the marginal lines of poverty and respectability because their lives were so 'unsatisfactory',[62] and like many other socialists showed an active dislike of those popular cultural forms, such as betting or drinking, which did not aid self-improvement, thrift or political activism.[63]

The anti-gambling movement had only the appearance of unity. Its supporters had very different aims and therefore different reasons for their involvement, even though the cacophony of voices, with its 'melange of prejudice, self-persuasion and proto-medical phraseology' allowed anti-gambling writers to see their attack on working-class betting as a crusade.[64] But, although arguments against betting and the changes and continuities in those arguments throughout the period are important in understanding the range of motivations behind the anti-race campaign, the movement did more than simply offer argument. Had the opposition to racing simply offered the arguments as theoretical ones little notice would have been taken of them. To be effective, the anti-racing groups had to engage in several sorts of action. Here again anti-race activities had elements both of continuity and of change.

II

What forms did anti-racing activity take? Preaching from the pulpit or elsewhere against the activities going on at meetings was the most common form of activity, and one found throughout the century, throughout England, Scotland and Wales, and in both nonconformist and Church of England places of worship. This was rarer than one might expect in some towns with race meetings, and it may well have been that where clergymen recognized the strong local support the races enjoyed, they were unwilling to challenge their congregations. It was rarer still in those towns such as Malton, Middleham or Newmarket where racehorse training was a key industry, and where, therefore, racing people were important members of congregations or gave financial support. At Newmarket, for example, most trainers were Church of England communicants, while the Jockey Club too had links with local churches. In 1872, for example, the Congregationalist Sunday school anniversary was held on the racecourse 'by the liberality of the Jockey Club' while the meeting of the deanery clergy was held in the Jockey Club subscription rooms.[65] Nevertheless, there were sporadic attempts to preach against the races throughout the century in the majority of towns. In Carlisle there always was strong religious opposition and in 1865, for example, Francis Close, by then Dean of Carlisle, renewed his earlier attacks, preaching a number of sermons which saw racing as 'a kind of pleasure which seemed to be unmitigatedly evil'.[66] Later Bishops of Carlisle followed in his footsteps, without any success.[67] At Richmond in 1889 the rector preached an anti-racing sermon attacking the presence of 'drunkards, gamblers and sharpers' at the races and condemning those who attended them as foolish, but this was at a time when Richmond races were in decline.[68] Such preaching was almost always entirely to those who were already converted opponents to racing, and in chapel, church or hall. It was rarely heard by the followers of racing and hence was singularly ineffective, except in marshalling existing opposition.

In order to influence (and directly confront) the unconverted, preaching and the distribution of tracts at courses was occasionally attempted, although some race meetings reacted to such activity by bill-posted warnings to itinerant preachers to keep off the course, threatening their prosecution. A primitive Methodist group bravely addressed the Manchester crowd and distributed tracts in 1838, holding forth with denunciations of the sinfulness and folly of the day.[69] A later description of Aintree described anti-racing tracts as being distributed to all who would take them, despite a notice forbidding this, by a loudly-spoken man who asked all who passed whether they had obtained permission from their minister to visit. This too was probably vain since the ground for several yards around was 'strewed with tracts'.[70] The Baptist F.B. Meyer, who had preached against the races in 1882, actually tried unsuccessfully to address the Leicester crowd in 1883, and escaped unmolested only with some difficulty.[71]

The publication of tracts against the races was a recognition that public opinion as a whole was not strongly opposed to the meetings, and needed changing. At Chester a Voluntary Association was set up especially to ascertain the views of the citizens and to publish small pamphlets presenting 'rational' arguments against the races.[72] Methodists often used reformed 'sinners' to influence people and there are occasional surviving tracts such as *What I Saw at Manchester Races*, by an 'Old Jockey', published in Manchester in 1851 and describing the evils of the scene, which show that this course of action was attempted. Public opinion was, however, markedly unswayed.

A common approach was therefore to keep the crowds away. Some nonconformist churches expelled members who went to the races, but more often churches organized counter-attractions. Such distractions came in several forms, often collectively organized by anti-race and temperance groups. The young were often prime targets. Schools generally suffered poor attendance during race weeks, so that it was hoped that by keeping children away from the races they would be less influenced by them. Even in the 1820s Sunday School managers were organizing 'treats' and other activities to keep their pupils from the races.[73] At Newcastle, the Sunday School Teachers Association, founded in 1835, had as one of its four key objectives the banning of 'the town races and their drinking, gambling and unruliness'.[74]

Rail excursions came early and Sunday school organizations were prominent in keeping children away. Indeed, the first recorded arrangement for a privately-organized, excursion train thus far traced was when about 150 members of the Bennett Street Sunday School visited Liverpool during the Manchester Race week of May 1831.[75] Thomas Cook's first temperance excursion in 1846 was another such Sunday school counter-attraction.[76]

To combat the processions associated with the races, anti-race protesters, including Sunday schools, organized their own processions or created alternative festivals. At Newcastle large strings of children from the local Sunday schools processed through the town *en route* to the station for their trips, excursions and picnics, some led by fife and flute bands. After the move of the races from the Moor to Gosforth Park in 1881, the Newcastle temperance organizations, who had previously unsuccessfully run opposition gatherings at Gosforth, held a series of meetings which resulted in the Town Moor being used from 1882 for alternative temperance meetings offering foot races, bicycle matches, assaults at arms, football matches and other sports, and a fair.[77] Consciously or unconsciously, its structure mirrored the races, and by 1883 it had stands, 24 large marquees, a long range of tents, tables and stalls.[78] In Middlesbrough and Stockton, as in many other places, a joint Sunday School Union was set up to offer activities 'as an antidote to the attractions provided by the races'.[79] Here prominent local industrialists and farmers lent facilities and support.[80] At Beverley a Minster Sunday School festival was held at the same time as the races by the 1870s.

By the end of the century such privately-organized alternatives had almost ceased, mainly due to funding difficulties. Private rail excursions had to be underwritten and sometimes lost money. The galas were also costly. At Stockton one organized by the Sunday School Union 'resulted in a heavy loss' and it was discontinued after the mid-1880s.[81] But it was also becoming clear that the policy of offering children alternatives to the races had been ineffective. Children could not be removed for each day of a two- or three-day meeting, and trips were therefore often added to race week activities, not substitutes for a visit. By the 1880s race meetings were enclosed and few children went, so there was less point in organizing alternatives except as symbols of opposition. Race weeks had become unofficial holidays in many towns, and increasingly trips were being offered by railway companies as commercial enterprises primarily for adults.

While opposition to the races themselves was largely unsuccessful, there were occasional victories which could be claimed. Sometimes a victory could be a partial one. Licensing magistrates were reluctant to refuse licences to grandstands and booths during customary race days, but it could be difficult for some meetings to extend to a further day. At Leicester the race committee tried unsuccessfully to acquire a Saturday licence in 1870, to the disappointment of the *Leicester Journal*.[82] At the Kingsbury course in London, founded in 1864 and which had seven meetings a year by 1869, magistrates refused licences to publicans in 1877 in an attempt to control it.[83]

There were occasional total victories after mid-century with courses or racehorse training grounds being closed down due to opposition, most usually when control over longstanding racing land fell into the hands of anti-racing owners, who terminated the leases. Examples include Malton, Durham, Hambleton and the Manchester Kersall Moor and Castle Irwell sites.[84] Anti-race groups had a better chance of succeeding where a newly enclosed meeting was setting up in an urban area without a strong racing tradition. At Halifax a new, enclosed course was set out in 1878, at a cost of nearly £40,000, attracting crowds of about 20,000. But there was strong opposition, led by a Congregationalist pastor, the vicar of Halifax and a number of local councillors including the mayor, and in 1879 they brought successful prosecutions for minor offences against members of the race company. The fines of £2 and £1 plus costs signalled that magistrates were unwilling to be punitive, but at a public meeting against the races the mayor moved a motion of 'regret and disapproval' against the 'recent establishment of races in the neighbourhood', considering them to be 'injurious to the moral and commercial interests of the community'. He then declared it carried even though many of the audience were racing supporters. Nevertheless, opposition to the races was strong enough to ensure that workmen were not able to absent themselves from work with impunity. To attend the races was to run the risk of job loss. By 1884 the meeting had such poor attendance it was forced to cease.[85]

In traditional racing towns, however, attempts at race closure were usually unsuccessful. A Doncaster solicitor who organized a public meeting in 1828 against the races and gambling there was met with a number of speeches opposing him and a pelting on the way home.[86] At Chester, when the Corporation was considering taking over the meeting fully in 1891, the watch committee were addressed by nonconformist clergy and middle-class opponents, including an accountant, an ironmonger, a baker and a solicitor; there was a letter from the Bishop, a memorial from the Dean, and a letter from Queen Street Congregational church, but all failed to influence the committee.[87]

The recognition that most racecourses could not be closed led to increased attacks on non-racecourse betting by the working classes. One way of combating this was by restricting betting information. A number of liberal nonconformist newspapers, by giving column inches to those who opposed the races, appeared to act as a key agent of indoctrination. Editors and owners were important therefore in determining policy. The *Newcastle Daily Telegraph* was reluctant to publish racing news, but on the death of the editor racing coverage was renewed. The *Northern Echo* set its typeface firmly against racing results and reports in the 1870s, and like other regional papers, gave strong support in the 1890s to the National Anti-Gambling League. The principle of restricting betting information was one thing, but in reality racing results were important for circulation. The *Northern Echo's* circulation was hit badly since regional rivals such as *The North-Eastern Daily Gazette* and the *Newcastle Daily Chronicle* boosted circulation with betting news and it was soon forced to resume. The later fate of the *Northern Daily Express* was salutory. It was anti-gambling and did not include racing news in its morning edition. It closed in 1886, complaining that what the people wanted was coverage of all race meetings, not just their local one.[88]

In Manchester there was also a short-lived attempt in 1870 to exclude betting news, but only the *Manchester Guardian* persevered and this action was only symbolic, since its sister paper the *Manchester Evening News* initially maintained full coverage of racing and betting. It tried a ban, briefly, and in the 1890s both papers lent strong support to the National Anti-Gambling League, but both were including betting information by 1902. The *Leeds Mercury* followed a similar pattern. In papers belonging to the Peases, the Rowntrees, the Cadburys and other newspaper-controlling anti-gamblers, the ambiguity of their attitude towards racing, with fulminations against betting in editorial columns often running alongside a full results service including starting prices, forced upon them by circulation pressure was something which caused them embarrassment and divided their ranks.

The restriction of information to the reading public who could not afford a paper was an alternative ploy. Libraries in a number of towns blacked out racing results before putting papers on display, usually at the instigation of local councillors or because of the attitude of the chief librarian.[89] There was wider discussion of whether to black out betting news, betting quotations and racing results on more than one occasion, and in 1893 a vote showed libraries to be equally divided on the subject.[90] This again was relatively ineffective and had a fairly symbolic impact.

Betting in list houses had been attacked spasmodically since the 1853 Act by local police forces throughout the country. Bookmakers responded by taking ready money bets in the street, and, in its turn, the introduction of by-laws concerned with obstruction reflects the response of anti-gambling magistrates and the police. Numbers of such by-laws date from the mid-1870s, although in some cases it is unclear whether they were aimed just at bookmakers. Some were more explicit. Manchester, for example, passed a by-law in 1875 which defined any three or more persons assembled together for the purpose of betting as obstructing the street.[91] Following the Municipal Corporations Act of 1882 Wolverhampton was probably the first to introduce a more specific local by-law to deal with street betting. A common form of words was:

> no person shall frequent or use any public place, on behalf of himself or any other person, for the purpose of wagering or agreeing to bet or wager with any person, or paying or receiving or settling bets

and offences were subject to a fine not exceeding £5. Following the success of the Blackpool Improvement Bill of 1901, second convictions could be subject to a fine of up to £10 and further convictions of up to £50.

Very occasionally resort was taken to legal measures which might attack racecourse betting direct. Following the 1853 Act it had at first been thought that betting on a racecourse was legal, but it came under renewed challenge in the early 1870s. Successful local prosecutions were made against bookmakers using a fixed spot, a wooden booth on the raceground (*Shaw* v. *Morley* 16 WR 763, 1871) and against bookmakers using an umbrella and a stool (*Bows* v. *Fenwick* 22 WR 804, 1872). Prosecutions followed spasmodically over the next two decades, but usually elicited unfavourable press reaction since crowds then turned to betting with less well-known and reputable bookmakers who often welshed. So although meetings upheld the law by posting notices banning such activities, they were tacitly allowed on almost all courses. In 1874 the magistrates at Edgeware fined the lessee of Kingsbury racecourse for permitting ready-money betting, although credit betting was still seen as legal,[92] and there was some brief panic among the courses. The next Goodwood meeting posted notices banning ready-money betting and tried police enforcement, but 'ready-money betting ... flourished as strongly as ever'.[93] The decision was reversed following the understandable failure of a later 1874 prosecution of Harry Chaplin, MP at Newmarket in front of local pro-racing magistrates for permitting ready-money betting in the rings, which was probably set up by the Jockey Club. More serious challenges to the legality of racecourse betting came with the more organized approach of the National Anti-Gambling League, founded in 1890 by F.D. Atkins with strong support from a coalition of nonconformist churches. The NAGL was a most significant pressure group which played a central part in channelling subsequent concerns about betting. It was, however, extremely fragmented, expressing anti-betting views from a variety of ideological perspectives. To begin with it favoured the prohibition of all betting, but it was soon realized that this was not possible in the light of popular opinion. This was a view reinforced during the 1895 election, when anti-betting speeches received adverse responses. It therefore attempted to move forward on two fronts simultaneously. Initially the stress was more on educational and propagandist work to change people's views. The twice-yearly *Bulletin* documented its activities, many of which were similar to temperance tactics – public meetings, lectures and sermons, the forming of local branches, pledges, petitions and subscription lists, and the reprinting of anti-gambling material from the press. The *Bulletin* also included accounts of the harm done to families by betting, crimes caused by it, analyses of the accuracy of betting tips and quotations from public figures denouncing betting. It was successful in getting its view into a range of the media, from the daily press to popular literature. The NAGL was active in lobbying watch committees, MPs and local politicians, and its actions were supported by the more liberal, nonconformist press. The NAGL's supporters brought out a number of books and other publications to stimulate discussion from the early 1890s.[94] A wide range of more ephemeral material was also circulated, including pamphlets, flysheets, leaflets and pledges. The NAGL had major branches in London, York, Manchester, the north-east and Scotland, together with membership granted to other groups which were subgroups of existing social and religious organizations, and had some smaller branches scattered across the country although the heart of its support was in the north. Its membership overlapped with that of other social reform groups, most particularly the temperance movement.

When Hawke took over the leadership of the NAGL in 1893 he placed a greater stress on the enforcement of existing laws and the creation of new and firmer ones against betting. Anti-betting by-laws were promoted and there was action against newspapers which encouraged betting. The NAGL also attempted organized prosecutions of racecourses, bookmakers, postal betting and betting clubs, although it had little success. Clubs, used by the upper classes as well as bookmakers, were a difficult target. A prosecution brought against the Albert Club (*Downs* v. *Johnson* [1895] 2QB 203) failed when it was argued that betting was confined to members and the club had been established for a purpose other than betting. Indeed, it merely formalized class distinction in the law, since attempts to establish working-class equivalents were banned. A second 1895 prosecution (*Queen* v. *Brown* 2QBD) attacking postal betting also failed.[95] While the taking of ready-money bets by bookmakers was recognized as clearly illegal, an 1897 case (*Bradford* v. *Dawson* QBD) made it clear that the payment of betting debts in public houses was not illegal.

The NAGL also initiated a number of prosecutions attempting to force an end to racecourse betting, posing a real threat to the courses. The suppression of racecourse bookmaking was seen as the 'first necessity',[96] which would reform upper-class betting habits, and it was the upper- and middle-class betting in the betting 'rings' or enclosures which were to be the target.

The legality of racecourse betting hinged on the lack of definition of the word 'place' in the 1853 Betting Act which stated that 'No ... place shall be opened, kept or used for the purpose of ... any person using the same ... [for] ... betting with persons resorting thereto'. The earlier prosecutions had been of bookmakers, but the NAGL decided to prosecute racecourse managers for allowing betting. On their first attempt against Messrs Trail at Northampton racecourse in 1893 the bookmaker was convicted but the magistrates acquitted the managers, accepting the defence that they had no knowledge of the bookmaker's activities. The NAGL sent a deputation to the Home Office, but while the Home Secretary was sympathetic, officials were less so. A further unsuccessful action in 1895 against the Jockey Club officials at Newmarket was dismissed on the same grounds as previously. However, this gave hope to the NAGL since both defences had failed to argue positively that betting was legal. To get round the defence of ignorance, the next prosecution, in 1896, was of one of the major shareholders at Hurst Park, the bookmaker Dick Dunn. Dunn was simply moving round the ring shouting his odds and taking bets and not using equipment. His defence was that he did not induce the improvident to bet, but merely dealt with those more wealthy betters who could afford entrance to Tattersall's. It was an appealing argument, which harked back to the class-based comment of the Attorney General when introducing the 1853 legislation, that the Bill would not 'interfere with that description of betting which had so long existed at Tattersall's', and it was accepted by the magistrates.

However, it went to appeal and in 1897 the Queen's Bench argued that the intention of the legislation was clear and that professional bookmaking in the rings was illegal. Dunn's case was referred back to the magistrates, who fined him £1. To the NAGL this now indicated that all betting could be seen as illegal, since a 'place' seemed to cover anywhere a bet was made. The *Bulletin* described it as 'a great triumph for social reform', and saw it as opening the way for further prosecutions.[97]

This caused panic among racecourse managers and shareholders. In his detailed study of the events surrounding the racecourse bookmaking campaign Dixon argues that it also caused concern to some police forces, who were not at all sanguine about the prospect of actively attempting to suppress racecourse betting and also had public order concerns.[98] In order to seek judicial reconsideration of the bookmaking issue a new action was needed where the racing authorities had some control over prosecution as well as defence. A clerk at Kempton Park, Charles Powell, was therefore given a single share in the company by a director. On 12 April 1897 he issued a writ against his company to get an injunction to restrain it from providing betting facilities. Following the temporary granting of an injunction by the Lord Chief Justice, it was rapidly referred to the Court of Appeal. A majority verdict on 5 July argued that the enclosure was not a 'place' under the 1853 Act, although they accepted that the company knew of the bookmaking; but the Master of the Rolls introduced a third element of judgment. He argued that even if the enclosure were a 'place', the bookmakers would have to have an exclusive 'use' of it, including clear elements of control and possession, which they did not, before they breached the 1853 Act. At this point police forces withdrew other prosecutions of racecourse betting and abandoned others under consideration.

There was then a two-year suppression of legal activity before the appeal reached the House of Lords. In the meanwhile the NAGL had gathered a large petition addressed to the Queen attacking the Court of Appeal and requesting redress, unsuccessfully arguing that the case was collusive and that the court had been misled. In 1899 their Lordships turned up in numbers, illustrating the importance of the issue, and by a large majority which included Lord Chancellor Halsbury, affirmed the Court of Appeal's decision, reaffirming the crucial point about the domination and control needed by bookmakers over the 'place' before they could be convicted. This judgment firmly established the legality of betting in racecourse enclosures, provided that bookmakers were not charged extra for entry, did not use paraphernalia which might be construed as creating a 'place' under the 1853 Act, and moved around the enclosure.

The propaganda victory of *Hawke* v. *Dunn* had now been reversed, but the NAGL was still optimistic. The defeat forced it to abandon its campaign against racecourse bookmaking and its attempts to halt upper-class betting in the rings. It nevertheless saw itself as having drawn attention to betting as a significant public issue. Its response was to turn its attention more to off-course, working-class gambling.[99] For some time local anti-gamblers had been active in putting pressure on local authorities to introduce more widely local government legislation originally set out in the Metropolitan Streets Act of 1867, which declared an assembly of three or more people in the street for the purpose of betting to be an obstruction. Bookmakers had tried to avoid this by dealing only with one better at a time, and by the mid-1890s specific by-laws specifically prohibiting the frequenting and use of streets for betting were being introduced by anti-gambling local authorities. By 1896, 25 towns and seven counties had such laws, and the NAGL was actively encouraging others to follow their lead.

Although the expansion of by-laws had been well under way before any real interest had been shown by the NAGL, the extra interest had a cumulative effect, increasing public awareness and generating a climate which encouraged the unsuccessful introduction by the Bishop of Hereford of a Bill, which was followed by an official enquiry – the House of Lords Select Committee on Betting of 1901–02. Although the NAGL played an important role in the provision of evidence, the Committee established an agenda which was only partially that of the NAGL, set firmly against street and public-house bookmaking but ignoring upper-class credit and racecourse betting. The several failed Street Betting Bills (1903–06) and the successful Street Betting Act (1906) were given strong support by the NAGL, which worked hard to encourage episcopal support, lobbied the government and organized meetings and conferences. Indeed, it attempted to take the credit for the Act itself and its successful parliamentary progress, presenting it as the culmination of a long campaign.[100]

But by 1906 the NAGL had also begun to realize the strength of inertia and establishment opposition and that the opportunities to tackle betting and on a broader front were limited, even with a new Liberal reformist government. It was also faced with competition for members from another national anti-gambling organization, the Society for the Suppression of Gambling, working in the moral and educational areas, using the services of the *Daily News* and largely funded by the Cadbury family. Other organizations had anti-gambling offshoots and denominational, regional and national friction was a constant problem. The NAGL responded by restructuring its organization and re-emphasizing its propagandist activity under the banner of a 'Forward Movement' campaign. From 1906–07 it claimed to have organized some 440 meetings and moved more from preaching to the converted to preaching to the unconverted inside factories such as Laird's shipbuilders or at their gates. Alongside this the NAGL targeted particular towns for intensive campaigns. Within its ranks there was now strong pressure to launch an attack against newspaper betting odds, which would have had a major impact on betting, but although there was support for this among some Liberal papers, the bulk of the press opposed it, while it was seen as impracticable by Home Office officials. Anti-gambling Bills in 1907 and 1912 both failed in part because they included bans on the publication of odds. The transmission of betting information by post, telegraph or telephone by the Post Office was another source of complaint, but this would have interfered with middle- and upper-class credit betting, while the Post Office was both unwilling to lose revenue and unwilling to infringe civil liberties by policing any measure. The NAGL therefore attempted as a more practical and realizable measure to tackle bookmakers' and tipsters' advertisements in the press, and a Betting Inducements Bill, introduced in 1912 and again in 1914, almost reached the statute book before the Great War intervened.

The problem for the NAGL was that legislation needed government support, but the government, facing constitutional difficulties, social, political and industrial conflict and other legislative pressures, was unwilling to lend support to private members' Bills which were controversial and took up much parliamentary time. At the same time, the Bills which were introduced were often overloaded, overambitious and lacked a clear and achievable focus.

Despite apparent support from a number of prominent politicians, industrialists and churchmen, the reality was that the NAGL's campaign was losing momentum by 1914. Liberalism and nonconformity were both losing support; the growth of betting had not been held back; the NAGL had not been able to introduce further legislation; and its subscription income since 1909 had been in slow but steady decline. Among informed parliamentarians and the police there was a growing appreciation that the problems of prohibition made a ban on betting unworkable, while the effect of the NAGL's activity had been to introduce legislation which forced the police into further attempts to suppress working-class betting, while ignoring the credit betting of wealthier groups, rendering the NAGL open to charges of hypocrisy and apparent class prejudice, both of which lost it sympathy.

As has been made clear, within the anti-gambling groups there was no consensus about racing and betting. Even at the end of the nineteenth century middle-class moralists, labour leaders or Liberal politicians each presented a range of arguments against them, and wanted to see a range of very different prohibitive legislation, educational and propagandist activity taking place. For many of its supporters, opposition to gambling was only one of a number of reformist social concerns. For most of the earlier period action was almost always localized and piecemeal and carried out by minority groups in the face of public apathy or antagonism, while the association with organized religion may have weakened, not helped, its impact. The activities associated with racing and betting changed little and although there were changes in the social, economic and moral estimation of such activities, opposition had little effect and anti-racing activities were simply incorporated into an existing recreational pattern. In the shorter run the reforming pressure groups which opposed betting had some victories, but they lost the war. The result was to consolidate the pattern of illegal but widespread betting in working-class communities which survived until the 1950s and the 1960s.

NOTES

1. S. Hardy (ed.), *The Diary of a Suffolk Farmer's Wife 1854–1869* (Basingstoke, 1992), pp.90–1.
2. For the later period see D. Dixon, *From Prohibition to Regulation, Bookmaking, Anti-gambling and the Law* (Oxford, 1991).
3. R. Holt, *Sport and the British* (Oxford, 1989), p.33.
4. *York Herald*, 26 August 1813.
5. The Druid, *The Post and the Paddock* (1862), p.13
6. See J. Raven, 'The abolition of the English state lotteries', *Historical Journal*, Vol.34, No.2, 1991, p.376. In lists of attendees after mid-century I have not so far come across any example of the clergy's attendance at meetings. There were, however, several clergy who bred and owned racehorses.
7. *Sporting Magazine*, August 1823, quoted by J. Fairfax-Blakeborough, *Extinct Race Meetings* (J.A. Allen, 1949), p.110.
8. J. Fairfax-Blakeborough, *Chester Races* (1951), p.13.
9. *Sporting Magazine*, November 1830, p.55.
10. Ibid., June 1844, p.474.
11. Quoted in J. Fairfax-Blakeborough, *Northern Turf History*, Vol.II (1949), p.153.
12. In 1832 in Carlisle the Lowther family and their connections withdrew their subscriptions to the races 'as a matter of course after the hostile feeling shown towards them by so many of the people of Carlisle' at the election. See *Westmorland Gazette,* 3 September 1832.
13. Report of the Select Committee of the House of Lords On the State of Agriculture, 1836 (79) VIII, Qs.5318–613.
14. For Lancashire examples see D. Foster, 'The Changing Social and Political Composition of the Lancashire Magistracy 1821–1851', PhD thesis, Lancaster University, 1971, pp.291–2.
15. F. Close, *The Evil Consequences of Attending the Racecourse* (1827).
16. O. Ashton, 'Clerical control and radical responses in Cheltenham Spa 1838–1848', *Midland History*, Vol.8, 1983, pp.121–47.
17. At Wolverhampton the magistrates attempted to ban the sale of alcohol at the races, but the races went ahead. See R. Swift, 'The English urban magistracy and the administration of justice during the early nineteenth century: Wolverhampton 1815–1860', *Midland History*, Vol.17, 1992, p.2.
18. A. Delves, 'Popular recreation and social conflict in Derby 1800–1850', in E. and S. Yeo, *Popular Culture and Class Conflict 1590–1914* (Brighton, 1981), p.111.
19. E.F. Calford, *Edinburgh: The Story of a City* (1975), p.236.
20. Quoted in A. Howkins, *Reshaping Rural England: a Social History 1850–1925* (1991), p.67.
21. E.g., the Revd Mr Dennis, 'well known as a most successful breeder ... his horses being generally entered in the name of John Scott', *Sporting Magazine,* August 1848, p.147.
22. *The Times*, 9 October 1874.
23. Ibid., 12 October and 23 October 1874.
24. W. Wilson, *Chester Races* (Chester, 1856), p.1.
25. T. Houston, *The Races: the Evils Associated with Horse Racing and the Steeplechase and Their Demoralising Effects* (Paisley, 1853).
26. M.J. Huggins, 'The growth of the enclosed courses on Teesside 1850–1902, *British Journal of Sports History*, Vol.3, No.2, 1986, provides a more extended discussion of this in the context of the Stockton and the Redcar meeting.
27. *Doncaster Gazette*, 4 September 1891.
28. A Chester Tradesman, *Chester Races: Do They Pay? Part 1: Direct Loss and Gain* (1871), p.6.
29. *Scarborough Gazette*, 16 September 1886.
30. See A Chester Tradesman, *Chester Races,* p.6
31. *Airdrie and Coatbridge Advertiser*, 3 August 1861.
32. E.g., *North-Eastern Daily Gazette*, 11 August 1885, 8 August 1890.
33. See R. Munting, 'Social opposition to gambling in Britain: a historical overview', *International Journal of the History of Sport*, Vol.10, No.3, 1993, pp.304–7.

34. E.g., *Redcar Gazette,* 12 August 1882.
35. See A Chester Trademan, *Chester Races,* p.4; see also Canon Kingsley, *Canon Kingsley on Betting* (n.d.), Chester Library.
36. See A Chester Tradesman, *Chester Races,* p.1.
37. *Stockton Herald*, 20 August 1881; *Redcar Gazette*, 12 August 1882.
38. *Stockton Herald*, 20 August 1894; 24 August 1895.
39. E.g., *Middlesborough Weekly News,* 23 April 1875.
40. *News of the World*, 23 February 1902.
41. *Burnley Express*, 27 August 1887.
42. The Liverpool *Porcupine* saw the Manchester Cotton Exchange as another form of gambling; e.g., *Porcupine*, 17 May 1862.
43. R.M. Bevan, *The Roodee: 450 years of Racing in Chester* (Northwich, 1989), p.30. The *Blackpool Gazette,* 16 May 1873, which spent some time discussing comments on his views in a *Liverpool Mercury* editorial, saw them as one-sided.
44. W. Wilson, *Chester Races* (Chester, 1856), p.3; address to the Watch committee at Chester 28 May 1891 in Racecourse Committee Minutes 1888–1902, Chester City Record Office.
45. For some Bolton examples of this see R. Poole, *Popular Leisure and the Music Hall in Nineteenth Century Bolton* (Lancaster, 1982), Ch.3.
46. See Wilson, *Chester Races*, p.1.
47. P. FitzGerald, ‘A letter addressed to a member of the Manchester Racing Association giving reasons for refusing to renew the lease of the present racecourse’ (1868); Salford Reference Library.
48. E.g., L.H. Curzon, ‘The horse as an instrument of gambling’, *Contemporary Review*, Vol.30, August 1877, p.392.
49. This and the following paragraphs draw heavily on the comprehensive treatment of the Victorian and Edwardian anti-gambling movement in Dixon’s *From Prohibition*, Ch.2.
50. D. Dixon, ‘Class act: The Street Betting Act of 1906’, *International Journal of the Sociology of Law*, Vol.8, 1980, p.114.
51. S. Churchill, *Betting and Gambling* (1894), p.45.
52. J.A. Hobson, ‘The ethics of gambling’, in B.S. Rowntree (ed.), *Betting and Gambling: a National Evil* (1905), pp.1–20.
53. J. Runciman, ‘The ethics of the turf’, *Contemporary Review*, Vol.55, 1889, p.608; H.H. Chamberlain, *Gambling and Betting* (1890), pp.24–5; J. Hawke, ‘Our principles and programme’, *New Review*, Vol.10, 1894, p.708.
54. See Churchill, *Betting and Gambling*; W.D. Mackenzie, *The Ethics of Gambling* (1895), p.43; Barnett, ‘Why are betting and gaming wrong?’, *Economic Review*, Vol.7, 1897, pp.168–81.
55. 1902 House of Lords Select Committee on Betting; evidence of Knight, Q.3638; Tannett-Walker, Qs.2848, 2861.
56. See Churchill, *Betting and Gambling*, pp.46, 49, 55.
57. See Dixon, *From Prohibition*, p.60, gives details.
58. J.M. Hogg, ‘Gambling among women’, in Rowntree (ed.), *Betting and Gambling*, pp.69–91.
59. Lady F. Bell, *At the Works: a Study of a Manufacturing Town* (1907), p.256. Her play, ‘The way the money goes’, produced in London in 1910, addressed the same theme.
60. See Churchill, *Betting and Gambling*.
61. Rowntree (ed.), *Betting and Gambling*, p.vii; A. Briggs, *A Study of the Work of Seebohm Roundtree, 1871–1954* (1961), p.79.
62. J.R. MacDonald, ‘Gambling and citizenship’, in Rowntree (ed.), *Betting and Gambling*, p.128.
63. See J. Burns, ‘Brains rather than beer or bets; the straight tip to the workers’, *Clarion Pamphlet*, No.36, 1902.
64. Dixon, ‘Class act’, p.117.
65. *Newmarket Monthly Illustrated Journal*, Vol.1, No.2, September 1872, pp.1–2; December 1872, p.1
66. *Carlisle Journal*, 10 June 1864; *Newcastle Daily Journal*, 31 May 65. For a Chester example see *Baily’s Magazine*, Vol.28, June 1876, p.421.
67. *The Times*, 1 November 1907.
68. *Darlington and Stockton Times*, 7 September 1889.
69. R.W. Proctor, *Our Turf, Our Stage and Our Ring* (Manchester, 1862), p.40; C. Ramsden,

Farewell Manchester (1964), p.164. Dickens, on his way from the Doncaster races in 1853, commented on 'the Itinerant personage in black ... telling him from the vantage ground of a legibly printed placard on a pole that for all these things the Lord will bring him to judgement.' C. Dickens, *Reprinted pieces and The Lazy Tour of Two Idle Apprentices* (1925), p.401.

70. 'The Aintree Carnival', in J.K. Walton and A. Wilcox (eds), *Low Life and Moral Improvement in Mid-Victorian England: Liverpool through the Journalism of Hugh Shimmin* (1991).
71. J. Crump 'The great carnival of the year: Leicester races in the nineteenth century', *Transactions, Leicestershire History & Archaeological Society*, Vol.58, 1982–83, p.7
72. J.S. Howson [Dean of Chester], *Chester Races* (Chester, 1870), p 9.
73. H. Curwen, *Kirkbie Kendal* (Kendal, 1900), p. 356, provides a Kendal example. Bolton Sunday schools instituted regular tea parties to keep their pupils from defecting on race days. See P. Bailey, *Leisure and Class in Victorian England* (1978), p.46.
74. R. Colls, *The Pitmen of the Northern Coalfield: Work, Culture and Protest 1790–1850* (Manchester, 1987).
75. R.H.G. Thompson, *The Liverpool and Manchester Railway* (1980), p.195.
76. Crump, 'The great carnival of the year', p.67.
77. *Newcastle Daily Journal*, 29 June 1865 describes an anti-race procession.; R.J. Charlton, *Newcastle Town* (London, 1885), p.356.
78. *Newcastle Daily Journal*, 17 March and 29 March 1882, 27 June 1883.
79. *Middlesbrough Weekly News*, 25 August 1865.
80. In 1880, for example, the ironmaster Charles Bolckow held a gala for the United Free Methodists. The primitive Methodists had a gala in a local farmer's field, the industrialist T.H. Richardson entertained the Newport Road Baptist School, and the owners of Blair's works entertained St. Andrew's Presbyterian scholars. See *North-Eastern Daily Gazette*, 19 August 1880.
81. *South Durham and Cleveland Mercury*, 20 August 1892.
82. *Leicester Journal*, 7 October 1870.
83. *The Times*, 6 July and 14 December 1877.
84. At Durham the University Senate refused to renew the lease; at Hambleton the training ground was closed when the non-conformist Sir Matthew Smith-Dodsworth succeeded his turf-loving brother; at Manchester P. Fitzgerald, MA, JP refused to renew the lease in 1868 (a letter addressed to the Manchester Racing Association giving his reasons is held in the Salford Archives). See also Ramsden, *Farewell Manchester*, pp.16–17.
85. Fairfax-Blakeborough, *Extinct Race Meetings*, pp.107–8.
86. Minutes of Evidence taken before the House of Lords Select Committee on Gambling; evidence of Robert Baxter, 12 March 1844, Qs.1019ff.
87. Chester City Record Office, Special Committee Minute Books 1888–91, meeting on 28 May 1891.
88. M. Milne, *The Newspapers of Northumberland and Durham* (1971), pp.85–7.
89. E.g., a Sheffield magistrate, associated with the local Social Questions League, was instrumental in persuading the city council to have all newspapers taken by Sheffield Free Library censored. See T. Mason, *Association Football and English Society 1863–1915* (1980), p.197.
90. *North East Daily Gazette*, 8 September 1893.
91. Evidence of R. Peacock [Manchester Chief Constable], 1902 Select Committee on Betting, Qs.152, 300.
92. *The Times*, 15 July 1874.
93. Ibid., 30 July 1874.
94. E.g., Churchill, *Betting and Gambling*; W.H. Norris, *A Hint to the Clergy and Other Anti-gambling Crusaders* (1894); J.M. Hogg, *Betting and Gambling* (Edinburgh, 1904).
95. References to these cases are made in evidence to the House of Lords Select Committee on Betting 1901; evidence of Hawke, Q.395 and Stutfield, Q.395.
96. J. Hawke, 'Our principles and programme', *New Review*, Vol.10 (1894), pp.705–17.
97. *The Bulletin of the Anti-Gambling League,* May 1897.
98. See Dixon, *From Prohibition*, Ch.3.
99. See W. Vamplew, *The Turf* (1976), pp.209–10. See Dixon, *From Prohibition*, Ch.4.
100. Dixon, *From Prohibition,* Ch.5.

9

Conclusion

The social and cultural meaning of non-work activities is a key element in any understanding of British society between 1800 and 1914. Involvement in or opposition to racing was a major factor in the lives of many people so the meanings given to racing are important. It cannot be dismissed as simply a rare event, a marginal feature, irrelevant to discussion about class formation, the rhetoric of social control or apparent attempts at the imposition of cultural hegemony. It could be found across Britain, in a range of towns, right through the period. The fortunes of horses, jockeys and owners were matters of interest to the press and to much of society. Nor was it an exception, a subculture, exhibiting structural and cultural features out of line with wider society, since support for racing came from across the social and much of the political spectrum. Racing expressed and distilled conflicts and stresses which were often hidden from view.

A study of horseracing therefore contributes to the examination and questioning of current views of the relationship between leisure and class. Leisure history is complex, with shifting patterns of power and interest, and the role of racing in a class society, with all its conflicts and relationships, is therefore difficult to establish. Previous models that historians have used to interpret the rise of commercialized leisure have tended to concentrate on attempts to prohibit and are therefore insensitive to some dimensions of participation and investment. The stress has instead been on the reformist group. Cunningham has argued that the examination of leisure activities involves the identification of leisure cultures, overlapping and influencing each other and in a constant state of change. Members of three of Cunningham's leisure cultures could be seen as wishing to reform aspects of convivial, pleasure-seeking and popular cultural forms such as racing. These would include those espousing his model of middle-class leisure culture, anxious to scrutinize and perhaps challenge the legitimacy of particular leisure pursuits; a working-class, religious, reformist culture; and a self-improving, rationalist, secular, reformist culture.[1] Their vociferousness made them apparently powerful in society.

Yet, as we have seen, horseracing experienced struggles over time and territory and was opposed by these groups, but their opposition was unsuccessful. Leisure was a major and often disputed frontier of social change and we need to examine racing in that light. Horseracing appears to have survived and flourished despite being associated with activities such as drinking of alcohol, prostitution and betting which ran counter to leisure reformist values.

Few meetings were closed because of opposition; in others noisy opposition was unsuccessful. Yet other towns, such as Leicester, had no organized opposition and no major campaign to abolish meetings.[2] Wider attacks on betting too were relatively unsuccessful. The impact of reformers both in terms of parliamentary legislation and on local meetings was slight in proportion to their efforts.

The reasons for racing's survival were inevitably complex and local as well as national in character. In the late eighteenth and the early nineteenth century the survival of the races was relatively unproblematical. The key factor was the linkage between race meetings and the upper-class, landed group who found racing and the matching of their thoroughbreds and the associated betting a pleasurable pursuit. Later nineteenth-century evidence suggests several reasons. The races were of financial benefit to sufficient people to ensure their survival either directly or through betting, while the strengthening position of the police force and magistracy led to the belief that the races were a nuisance but not a threat. Much more importantly, however, a study of racing reveals its support at all levels in the class system, which allowed sectional interests to be more sternly resisted.

We need to distinguish here between the rhetorical justifications for racing and the reality. Apologists for racing associated it with manliness, with British heritage and with liberty. William IV's speech in Egham in 1836, where he described racing as 'the manly and noble sport of a free people', was often quoted in this regard.[3] Even an anti-racing paper admitted that racing was 'a national sport' before claiming it was one on which 'some difference of opinion may and does exist among all classes'.[4] The principles of freedom of choice in leisure were codified late in the nineteenth century by the Sporting League, the pro-racing organization created in direct opposition to the National Anti-Gambling League. It devised test questions for candidates to county councils and Parliament which sought agreement with the principles that the people

> should have liberty in their sports, pastimes and recreations (under such rules as are from time to time laid down by those who practically understand the same) and that such liberty, while regulated by the law of the land should be exempt from any interference

and that

> persons or bodies of persons seeking in any way to obstruct, interfere with or suppress any sport, pastime or regulation ... should be discouraged and discountenanced by magistrates, County Councils or other authorities.[5]

Such arguments were ideologies of justification for racing. Yet they also indicate that racing was part of everyday life and that attempts at prohibition were part of a declaredly ideological project.

As we have seen, racing also sometimes made a significant contribution to the local economy of a number of towns, although this depended in part on the size and importance of the races. Corporations could benefit and the money spent by visitors went mostly to certain groups which included innkeepers and other refreshment-house keepers, stand proprietors, the owners of hotel and other accommodation, cab proprietors and some tradesmen. Provided that the managers of the course showed appropriate economic and commercial acumen, profits could be made and investment in the grandstands, and in the later enclosed courses, was predominantly local. Further down the social scale, excursionists often sought sustenance in town before the races, and at Doncaster in 1860 it was said that at almost every house banners were hung out bearing the inscription 'refreshments may be had here'.[6] The social events in the towns and at assemblies, balls and theatrical performances allowed the urban and rural elites to mix and attracted further spending. Such economic arguments should not be overstated since, as we have seen, there were also those industrialists, shopkeepers and tradesmen opposed to the races who argued that the closing down of industries, loss of income and crime were damaging to the local economy. But both sets of arguments were exaggerated. When races were attended by the county gentry and were a local festival, money was certainly circulated to the benefit of the town. But by the later nineteenth century for many towns the gains must have been marginal, with those by some groups being almost balanced by the losses of others. The enclosed races attracted mainly betting men and there was less local interest. The local economic arguments cannot therefore be seen as central to racing's survival.

Racing also provided a key setting for gambling, although it cannot be argued that betting was the sole reason for racing's survival, as did the National Anti-Gambling League. Gaming activities such as pitch and toss, card games and the like were common in all working-class communities. Whippet and greyhound racing, potshare bowling, pedestrianism and other betting sports were a feature of the early enclosed recreation grounds from the 1860s, and by the 1890s football and later the pools provided alternatives.[7] Yet regular betting on horse races grew from being an activity for a turfite minority at the start of the nineteenth century to being among the most common of British male leisure activities by 1914. The middle classes were divided in their attitudes. While a vociferous group opposed it, many gave it their support and many others their tacit approval. Many newspapers gave consistent support to local meetings and even at the height of the anti-betting period argued that betting prosecutions were pointless. The *Clitheroe Times* spoke for many in arguing that 'the nation is a gambling one at heart', with an 'extremely flexible conscience' and that prosecutions were 'a solemn farce'.[8] Even when it came to illegal betting in public houses not all magistrates were prepared to uphold the law.[9] The complaints that police, Post Office and telegraph officials were often prepared to ignore plainly illegal betting acts all illustrate the same point.[10] In the evidence presented to the 1902 Select Committee on Betting there was rarely any denial that betting was popular. Even the Chief Constable of Manchester, a strong opponent of it, recognized the difficulty in dealing with it and the tensions it created in society. His claims that neither the leading men of the provincial towns nor the leaders of the working class would go on a platform and support betting were exaggerated, and he accepted that his opposition had made him unpopular. Sir James Lowther, by contrast, claimed that the promoters of repressive legislation had 'failed to realize the great force of public opinion against them'.[11]

Another explanation of racing's survival may be that a strengthening of the forces of law and order in the nineteenth century led to fewer concerns over the policing of the race meetings, as was the case with the fairs. There is some truth in this. The control of races was in the hands of the police at most courses by the 1830s, and the maintenance of order was of concern to all race committees. Control over the regional crowds could be carried out by local police, but the controlling of travelling pickpockets, owners of gaming activities or other criminals was more difficult since they were skilled in avoiding detection. Travelling police who knew the 'swell mob' were therefore hired by the major courses. London detectives were specializing in this from quite early on. Doncaster hired Bishop of Bow Street to help to 'keep the pickpockets at bay' by 1829,[12] and had Leadbitter, another tough, well-travelled (and 19-stones) London officer in the 1840s and the 1850s.[13] Large numbers of police were soon at the major meetings. Epsom, for example, had over 500 on the course by 1856, and over a thousand by 1865.[14] Systems of control also emerged. At Newcastle by 1847 the police had a spacious marquee erected as a rendezvous and kept delinquents there before their being confined to the cells.[15] Courses soon began importing detectives from the industrial conurbations, whence the majority of racecourse criminals came, to help in recognizing such groups. By the mid-nineteenth century Doncaster had detectives from London, Birmingham, Barnsley, Wakefield, Manchester and Goole.[16] In 1851 York had detectives from Manchester, Newcastle, Hull, Leeds and Sheffield for the August meeting, but suffered from its failure to engage metropolitan detectives when 'cheap trains from London' carrying pickpockets arrived. The increased incidence of enclosed courses, with their separate enclosures, made control easier for the police and the gatekeepers and by the 1900s there were few complaints. Right through the period race meetings generated few arrests. The types of prosecution showed large elements of continuity, while prosecutions were spasmodic, suggesting tolerant policing, an unwillingness to prosecute or the turning of blind eyes. Firm police handling was uncommon. The police presence however, may have played a part in making those opposed to the races, who were unlikely to attend, feel that racing was under control.

The same point holds good for the management of racing by the Jockey Club, an elite of upper-class noblemen, politicians and statesmen, who appeared to have a large measure of control over the sport. Its occasional, well-publicized actions over dishonesty created the impression of power and authority even though this was more apparent than real at individual meetings, and it only significantly began to extend its power beyond a small group of elite meetings from 1870. By the early twentieth century it presided over some 50 high-status, highly commercialized race meetings, the results of which were critical for working-class betters.

More importantly, racing embodied shared community values, notions of male sociability, a social cement where high and low could meet together in joint enjoyment of sport.[17] Grandstands provided segregated areas and the classes did not need to mix in a free and unconstrained way unless they wished, while some meetings even had special railway halts nearby so that upper-class attendees could avoid the 'roughs'.[18] Nevertheless, such sharing of mutual enjoyment may be seen in a variety of contexts, from attendance at meetings, to the cross-class readership of many racing magazines and newspapers. Women (and children) of all classes attended the earlier open meetings in significant numbers, although, following enclosure, the numbers of upper and upper-middle-class women in the stands rose while their numbers overall declined. But there is also evidence of increasing female involvement in betting from the later nineteenth century.

This brings us to perhaps the most important finding of this study. Racing had cross-class support. One of the points made consistently by Joyce is that the possibility of all manner of cross-class alliances and reciprocities is only to be expected when class itself was so incompletely developed in British life.[19] Notions of class cannot be ignored, but what comes through again and again is that the world of racing allowed social exclusivity if it were desired, but also relied heavily on cross-class connections. Owners, trainers, jockeys and betters were all linked together in a range of ways. Racing insiders shared values, loyalties and attitudes with racing insiders from other classes. So class was not all-important. Working people possessed a spectrum of identities which were not just those of class but included those of the workplace and the community in a non-class sense, the county or the region, and this allowed participation in racing.[20] Racing does carry class meanings, although these could be speculative and somewhat inconclusive, but, at the same time, it had broad appeal across class boundaries.[21] Perhaps, it might be argued, the real division was between the respectable and rough, and the rough of all classes met at the races. In reality, however, as has been demonstrated, the range of groups and individuals attending meetings militates against any such oversimple analysis.

As we have seen, racing was also supported by the upper classes, and this study confirms a renewed expansion of interest in racing among these classes in the later nineteenth century, following a temporary decline in interest around the 1840s. Interestingly here, while voluntary organizations were a major vehicle for much leisure activity, the earlier non-commercialized, voluntary associations in the forms of the Jockey Club and other select racing clubs were being replaced later in the century by more informal, country house parties. Racing was also supported by the British royal family, the most socially prominent of upper-class supporters of racing. This provides both clear examples of racing continuity and a clear context of patronage, ritual display and support for racing itself. In the early nineteenth century, George IV, both as Prince of Wales and King, was a regular visitor to race meetings, using them as opportunities both for pleasure and to enlist popular support.[22] As King he supported Ascot, where he instituted the first, more formal, royal procession in 1825 and was heavily involved in racing.[23] Although William IV raced his horses and allowed himself to be advertised as the ‘patron’ of the Jockey Club, in reality he had less interest in racing. Nevertheless, he improved the royal stud at Hampton, attended Ascot and increased the number of royal plates. Queen Victoria also had only a limited interest, although she attended Doncaster in 1835 and Epsom on a number of occasions.[24] Her most consistent attendance was at Ascot, near to Windsor, where she maintained the procession to the course and attended the races fairly regularly until the death of Prince Albert in 1861, after which she lost interest and tried to dissuade her son from involvement.[25] Nevertheless, she revived the Hampton Court stud, and subscribed to the *Racing Calendar*.[26]

The Prince of Wales helped to improve the respectability of racing more indirectly. His support may have affected the view of those who never went racing or attended only the higher-status events, and his patronage gained racing further support through social emulation.[27] He attended his first Derby in 1863, became a member of the Jockey Club in 1864 and was regularly at meetings by the 1870s.[28] He became a registered owner in 1875 and gave public support to racing thereafter.[29] By 1890 he was attending 28 meetings a year.[30] His 1896 Derby and St. Leger wins with Persimmon were highly popular and his subsequent 1909 Derby success with Minoru was greeted with 'great enthusiasm'.[31] The press hailed the victory as a national triumph and his victories on the turf added significantly to his personal popularity, which was almost certainly due in part to his enjoyment of life – good food, good wine, racing and betting and the company of personable women. The month after his death in 1910 Royal Ascot was held with those in the enclosure wearing black, the Royal Stand closed and racecards edged in black. King George V, although less keen on racing, owned horses before his succession and carried on Edward's racing establishment, regularly attending Ascot with his Queen.[32]

Major political figures, including many prime ministers, were also prepared to be seen at meetings and support the turf through their ownership and breeding activities. Further down the political ladder, attitudes in local government to local races, as to betting, were much less straightforward, and magistrates, local boards and corporations were split. In some racing towns support shifts in local political dominance affected attitudes. Even at Doncaster, which was always dominated by a pro-racing group, there were times when anti-race views came near to achieving a majority. The early 1850s, for example, saw examples of what one writer described as 'the anti-bigotry conflict', those 'periodical fierce racing rows in their council chamber which have become part and parcel of their turf history'.[33] In 1853 race supporters only narrowly won the day after promising to donate £1,000 a year for five years to the church out of stand receipts, but by 1856 the solicitor and auctioneer most active in anti-race campaigning had both been voted off the council. In 1867, and again in 1875, the editor of the *Doncaster Reporter* tried to bring an end to the widespread, illegal bookmaking on the course carried out on land let by the Corporation, but with little success and no significant Corporation support.

We have seen too how strong support was among certain groups within the middle classes. Many of these had direct involvement in racing as attendees, shareholders, organizers and managers, owners or betters.

Others, perhaps even a majority, did not have strong views either way. The strongly anti-racing Dean of Chester was prepared to concede that there were people who supported the races because they were under the impression that they were beneficial, and that there were 'large numbers who simply acquiesce in things as they are'.[34] This underestimated the popular interest in racing. When Frith's painting of Derby Day was exhibited at the Royal Academy in May 1858 it caused a sensation and subsequently generated interest and popularity throughout the world, with engravings selling in large numbers.[35]

For the working classes, the races were seen as a holiday from 'the dull and wearying round of daily work', giving freedom from 'buzzers, benches and exacting timekeepers'.[36] During the period of unrest in the 1820s and again during the 1840s some of the upper classes saw race-meetings as a potential social antidote, a way of distracting the working classes from revolution, a kind of bread-and-circuses experience, and Sir William Gregory argued strongly for the turf's use as 'a safety valve for the lower orders' in Britain.[37] Local meetings made a contribution to local and regional identity, and racecourse drinking, eating and other forms of sociability were enjoyed by many. Working-class betting, generated by local interest and sustained by local, working-class bookmakers, had become a mass leisure activity by the 1880s after a slow but steady build up from the 1840s. Betting provided a cohesive, informal, social network.

Untangling the state's role in racing is more difficult. In general, it proved reluctant to legislate, and even more reluctant to enforce laws in relation to racing and betting. Racing provided revenue through taxes on racehorses, while the state provided Royal Plates to encourage breeding. Most legislation was paternalistic, directed against working-class betting rather than racing itself. The most significant interventions were the 1853 Betting House Act, and the 1906 Street Betting Act, both of which ignored betting on racecourses and upper-class credit betting.

What also comes out quite clearly is the complex reality of diverse local and regional experience. Although examples have been drawn from a wide variety of geographical areas and social contexts, this does not do full justice to the range of reasons lying behind the survival or cessation of individual race meetings, while regional differences in particular have received less attention than their importance deserves. In Yorkshire, for example, the North Riding and York provided support for a significant number of meetings. By contrast, the much more densely populated and industrially developed West Riding sustained only Pontefract and Doncaster, and attempts to preserve meetings at Leeds, Rotherham, Sheffield, and elsewhere were unsuccessful.

It might be argued that the North Riding's early association with breeding and training in the seventeenth and the eighteenth century and its high proportion of large, landed estates gave it a positive environment for race meetings, while the rapid industrialization of the West Riding towns and the Riding's lower proportion of landed estates created a more negative environment for racing, although the Earls Fitzwilliam and Scarborough and Lord Wharncliffe all owned substantial land in the West Riding, and the first two families had an interest in racing. Certainly some towns which experienced rapid industrialization, such as Bradford or Leeds, struggled to sustain a meeting.[38] Yet others elsewhere, such as Manchester or Liverpool, were always able to offer substantial prize money. We need to examine more closely the reasons lying behind such different experiences. Even rural counties differed in their experience of racing. The North Riding of Yorkshire contrasts significantly with Westmorland, which failed to sustain regular meetings even at Appleby or Kendal. There have as yet been insufficient detailed case studies at a local level to extend the basic question of why racing survived or failed to take root in particular localities and we need to look more closely at individual towns or regions, in order to provide a more informed, contextually-aware set of satisfactory explanations. Was the survival of racing in Newcastle, for example, as against Leeds, because a greater proportion of Newcastle's leading citizens had family or property links with race-going, county society and was there perhaps more gentrification of the bourgeoisie there as against the apparently greater development of an independent, middle-class culture with strong sectarian and evangelical roots in Leeds?[39] Racing had different patterns of development and success in different settings, and the range and complexity of cross-currents acting upon it require more work at the local level to confirm or challenge the general patterns indicated here.

At the national level, racing, like the drink question, was apparently a battleground, and appeared to be opposed by repressive and manipulative forms of middle-class authority. Morris has pointed out the role of voluntary societies in establishing the ideological, cultural and moral dominance of a middle-class reformist group, although the membership of the groups opposed to racing was not confined to the middle classes and such groups also contained working-class men and women with more respectable, nonconformist backgrounds, publicly espousing similar views.[40] But, in the case of racing, the Sunday schools, the National Anti-Gambling League and other similar groups were conspicuously unsuccessful. Although the rhetoric and legitimating ideology of the apparently dominant reformist leisure culture was powerful, it is increasingly clear that it was less effective than it appeared and, once more, further research is needed.

In beginning to redefine how we understand the culture of Victorian Britain we need to pay less attention to the acts and voices of well-publicized reformist groups. This contextualizes racing as a marginal and illicit practice. Racing and other forms of leisure were more powerful in society than the reformist groups. Both meetings and betting reveal British society's ability to achieve a broad consensus and to organize itself effectively for both pleasure and reward.

Previously, in the 1970s and the 1980s, the focus of research has been on those leisure activities in the early- and the mid-Victorian period which suffered attacks as there were attempts to lead the working classes towards more wholesome and supposedly rational recreations. Although many sports made apparent attempts to renew, revise and regulate themselves to avoid attack, the extent of their transformation is still a matter of debate.[41] In some cases, such as bullbaiting or cockfighting, opposition to them was relatively successful, especially when suppression was intensified by legislation and the new police forces.[42] Pugilism had all but disappeared by the 1860s.[43] Counter-attractions such as the mechanics' institutes or new commercial leisure forms such as skating rinks emerged as more respectable recreations. Other traditional forms of leisure which continued, but according to Cunningham – in a view whose validity has been generally accepted, these persisted only under duress.[44]

But such historiographical preoccupations were strongly influenced by source availability. Attempts at repression and control generated easily accessible evidence in Parliamentary Papers, the archives of voluntary organizations and local government, and led to an initial stress on more obvious aspects of the relationship between class and leisure and an impression of the powerful and all-encompassing nature of middle-class hegemony. Some leisure activities certainly struggled to survive despite popular resistance, but evidence is now emerging that attempts at control were quite often partial and incomplete.

As a wider range of source materials were tapped, it has become clearer that nonconformist and evangelical reformist values were by no means all-pervading and that notions of a cataclysmic destruction of popular leisure forms in the mid-Victorian period are incorrect. F.M.L. Thompson has argued persuasively that even in the 1840s and the 1850s respectability's hold over behaviour was 'partial and vulnerable to the pressures of affluence and self-indulgence'.[45] Even in the world of 1860s religiosity some contemporaries were prepared to admit that there was 'a good deal of deliberate hypocrisy'.[46] Golby and Purdue took the view that enjoyment, entertainment and sport were already by then becoming more attractive to the middle classes.[47] Bailey has argued powerfully that *working-class* men and their families for whom respectability was a staple and regular way of life were 'rarer birds than contemporaries or today's historians have allowed'.[48] Respectability was practised in a much more limited sense, and was limited in a number of ways, by sex, by age, by situation and by role, so that there could be different modes of behaviour within a single lifestyle, at different times and in different contexts.

Such an argument may also be applied to the middle classes. The mass of early- and mid-Victorian material trying to specify appropriate conduct for the middle classes was only necessary because of the underlying anxieties about the existence of middle-class enjoyment of less respectable pleasures. Any notions of a unified middle class are open to strong challenge. Bailey has argued that 'there was as much disagreement as consensus among dominant groups'.[49] There is a growing recognition among historians that, like the working classes, the mid-Victorian middle classes were divided among themselves in attitudes to leisure.[50] Many never accepted nonconformist, evangelical canons of behaviour in their leisure lives. A more convincing explanation is that middle-class, reforming hegemony was only partly powerful, much more rhetoric than reality, and that its influence was limited to certain settings. The more we examine this theoretically dominant middle-class culture the more problematic it becomes. Racing provides a clear example of an activity under attack where the reformers failed even to convince the majority of their own class, which was split in its attitudes.

Paradoxically, however, racing was characterized internally by elements of conflict and competition. Although this competition was not at its heart one of class, there were elements of class conflict embedded in it and some aspects of racing reflected the class tensions of society at large. It was generally individualistic rather than associational, and there were few organized groups of like-minded individuals. Some participants wanted to make a profit from their activities, whether breeding, training, owning, betting or otherwise; some wanted to see a particular horse win; some wanted to win more money or more races than others. But competition and conflict were most often intra- not inter-class. Competition about racing's survival was certainly intra-class. Competition on the turf itself was between individuals and groups, often of mixed class origins. It required quick thinking, at other times long-term strategic and tactical astuteness. Success on the turf often required a quite different morality from that of the amateur, middle-class sportsman.

Another set of questions concerned the process of commercialization and the extent to which local race meetings in the earlier pre- and proto-industialization period could be seen to be commercial in their approach.

The chronology of racing has been previously insufficiently clear and this study adds further weight to the claims being made for locating the birth of modern, commercialized leisure in the eighteenth century if not before.[51] At the beginning of the following century racing was already shaped by entrepreneurial initiatives, and the growth of regional and national, printed support in the form of racing calendars, stud books, turf reports in the press and *The Sporting Magazine,* which turned it into an industry. At the same time, even at the end of the period racing was only partially organized for profit, although it had become a much more highly capitalized form of mass entertainment. In part racing was an example of conspicuous consumption and many apparently commercial moves were actually no more than attempts to reduce the costs of racehorse ownership. This also applied to breeding, which was only profitable to a minority. Even betting may be seen simply as a means of redistributing wealth within the sport.

The chronology of betting, an emergent example of mass culture and mass consumption among many men and some women by the beginning of the twentieth century, has also to be pushed back. It already had a significant popular following as early as the 1840s, with antecedents in the early state lottery and in earlier betting activities and, despite the 1853 Act, off-course betting developed in local communities from the 1840s onwards. Working-class bookmakers emerged as betting became increasingly a commercialized industry, added to which betting provided opportunities for working-class women.

In part, racing offers us an example of leisure continuity amid change. In the 1840s and the 1850s, for example, while some popular recreations were under pressure from middle-class evangelicalism, urbanization and industrial capitalism and were often suppressed by legislation and the police, racing survived any such duress, re-emphasizing the role of continuities in cultural formation. From then onwards the counter-attractions of rational recreations were meant to lure the working classes away from drink, betting and sensuality. Race meetings offered all of these, yet the complexity of motive among its supporters and the division of interest between the middle and the working classes, some of whom opposed it, others of whom supported it or modified it to meet their own needs, helped to ensure racing's survival.

At the same time racing itself changed in response to outside demands. It shifted from a regional to a national pursuit. The number of horses and their owners increased, horses began racing earlier and over shorter distances, and selling plates and handicaps became more common than gold cups, sweepstakes and weight-for-age races. Betting grew to become a central part of working-class life.

Racing cannot be treated in isolation and where possible here it has been related to culture in the sense of a particular way of living, seeing how in its complexity it fitted into working-, middle- or upper-class life. It demonstrates, for example, how race meetings provided a holiday for the working classes, despite the wishes of their employers, and the ways they organized themselves to do so. But racing was transformed not in conflict between classes or in subordination but through its ability to adapt to social and economic change. This was linked to significant elements of hedonism in terms of attendance at meetings themselves, in the activities associated with the meetings and in betting. Betting, for example, could offer rationality, competition or high-stake plunging. The activities taking place on the course ranged from the display of patronage or networking, to drinking, fighting or sexual dalliance.

Studies of British society need to take more account of racing, both as a major source of employment and as a central leisure activity. It was a highly-adaptable leisure form, capable of offering different satisfactions to different individuals and groups. For some it was a focus for contested meanings. For others it was a source of integrative social and cultural experiences. It was unashamedly populist, yet also elitist. This book has concentrated on its relation to social structure, but its relationship to the state, political life, the military and to nonconformist religious movements are all strands which merit further exploration. The coming together of steeplechasing and related sports under the National Hunt Committee (whose membership overlapped with that of the Jockey Club) is another socially fascinating area yet to be fully explored in terms of social structure.[52] Here gentlemen riders survived and the struggles to accommodate middle-class values in the clash between amateur and professional jockeys is interesting and illuminating. Flat racing in Ireland, although relatively unimportant in terms of betting and its level of turnover, also deserves more treatment.

More important, however, is the need to explore much further the gap between rhetoric and reality in the leisure life of Victorian Britain. The power and pervasiveness of reformist ideology needs to be examined much more critically and the current chronology re-evaluated. There is a need to begin a critical reassessment of class, respectability and culture, and to develop an agenda for future research, based on more detailed explorations of private practice rather than public rhetoric and regulatory activity. Racing and betting provide examples of the latter's weakness in practice. Social historians examining social structure and class relationships have too often marginalized leisure or used hegemonic blinkers. Both racing and betting could be found playing a role in many of Cunningham's leisure cultures: the culture of the aristocratic leisured classes, urban middle-class culture, artisan culture, rural popular culture and urban popular culture. Other activities such as excessive drinking may also be found in a range of contexts throughout the period at all levels of society. Up until now their extent has received only limited attention, but if we are to understand the social history of leisure more fully and avoid the oversimplification of existing models their study may well prove satisfactory and rewarding, especially in relation to the middle classes. Historians need to study the relationship between respectable and less respectable leisure forms in terms of the lived experience of individuals, the intra-class plurality of leisure interests and the ways in which different contexts contributed to different behaviours. This study of racing has implications for how we interpret the broader history of class and leisure.

NOTES

1. H. Cunningham, 'Leisure and culture', in F.M.L. Thompson (ed.), *The Cambridge Social History of Britain 1750–1950*, Vol.2, *People and Their Environment* (1990), pp.289–320.
2. J. Crump, 'The great carnival year: Leicester races in the nineteenth century', *Transactions, Leicestershire History & Archaeological Society*, Vol.58, 1982–83, p.65.
3. J. Whyte, *History of the British Turf*, Vol.1 (1840), p.xvii.
4. *Doncaster Reporter*, 4 September 1867.
5. W. Allison, *My Kingdom for a Horse* (1919), p.345.
6. *The Times,* 13 September 1860.
7. For northern examples see M.J. Huggins, 'Leisure and sport in Middlesbrough 1840–1914', in A.J. Pollard (ed.), *Middlesbrough: Town and Community 1830–1950* (Stroud, 1996), pp.47–8, and Metcalfe 'Potshare bowling in the mining communities of east Northumberland 1800–1914', in R. Holt (ed.), *Sport and the Working Class in Modern Britain* (Manchester, 1990), pp.29–44. For football betting see T. Mason, *Association Football and English Society 1863–1915* (Brighton, 1980), p.182.
8. *Clitheroe Times*, 31 May 1889.
9. This was an admission of Hawke in his evidence on behalf of the Anti-Gambling League in 1901. Select Committee of the House of Lords on Betting 1901 (370) v.347.
10. Ibid., evidence of Hawke, Q.206.
11. Ibid., evidence of Chief Constable Peacock, Q.450; Sir James Lowther, Q.2143.
12. *The Times*, 21 September 1829.
13. *Leeds Times*, 18 September 1841; *Doncaster Gazette,* 19 September 1851; 'Turf pencillings', *Sporting Magazine*, October 1853, p.277.
14. *The Times*, 29 May 1856, 1 June 1865.
15. *Newcastle Journal*, 26 June 1847.
16. *Doncaster Gazette*, 19 September 1851.
17. P. Bailey, *Leisure and Class in Victorian England: Rational Recreation and the Contest for Control 1830–1885* (1978), p.23.
18. J. Fairfax-Blakeborough, *A Short History of Redcar Racecourse* (Ripon, 1950), p.9.
19. P. Joyce, 'Work', in Thompson, *Cambridge Social History of Britain*, Vol.2.
20. Idem, *Visions of the People: Industrial England and the Question of Class 1848–1914* (Cambridge, 1991). See also J. Hill and J. Williams (eds), *Sport and Identity in the North of England* (Keele, 1996).
21. This was a point brought out consistently by northern conservative papers such as the *North Star*, the *South Durham and Cleveland Mercury* and the *Middlesbrough Exchange* in the second half of the nineteenth century.

22. In 1806, for example, he and the Duke of Clarence went to Doncaster by carriage from Knowsley (Lord Derby's estate) and stayed in lodgings there for the races. Volunteer cavalry regiments were drawn up outside, there was an address by the mayor and corporation, and they dined with the county gentry. *York Herald*, 27 September 1806.
23. There had been more informal royal drives before this date. See D. Laird, *Royal Ascot* (1976), pp.46, 68.
24. Prince Albert took the Prince of Prussia to the Derby in 1856; *The Times*, 29 May 1856.
25. G.J. Cawthorne and R.S. Herod, *Royal Ascot* (1902), p.104; *The Times*, 8 June 1853.
26. For details of the royal studs see A. Fitzgerald, *Royal Thoroughbreds: a History of the Royal Studs* (1990), which draws heavily on the Royal Archives at Windsor.
27. E.g., D. Brailsford, *British Sport: a Social History* (Cambridge, 1992), p.72.
28. *Newmarket Monthly Illustrated Journal*, November 1872, November 1873.
29. 'King Edward as a sportsman', *The Times,* 11 May 1910.
30. P. Horn, *High Society: the English Social Elite 1880–1914* (1992), p.143.
31. *Sportsman,* 27 May 1909.
32. 'Racing; the King's horses', *The Times,* 19 December 1910.
33. See *Sporting Magazine,* June 1853, p.450. See also November 1856, p.352, December 1856, pp. 387ff.
34. J.S. Howson [Dean of Chester], *Chester Races* (1870), p.1.
35. A. Noakes, *William Frith: Extraordinary Victorian Painter* (1978), pp. 65–8.
36. *North-Eastern Daily Gazette*, 18 August 1880.
37. J. Kent, *The Racing Life of Lord George Cavendish Bentinck, MP* (1892), p.398.
38. Bradford had only occasional, poor quality meetings on the moor, which ended in 1878 when the moor was enclosed; see D. Russell, 'The pursuit of pleasure', in D.G. Wright and J.A. Jowett (eds), *Victorian Bradford* (1982), pp.199–221. For Leeds see J. Fairfax-Blakeborough, *Extinct Race Meetings: Northern Turf History*, Vol.II (1949), pp. 57–160.
39. For gentrification see L. Stone and J.C. Stone, *An Open Elite? England 1540–1880* (Oxford, 1984), pp.409–11. For an independent evangelical culture see L. Davidoff and C. Hall, *Family Fortunes: Men and Women of the English Middle Class 1780–1850* (1987); R.J. Morris, 'Middle-class culture 1700–1914', in D. Fraser (ed.), *A History of Modern Leeds* (Manchester, 1980), pp.212–14.
40. Morris, 'Middle-class culture'.
41. See Cunningham, 'Leisure and culture', in Thompson, *Cambridge Social History of Britain*, Vol.2, p.336.
42. D. Read, 'Beasts and brutes: popular blood sports c.1780–1860', in R. Holt (ed.), *Sport and the Working Class in Modern Britain* (Manchester, 1990), pp.12–28. More generally see Bailey, *Leisure and Class in Victorian England*; H. Cunningham, *Leisure in the Industrial Revolution c.1780–c1880* (1980); R.D. Storch (ed.), *Popular Culture and Custom in Nineteenth Century England* (1982).
43. See Brailsford, *British Sport*, p.73.
44. See P. Bailey, 'Leisure and the Historian', *Leisure Studies*, Vol.8, No.2, May 1989, pp.107–21.
45. F.M.L. Thompson, *The Rise of Respectable Society: a Social History of Victorian Britain 1830–1900* (1988), p.260.
46. E.B. Bax, *Reminiscences and Reflections of a Middle and Late Victorian* (1918), p.17.
47. J. Golby and B. Purdue, *The Emergence of an Urban Popular Culture* (Milton Keynes, 1981), pp.30–3.
48. P. Bailey, 'Will the real Bill Banks stand up? A role analysis of mid-Victorian working-class respectability', *Journal of Social History,* Vol.12, 1979, p.346. However, some years later in *Leisure and Class in Victorian England* (1987 edn), p.20, he felt somewhat more confident that respectability was situationally adopted for instrumental advantage in the later nineteenth century.
49. Idem, *Music Hall: the Business of Pleasure* (1986), p.xvi.
50. J.K. Walton, *The English Seaside Resort: a Social History 1750–1914* (Leicester, 1983), p.180.
51. J.H. Plumb, 'The commercialisation of leisure in eighteenth century England', in N. McKendrick (ed.), *The Birth of a Consumer Society* (Bloomington, 1982).
52. See R. Munting, *Hedges and Hurdles: a Social and Economic History of National Hunt Racing* (1987).

Bibliography

MANUSCRIPT SOURCES

Cambridge County Record Office, R83/27, Horse Accounts of George Milne of Newmarket 1876–89

296/B933, Sale Book; horse for Royston Racing Club, 1874

101/P6, Plan of Newmarket Race Ground, 1852

Chester City Record Office, CR 543, Chester Race Company Articles of Association, 1892

Cheshire County Record Office, D4222/24, Knutsford Race Committee Minutes, 1849–52

Census enumerators' books for Croft, Malton, Middleham, Richmond, Hambleton, Beverley and Newmarket, 1841–91

Doncaster Archives, Minutes of Doncaster Race Committee

Durham County Record Office, D/St/CI, Bowes papers relating to racing and betting.

D/X/872/1, Diary of P. Greathead, servant to the Earl of Strathmore

Durham University Library Archives, Gibby Papers file on Durham City Races

Hull University Archives, DDBC/4/8, letter from E. Crosskill

Humberside County Archives, DDSY, Sykes Papers

Jockey Club Rooms, Newmarket, Betting Books of John Gully, 1810–25; Jockey Club Accounts

Lancashire Record Office, DDX 103/4, Minutes of Preston Racecourse proprietors

DDC 1, Box 3, Accounts of the Fylde Horse Breeding Improvement Company

Race bills

Liverpool Record Office Records of the 14th Earl of Derby

Diaries and papers of the Molyneux of Sefton

Manchester Reference Library, Minutes of the Manchester Racecourse

Middlesbrough Archives, Theatre Royal playbills

North Riding Record Office, ZPB III 6/4, Mr Allen's accounts relating to racing
ZCO, Riddell archives
ZNK, Zetland archives
Northumberland Record Office, NRO 1356/D, Orde racing correspondence
Will of Antony Nichol, 1881
ZMI, S.57, Moncke archives
Public Record Office, BT31, Records relating to failed grandstand, racecourse and stud companies
Sheffield Archives, WWM, Fitzwilliam archives, references relating to horse racing.
Suffolk Record Office, HA 513/5, Grafton papers
HD/1325, Papers relating to sale particulars of racing and stud stables
EF/506/6/1, Newmarket Urban District Council records
University of Durham Archives and Special Collections, Durham University Surveyors Department, Bundle 178, Leases of the racecourse
York City Archives, Papers relating to racing
West Yorkshire Archive Service, Leeds District, Vyner family records
DB213/111, Proposed racecourse near Leeds, 1882–84

PARLIAMENTARY PAPERS AND PUBLICATIONS

Account of the Amount of Stamp Duty Received 1811–30 (405) XXV
Account of Duty Collected on Racehorses Yearly 1850–56 (385) XXXVIII.513
Bill for the Suppression of Betting houses 1852–53 (761) I.127
Bill to Repeal and Re-impose under New Regulations the Duty on Racehorses 1856 (243) VI.1
Bill to Mend the Laws Relating to Horseracing 1870 (155) II.205
Bill to Amend the Law Relating to Betting 1871 (213) I.179
Bill to Amend the Law Relating to Betting 1872 (186) I.141
Bill to Amend the Act of 16th and 17th Vict. An Act for the Suppression of Betting Houses 1874 (4) I.79
Bill to Extend to Scotland the Act for the Suppression of Betting Houses 1873 (185) I.57
Bill for Licensing Racecourses 1877 (54) VI.5
Bill for Licensing Racecourses round the Metropolis 1878 (76) VII.43
Bill for Licensing Metropolitan Suburban Courses 1878–9 (48) V.491
Copy of Reports from Mr Scudamore to the Postmaster General with Appendices 1867–68 (202) XLI

Hansard

Report of the Select Committee on the Post Office Telegraph Department 1876 (357) XIII

Return Showing the Number of Stamps for Newspapers 1831–32 (30) XXXIV

Return Relating to the Number of Advertisements in London Newspapers and the Amount of Duty Paid 1831–34, 1835 (108) XXXVII

Return Relating to the Number of Stamps Issued for Newspapers in Great Britain and Ireland 1836–38, 1839 (548) XXV
1838–40, 1841 (407) XII

Return Relating to the Number of Stamps Issued for Newspapers in the United Kingdom 1837–50, 1852 (42) XXVIII

Royal Commission on the Municipal Corporations of England and Wales, First Report 1835 XXV

Royal Commission on Horse-Breeding, First Report 1888 (C5419) XLVIII.I;
Second Report 1888 (C5595) XLVIII.II;
Third Report, Minutes of Evidence and Index (C6034-I) XXVII.319,327;
Fourth Report, Appendices 1893–94 (C6897)XXXI.871;
Fifth Report 1895 (C7811) XXXV.365;
Sixth Report 1897 (C8593) XXXIV.233
Seventh Report 1899 (C9487) XXXIII.1029

Select Committee of the House of Commons on the Post Office Telegraph 1876 (357) XIII

Select Committee of the House of Lords on Betting 1901 (370) v.347

Select Committee of the House of Lords on Betting 1902 (389) v.445

Select Committee of the House of Lords on the Laws Respecting Gaming First Report 1844 (468) VI; Second Report 1844 (544) VI Third Report (604) VI

Select Committee of the House of Lords on the State of Agriculture 1836 (79) VIII

BOOKS AND ARTICLES IN BOOKS

Anon., *Horse Racing: Its History and Early Records* (Saunders, Otley, 1863)

—, *Racing at Home and Abroad* (London & County Press Association, 1927)

—, *Lancaster Records 1801–1850* (Lancaster, 1869)

—, *An Official History of Stockton Racecourse* (Stockton, 1955)

C.R. Acton, *Silk and Spur* (Richards, 1935)

J. Alexander (ed.), *Culture and Society: Contemporary Debates* (1990)

H. Allingham and D. Radford, *William Allingham: a Diary 1824–1889* (1907)

W. Allison, *My Kingdom for a Horse* (Grant Richards, 1919)

—, *Memories of Men and Horses* (Grant Richards, 1922)

K.J. Allinson, *The Victoria History of the Counties of England: A History of the County of York East Riding*. Vol.VI. *The Borough and Liberties of Beverley* (Oxford, 1989)

An Octogenarian, *Reminiscences of Old Manchester and Salford with An Account of Manchester Races in the Time of George III* (Manchester, 1887)

An Old Jockey, *What I Saw at Manchester Races* (Manchester, 1851)

M.Y. Ashcroft, *Letters and Papers of Henrietta Matilda Crompton and Her Family* (North Riding Record Office, Northallerton, 1994)

J.D. Astley, *Fifty Years of My Life* (Hurst & Blackett, 1894)

W.E.A. Axon, *The Annals of Manchester* (Manchester, 1886)

J.J. Bagley, *Lancashire* (1972)

E.C. Baker, *Sir William Preece FRS: Victorian Engineer Extraordinary* (1976)

D. Batchelor, *The Turf of Old* (Witherby, 1951)

P.S. Bagwell, *The Transport Revolution from 1770* (1974)

P. Bailey, *Leisure and Class in Victorian England* (1978)

J.B. Baker, *History of Scarborough* (Scarborough, 1882)

J.W. Bateman, *The Greater Landowners of Great Britain and Ireland* (1883)

F.H. Bayles, *Race Courses Atlas of Great Britain and Ireland* (1903)

E.B. Bax, *Reminiscences and Reflections of a Middle and Late Victorian* (Allen & Unwin, 1918)

J.V. Beckett, *The Aristocracy in England 1660–1914* (1986)

O. Beckett, *J.F. Herring and Sons* (J.A. Allen, 1981)

Lady Florence Bell, *At the Works: a Study of a Manufacturing Town* (1985 edn)

J.M. Bellamy, *The Trade and Shipping of Nineteenth Century Hull* (Beverley, 1979)

T. Bennett, *Popular Culture: History and Theory* (Open University, 1981)

W. Bennett, *The History of Burnley from 1850* (Burnley, n.d.)

S. Bent, *Criminal Life: Reminiscences of 42 Years as a Police Officer* (Manchester, n.d.)

R.M. Bevan, *The Roodee* (Cheshire Country Publishing, 1989)

A.M. Binstead, *Pitcher in Paradise* (Bliss, Sands, London, 1903)
—, *A Pink 'Un and a Pelican* (Bliss, Sands, London, 1898)
T.H. Bird, *Admiral Rous and the English Turf* (1939)
R. Black, *Horse-Racing in England* (R. Bentley, 1893)
—, *The Jockey Club and its Founders* (Smith Elder, 1891)
E. Bland (ed.), *Flat Racing Since 1900* (Andrew Dakers, 1950)
B. Blunt, *Arthur Yates: Trainer and Gentleman Rider* (Grant Richards, 1922)
R.F.L. Blunt, *Betting and Gambling* (1902)
J.B. Booth, *Old Pink 'Un Days* (Grant Richards, 1924)
—, *Sporting Times: the Pink 'Un World* (T. Werner Laurie, 1938)
P. Borsay, *The English Urban Renaissance* (Oxford, 1989)
T. Bowman, *History of Richmond* (Richmond, 1814)
E.W. Bovill, *The England of Nimrod and Surtees* (1959)
T. Bradley, *The Old Coaching Days in Yorkshire* (Leeds, 1887)
D. Brailsford, *Bareknuckles: a Social History of Prize Fighting* (Cambridge, 1988)
—, *British Sport: a Social History* (Cambridge, 1992)
A. Briggs, *A Study of the Work of Seebohm Rowntree 1871–1954* (Longmans, 1961)
C. Brindley, *Stable Talk and Table Talk* (1846)
P. Brett, *The Rise and Fall of the York Whig Club 1818–1830* (York, 1990)
D.W.E. Brock, *The Racing Man's Weekend Book* (n.d.)
G.A. Brown, *A Useful Chronology of Local Events* (Norton, 1899)
T.H. Browne, *History of the English Turf 1904–1930* (Virtue, 1931)
J. Buckmaster, *A Village Politician: the Life Story of John Buckley* (Caliban Books, Horsham, 1982)
R. Butch (ed.), *For Fun and Profit: the Transformation of Leisure into Consumption* (Philadelphia, 1990)
E.F. Calford, *Edinburgh: the Story of a City* (1975)
J. Caminada, *Twenty-five Years of Detective Life: a Fascinating Account of Crime in Victorian Manchester* (Manchester, 1985)
R. Cashman and M. McKernan (eds), *Sport in History* (Queensland, 1989)
S. Caunce, *Amongst Farm Horses: the Horselads of East Yorkshire* (Stroud, 1991)
G.J. Cawthorne and R.S. Herod, *Royal Ascot* (Treherne, London, 1902)
V. Chancellor (ed.), *Master and Artisan in Victorian England* (1969)
Chester Tradesman, *Chester Races: Do they Pay?* Chester, 1871)
K. Chesney, *The Victorian Underworld* (1970)
G. Chetwynd, *Racing Reminiscences* (Longmans, Green, 2 vols., 1891)
C. Chinn, *Better Betting with a Decent Feller* (Hemel Hempstead, 1991)

S. Churchill, *Betting and Gambling* (1894)
M. Clapson, *A Bit of a Flutter: Popular Gambling in England c.1820–1961* (Manchester, 1991)
J. Clarke and C. Critcher, *The Devil Makes Work: Leisure in Capitalist Britain* (1985)
C. Clarkson, *History of Richmond* (Richmond, 1814)
F. Close, *The Evil Consequences of Attending the Racecourse* (1827)
M. Cobbett, *Wayfaring Notions* (Sands, London, 1906)
R. Colls, *The Collier's Rant* (1977)
—, *The Pitmen of the Northern Coalfield: Work, Culture and Protest 1790–1850* (Manchester, 1987)
E. Conran, *John Bowes, Mystery Man of the British Turf* (Bowes Museum, 1985)
T.A. Cook, *A History of the British Turf* (Virtue, 3 vols., 1905)
H. Cox, *Chasing and Racing: Some Sporting Reminiscences* (John Lane, London, 1922)
M. Cox, *Derby: the Life and Times of the 12th Earl of Derby* (J.A. Allen, London, 1974)
D. Craig, *Horse-racing* (1963)
T.W.H Crossland, *Who Goes Racing* (Crossland, 1907)
J. Crowther, *Beverley in Mid-Victorian Times* (Beverley, 1990)
E.D. Cuming (ed.), *Squire Osbaldeston: His Autobiography* (1926)
H. Cunningham, *Leisure in the Industrial Revolution* (1980)
—, 'The metropolitan fairs: a case study in the social control of leisure', in A.P. Donajgrodski (ed.), *Social control in Nineteenth-century Britain* (1978)
H. Curwen, *Kirkbie Kendal* (Kendal, 1900)
L.H. Curzon, *The Blue Riband of the Turf* (Chatto & Windus, 1890)
—, *A Mirror of the Turf* (Chapman & Hall, 1892)
H. Custance, *Riding Recollections and Turf Stories* (News of the World, 1894)
R. Darvill, *A Treatise on the Care, Treatment and Training of the Racehorse* (1846 edn)
B. Darwin, *John Gully and His Times* (Cassell, 1935)
W. Day, *The Racehorse in Training* (Chapman & Hall, 1880)
—, *Reminiscences of the Turf* (Richard Bentley, 1886)
—, *Turf Celebrities I have Known* (F.V. White, 1891)
A. Delves, 'Popular recreation and social conflict in Derby 1800–1850', in E. and A. Yeo (eds.), *Popular Culture and Class Conflict* (Harvester Press, Brighton, 1981), pp.89–127
C. Dickens, *The Lazy Tour of Two Idle Apprentices* (1954 edn)

D. Dixon, *The State and Gambling: Developments in the Legal Control of Gambling in England* (Hull, 1981)

—, *Illegal Gambling and Histories of Policing in England* (Hull, 1984)

—, *From Prohibition to Regulation: Bookmaking, Anti-gambling and the Law* (1991)

W. Scarth Dixon, *In the North Countree. Annals and Anecdotes of Horse, Hound and Hero* (1889)

—, *The Influence of Racing and the Thoroughbred Horse on Light Horse Breeding* (Hurst & Blackett, 1924)

S. Dixon, *From Gladiateur to Persimmon* (Grant Richards, 1901)

A.P. Donajgrodski (ed.), *Social Control in Nineteenth Century Britain* (1978)

E.E. Dorling, *Epsom and the Dorlings* (Stanley Paul, Plymouth, 1939)

The Druid [H.H. Dixon], *Saddle and Sirloin* (Vinton, 1870)

—, *The Post and the Paddock* (Vinton, 1856)

—, *Scott and Sebright* (Vinton, 1862)

—, *Silk and Scarlet* (Vinton, 1859)

F. Engels, *Condition of the Working Class in England* (1969 edn)

B. English, *The Great Landowners of East Yorkshire 1530–1910* (1990)

R.H. Eddleston, *Some Northern Thoroughbreds: Teesdale Horses and Their Owners* (Gainford 1942)

J. Fairfax-Blakeborough, *A Short History of Redcar Racecourse* (Ripon, 1950)

—, *Chester Races* (1951)

—, *Malton Memories and I'Anson Triumphs* (Truslove & Bray, 1925)

—, *Northern Sport and Sportsmen* (Stockton, 1916)

—, *Northern Turf History*, Vol.1, *Hambleton and Richmond* (J.A. Allen, 1948)

—, *Northern Turf History*, Vol.2, *Extinct Race Meetings* (J.A. Allen, 1949)

—, *Northern Turf History*, Vol.3, *York and Doncaster Races* (J.A. Allen, n.d.)

—, *Northern Turf History*, Vol.4, *History of Horse Racing in Scotland* (J.A. Allen, 1973)

—, *Paddock Personalities* (n.d.)

—, *The Analysis of the Turf* (Philip Allen, 1927)

N. Fairfax-Blakeborough, *J.F.-B.: Memoirs of Jack Fairfax-Blakeborough* (J.A. Allen, 1978)

R. Fieldhouse and B. Jennings, *A History of Richmond and Swaledale* (1978)

F. Finnegan, *Poverty and Prostitution: a Study of Victorian Prostitutes in York* (Cambridge, 1979)

A. Fitzgerald, *Royal Thoroughbreds* (Sidgwick & Jackson, 1990)
J.S. Fletcher, *The History of the St. Leger Stakes* (Hutchinson, 1926)
Fraser, *Guide to Liverpool* (n.d.)
J. Gale, *The Blaydon Races* (Newcastle, 1970)
M. Girouard, *The English Town* (Milan, 1990)
J. Golby and A.W. Purdue, *The Civilisation of the Crowd: Popular Culture in England 1750–1900* (1984)
—, *The Emergence of an Urban Popular Culture* (Open University, 1981)
J.H. Goldstein (ed.), *Sports Violence* (New York, 1983)
E.J. Gorn, *The Manly Art: The Lives and Times of the Great Bareknuckle Champions* (1986)
R. Gruneau, *Class, Sports and Social Development* (University of Massachusetts Press, Amherst, 1983)
A. Guttman, *From Ritual to Record: the Nature of Modern Sports* (New York, 1978)
C.S. Hallas, *The Wensleydale Railway* (Clapham, 1984)
T. Hampton, *History of Horwich* (Wigan, 1883)
C.E. Hardy, *John Bowes and the Bowes Museum* (Frank Graham, Newcastle, 1970)
S. Hardy (ed.), *The Diary of a Suffolk Farmer's Wife 1854–1869* (Basingstoke, 1992)
B. Harrison, *Drink and the Victorians* (1971)
G. Hart, *A History of Cheltenham* (n.d.)
T. Heywood, *New Annals of Rochdale* (Rochdale, 1931)
C.R. Hill, *Horse Power: the Politics of the Turf* (Manchester, 1988)
J. Hill and J. Williams, *Sport and Identity in the North of England* (Keele, 1996)
J. Hislop and D. Swannell (eds), *The Faber Book of the Turf* (1990)
G. Hodgman, *Sixty Years on the Turf* (1901)
J.M. Hogg, *Betting and Gambling* (Edinburgh, 1904)
G.O. Holt, *A Regional History of the Railways of Great Britain*, Vol.10, *The North-West* (1986)
R. Holt, *Sport and the British* (Oxford University Press, 1989)
— (ed.), *Sport and the Working Class in Modern Britain* (Manchester, 1990)
J.P. Hore, *The History of Newmarket and the Annals of the Turf* (A.H. Bailey, 3 vols., 1886)
—, *Sporting and Rural Records of the Cheveley Estate* (S.N. Press, 1899)
P. Horn, *High Society: the English Social Elite 1880–1914* (1992)
T. Houston, *The Races: the Evils Connected with Horse Racing and the Steeplechase* (Paisley, 1853)

A. Howkins, *Reshaping Rural England: a Social History 1850–1925* (1991)

J.S. Howson [Dean of Chester], *Chester Races* (Chester, 1870)

N. Hudleston, *History of Malton and Norton* (Scarborough, 1962)

M.J. Huggins, *Kings of the Moor: North Yorkshire Racehorse Trainers 1760–1900* (Middlesbrough, 1991)

E.M. Humphris, *The Life of Fred Archer* (Hutchinson, 1923)

—, *The Life of Mathew Dawson* (Witherby, 1928)

C.J. Ingledew, *History and Antiquities of North Allerton* (1858)

G. Jackson, *Hull in the 18th Century: a Study in Economic and Social History* (Oxford University Press, 1972)

D.J.V. Jones, *Rebecca's Children: a Study of Rural Society, Crime and Protest* (Oxford, 1989)

A. and E. Jordan, *Away for the Day: the Railway Excursion in Britain* (Silver Link Publishing, 1991)

P. Joyce, *Work, Society and Politics: the Culture of the Factory in Late Victorian England* (Brighton, 1980)

—, *Visions of the People: Industrial England and the Question of Class 1848–1914* (Cambridge, 1991)

J. Kent, *The Racing Life of Lord George Cavendish Bentinck, M.P.* (Blackwood, 1892)

—, *Records and Reminiscences of Goodwood and the Dukes of Richmond* (Sampson, Low, 1896)

J.L. Kieve, *The Electric Telegraph: a Social and Economic History* (1973)

C. Kingsley, *Betting: a Letter to the Young Men of Chester* (Chester, 1871)

T. Koditschek, *Class Formation and Urban Industrial Society Bradford 1750–1850* (Cambridge, 1990)

D. Laird, *Royal Ascot* (Hodder & Stoughton, 1976)

G. Lambton, *Men and Horses I Have Known* (J.A. Allen, 1924)

G. Lehndorff, *Horse Breeding Recollections* (Horace Cox, 1883)

S. Lewis, *A Topographical Dictionary of England*, Vol.II (1849)

E.P. Loder, *Bibliography of the History and Organisation of Horse Racing and Thoroughbred Breeding in Great Britain and Ireland* (J.A. Allen, 1978)

Marquess of Londonderry, *The Londonderry Album: Portraits from a Great House in the 1890s* (1978)

R. Longrigg, *The History of Horse Racing* (Macmillan, 1972)

C. Bruce Lowe, *Breeding Horses by the Figure System* (Horace Cox, 1895)

J. Lowerson, *Sport and the English Middle Classes 1870–1914* (Manchester University Press, 1993)

— and J. Myerscough, *Time to Spare in Victorian England* (Brighton, 1971)

A.D. Luckerman, *Sharps, Flats, Gamblers and Racehorses* (Grant Richards, 1914)

R.C. Lyce, *Royal Newmarket* (1945)

J.M. MacKenzie, *Propaganda and Empire: the Manipulation of British Public Opinion 1880–1900* (Manchester, 1984)

K.A. MacMahon, *The Beginnings of the East Yorkshire Railways* (Beverley, 1977)

R. McKibbin, *The Ideologies of Class* (Oxford University Press, 1991)

H.L. Malchow, *Gentlemen Capitalists: the Social and Political World of the Victorian Business Man* (1991)

R.W. Malcolmson, *Popular Recreations in English Society 1700–1850* (Cambridge, 1977)

J. Mangan and J. Walvin (eds), *Manliness and Morality: Middle Class Masculinity in Britain and America 1800–1940* (Manchester, 1987)

S. Margetson, *Leisure and Pleasure in the Nineteenth Century* (Newton Abbot, 1971)

R. Marsh, *A Trainer to Two Kings* (Cassell, 1925)

W. Marshall, *Review and Abstract of the County Reports to the Board of Agriculture*, Vol.1, *Northern Department* (1818)

T. Mason, *Association Football and English Society 1863–1915* (Brighton, 1980)

— (ed.), *Sport in Britain: a Social History* (1988)

P. Mathieu, *The Druid Lodge Confederacy* (J.A. Allen, 1990)

H. Mayhew, *London Labour and the London Poor*, Vol.IV, *Those That Will Not Work* (Frank Cass, 1967)

H. Meller, *Leisure and the Changing City 1870–1914* (1976)

G. Miller, *Blackburn: the Evolution of a Cotton Town* (Blackburn, 1951)

M. Milne, *The Newspapers of Northumberland and Durham* (1971)

C.F. Moffatt, *For a Purse of Gold* (Newcastle, 1986)

M.G. Moore, *An Irish Gentleman: George Henry Moore* (T.Werner Laurce, London, n.d.)

R. Moore, *Pitmen, Preachers and Politics: the Effects of Methodism in a Durham Mining Community* (Cambridge, 1976)

E. Moorhouse, *The History and Romance of the Derby* (Biographical Press, 2 vols., 1911)

J. Morris (ed.), *Class, Power and Social Structure in British Nineteenth Century Towns* (Leicester, 1986)

—, *Class, Sect and Party: the Making of the British Middle Class in Leeds 1820–1850* (Manchester University Press, 1990)

R. Mortimer *et al.*, *Bibliographical Encyclopaedia of British Flat Racing* (Macdonald & Jane's, 1978)

— and M. Seth-Smith, *Derby 200* (1979)
—, *The History of the Derby Stakes* (Cassell, 1962)
—, *The Jockey Club* (1958)
C. Morton, *My Sixty Years on the Turf* (Hutchinson, n.d.)
R. Munting, *Hedges and Hurdles, a Social and Economic History of National Hunt Racing* (1987)
—, *An Economic and Social History of Gambling in Britain and the USA* (Manchester, 1996)
C.N. New, *Lord Durham: a Biography of John George Lambton* (1968)
Nimrod, *Memoirs of the Life of John Mytton* (Methuen, 1903)
—, *The Chace, the Road and the Turf* (John Lane, 1927 edn)
A. Noakes, *Sportsmen in a Landscape* (1954)
—, *William Frith: Extraordinary Victorian Painter* (1978)
W.H. Norris, *A Hint to the Clergy and Other Anti-Gambling Crusaders* (1894)
R. Onslow, *The Squire: George Alexander Baird, Gentleman Rider 1861–1893* (Harrap, 1980)
—, *Headquarters* (Great Ouse Press, Cambridge, 1983)
—, *Royal Ascot* (Marlborough, 1990)
—, *The Squire* (1980)
V. Orchard, *Tattersalls: 200 Years of Sporting History* (Hutchinson, 1953)
J. Orton, *Turf Annals of York and Doncaster* (T. Empson, York, 1844)
J. Osbourne, *The Horsebreeders' Handbook* (1898)
A.E. Pease, *Half a Century of Sport* (1932)
J. Peddie, *Racing for Gold* (1891)
G. Plumtre, *The Fast Set* (Fores, 1985)
A.J. Pollard (ed.), *Middlesbrough: Town and Community 1830–1950* (Stroud, 1996)
W. Pollard, *History of the Stanleys of Knowsley* (Liverpool, 1868)
R. Poole, *Popular Leisure and the Music Hall in 19th Century Bolton* (Lancaster, 1982)
J. Porter, *John Porter of Kingsclere* (Grant Richards, 1896)
—, *Kingsclere* (Chatto & Windus, 1896)
Duke of Portland, *Memoirs of Racing and Hunting* (London, 1935)
C.M. Prior, *The History of the Racing Calendar and Stud Book* (Sporting Life, 1926)
—, *Stud Book Lore* (F.M. Prior, 1951)
R.W. Proctor, *Our Turf, Our Stage, Our Ring* (Manchester, 1862)
—, *Memorials of Manchester Streets* (Manchester, 1874)
J. Radcliffe, *Ashgill: or The Life and Times of John Osborne* (Sands, 1900)
C. Ramsden, *Farewell Manchester* (J.A. Allen, 1966)

—, *Ladies in Racing* (Stanley Paul, 1973)
L. Rasmussen and M. Napier, *Treasures of the Bloodstock Breeders' Review* (J.A. Allen, 1990)
M. Reed and R. Wells (eds), *Class, Conflict and Protest in the English Countryside 1700 – 1880* (1990)
H. Reeve (cd.), *The Greville Memoirs*, Vol.2 (1885)
J. Rice, *The History of the British Turf* (Sampson Low, 2 vols., 1879)
C. Richardson, *The English Turf* (Methuen, 1901)
Ripon Civic Society, *Ripon: Some Aspects of its History* (Clapham, 1972)
J.M. Robinson, *The English Country Estate* (1988)
T. Rogerson, *Lancashire General Directory for 1818*, Pt 1 (Manchester, 1818)
F. Ross, *Celebrations of the Yorkshire Wolds* (1878)
Lord Rossmore, *Things I Can Tell* (Eveleigh Nash, London, 1912)
B.S. Rowntree, *Betting and Gambling* (1905)
J. Rule, *Albion's People: English Society 1714–1815* (1992)
R. Samuel (ed.), *East End Underworld: Chapters in the Life of Arthur Harding* (1981)
J.L. Saywell, *History and Annals of Northallerton* (Northallerton, 1885)
A. Scott, *Turf Memories of Sixty Years* (Hutchinson, 1925)
S. Scott, *A Westmorland Village* (London, 1904)
M. Seth-Smith, *A Classic Connection* (1983)
—, *Bred for the Purple* (Frewin, 1969)
—, *Lord Paramount of the Turf* (Faber, 1971)
— (ed.), *Steeplechasing and Foxhunting* (1977)
H. Shimmin, *Liverpool Life, Its Pleasures, Practices and Pastimes* (Liverpool, 1856)
C. Sydney, *The Art of Legging* (Maxline International, 1976)
F. Simpson, *Chester Races, Their Early History* (Chester, 1925)
R. Sissons, *The Players: a Social History of the Professional Cricketer* (1988)
T. Sloan, *Tod Sloan* (Grant Richards, 1915)
J.T. Slugg, *Reminiscences of Manchester 50 Years Ago* (Manchester, 1881)
W. Smith (ed.), *Old Yorkshire* (1884)
J. Stevens, *Knavesmire* (Pelham Books, York, 1984)
R.D. Storch (ed.), *Popular Culture and Custom in Nineteenth Century England* (1982)
Earl of Suffolk and Berkshire (ed.), *Racing and Steeplechasing* (Longmans, Green, 1886)
— and W.G. Craven, *The Badminton Library: Racing* (1886)
D. Sutherland, *The Yellow Earl* (1965)

—, *The Landowners* (1988)
Sylvanus, *The Bye-Lanes and Downs of England* (Richard Bentley, 1850)
R Taine, *Notes on England* (New Jersey, 1958)
R.V. Taylor, *Yorkshire Anecdotes* (1887)
R.H.G. Thomas, *The Liverpool and Manchester Railway* (1980)
E.P. Thompson, *The Making of the English Working Class* (1968)
F.M.L. Thompson, *English Landed Society in the Nineteenth Century* (1963)
— (ed.), *The Cambridge Social History of Britain 1750–1950*, 3 vols. (1990)
—, *The Rise of Respectable Society* (1988)
Thormanby, *Famous Racing Men* (James Hogg, 1882)
—, *Kings of the Turf* (Hutchinson, 1898)
J. Tyrrel, *Racecourses on the Flat* (Marlborough, 1989)
W. Vamplew, *The Turf: a Social and Economic History of Horse Racing* (Allen Lane, 1976)
—, *Pay Up and Play the Game: Professional Sport in Britain 1975–1914* (Cambridge University Press, 1988)
B. Waites, *Popular Culture in Late 19th Century and Early Twentieth Century Lancashire* (Milton Keynes, 1981)
J.K. Walton, *The English Seaside Resort: a Social History 1759–1914* (Leicester, 1983)
— and J. Walvin, *Leisure in Britain 1780–1939* (Manchester, 1983)
— and A. Wilcox (eds), *Low Life and Moral Improvement in Mid-Victorian England: Liverpool through the Journalism of H. Shimmin* (1991)
J. Walvin, *Leisure and Society, 1830–1950* (1978)
C.R. Warren, *Sixty Years on the Turf* (Grant Richards, 1901)
A.E.T. Watson, *The Racing World and Its Inhabitants* (Macmillan, 1904)
—, *The Turf* (Lawrence & Bullen, 1898)
J. Welcome, *Fred Archer: His Life and Times* (Faber, 1967)
—, *Neck or Nothing: the Extraordinary Life and Times of Bob Sievier* (1970)
—, *The Sporting World of R.S. Surtees* (Oxford, 1982)
J. Wigley, *The Rise and Fall of the Victorian Sunday* (Manchester, 1980)
J.C. Whyte, *History of the British Turf*, Vols.I and II (Henry Coburn, 1839–40)
F.L. Wilder, *English Sporting Prints* (1974)
O. Wilkinson, *The Agricultural Revolution in the East Riding of Yorkshire* (Guisborough, 1980)
P. Willett, *The Classic Racehorse* (Stanley Paul, 1989)
—, *The Thoroughbred* (Weidenfeld & Nicolson, 1970)

—, *The Story of Tattersall's* (Stanley Paul, 1987)
F.S. Williams, *Our Iron Roads*, Vol.1 (1883)
P.W. Wilson (ed.), *The Greville Diaries* (1927)
W. Wilson, *Chester Races* (Chester, 1856)
W. Wise, *Richmond and Yorkshire in the 1830s* (Richmond, 1977)
D.G. Wright and J.A. Jowitt (eds), *Victorian Bradford* (1982)
M. Wynn Jones, *The Derby* (1979)
E. Yeo and S. Yeo (eds), *Popular Culture and Class Conflict 1590–1914* (Brighton, 1981)

THESES

C. Case, 'Subculture as Adaptation to Strain: the Occupational Arena of Horseracing', PhD thesis, State University of New York (1988)
M. Clapson, 'Popular Gambling and English Culture *c.*1845 to 1961, with special reference to Lancashire', PhD thesis, Open University (1989)
J. Crump, 'Amusements of the People: the Provision of Recreation in Leicester 1850–1914', PhD thesis, University of Warwick (1985)
G. Deacon, 'Popular Song and Social History: a Study of the Miners of the North East', PhD thesis, University of Essex (1987)
M.P. Filby, 'A Sociology of Horse Racing in Britain', PhD thesis, University of Warwick (1983)
D.W. Hadfield, 'Political and Social Attitudes in Middlesbrough with Special Reference to the Role of the Middlesbrough Ironmasters', PhD thesis, Teesside Polytechnic (1981)
R. Hale, 'The Demise of Horseracing in Lancaster and Preston', Undergraduate dissertation, Lancaster University (1991)
—, 'Horse Racing in Cumbria: the Development and Survival of Racing in Carlisle', Undergraduate dissertation (1992)
P. Khan, 'The Sport of Kings: a Study of Traditional Social Structure under Threat', PhD thesis, University of Wales (1980)
R. Miller, 'Gambling and the British Working Class 1870–1914', MA thesis, University of Edinburgh (1974)
J. Tolson, 'The Railways and Racing', PhD thesis (in draft), De Montfort University, Leicester

ARTICLES

N. Ashton, 'Clerical Control and Radical Response: Cheltenham Spa 1838–1848', *Midland History*, Vol.8 (1983), pp.121–47

P. Bailey, 'Leisure, Culture and the Historian: Reviewing the First Generation of Leisure Historiography in Britain', *Leisure Studies*, Vol.8 (1989), pp.107–27

E. Bowden Rowlands, 'A Glance at the History of Gambling', *Westminster Review*, Vol.135 (1891)

M. Clapson, 'A Bit of a Flutter', *History Today*, October 1991, pp.38–44

J. Crump, '"The Great Carnival of the Year": the Leicester Races in the Nineteenth Century', *Transactions of the Leicestershire Historical and Archaeological Society*, Vol.58 (1982–83), pp.58–74

L. Curzon, 'The Horse as an Instrument of Gambling', *Contemporary Review*, 30 August 1877 pp.376–94

C. Dickens, 'Epsom', *Household Words*, Vol.3, No.63 (7 June 1851)

D. Dixon, 'Class Law: the Street Betting Act of 1906', *International Journal of the Sociology of Law*, Vol.8 (1980) pp.101–28

K. Gregson, 'Songs of Horse Racing on Tyneside', *North-East Labour History*, No.17 (1983), pp.11–14

M.J. Huggins, '"Mingled Pleasure and Speculation": the Survival of the Enclosed Racecourses on Teesside 1855–1902', *British Journal of Sports History*, Vol.3, No.2 (September 1986)

—, 'Thoroughbred Breeding in the North and East Ridings of Yorkshire in the Nineteenth Century', *Agricultural History Review*, Vol.42 (1994)

—, 'Culture, Class and Respectability: Racing and the Middle Classes in the Nineteenth Century', *International Journal of the History of Sport*, Vol.11, No.1 (1994)

—, 'Lord Bentinck, the Jockey Club and Racing Morality in Nineteenth-century England', *International Journal of the History of Sport* Vol.13, No.3 (December 1996)

D.C. Itzkovitz, 'Victorian Bookmakers and Their Customers', *Victorian Studies*, Vol.32, No.1 (Autumn 1988)

G. Jobey, 'Cock-fighting in Northumberland and Durham during the Eighteenth and Nineteenth Centuries', *Archaealogia Aeliana*, Vol.20 (1992), pp.1–25

R.J. Moore-Colyer, 'Gentlemen, Horses and the Turf in Nineteenth Century Wales', *Welsh History Review* Vol.16 (1992), pp.47–62

—, 'Field Sports, Conservation and the Countryside in Georgian and Victorian Wales', *Welsh History Review*, Vol.16, No.2 (June 1993), pp.308–23

J. Raven, 'The Abolition of the English State Lottery', *Historical Journal*, Vol.34, No.2 (1991), pp.371–90

J. Runciman, 'The Ethics of the Turf', *Contemporary Review*, Vol.55 (1889)

K.A. Sandiford, 'The Victorians at Play: Problems in Historical Methodology', *Journal of Social History*, Vol.15 (Winter 1981), pp.271–88

G.H. Strutfield, 'Racing in 1890', *Nineteenth Century*, Vol.27 (1890)

F.M.L. Thompson, 'Some Nineteenth Century Horse Sense', *Economic History Review*, Vol.29 (1976)

R.W. Tomlinson, 'A Geography of Flat Racing in England', *Geography*, Vol.71, No.3 (June 1976), pp.228–39

NEWSPAPERS AND PERIODICAL PUBLICATIONS

Airdrie and Coatbridge Advertiser
Baily's Magazine of Sports and Pastimes
Bell's Life in London
Beverley Guardian
Bloodstock Breeders' Review
Burnley Advertiser
Carlisle Patriot
Carlisle Journal
Clarion Pamphlet
Cleveland News
Colne and Nelson Guardian
Darlington and Stockton Times
Doncaster Gazette
Doncaster Reporter
Durham County Advertiser
Free Lance
Leeds Mercury
Lonsdale Magazine
Illustrated London News
International Journal of the History of Sport
International Journal of the Sociology of Law
Leicester Journal
Licensed Victuallers Gazette
Malton Messenger
Manchester and Salford Advertiser
Manchester Courier

Manchester Free Lance
Manchester Guardian
Middlesbrough Temperance Visitor
Middlesbrough Times
Middlesbrough Weekly News and Cleveland Advertiser
Morpeth Herald
New Sporting Magazine
Newcastle Daily Chronicle
Newmarket Journal
News of the World
North Eastern Daily Gazette
North Star
Northern Echo
Northumbrian
Penny Bell's Life
Porcupine
Prophetic Bell
Racing Calendar
Racing Illustrated
Redcar Gazette
Redcar News
Ripon Chronicle and Richmond Weekly News
Ruff's Guide to the Turf
Scarborough Gazette
South Durham Herald
South Durham and Cleveland Mercury
Sporting Chronicle
Sporting Kalendar
Sporting Life
Sporting Magazine
Sporting Review
Sportsman
Stockton Herald
Stokesley News and Cleveland Reporter
Sunday Times
The Times
Wensleydale Advertiser
Westmorland Gazette
York Chronicle
York Herald
Yorkshire Gazette
Yorkshireman

Index